5th Edition

Texas
Real Estate Contracts

By Michelle Evans

Texas Real Estate Contracts, Fifth Edition

Michelle Evans

Executive Editor: Sara Glassmeyer

Production Managers: Elizabeth King and Linda Francis, KnowledgeWorks Global Ltd

Cover Designer: Brian Brogaard

Cover image:

Thinkstock by Getty Images
The Texas Capitol at Sunset

Credit: TriciaDaniel

Product Specialist: Deborah Miller

Chapter Opener Image Credits:

Natee Meepian, FabioBalbi

For product information and technology assistance, contact us at
Mbition Customer Support, 800-532-7649.
For permission to use material from this text or product, please contact
publishingsupport@mbitiontolearn.com.

Library of Congress Control Number: 2018965626
Student Edition:
ISBN-13: 978-1-62980-233-6
ISBN-10: 1-62980-233-6

Mbition, LLC
18500 W Corporate Drive, Suite 250
Brookfield, WI 53045, USA

Visit us at **www.mbitiontolearn.com**

Printed in the United States of America
1 2 3 4 5 6 24 23 22 21 20 19

BRIEF CONTENTS

CONTENTS

TABLE OF FIGURES

PREFACE

As with many issues in real estate, the law of real estate contracts is constantly changing. Because of the rapid growth in this area, the Texas Real Estate Commission requires all real estate licensees to have training in the law of contracts and promulgated contract forms. This text was designed to comply with the requirements of the law and includes all of the elements specified by the Texas Real Estate Commission for inclusion in the Law of Contracts course.

The Law of Contracts course is a **documentation** course, but it is not just about the documents. It is important to learn something about the documents (contracts) used in the field; however, a person should know more than just how to "put marks on the paper" or "fill in the blanks."

To the extent of that conviction, an attempt was made to prepare for the reader a book that will provide general information on contracts, as well as offer an understanding of the contract forms themselves. This approach has worked well through numerous sections of coursework for several years in more than one educational setting with a diversity of students.

NEW TO THIS EDITION

This edition has been updated to reflect the latest legislative changes and form changes from the Texas Real Estate Commission through 2019. In addition, this edition has been updated to meet the requirements addressed in the TREC Core Course Approval Form effective January 17, 2017 for Law of Contracts. Specifically, these changes include:

Chapter 1 – Texas Contract Law

This chapter was rewritten to focus on Texas contract law. Detail has been provided about the Texas Real Estate License Act, unauthorized practice of law, authorized practices, the Broker-Lawyer Committee, use of promulgated contract forms and exceptions, Deceptive Trade Practices Consumer Protection Act (DTPA), fraud, and Texas real estate fraud.

Chapter 2 – Basics of Real Estate Law

This chapter now addresses the basics of real estate law. More specifically, this chapter focuses on real property and the law, land, real estate, and real property, real property vs. personal property, characteristics of real property, forms of real estate ownership, ownership of real estate by business organizations, property descriptions and condominiums, cooperatives, townhouses, and time-shares, and laws affecting real estate.

Chapter 3 – Introduction to Contracts

Chapter 3 now provides an introduction to contracts. This chapter focuses on elements of a valid contract, express or implied contracts, unilateral or bilateral contracts, valid, void, voidable, and unenforceable contracts, and executed or executory contracts.

Chapter 4 – Ownership Rights and Limitations

This chapter now focuses on ownership rights and limitations. Specifically, this chapter looks at interests in real estate, government powers, estates in land, encumbrances, water rights, mineral rights, environmental issues, and homestead.

Chapter 5 – Contracts Used in Real Estate

Chapter 5 looks at the contracts used in real estate. This chapter covers real estate contracts, contract law, discharge of contracts, contracts used in the real estate business, Listing Agreements, Buyer Agency Agreement, leasing real estate, leasehold estates, lease agreements, types of leases, discharge of leases, options, Contract for Deed, and Lease Purchase Agreements.

Chapter 6 – The Sales Contract

Chapter 6 now provides details about the sales contract. This includes the offer and acceptance, the document, financing information, disclosures, conveyance of the property, signatures, Statute of Frauds, default and breach of contract, and remedies.

Chapter 7 – Contingencies, Addenda, and Amendments

This chapter focuses on contingencies, addenda, and amendments. More specifically, this chapter looks at contingencies, amendments, and addenda not addressed elsewhere.

Chapter 8 – Financing Real Estate

Chapter 8 looks at financing real estate. This chapter covers mortgage law, security and debt, promissory note, mortgages or deeds of trust, owner financing, foreclosures and short sales, liens, the real estate financing market, techniques and loan programs, financing legislation, and Computerized Loan Origination (CLO).

Chapter 9 – Financing Real Estate

This chapter now looks at conveyance of title. This includes title, voluntary alienation, involuntary alienation, conveyance of estates, public records, and proof of ownership.

Chapter 10 – Transaction Process and Closing

Chapter 10 now focuses on the transaction process and closing. More specifically, this chapter looks at the transaction process, sample checklist, loan approval, Real Estate Settlement Procedures Act (RESPA), inspections, title work, preparation for closing, prorations, and closing and funding.

Appendix

The appendix includes some contract examples addressing common areas of concern. Although, common areas of concern are also addressed throughout the text.

Some caveats must be stated. Although this book is using the most current forms available at the time of publication, it will become dated. Contracts, especially those promulgated by the Texas Real Estate Commission, change and hopefully improve constantly. That is just a fact of life, so it is recommended that you investigate to determine the most current documents available at the time you use the book. In addition, certain forms, such as the deed and deed of trust, may not be completed by the real estate licensee and must be drafted and completed by a licensed attorney. The material found here is no substitute for the professional help provided by an attorney at law. The unique facts of a particular situation cannot always be directly linked to the generalizations that are required when a text is created. Seek legal advice when you first realize you are entering unsafe areas. Don't wait until you have already made some poor choices to get help. Best wishes in your real estate endeavors!

Michelle Evans

ABOUT THE AUTHOR

Michelle Evans is an attorney who has practiced in South Texas for 23 years. She is a former adjunct professor at San Antonio College, where she taught both contract law and real estate law for the Real Estate Program. Educationally, Ms. Evans holds a BS from the University of Texas at San Antonio and a JD from St. Mary's University School of Law. She is a frequent speaker on contract matters and has authored numerous legal articles on real estate and contract law issues.

ACKNOWLEDGMENTS

Almost no book is created by just the author. Certainly, I did not make this book without lots of great help. Many thanks to Sara Glassmeyer, Elizabeth King, and Linda Francis, whose support and patience were vital.

On a personal level, I would like to dedicate this book to my husband, Richard.

CHAPTER

1

TEXAS CONTRACT LAW

KEY TERMS

Broker-Lawyer Committee
common law fraud
contribution
Deceptive Trade Practices Consumer Protection Act (DTPA)
indemnity
promulgated
Texas Real Estate License Act (TRELA)
Texas Real Estate Commission (TREC)

A discussion of Texas real estate contract law must begin with the history of the laws and entities involved in the residential real estate industry. The real estate industry has been regulated in Texas for several decades. In 1939, Texas passed the Texas Real Estate Dealer's License Act, which required real estate professionals to be licensed by the Texas secretary of state. A decade later in 1949 the licensing responsibility fell to the newly created Texas Real Estate Commission. The name of the Act regulating the industry was changed shortly thereafter to the Texas Real Estate License Act.

This chapter provides more detail about the Texas Real Estate License Act, particularly what constitutes the unauthorized practice of law by real estate license holders. The Broker-Lawyer Committee of the Texas Real Estate Commission is introduced along with the Commission's guidelines concerning the use of required "promulgated" contract forms in residential real estate transactions. The chapter concludes with a discussion of fraud, including violations of the Texas Deceptive Trade Practices Consumer Protection Act that may be alleged against real estate license holders as well as against others involved in the real estate transaction.

TEXAS REAL ESTATE LICENSE ACT

The **Texas Real Estate License Act** (TRELA) codified in the Texas Occupations Code was created to govern the real estate profession. The administration of the Texas Real Estate License Act was vested

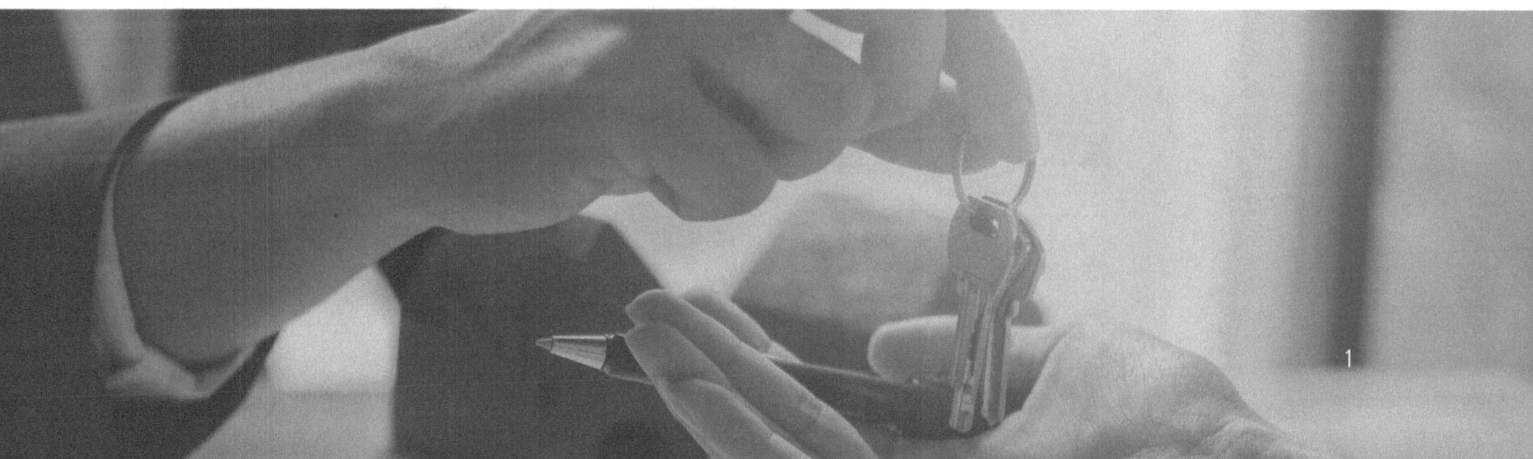

in the Texas Real Estate Commission. The **Texas Real Estate Commission (TREC)** consists of nine members appointed for six-year terms by the governor with the advice and consent of the Texas senate. Six of these members are required to have operated as real estate brokers for at least five years preceding their appointments. The remaining three members must be representatives of the general public who are not real estate license holders.

The Texas Real Estate Commission has the authority and power to make and enforce all rules and regulations necessary for the performance of its duties, to establish standards of conduct for real estate license holders, and to insure license holder compliance with the provisions of the Texas Real Estate License Act. In addition, the Texas Real Estate Commission is empowered to investigate the actions of real estate license holders and to suspend or revoke real estate licenses for violations of the Texas Real Estate License Act. Real estate license holders must be especially careful not to go beyond the scope of their real estate license and practice law.

UNAUTHORIZED PRACTICE OF LAW

In General

The Texas Real Estate Commission has drafted rules specifying what constitutes the unauthorized practice of law by real estate license holders. The pertinent provisions are as follows:

> A license holder may not practice law, directly or indirectly offer, give or attempt to give legal advice, directly or indirectly, give advice or opinions as to the legal effect of any contracts or other such instruments which may affect the title to real estate, give opinions concerning the status or validity of title to real estate, attempt to prevent or in any manner whatsoever discourage any principal to a real estate transaction from employing a lawyer.[1]
>
> A license holder may not draft language defining or affecting the rights, obligations or remedies of the principals of a real estate transaction, including escalation, appraisal or other contingency clauses; or add factual statements or business details to a form approved by the Commission if the Commission has approved a form or addendum for mandatory use for that purpose.[2]

[1] 22 T.A.C. § 537.11 (b)(1)-(4), (7).

[2] 22 T.A.C. § 537.11(b)(5) and (6).

In the standard promulgated residential sales contracts and addenda all of the blanks provided can be filled in with "factual statements and business details desired by the principals."[3] Each of the promulgated residential sales contract forms contains a special provisions paragraph, paragraph 11, which provides additional space to indicate the specific desires of the principals. However, the Rules of the Texas Real Estate Commission prohibit license holders from adding additional information for which a form has been approved by the Commission for mandatory use.

Note also that the license holder is permitted to strike items from the contract that are desired by the parties.[4] It is of paramount importance that if a term is crossed out as desired by a party to the negotiations, then the license holder should make sure that the party initials the change and indicates the date and time on the change. Also, even though the rules allow for items to be crossed out if a party desires, the license holder should use caution and not allow entire sentences to be crossed out.

In addition, note that the license holder cannot practice law and practicing law includes "drafting language defining or affecting the rights of the principals." Such legal documents include deeds. Because of the large supply of lawyer software programs, the license holder may see an opportunity to make a little extra money by preparing a deed for the parties. Since a standard general warranty deed exists in most of these software programs, the license holder may believe there is nothing wrong with using a computer generated form. However, the law specifically prohibits this activity. Furthermore, the form chosen may not comply with Texas law.

The Texas Real Estate Commission takes the unauthorized practice of law very seriously and there are significant penalties for violation. The Texas Real Estate License Act provides that:

> [t]he Commission shall suspend or revoke the license or certificate of registration of a license or certificate holder who is not a licensed attorney in this state and who, for consideration, a reward, or a pecuniary benefit, present or anticipated, direct or indirect, or in connection with the person's employment, agency, or fiduciary relationship as a license or certificate holder: (1) drafts an instrument, other than a form described by section 1101.155, that transfers or otherwise affects an interest in real property; or (2) advises a person regarding the validity or legal sufficiency of an instrument or the validity of title to real property.[5]

---

[3] 22 T.A.C. § 537.11(d).

[4] 22 T.A.C. § 537.11(d).

[5] Tex. Occ. Code § 1101.654(a).

Authorized Practices

The Texas Real Estate Commission, however, does authorize certain practices by the license holder. The pertinent provisions are as follows:

> This section does not limit a license holder's fiduciary obligation to disclose to the license holder's principals all pertinent facts that are within the knowledge of the license holder, including such facts which might affect the status of or title to real estate.[6]
>
> This section does not prevent the license holder from explaining to the principals the meaning of the alternative choices, factual statements and business details contained in an instrument so long as the license holder does not offer or give legal advice.[7] It is not the practice of law for a license holder to fill in the blanks in a contract form authorized for use by this section.[8]

The Rules of the Texas Real Estate Commission, however, do limit the license holder's practices. For example, a license holder may disclose facts to his or her principal, but he or she may not disclose the legal implication or effect of those facts because this would be considered practicing law. With regard to the sales contracts, there are certain provisions that cannot be eliminated in the existing contract or included by the real estate license holder because this would call for the license holder to make a legal conclusion or it may affect the legal rights of the parties involved. Certain deletions by a license holder may include whole sentences or paragraphs that directly relate to the transaction at hand. Where the addition or deletion of a provision calls for the license holder to draw a legal conclusion or may affect the rights of the parties, the parties must be allowed to consult with an attorney as follows:

> When a transaction involves unusual matters that should be reviewed by a lawyer before an instrument is executed, or if the instrument must be acknowledged and filed of record, the license holder shall advise the principals that each should consult a lawyer of the principal's choice before executing the instrument.[9]

Note that the parties must be allowed to consult with an attorney *prior* to signing the agreement. Because this is so important, the promulgated residential contracts provide a final warning that license holders cannot give legal advice so if the parties do not understand the contract they should consult an

---

[6] 22 T.A.C. § 537.11(c).
[7] 22 T.A.C. § 537.11(e).
[8] 22 T.A.C. § 537.11(d).
[9] 22 T.A.C. § 537.11(f).

attorney before signing. If a party wants to see an attorney, he or she has the right to go to an attorney. If the contract form is already completed, make an extra copy for the person to take to an attorney. Space is provided for the parties to list their respective attorneys. If one or both parties to the agreement do not have an attorney, a license holder may simply list "Attorney not Selected" in the space provided.

Once the agreement is signed, it is too late to protect their rights. Once a party is notified that he or she must consult an attorney, however, he or she may ask several questions, like "Do you know an attorney I could consult with?" or "I would like to talk with an attorney, but I can't afford one. Could you talk to a lawyer for me?" or "If I give you a higher commission, could you pay for the lawyer?" Because of the inherent conflict of interest involved, the Rules of the Texas Real Estate Commission provide as follows:

> A license holder may not employ or pay for the services of a lawyer, directly or indirectly, to represent a principal to a real estate transaction in which the license holder is acting as an agent.[10] A license holder may employ and pay for the services of a lawyer to represent only the license holder in a real estate transaction.[11]

Because of the rules prohibiting the license holder from employing a lawyer on the principal's behalf, a license holder must be careful when recommending a lawyer. It is always good practice, if the principal asks for a referral, that the license holder give the principal a list of about five attorneys with whom he or she, the license holder, has dealt in the past. This same basic rule applies in any circumstances in which the client asks for a referral of the services of another professional. The ultimate decision should be left to the principal. If the principal chooses not to consult with an attorney, then some type of in-house waiver or notice form should be used to indicate that the license holder gave notice to the principal of the potential need for legal services and the principal waived his or her rights to seek consultation. Note that rule also provides that a license holder may employ an attorney to act on his or her own behalf in the real estate transaction.

Once an attorney has been consulted or the principal waived his or her rights to consultation, the parties may go forward with execution of the contract. However, before the principals sign the contract, under the Rules of the Texas Real Estate Commission, the license holder must notify the principals that the instrument they are about to execute *is binding on them*.[12]

---

[10] 22 T.A.C. § 537.11(b)(8).
[11] T.A.C. § 537.11(g).
[12] 22 T.A.C. § 537.11(h).

THE BROKER-LAWYER COMMITTEE

In keeping with the general purpose of the Texas Real Estate Commission and its powers under the Texas Real Estate License Act, the Texas Real Estate **Broker-Lawyer Committee** was created, in part, to draft and revise contract forms and addenda capable of uniform use by real estate license holders. These forms for the most part are mandatory and are often referred to as **promulgated** forms. However, a portion of the forms created are merely approved forms and as such are discretionary. These forms contain uniform language for use in various real estate transactions with blanks for the license holder to fill in to conform the contract to the particular facts of the transaction. This text will discuss the most current TREC forms as of the date of submission. However, the reader should be aware that these forms are constantly in flux. Therefore, the reader should always confirm that the forms discussed herein are still current. The Texas Real Estate Commission maintains a website, www.trec.texas.gov, where this information can be obtained.

Although real estate license holders fill in the forms, they often do not understand the legal effect of the entries that they make on the contract. In order to complete the contracts successfully, the real estate license holders must have a practical knowledge of the contract itself and of the law concerning the contracts. For complex transactions, however, an attorney should be consulted. It is important for the license holder to avoid any action that a consumer could interpret as the practice of law.

USE OF PROMULGATED CONTRACT FORMS

In General

The general rule for the use of promulgated forms is as follows:

> When negotiating contracts binding the sale, exchange, option, lease or rental of any interest in real property, a real estate license holder shall use only those contract forms approved for mandatory use by the Texas Real Estate Commission (the Commission) for that type of transaction.[13]

Exceptions

Generally, there are four situations where the real estate license holder is not required to use a promulgated form. The Texas Real Estate Commission lays the exceptions out as follows:

(1) transactions in which the license holder is functioning solely as a principal, not as an agent;

[13] 22 T.A.C. § 537.11(a).

(2) transactions in which an agency of the United States government requires a different form to be used;

(3) transactions for which a contract form, or addendum to a contract form, has been prepared by a property owner or prepared by a lawyer and required by a property owner;

(4) transactions for which no mandatory contract form or addendum has been approved by the Commission, and the license holder uses a form prepared by a lawyer licensed by this state, or a trade association in consultation with one or more lawyers licensed by this state, for the particular type of transactions involved that meets certain requirements or prepared by the Texas Real Estate Broker-Lawyer Committee (the Committee) and approved by the Commission for voluntary use by license holders.[14]

Section (1) simply deals with those transactions in which the license holder is either selling his or her own property or purchasing property for his or her own benefit. Keep in mind that even though the license holder does not have to use a promulgated form when acting as a seller or purchaser, he or she is required to notify any other person with whom he or she deals that he or she is a licensed real estate broker or sales agent acting on his or her own behalf either by disclosure in the sales contract or rental agreement or by disclosure in any other writing given prior to entering into a sales contract or rental agreement.[15] This notice must also be given when the license holder is acting on behalf of the license holder's spouse, parent, or child; a business entity in which the license holder is more than a 10% owner; or a trust for which the license holder acts as trustee or of which the license holder or the license holder's spouse, parent, or child is a beneficiary.[16] Typically, the license holder will indicate his or her direct or indirect interest in the transaction in the sales contract itself in paragraph 4 addressing license holder disclosure.

Section (2) of the exceptions is self-explanatory and needs no further discussion.

Section (3) seems straightforward; however, a problem exists where a property owner presents his or her own form, and it is either a form that was used by the property owner in another state or a form that the property owner downloaded

4. LICENSE HOLDER DISCLOSURE: Texas law requires a real estate license holder who is a party to a transaction or acting on behalf of a spouse, parent, child, business entity in which the license holder owns more than 10%, or a trust for which the license holder acts as a trustee or of which the license holder or the license holder's spouse, parent or child is a beneficiary, to notify the other party in writing before entering into a contract of sale. Disclose if applicable:_______________.

FIGURE 1-1 License Holder Disclosure

[14] 22 T.A.C. § 537.11(a).

[15] 22 T.A.C. § 535.144.

[16] 22 T.A.C. § 535.144(a).

from the internet or from a standard consumer legal form software program. To protect themselves, some brokers have established in house policies that prohibit the use of any contract forms other than the standard promulgated TREC contract forms. This is done primarily to limit future liability. For those brokerages that have not established a specific policy against the use of property owner forms, some prefer to ask the property owner to have the contract reviewed by an attorney of his or her choice. If the form is reviewed by an attorney, the license holder should request that the attorney issue a written certification that the form is appropriate for use in the transaction. If the property owner refuses or simply prefers not to seek an attorney, then most brokerages have a standard waiver of counsel form that they have signed by the property owner and keep in the transaction file. Where a form has been prepared by an attorney and required by the property owner, in-house brokerage policy may still limit the use of such a form. Where there is no in-house policy, it is still a good idea to get a written certificate of a particular use of the form from the attorney. All written attorney certifications should be maintained in the transaction file in case of future problems.

In section (4), there are several instances in which there is no promulgated form available and the license holder uses a form prepared by in-house counsel or outside counsel for the brokerage, or by counsel for a trade organization of which the broker is a member, and certified for a particular use. In addition, at certain times, trial use forms are made available through the Texas Real Estate Commission.

Failure to use the required promulgated form or to meet one of the four exceptions to the use of the promulgated forms is a violation of the Rules of the Texas Real Estate Commission and can result in license suspension or revocation. A violation also occurs when the license holder fails to use a current promulgated form. This problem arises most often in brokerage firms that use computer-generated TREC forms where the brokerage fails to update the forms on the computer when new forms become mandatory. Since the TREC forms have been made available over the internet, this no longer appears to be a problem.

DECEPTIVE TRADE PRACTICES CONSUMER PROTECTION ACT (DTPA)

In addition to the administrative penalties that can be assessed against a license holder who violates the Rules of the Texas Real Estate Commission or the Texas Real Estate License Act, the license holder may face civil liability for violating his or her responsibilities to clients or other third parties. Civil liability can arise if the license holder commits fraud or misrepresentation.

Fraud

Common law fraud is simply fraud that arises under case decisions. In order for an injured party to establish that a common law fraud occurred in a real estate transaction, certain elements must be established. The elements of a **common law fraud** claim are that the speaker made (1) a material representation, (2) that was false, (3) that the speaker knew was false at the time it was made, (4) that was made with the intention of being acted upon, (5) the party acted in reliance, and (6) injury was suffered.[17]

Texas Real Estate Fraud

Another law that may aid the injured party in establishing fraud is actually part of Texas statutory law. Section 27.01 of the Texas Business and Commerce Code deals specifically with fraud in real estate transactions. Fraud and the remedies for the fraud are defined under this law as follows:

> (a) Fraud in a transaction involving real estate consists of a
>
> (1) false representation of a past or existing material fact, when the false representation is
>
> (A) made to a person for the purpose of inducing that person to enter into a contract; and
>
> (B) relied on by that person in entering into that contract; or
>
> (2) false promise to do an act, when the false promise is
>
> (A) material;
>
> (B) made with the intention of not fulfilling it;
>
> (C) made to a person for the purpose of inducing that person to enter into a contract; and
>
> (D) relied on by that person in entering into that contract.
>
> (b) A person who makes a false representation or false promise commits the fraud described in subsection (a) of this section and is liable to the person defrauded for actual damages.
>
> (c) A person who makes a false representation or false promise with actual awareness of the falsity thereof commits the fraud described in subsection (a) of this section and is liable to the person defrauded for exemplary damages. Actual awareness may be inferred where objective manifestations indicate that a person acted with actual awareness.
>
> (d) A person who (1) has actual awareness of the falsity of a representation or promise made by another person and (2) fails to disclose the falsity of the representation or promise to the person defrauded, and (3) benefits from the false representation or promise commits the fraud described in subsection (a) of this section and is liable to the person defrauded for exemplary damages. Actual awareness may be inferred where objective manifestations indicate that a person acted with actual awareness.

---

[17] Trenholm v. Ratcliff, 646 S.W.2d 927 (Tex. 1983).

(e) Any person who violates the provisions of this section shall be liable to the person defrauded for reasonable and necessary attorney's fees, expert witness fees, costs for copies of depositions, and costs of court.

Texas Deceptive Trade Practices Consumer Protection Act (DTPA)

Another law that has great importance to consumers victimized by fraud or misrepresentation, particularly in real estate transactions, is the **Texas Deceptive Trade Practices Consumer Protection Act (DTPA)** contained in chapter 17 of the Texas Business and Commerce Code. The DTPA was enacted to protect consumers against false, misleading, and deceptive business practices; unconscionable actions; and breaches of warranty and to provide efficient and economical procedures to secure such protection.[18]

Definitions

Certain definitions were drafted to aid in the effectuation of the law. These definitions are listed as follows in Tex. Bus. and Comm. Code § 17.45.

(1) "Goods" means tangible chattels or real property purchased or leased for use.

(2) "Services" means work, labor, or service purchased or leased for use, including services furnished in connection with the sale or repair of goods.

(3) "Person" means an individual, partnership, corporation, association, or other group, however organized.

(4) "Consumer" means an individual, partnership, corporation, this state, or a subdivision or agency of this state who seeks or acquires by purchase or lease, any goods or services, except that the term does not include a business consumer that has assets of $25 million or more, or that is owned or controlled by a corporation or entity with assets of $25 million or more.

(5) "Unconscionable action or course of action" means an act or practice which, to a consumer's detriment, takes advantage of the lack of knowledge, ability, experience, or capacity of the consumer to a grossly unfair degree.

(6) "Trade" and "commerce" mean the advertising, offering for sale, sale, lease, or distribution of any good or service, of any property, tangible or intangible, real, personal, or mixed, and any other article, commodity, or thing of value, wherever situated, and shall include any

[18] Tex. Bus. and Comm. Code § 17.44(a).

trade or commerce directly or indirectly affecting the people of this state.

(7) "Documentary material" includes the original or a copy of any book, record, report, memorandum, paper, communication, tabulation, map, chart, photograph, mechanical transcription, or other tangible document or recording, wherever situated.

(8) "Consumer protection division" means the consumer protection division of the attorney general's office.

(9) "Knowingly" means actual awareness, at the time of the act or practice complained of, of the falsity, deception, or unfairness of the act or practice giving rise to the consumer's claim or, in an action brought under subdivision (2) of subsection (a) of section 17.50, actual awareness of the act, practice, condition, defect, or failure constituting the breach of warranty, but actual awareness may be inferred where objective manifestations indicate that a person acted with actual awareness.

(10) "Business consumer" means an individual, partnership, or corporation who seeks or acquires by purchase or lease, any goods or services for commercial or business use. The term does not include this state or a subdivision or agency of this state.

(11) "Economic damages" means compensatory damages for pecuniary loss, including costs of repair and replacement. The term does not include exemplary damages or damages for physical pain and mental anguish, loss of consortium, disfigurement, physical impairment, or loss of companionship and society.

(12) "Residence" means a building:

(A) that is a single-family house, duplex, triplex, or quadruplex or a unit in a multiunit residential structure in which title to the individual units is transferred to the owners under a condominium or cooperative system; and

(B) that is occupied or to be occupied as the consumer's residence.

(13) "Intentionally" means actual awareness of the falsity, deception, or unfairness of the act or practice, or the condition, defect, or failure constituting a breach of warranty giving rise to the consumer's claim, coupled with the specific intent that the consumer act in detrimental reliance on the falsity or deception or in detrimental ignorance of the unfairness. Intention may be inferred from objective manifestations that indicate that the person acted intentionally or from facts showing that a defendant acted with flagrant disregard of prudent and fair business practices to the extent that the defendant should be treated as having acted intentionally.

Unlawful Deceptive Trade Practices

A laundry list of unlawful deceptive trade practices is included in section 17.46. "False, misleading, or deceptive acts or practices" in the real estate industry include, but are not limited to, the following partial list of acts:

(1) passing off goods or services as those of another;

(2) causing confusion or misunderstanding as to the source, sponsorship, approval, or certification of goods or services;

(3) causing confusion or misunderstanding as to affiliation, connection, or association with, or certification by, another;

(4) using deceptive representations or designations of geographic origin in connection with goods or services;

(5) representing that goods or services have sponsorship, approval, characteristics, ingredients, uses, benefits, or quantities which they do not have or that a person has a sponsorship, approval, status, affiliation, or connection which the person does not;

(6) representing that goods are original or new if they are deteriorated, reconditioned, reclaimed, used, or secondhand;

(7) representing that goods or services are of a particular standard, quality, or grade, or that goods are of a particular style or model, if they are of another;

(8) disparaging the goods, services, or business of another by false or misleading representation of facts;

(9) advertising goods or services with intent not to sell them as advertised;

(10) advertising goods or services with intent not to supply a reasonable expectable public demand, unless the advertisements disclosed a limitation of quantity;

(11) making false or misleading statements of fact concerning the reasons for, existence of, or amount of price reductions;

(12) representing that an agreement confers or involves rights, remedies, or obligations which it does not have or involve, or which are prohibited by law;

(13) knowingly making false or misleading statements of fact concerning the need for parts, replacement, or repair service;

(14) misrepresenting the authority of a salesman, representative or agent to negotiate the final terms of a consumer transaction;

(22) representing that work or services have been performed on, or parts replaced in, goods when the work or services were not performed or the parts replaced;

(24) failing to disclose information concerning goods or services which was known at the time of the transaction if such failure to disclose such information was intended to induce the consumer into a transaction into which the consumer would not have entered had the information been disclosed;

(25) using the term "corporation," "incorporated," or an abbreviation of either of those terms in the name of a business entity that is not incorporated under the laws of this state or another jurisdiction;

(28) using the translation into a foreign language of a title or other word, including "attorney," "immigration consultant," "immigration expert," "lawyer," "licensed," "notary," and "notary public," in any written or electronic material, including an advertisement, a business card, a letterhead, stationery, a website, or an online video, in reference to a person who is not an attorney in order to imply that the person is authorized to practice law in the United States.

Actions

The Act provides relief for injured consumers. A consumer may maintain an action where any of the following constitute a producing cause of economic damages or damages for mental anguish:

(1) the use or employment by any person of a false, misleading, or deceptive act or practice that is:
   (A) specifically enumerated in a subdivision of subsection (b) of section 17.46 of this subchapter; and
   (B) relied on by a consumer to the consumer's detriment;

(2) breach of an express or implied warranty;

(3) any unconscionable action or course of action by any person; or

(4) the use or employment by any person of an act or practice in violation of chapter 541, Insurance Code.[19]

Damages recoverable by the consumer include economic damages, which may be trebled if the conduct was committed intentionally. The consumer may also seek an injunction. An injunction is an order by the court that prohibits specified acts. The consumer may also seek court costs and reasonable attorney's fees.[20]

In addition, an action can be brought by the attorney general's office, consumer protection division. This action is brought if the division has reason to believe that a person is engaging in, has engaged in, or is about to engage in

[19] Tex. Bus. and Comm. Code § 17.50(a).

[20] Tex. Bus. and Comm. Code § 17.50(b)&(d).

any unlawful act or practice.[21] This action will be brought in the name of the state against the defendant and is designed to restrain the defendant's unlawful activities. In addition, the division may request a civil penalty of not more than $20,000 per violation.[22]

Waiver

The general rule is that a waiver by a consumer of the provisions of the Act is contrary to public policy and is unenforceable and void. However, a waiver is valid and enforceable if: (1) the waiver is in writing and is signed by the consumer; (2) the consumer is not in a significantly disparate bargaining position; and (3) the consumer is represented by legal counsel in seeking or acquiring the goods or services.[23] Note, however, that the waiver is not effective if the consumer's legal counsel was "directly or indirectly identified, suggested, or selected by a defendant or an agent of the defendant."[24] In addition, the waiver does not act as a defense to an action brought by the attorney general.[25]

The waiver must be: (1) conspicuous and in bold-face type of at least 10 points in size; (2) identified by the heading "Waiver of Consumer Rights," or words of similar meaning; and (3) in substantially the following form:

> "I waive my rights under the Deceptive Trade Practices Consumer Protection Act, Section 17.41 et seq., Business & Commerce Code, a law that gives consumers special rights and protections. After consultation with an attorney of my own selection, I voluntarily consent to this waiver."

Defenses and Indemnity

The Act provides for certain defenses. In an action under the Act, it is a valid defense to the award of any damages or attorneys' fees if the defendant proves that before consummation of the transaction he or she gave reasonable and timely written notice to the plaintiff of the defendant's reliance on:

(1) written information relating to the particular goods or service in question obtained from official government records if the written information was false or inaccurate and the defendant did not know and could not reasonably have known of the falsity or inaccuracy of the information;

---

[21] Tex. Bus. and Comm. Code § 17.47(a).
[22] Tex. Bus. and Comm. Code § 17.47(c).
[23] Tex. Bus. and Comm. Code § 17.42(a).
[24] Tex. Bus. and Comm. Code § 17.42(b).
[25] Tex. Bus. and Comm. Code § 17.42(e).

(2) written information relating to the particular goods or service in question obtained from another source if the information was false or inaccurate and the defendant did not know and could not reasonably have known of the falsity or inaccuracy of the information; or
(3) written information concerning a test required or prescribed by a government agency if the information from the test was false or inaccurate and the defendant did not know and could not reasonably have known of the falsity or inaccuracy of the information.[26]

In addition, it is a defense to a cause of action if the defendant proves that he or she received notice from the consumer advising the defendant of the nature of the consumer's complaint and of the amount of economic damages, damages for mental anguish, and expenses, including attorneys' fees, if any, reasonably incurred by the consumer in asserting the claim against the defendant, and that within 30 days after the day on which the defendant received the notice the defendant tendered to the consumer:

(1) the amount of economic damages and damages for mental anguish claimed; and
(2) the expenses, including attorneys' fees, if any, reasonably incurred by the consumer in asserting the claim against the defendant.

A defendant in an action under the Act may be able to seek contribution or indemnity from one who may have been liable for the damaging event.[27] **Contribution** is the right of a defendant to recover proportional shares of a judgment from others whose negligence contributed to the injury of the consumer. **Indemnity**, on the other hand, refers to a right whereby one party agrees to indemnify, or restore, another upon the occurrence of some anticipated loss.

Statute of Limitations

All actions brought under this Act must be commenced within two years after the date on which the false, misleading, or deceptive act or practice occurred or within two years after the consumer discovered or, in the exercise of reasonable diligence, should have discovered the occurrence of the false, misleading, or deceptive act or practice.[28]

One important distinction in the DTPA from that of both common law fraud and statutory real estate fraud is that there is no requirement that the injured party show that the offender acted knowingly or purposefully. As a result, an accidental misrepresentation can result in DTPA liability. The Deceptive Trade Practices

[26] Tex. Bus. and Comm. Code § 17.506(a).
[27] Tex. Bus. and Comm. Code § 17.555.
[28] Tex. Bus. and Comm. Code § 17.565.

Act is one of the reasons it is a good idea to maintain complete and accurate records of all transactions. Everything that occurs should be documented and the transaction files should be kept for a significant period of time.

Discussion Questions

1. Discuss some tasks that a real estate professional is permitted to do within the scope of his or her license.
2. Discuss some tasks that would be considered the unauthorized practice of law by a real estate professional.
3. Identify the four exceptions to the requirement that a real estate professional use a promulgated contract form if one is available.
4. What is the Texas Deceptive Trade Practices Consumer Protection Act and what is its purpose?
5. How does the Texas Deceptive Trade Practices Consumer Protection Act apply to real estate license holders? List three instances where a deceptive trade practices action might be brought against a real estate license holder.
6. What are the damages available to an injured consumer under the Texas Deceptive Trade Practices Consumer Protection Act and what defenses are available to the license holder?

CHAPTER

2

BASICS OF REAL ESTATE LAW

KEY TERMS

bill of sale
common law marriage
community property
condominium ownership
constitutional county court
contract clause
cooperative
co-ownership
county court at law
district court
diversity of citizenship jurisdiction
federal question jurisdiction
fixity
fixtures
Full Faith and Credit clause
general partnership
immobile
inception of title doctrine
indestructibility
Declaration of Informal Marriage
interest
joint tenancy
justice court
land
limited partnership
modification
non-realty items
partnership
personal property
plat
real estate
real property
scarcity
separate property
situs
sole proprietorship
survey
tenancy in common
Texas Constitution
uniqueness
U.S. Constitution

REAL PROPERTY AND THE LAW

In order to understand contracts in the real estate industry, it is important to address various aspects of the law concerning real property. This chapter will expand upon numerous aspects of real property law including the distinction between real property and personal property, the characteristics of real property, forms of ownership, including ownership by business entities, condominiums,

cooperatives, townhouses, and timeshares, and laws affecting real estate. But first it is important to clarify what constitutes real property.

LAND, REAL ESTATE, AND REAL PROPERTY

The terms "land," "real estate," and "real property" are often used interchangeably, but they have slightly different definitions. "**Land**" is the "ground, soil, or earth." It also includes the underlying subsurface as well as the overlying air, subject to limitations on use of that air imposed for air travel. "**Real estate**" however is the "land and anything permanently affixed to the land, such as buildings, fences, and those things attached to the buildings, such as light fixtures, plumbing and heating fixtures, or other such items which would be personal property (movable property) if not attached."[1] The Texas Real Estate License Act defines "real estate" as "any interest in real property, including a leasehold, located in or outside this state."[2] "Real estate" and "real property" are generally used synonymously. However, "real property" is land, whatever is erected, growing, or affixed to the land, and the rights associated with that land.[3]

Ownership, or title, to real property is often referred to as a bundle of rights and each of these rights will be expressed in the legal doctrines and contracts discussed throughout this text. Some of the key rights within this bundle include the right to possess, use, transfer, and exclude others.[4] The right of possession is the right to occupy the property in person. The right to use the property includes the right to enjoy the property as well as the right to control any use made of the property. However, local ordinances or homeowners association regulations may place additional restrictions on the property owner's right to use the property. The right to transfer the property is the right of the owner to dispose of the property either temporarily, such as with a lease, or permanently through a sale. And the right to exclude others allows the property owner to limit who enters his or her property. This right to exclude is limited, however, when easements are in place to permit others, such as utility company employees, to access the property. Possession of some, but not all, of these rights will give the possessor a right or **interest** in the property, but not ownership. Only an owner of real property can sell, or otherwise dispose of, that property.

REAL PROPERTY VS. PERSONAL PROPERTY

When considering what property is included in a sale, one must also be able to distinguish between real property and personal property. **Personal property** consists of movable property and would be conveyed with either a bill of sale or a

---

[1] Bryan A. Garner, *Black's Law Dictionary*, 10th ed. (St. Paul, MN: Thomson West, 2014).
[2] Tex. Occ. Code § 1101.002(5).
[3] Bryan A. Garner, *Black's Law Dictionary*, 10th ed. (St. Paul, MN: Thomson West, 2014).
[4] See Evanston Ins. Co. v. Legacy of Life, Inc., 370 S.W.3d 377 (Tex. 2012).

non-realty items addendum associated with a promulgated sales contract. A **bill of sale** is a written instrument that may be used by the parties to a real estate sales contract to transfer title of personal property from the seller to the purchaser. When a bill of sale is used, the personal property is conveyed outside of the real estate sales transaction. For this reason, the bill of sale is used in Federal Housing Administration (FHA) transactions as the means by which to transfer personal property. A sample bill of sale is contained in figure 2-1. It is usually preferred that the transfer of the personal property be kept separate from the transfer of the real property.

However, several real estate trade organizations have drafted what are referred to as **non-realty items** addenda used as attachments to the sales contract. A sample Non-realty Items Addendum (TREC OP-M) from the Texas Real Estate Commission is provided in figure 2-2. This document allows the transfer of the personal property to occur almost simultaneously with the transfer of the real property in the same transaction. This is in contrast to the bill of sale. This type of addendum; however, is not allowed in FHA-insured loans.

For both documents, a description of the property is required. When completing the description, a great deal of detail is necessary. For example, if "the coffee table" is part of the sale and there are three coffee tables, then the color, dimensions, and location of the specific coffee table should be included. If the

BILL OF SALE

I, ______________, [Seller] of the City of ______________, County of ___________, State of Texas, in consideration of ____________ Dollars ($______) paid to me by ______________, [Buyer], of the City of ______________, County of ___________, State of Texas, the receipt of which is acknowledged, sell to _____________ the following described goods:

____

____

____

I covenant and warrant that I am the lawful owner of the goods and that the goods are free from all encumbrances. I further covenant and warrant that I have the right to sell the goods and will warrant and defend that right against the lawful claims and demands of all persons.

This bill of sale is effective as to the transfer of all property listed above as of __________________ [date]. Delivery is to be made at __________________ [location] on ________________[date].

This bill of sale is executed the ________________ day of _________, ________________.

____

Seller

FIGURE 2-1 Bill of Sale
Source: © 2021 Mbition LLC

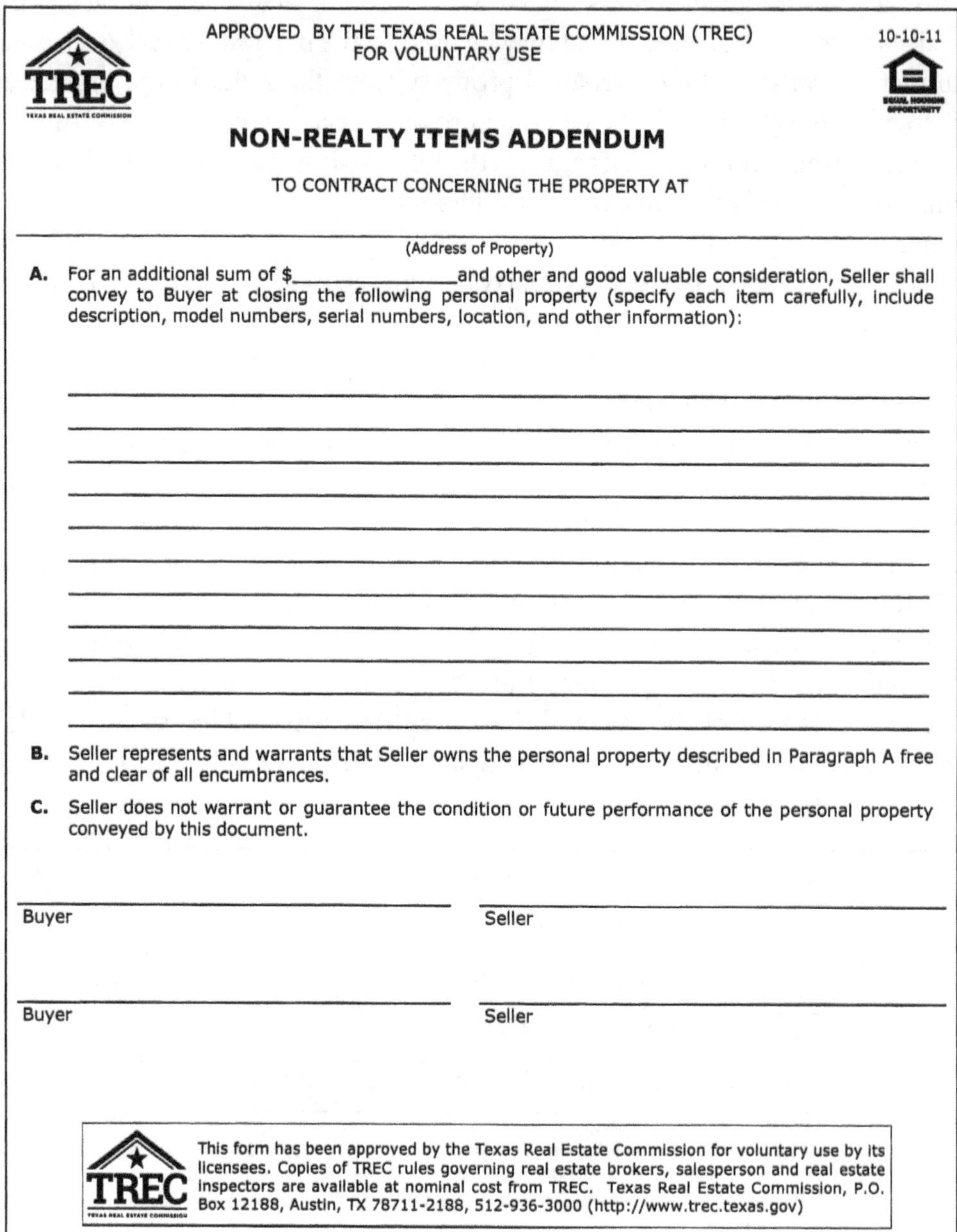

TREC TEXAS REAL ESTATE COMMISSION

APPROVED BY THE TEXAS REAL ESTATE COMMISSION (TREC)
FOR VOLUNTARY USE

10-10-11

EQUAL HOUSING OPPORTUNITY

NON-REALTY ITEMS ADDENDUM

TO CONTRACT CONCERNING THE PROPERTY AT

____
(Address of Property)

A. For an additional sum of $______________ and other and good valuable consideration, Seller shall convey to Buyer at closing the following personal property (specify each item carefully, include description, model numbers, serial numbers, location, and other information):

____

B. Seller represents and warrants that Seller owns the personal property described in Paragraph A free and clear of all encumbrances.

C. Seller does not warrant or guarantee the condition or future performance of the personal property conveyed by this document.

Buyer	Seller
Buyer	Seller

This form has been approved by the Texas Real Estate Commission for voluntary use by its licensees. Copies of TREC rules governing real estate brokers, salesperson and real estate inspectors are available at nominal cost from TREC. Texas Real Estate Commission, P.O. Box 12188, Austin, TX 78711-2188, 512-936-3000 (http://www.trec.texas.gov)

TREC NO. OP-M

FIGURE 2-2 Non-realty Items Addendum
Source: Reprinted with permission of Texas Real Estate Commission

refrigerator is to be included in the sale, then the model number, serial number, color, and dimensions should be included. The parties can indicate whether or not additional monies will be paid for the personal property. In addition, the property will generally be conveyed to the buyer as is with no warranties. The buyer can request a transfer of any warranties the seller may have on the property. A small fee may need be paid to the warranty company in most cases to transfer the warranty. Bear in mind that not all warranties are transferable.

As mentioned, **real property** consists of the land, everything attached to the land, and the rights associated with that land. Personal property items attached to the land are referred to as **fixtures**. In the residential sales contract, title to the real property is what is conveyed. The legal description identifies the real property for sale and all fixtures attached to that property. There are two types of property descriptions often associated with land—the metes and bounds and lot and block descriptions. These will be discussed in greater detail later in this chapter. A certified copy of the seller's deed should be obtained to make sure the proper property description is used.

The fixtures associated with the real property are contractually defined as improvements and accessories. Generally, the fixtures indicated in the promulgated residential sales contract address the most common fixtures found on the property. However, there may be instances when the item is not included within the list. In these situations, Texas law requires consideration of three elements for determining whether the property constitutes a fixture. These elements are (1) the mode of annexation, (2) adaptation of the personalty to the purpose of the realty, and (3) intent of the owner.[5] This distinction between whether property is personal or real is not only important for purposes of the residential sales contract, but it is also important for identifying which law applies if there is a problem. For instance, if the property is considered a fixture, then Texas real estate law will be applied. However, if the property is considered personal property, then the Texas Uniform Commercial Code will be applied.

A seller can also contractually define what personal property is not to be included in the sale in a listing agreement as well as in the promulgated residential sales contract. Ideally, the seller should have already made this preference known at the time of listing the property. It is not a good idea to give notice of an exclusion of personal property for the first time after a buyer has proposed an offer. Including such an exclusion at that point would be treated as a counteroffer and thus a rejection of the buyer's offer. It is possible to notify a prospective buyer that certain property is not to be included in the sale by telling him or her at the showing which property is excluded, by removing the excluded property before showing, or by putting a large sign on the item that is excluded from the sale. The idea is to prevent the prospective buyer from falling in love with the item before an offer is proposed.

CHARACTERISTICS OF REAL PROPERTY

Real property has both physical and economic characteristics. The physical characteristics are the defining features of real property that determine how it is used. There are three physical characteristics of real property. These physical characteristics are its immobility, indestructibility, and uniqueness. Real property is

[5] Reames v. Hawthorne-Seving, Inc., 949 S.W.2d 758, 762 (Tex. App.–Dallas 1997).

immobile because it cannot be moved from place to place. Thus, a real property owner cannot carry the real property with him or her like personal property and instead the owner must go to the property to use and enjoy it. In addition, when a sale takes place, the seller cannot hand the real property directly to the purchaser to change ownership. Instead, a deed is used as a representation of this ownership transfer. This is unlike a sale of personal property where the money and goods can be directly exchanged.

The **indestructibility** of real property, specifically land, means that it cannot be destroyed and; therefore, it will last forever. The boundaries; however, might change over time due to natural causes, such as accretion or erosion. This characteristic allows real property to maintain value over time because it can continue to be used compared to personal property that will eventually wear out.

The **uniqueness**, or heterogeneity (nonhomogeneity), of property means that no two pieces of property are exactly the same because no two pieces of property can occupy the same space. Unfortunately, if property is one of a kind, then there can be no substitutes. This is unlike personal property, where substitutes are readily available. The uniqueness of real property is reflected in the default remedies available for breach of contract. Specifically, the promulgated residential sales contracts provide for specific performance among the remedies for default. Specific performance can be used to force the seller to sell the property as he or she promised under the sales contract.

Unlike the physical characteristics of real property, the economic characteristics of real property are the features that affect its value as a product in the marketplace. There are four economic characteristics of real property that are influenced by the physical characteristics. These economic characteristics are its scarcity, modification, fixity, and situs. The **scarcity** of property relates to the supply and demand for a property. More specifically, scarcity occurs when there is an increased demand for land in a particular area, but the supply is low. The determination of whether property in a given area is considered scarce will fluctuate over time, but when it exists it will drive up the market price.

Modification refers to improvements made in a given geographic area that influence value and how property owners use their property. For example, construction of a movie theater complex with shopping centers and restaurants might increase the value of neighboring farm land and influence the property owner to sell the property to a subdivision or apartment complex developer.

The characteristic of **fixity** refers to the permanence of the property as an investment. This investment permanence means that an investment in real property will take several years before the property owner obtains a benefit. Therefore, the property owner must take this into account when determining the use for the land or making any improvements to the land. Mortgage companies take this fixity into account when setting the terms for property loans. For residential loans, the loan term for unimproved property is often 10 years compared to 20 or 30 years for improved property. Both loan terms would still permit a property owner to obtain a financial benefit from the property as these terms are not unreasonably long. However, it is unlikely that a property owner could obtain a financial benefit after a 40- or 50-year loan term.

In addition, fixity refers to the value impact that immobility has on real property. This characteristic is beneficial when the market in a given area is doing well because there is no risk of other real estate moving in to create competition like there could be with personal property. However, this characteristic can hurt the property value when the market is not doing well because the appeal of the property will only be able to reach those interested in moving to that market.

Finally, **situs** refers to people's preference for property in a particular location. This preference may be due to such factors as geography, climate, economy and job market, demographics, culture, education, healthcare, and transportation. Over time, however, people weigh these factors differently, which can impact their location preferences.

FORMS OF REAL ESTATE OWNERSHIP

It is important to understand the forms of real estate ownership held or to be held by the parties when completing real estate contracts. The parties to the sales contract will consist of the buyer and the seller. The name used for the seller should be the name as it appears on the deed of record. The name used by the buyer will be the legal name of the buyer. When listing the parties' names on the contract, the parties must be capable of identification. Therefore, the parties' full legal names should be used. Care should be taken to avoid nicknames and abbreviations. For example, "John Lloyd Smith" is better than "J.L. Smith." Further, the legal status of the parties should be indicated. If a married couple is involved in the transaction, they should be indicated as such. For example, "Jeff Doe and wife, Mary Ann Wilcox-Doe." Use of the older phrase "et ux" should be avoided in reference to the wife without inclusion of the wife's name, for instance "Jeff Doe et ux." If Jeff Doe had been married several times or if he at some point had taken a common law wife, it would be unclear which wife "et ux" referred to. If a business entity is involved in the transaction, the legal status of the business should be indicated.

Individual Ownership of Property

Real property can be owned by an individual, a married couple, unmarried co-owners, or a business. Real property owned by one individual is straightforward. The documentation in this case can include language such as "John Brown, a single person" or "Jane Brown, an individual."

Community Property Ownership and Informal Marriages

In General

The law concerning property ownership by a married couple is also important to the law of contracts. **Community property** is property owned in common between spouses, each having a one-half undivided interest in the property by virtue of their marital status. In Texas, all property owned during marriage is presumed to be community property.[6] In order to overcome this presumption, the burden is on the one who wants to show that the property is separate property, not community property. **Separate property** is property owned during marriage by a spouse in his or her own name or right. Separate property, in Texas, includes (1) all property owned before marriage; (2) property gained through gift, devise, or descent; (3) personal injury recoveries except for lost wages; and (4) property made separate by agreement.[7]

Inception of Title Doctrine

A key element to distinguishing community property from separate property is when title arose. This is of importance when property is acquired over a period of time, as is the case with real estate. The rule applicable in these situations is referred to as the **inception of title doctrine**. According to the inception of title doctrine, property is considered either separate or community at the beginning of title. If in the first moment a legal right is acquired in property the person is single, then the property is separate property. If he or she is married at that time, then the property is community property. It doesn't matter who pays the monthly mortgage installments. This doctrine typically characterizes property acquired on credit. For example, if a person purchases real estate as his or her separate property and subsequently gets married, the property in title is separate property. This is the case even if the non-owner spouse makes the mortgage payments. In Texas, if a non-title spouse makes payments on the property, the title interest does not change, but the non-title spouse may be entitled to reimbursement upon death of the title holder or upon divorce.

Informal Marriages

Community property laws apply to all married couples in the state of Texas. This includes couples who have been formally married by a priest, rabbi, or justice of the peace, as well as couples who have been informally married. An informal marriage in Texas, often referred to as a common law marriage, is a legal marriage. In order to establish the existence of a **common law marriage**, a person claiming to have been a spouse must show three elements. First, the alleged spouse

[6] Tex. Fam. Code §3.003.

[7] Tex. Fam. Code § 3.001.

must prove that there was an agreement. This agreement can be either verbal or written. Second, he or she must establish that there was cohabitation with the other spouse. There is no minimum amount of time required in order to establish cohabitation. Living together for any length of time is sufficient. Third, the alleged spouse must establish that the couple represented themselves as a married couple.[8] If one is unsure if a couple is married, there is no requirement to obtain a copy of the marriage license. Under Texas law, if the couple discloses that they are married, in most cases that will be sufficient to presume they are married. If a lender or title company is involved in the transaction and no marriage license is of record, the company may require additional proof of marital status in the form of an affidavit that is sometimes referred to as a **Declaration of Informal Marriage**.

The issue of marital property is important for license holders to understand because Texas law requires that all contracts for the sale of community real property be signed by both spouses. In contracts for the purchase of real property by both spouses, marital status should be noted because the resulting deed will usually reflect the legal status of the parties. Marital status might be demonstrated in the contract when describing the parties and might contain special language noted after the parties' names, such as "a married couple" or "________________ (husband's name) and wife, ________________ (wife's name)."

At this point, it is also important to note that even though the real property may be in both parties' names, this detail alone is insufficient to establish survivorship rights to the property in one spouse if the other spouse dies. If survivorship rights are in place, then a deceased spouse's share in the property upon death will pass automatically to the surviving spouse. Without these rights, the deceased spouse's share will pass to his or her estate, which may or may not be the surviving spouse. If the parties are interested in survivorship rights in case of death, it must be indicated in the residential sales contract and addressed in the closing documents. The addition of language such as "with rights of survivorship," in addition to the parties' description, should be used.[9]

Co-Ownership

Tenancy in Common

Co-ownership is ownership of real or personal property by two or more persons. The type of co-ownership between unmarried persons recognized in Texas is called the **tenancy in common**. The tenant in common holds an undivided interest in the property, and there is no automatic right of survivorship between the parties. For example, Betty Jones and Bobby Smither purchase a 20-acre estate in Texas as "tenants in common." Betty Jones dies two years later. Her interest in the property would not go to Bobby Smither, but instead would pass to her estate.

---

[8] Tex. Fam. Code § 2.401.

[9] Tex. Est. Code Ch. 112.

However, a co-owner may establish the right of survivorship in the remaining co-owners by indicating in writing that the co-owners take the property with rights of survivorship. For example, Frank Brown and Barney Red purchase a condominium in Texas as "tenants in common with rights of survivorship." Under this type of ownership, if Frank Brown dies, his interest will pass to Barney Red rather than to his estate.

Joint Tenancy

Another type of co-ownership, which is not recognized in Texas, is the **joint tenancy**. This relationship was recognized at common law and created under the four unities: time, title, interest, and possession. The unity of time requires the joint tenants to take their interests at the same time. The unity of title requires that the joint tenants receive their interests in property under the same instrument. The unity of interest requires that the owners take the same interest in the property, such as fee simple, a life interest, or a defeasible fee. Last, the unity of possession means that each tenant has an undivided right of possession. In addition, the joint tenant has an automatic right of survivorship. That is, the entire tenancy of a deceased co-owner passes to the survivors by default rather than the estate of the deceased. A document in Texas that refers to the parties as "joint tenants" is presumed to create a tenancy in common, but *without* automatic rights of survivorship.

Co-ownership issues often arise in real estate transactions. Since the owners can take the title to the property either with or without rights of survivorship, it is important that co-owners be told they must seek an attorney so that the parties' intent in the co-ownership is established in the contract, as well as in the resulting title documents. Some brokers have in-house checklists drafted by attorneys to be used in this instance. These checklists indicate the parties' preference for survivorship similar to the checklists used by banks to set up survivorship in joint bank accounts.

OWNERSHIP OF REAL ESTATE BY BUSINESS ORGANIZATIONS

Sole Proprietorship

A real estate professional will often work with a business entity in the real estate transaction; therefore, it is important to have some background of the various types of business entities that are available in Texas. The most common type of business entity is a **sole proprietorship.** When a sole proprietorship is involved in the transaction, it may be identified, for example, as "_______ (name of individual) d.b.a. _________________(name of sole proprietorship)." The "d.b.a." is an abbreviation for "doing business as" and is seen typically when one person creates an assumed name in the local county clerk's office. It is considered to be a quick and easy entity to create by an individual as no formal papers need to be filed with the Texas Secretary of State's Office. However, the sole proprietorship is just a different hat for the underlying owner. As a result, there may be underlying community property issues that need to be considered with this type of entity.

Partnerships

In General

A **partnership** in Texas is defined as an association of two or more persons to carry on a business for profit.[10] There are three types of partnerships in Texas. These are the (1) general partnership, (2) limited partnership, and (3) limited liability partnership.

General Partnership

An entity similar to the sole proprietorship, but with the involvement of two or more persons is a **general partnership**. For example, if a general partnership is involved in the transaction, it may be identified as "________________ (name of the partnership), a partnership (or general partnership) consisting of ______________(first partner) and ____________(second partner)." Just like with the sole proprietorship, the general partnership is created by filing for an assumed name certificate in the local county clerk's office. It is considered to be a quick and easy entity to create as no formal papers need to be filed with the Texas Secretary of State's Office. However, the general partnership is just a different hat for the underlying owners. As with the sole proprietorship, there may be underlying community property issues that need to be considered with this type of entity.

Limited Partnership (LP)

A second type of partnership is the limited partnership. The **limited partnership** is similar to the general partnership because it involves two or more persons; however, the partners involved can have a different role as either general partners or limited partners.[11] The general partners are typically the managers of the company, while the limited partners are typically investors. The paperwork for creating this entity is filed with the Texas Secretary of State's Office instead of the local county clerk's office. However, only the general partners are named in the paperwork filed with the Texas Secretary of State's Office as well as on any subsequent real estate transaction paperwork. When a limited partnership is involved in a transaction, for example, it may be identified as "_______________(name of partnership), a limited partnership consisting of ___________(first partner) and ____________(second partner), general partners." Unfortunately, the limited

[10] Tex. Bus. Org. Code § 152.051(b).

[11] Tex. Bus. Org. Code Ch. 153.

partnership is still just a different hat for the underlying owners; therefore, there may still be underlying community property issues.

Limited Liability Partnership (LLP)

A third type of partnership is the limited liability partnership. A **limited liability partnership** is similar to a general partnership because it involves two or more persons, but the partners involved are not responsible for each other's misconduct.[12] This type of partnership is seen with professional organizations, such as law firms, in Texas. Just like with the limited partnership, the paperwork for creating this entity is filed with the Texas Secretary of State's Office instead of the local county clerk's office. When a limited liability partnership is involved in a transaction, for example, it may be identified as "___________(name of partnership), a limited liability partnership consisting of ___________(name of first partner) and _______________(name of second partner)." Just like with the other types of partnerships, the limited liability partnership is still just a different hat for the underlying owners; therefore, there may still be underlying community property issues.

Corporations

Another business entity seen in Texas is the **corporation.**[13] When a Texas corporation is involved in the transaction, for example, it may be identified as "__________(name of corporation), a domestic (or Texas) corporation." If a foreign corporation is involved, such as a corporation from Delaware for example, it may be identified as "_______(name of corporation), a foreign (or Delaware) corporation." Just like with the limited partnership and limited liability partnerships, the paperwork for creating this entity is filed with the Texas Secretary of State's Office instead of the local county clerk's office. A significant benefit over the limited partnerships; however, is that the corporation is considered a separate entity from that of the underlying owners so the owners in a corporation are not just simply wearing a different hat. Therefore, there are no underlying community property issues for the entity.

Limited Liability Companies (LLC)

The last type of Texas business entity is the **limited liability company.**[14] When a limited liability company is involved in a transaction, for example, it may be identified as "_______________(name of company), a Texas limited liability company." Just like with the corporation, the paperwork for creating this entity

[12] Tex. Bus. Org. Code Ch. 153, Subch. H.

[13] Tex. Bus. Org. Code Ch. 21.

[14] Tex. Bus. Org. Code Ch. 101.

is filed with the Texas Secretary of State's Office instead of the local county clerk's office.

PROPERTY DESCRIPTIONS AND CONDOMINIUMS, COOPERATIVES, TOWNHOUSES, AND TIME-SHARES

The legal description of real property is important for determining ownership of that real property. Therefore, the sales contract and the deed must describe the premises with reasonable certainty in order to constitute a valid property description. When listing the real estate, the license holder should use the property description from the seller's deed. Tax statements are not always accurate, and the street address alone is insufficient. A **survey** is often used to measure the real estate to determine boundaries in addition to total size, but it is not required in all situations. The promulgated sales contract addresses the survey options available to the buyer.

In Texas, there are several methods used to describe property, and this property description will often dictate which residential sales contract form is used. These descriptions include the metes and bounds description, the recorded lot and block description, and the condominium description.

Metes and Bounds

Metes and bounds is a common method for describing rural property in Texas. A metes and bounds description may also be used to describe urban property that is not part of a subdivision. The process of describing property by metes and bounds involves delineating the exterior boundaries of the property by making reference to landmarks, distances, and directions. It begins and ends at an established point of beginning (POB). Because the metes and bounds description can be very long, the actual description is typically copied from the deed and attached as an exhibit to the sales contract.

Lot and Block

Subdivisions of property are quite common in urban areas. In order to create a subdivision, however, a plat must be drafted and recorded in the county deed records. A **plat** is a map of an area of land that incorporates the rural metes and bounds description of the entire property, but is subdivided as necessary for the subdivision project. Subdivisions can be created for both houses and townhouses. **Townhouses** are merely houses with several floors that can be constructed within a smaller footprint of land. Sales of townhouses involve the building as well as the underlying land so they are treated the same as houses for purposes of the sales contracts. It is also possible to have a townhouse apartment, which involves a lease arrangement rather than an ownership interest. Leases are discussed in more detail in a later chapter.

Once the property is subdivided, each lot retains its own property description. For houses, this property description is typically in the form of "lot ____, block ____, NCB ___, ______________ subdivision." For townhouses; however, there might not be a "block" designation as townhouse projects don't typically involve streets like the subdivisions for houses. In the lot and block description, the term NCB refers to a "new city block." If a lot and block description does not use the NCB designation, then it may use a CB designation. In this case, CB simply refers to "county block." The lot and block description is seen in the One- to Four-Family Residential Contract (TREC 20-14). Using this contract description as a guide, the description of a house within a subdivision might read:

> Lot 10, Block 20, NCB 1020 Springfeld Subdivision Addition, City of San Antonio, County of Bexar, Texas, known as 1234 Carter Way 78244, or as described on the attached exhibit.

Condominiums

Condominiums are quite popular because they give the joy of real property ownership without the burden of upkeep. **Condominium ownership** involves ownership of the unit plus an undivided ownership in the land underneath and an undivided ownership interest in the common elements on the premises, such as the stairways and the sidewalks. According to the Uniform Condominium Act, which applies to Texas condominiums established on or after January 1, 1994, a condominium is defined as "a form of real property with portions of the real property designated for separate ownership or occupancy, and the remainder of the real property designated for common ownership or occupancy solely by the owners of those portions." Real property is a condominium only if one or more of the common elements are directly owned in undivided interests by the unit owners.[15] The "unit" within the condominium is defined as "the physical portion of the condominium designated for separate ownership or occupancy, the boundaries of which are described by the declaration."[16] Whereas, the "common elements" are defined as "all portions of a condominium other than the units and includes both general and limited common elements."[17]

Real property is not a condominium if all of the common elements are owned by a legal entity separate from the unit owners, such as a corporation, even if the separate legal entity is owned by the unit owners.[18] This provision serves to distinguish a condominium from a cooperative. A **cooperative** is similar to

[15] Tex. Prop. Code § 82.003(8).
[16] Tex. Prop. Code § 82.003(23).
[17] Tex. Prop. Code § 82.003(5).
[18] Tex. Prop. Code § 82.003(8).

a condominium because it involves ownership of the unit and the common areas, but the ownership is not by the residents as is the case for condominiums. Instead, the ownership is held by a corporation. The individual residents own a stock share in the corporation, which entitles them to reside in the unit and share the common areas. The corporation maintains the premises so a cooperative is similar to a lease arrangement.

When a transaction involves the sale or purchase of a condominium, there is one contract that can be used—the Residential Condominium Contract (Resale) (TREC 30-13). In this contract, the condominium property description may look as follows:

> Condominium Unit 06, in Building 12, of Lone Oak Condominiums, a condominium project, located at 100 West Sard, 72222, City of Castle, Bravo County, Texas, described in the Condominium Declaration and Plat and any amendments thereto of record in said County; together with such Unit's undivided interest in the Common Elements designated by the Declaration, including those areas reserved as Limited Common Elements appurtenant to the Unit and such other rights to use the Common Elements which have been specifically assigned to the Unit in any other manner.

Condominiums can also be leased. In fact, the Uniform Condominium Act defines a "leasehold condominium" as "a condominium in which all or a portion of the real property is subject to a lease the expiration or termination of which will terminate the condominium or reduce its size." Leases will be discussed in more detail in a later chapter.

Another common use for condominiums is as time-share properties. Although just about anything (apartment, condominium or cooperative unit, hotel or motel room, cabin, lodge, or other private or commercial structure) will suffice for time-share purposes as long as it (a) is affixed to real property; (b) is designed for occupancy or use by one or more individuals; and (c) is part of a timeshare plan.[19] Time-shares in Texas are governed by the Texas Timeshare Act and are considered real estate according to the Texas Real Estate License Act.[20] However, the real estate interest is a co-ownership interest among multiple owners whereby the co-owners agree that their ownership is limited to a certain time period each year. Given the complexities involved with a time-share transaction, the developer typically provides his or her own contract for the transaction rather than use the standard promulgated Texas Real Estate Commission forms. However, the time-share plan must be approved by the Texas Real Estate Commission.

---

[19] Tex. Prop. Code § 221.002(1).

[20] Tex. Prop. Code § 221.011(c); Tex. Occ. Code § 1101.002(5).

LAWS AFFECTING REAL ESTATE

Depending on the type of contract involved in a given real estate situation, there may be many different laws that affect the use and application of the contract as well as the parties' rights and obligations under the contract. In addition, there may be many different real estate laws that may affect the underlying transaction, but that may or may not be addressed in the contract. These laws may come from several different sources. Laws may be classified as either federal law or state law. Both federal and state laws may be further classified according to constitutional law, statutory law, regulatory law, and case law, as discussed next.

Constitutional Law

The primary source of law at the federal level is the **United States Constitution**. This constitution sets forth the fundamental law of the nation and sets forth the principles relating to the organization and regulation of the federal government. Within the federal constitution, there are a few provisions that relate directly to contract and real estate law. For example, the **Contract clause** of the United States Constitution provides that no state shall pass a law that impairs the obligation under a contract. In addition, the **Full Faith and Credit clause** of the federal constitution essentially states that contracts and other legal documents executed in one state are valid in all other states. The United States Constitution can be found in the *United States Code (U.S.C.), Constitution Volumes.*

The equivalent source of constitutional law at the state level is the **Texas Constitution**. The Texas Constitution sets forth the primary law of the state as well as the organization and regulation of the state government. Of great importance to Texans, the Texas Constitution provides for a homestead exemption, which protects the family home from forced sale by general creditors. This provision is also important to real estate license holders as it relates to the listing and sale of homestead property. The text of the Texas Constitution can be found in *Vernon's Texas Constitution* or online on the Texas legislature website, www.constitution.legis.state.tx.us.

Statutory Law

Another source of law in the United States is federal statutory law. Federal statutes are Acts of Congress that command or prohibit some type of action. Several federal statutes have application to the real estate business as well as to real estate license holders. For example, the Real Estate Settlement Procedures Act requires that borrowers receive disclosures from their lenders at specified times to allow them to comparison shop when seeking a mortgage. In addition, the federal Fair Housing Act prohibits discrimination in the sale or lease of residential real property on the basis of race, color, religion, national origin, sex, handicap, or familial status. Federal statutory law can be found in the *United States Code (U.S.C.), Statutes Volumes.*

Several Texas statutes play a key role in the real estate business and real estate transactions in general. The Texas Property Code relates entirely to transactions involving properties, particularly conveyances of real estate. The Texas Natural Resources Code and Texas Water Code deal with interests in subsurface estates such as minerals and water rights. The Texas Estates Code dictates what the practice and procedure is for the disposition of assets, including real property, and the clearing of title to land upon death. And the Texas Real Estate License Act, found in the Texas Occupations Code, governs the practice and procedure of real estate license holders and provides for penalties for violations of the licensing act. Statutory law can be found in two locations in Texas—*Vernon's Texas Codes* and *Vernon's Texas Civil Statutes*. Both of these resources are available on the Texas Legislature website, www.statutes.legis.state.tx.us.

Agency Rules and Regulations

Rules and regulations provide much of the guidance for the real estate industry. Rules are standards of practice established by an agency, whereas regulations are the means by which the standards are enforced. At the federal level, the Department of Housing and Urban Development (HUD) implements rules and regulations that affect federal housing programs. HUD investigates instances of housing discrimination as well as unsafe housing conditions. In addition, the Environmental Protection Agency (EPA) implements rules and regulations concerning environmental issues. Federal agency rules and regulations are located in the *Code of Federal Regulations* (C.F.R.), an annual publication, which incorporates the final rules outlined in the *Federal Register* (Fed. Reg.), a daily publication. The text of both of these publications can be found on the Government Printing Office's website, www.gpo.gov.

The Texas agency of great importance to license holders is the Texas Real Estate Commission. The Texas Real Estate Commission (TREC) is the state agency that issues real estate licenses in Texas. The Commission is also responsible for drafting rules and regulations that govern license holder behavior and enforce violations of the Texas Real Estate License Act. This authority is given to TREC from the state legislature. Texas agency rules and regulations are located in the *Texas Administrative Code* (T.A.C), an annual publication, which incorporates the final rules outlined in the *Texas Register* (Tex. Reg.), a daily publication. The text of both of these publications can be found on the Texas Secretary of State's website, www.sos.state.tx.us.

Case Law

Both federal and state case law play an important role in creating uniformity for license holder behavior and for the real estate industry as a whole. Case law takes the facts and results of previous similar cases, often referred to as precedent, and applies them to the case at hand to reach a similar result. However, jurisdiction in a federal court is more limited than that of a Texas court. There are only two ways to establish jurisdiction in a federal court. These two methods are federal question jurisdiction and diversity of citizenship jurisdiction. In **federal question jurisdiction**, there must be a federal question involved. That is, some federal law must have an implication in the case.[21] For example, a farmer is sent notice by the federal government that he or she can no longer plant crops on the back 50 acres of his or her land because it might upset the habitat of the golden-cheeked warbler. The protection of the bird involves the federal Endangered Species Act and, as a taking for which compensation was not provided, implicates the Fifth Amendment to the U.S. Constitution. Therefore, a federal question is involved that can be handled in the federal courts.

If there is no federal question involved, then the only other means of establishing jurisdiction would be based on diversity of citizenship. In order to establish **diversity of citizenship jurisdiction**, the suit must involve citizens from different states, and there must be an amount in controversy in excess of $75,000.[22] For example, Jenny Seller of Sunny, California, places an ad on the internet that states, "Beautiful waterfront lots for sale—only $80,000." Betty Buyer of Pensacola, Florida, sees the ad and sends $80,000 with a letter that says, "Just send me the title." Betty Buyer never receives the title and files suit in federal court. The diversity of citizenship can be established in this case.

If federal jurisdiction can be established, then trial can be brought in a federal district court. The four major federal district courts in Texas are the Eastern District, the Western District, the Southern District, and the Northern District. Each of these courts maintains a website where recent court decisions can be retrieved. In addition, published decisions from these courts can be obtained through a publication called the *Federal Supplement* (F. Supp., F.Supp.2d, F.Supp.3d). If an adverse judgment is obtained in the federal district court, then the losing party may choose to appeal to a federal appellate court. Appeals from the federal district courts in Texas are to the Fifth Circuit, an intermediate appellate court. The Fifth Circuit also maintains a website where recent court decisions can be retrieved. Published decisions for the Fifth Circuit, along with those from other federal intermediate appellate courts, are found in the *Federal Reporter* (F., F.2d, F.3d). An appeal from an adverse judgment at the intermediate appellate level will progress the losing party to the United States Supreme Court, where review is limited. The United States Supreme Court also maintains its own website for recent opinions. Published decisions for the United States Supreme Court are also found in the *United States Reports* (U.S.).

Trial in the Texas court system begins in a Texas lower court. Four types of primary civil trial courts are found in Texas—the justice court, constitutional

---

[21] 28 U.S.C. § 1331.

[22] 28 U.S.C. § 1332.

county court, statutory county court, and district court. The lower courts are county-specific and the county where the legal issue arose dictates the court chosen. The lowest of these courts is the justice court. The **justice court** has a jurisdictional amount of between $0.01 and $10,000.[23] In addition to an exclusive jurisdictional amount, the justice court has exclusive subject matter jurisdiction over forcible entry and detainer actions, more commonly referred to as eviction proceedings. These evictions are cases that deal with the struggle over possession of real property between a landlord and a tenant. Cases dealing with rent disputes will be settled in the court with adequate jurisdictional amounts. An appeal from the justice court is always to the county court at law where the parties receive a trial de novo, that is, a new trial. The justice court also has concurrent jurisdiction with the district court over suits relating to enforcement of residential subdivision deed restrictions that do not concern a structural change to a dwelling.[24] However, a justice court does not have jurisdiction of: (1) a suit in behalf of the state to recover a penalty, forfeiture, or escheat; (2) a suit for divorce; (3) a suit to recover damages for slander or defamation of character; (4) a suit for trial of title to land; or (5) a suit for the enforcement of a lien on land.[25]

The **constitutional county court** is the next available trial court. This court has a jurisdictional amount of between $200.01 and $10,000 and therefore overlaps the jurisdiction of the justice court.[26] A county court has appellate jurisdiction in civil cases over which the justice courts have original jurisdiction in cases in which the judgment appealed from or the amount in controversy exceeds $250.[27]

The third trial court is the **county court at law**. This court has a jurisdictional amount of between $500.01 and $200,000.[28] It also has subject matter jurisdiction in probate proceedings where there is no statutory probate court.

The highest trial court is the **district court**. This court has a jurisdictional amount in excess of $500.[29] This court has subject matter jurisdiction over suits (1) to recover damages for slander or defamation of character; (2) for the enforcement of a lien on land; (3) on behalf of the state for escheat; (4) for divorce; (5) for the forfeiture of a corporate charter; (6) for the trial of the right to property valued at $500 or more and levied on under a writ of execution, sequestration, or attachment; (7) for eminent domain; or (8) for the recovery of land (trespass to try title).[30] An appeal taken from this court will be made to the court of appeals.[31]

---

[23] Tex. Gov't Code § 27.031(a).
[24] Tex. Gov't Code § 27.034(a).
[25] Tex. Gov't Code § 27.031(b).
[26] Tex. Gov't Code § 26.042.
[27] Tex. Gov't Code § 26.042(e).
[28] Tex. Gov't Code § 25.0003.
[29] Tex. Gov't Code § 24.007.
[30] Tex. Gov't Code § 26.043.
[31] Tex. Gov't Code § 22.220.

Most real estate and contract issues are resolved in the district court. District court opinions, however, cannot be found online nor are they published in any other form. Appeal from the district court is to an intermediate appellate court. There are multiple appellate courts in Texas determined by region. In this intermediate appellate court, there is no trial per se, but rather a review by the court of the trial court proceedings to determine if there was any error. This court may either affirm, or agree to, the decision of the lower court; or reverse the decision of the trial court and render its own opinion; or reverse and remand the case to the trial court to reissue an opinion consistent with that of the court of appeals. Both issues of fact and issues of law are considered at this level. Intermediate appellate court decisions may be found on the individual court's website. Published decisions are also found in the *South Western Reporter* (S.W., S.W.2d, S.W.3d).

Civil appeals from the intermediate appellate court are made to the Texas Supreme Court. However, review of cases by the Texas Supreme Court is limited to questions of law that are important to the jurisprudence of the state.[32] Recent Texas Supreme Court decisions can be found on the court's website. In addition, published decisions from this court can also be found in the *South Western Reporter*. The different levels of both the federal and state court system are shown in figure 2-3.

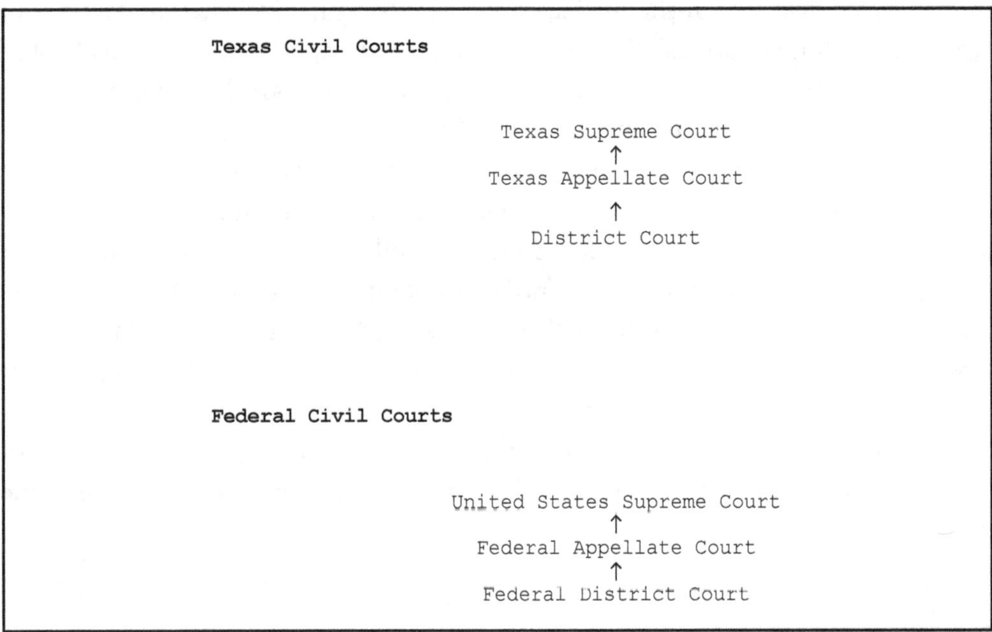

FIGURE 2-3 The Texas and Federal Civil Court Systems
Source: © 2021 Mbition LLC

[32] Tex. Gov't Code § 22.001.

Discussion Questions

1. List three Texas statutes that concern real estate.
2. List the hierarchy of the federal civil court system.
3. What is the distinction between community property and separate property? Give an example of each. Why is it necessary to know whether property is community property or separate property when listing a property for sale?
4. What is an example of a form of co-ownership recognized in Texas? Describe this form of co-ownership and how a listing might be affected by this type of ownership or potential ownership?
5. When might a bill of sale be used in a real estate sales contract?
6. What are the types of property descriptions used in Texas, and when might each be used?

CHAPTER

3

INTRODUCTION TO CONTRACTS

KEY TERMS

bilateral contract
consideration
contract
durable power of attorney
executed contract
executory contract
express contract
gratuitous consideration
guardianship
implied contract
intoxicated individuals
letters of guardianship
lis pendens
mental capacity
mentally infirm
minors
misrepresentation
necessaries
nominal consideration
option contract
past consideration
pecuniary consideration
power of attorney
preexisting legal duty
promissory estoppel
ratification
unenforceable contract
Uniform Vendor and Purchaser Risk Act
unilateral contract
valid contract
valuable consideration
voidable contract
void contract

ELEMENTS OF A VALID CONTRACT

For purposes of this text, a **contract** is "a promise or a set of promises for the breach of which the law gives a remedy, or the performance of which the law in some way recognizes as a duty."[1] The promises set out in the contract can be either verbal or written. In order for the promises to constitute a valid contract, certain essential elements must be present. These essential elements include the mutual assent of the parties, which is evidenced by an offer and an acceptance, consideration,

[1] *Restatement (Second) of Contracts §1 (1981).*

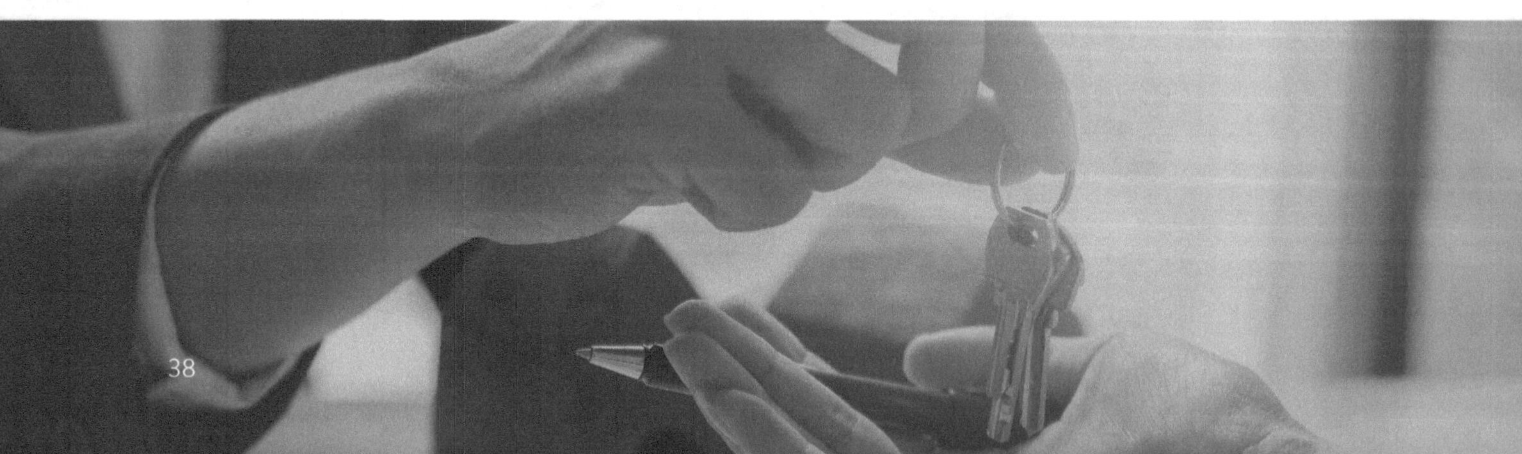

capacity of the parties, and legality. For contracts involving the sale of real estate, for example, a doctrine called the Statute of Frauds requires that the contracts be in writing to be enforceable in a court of law. Mutual assent, in the form of an offer and an acceptance, as well as the Statute of Frauds will be discussed in later chapters. Consideration, capacity of the parties, and legality of the contract, however, will be addressed.

Consideration

Consideration is simply the inducement to a contract, often referred to as a bargained for exchange between the parties to an agreement. Therefore promises that are the result of a bargained for exchange are enforceable. Further, in this bargained-for exchange, each party must experience both a benefit and a detriment. In figure 3-1, A gives a benefit to B, which results in a detriment to A. In addition, B gives a benefit to A, which results in a detriment to B. In real estate transactions, there are various types of consideration.

The first type of consideration commonly found in real estate transactions is a promise given in exchange for a promise. The promise in exchange for a promise is used as the consideration present in a bilateral contract. For example, in a contract for the purchase and sale of real estate, a prospective purchaser promises to pay the sales price in exchange for the seller's promise to transfer the title to the property, as shown in figure 3-2. This promise in exchange for a promise constitutes sufficient consideration to establish a valid contract. This means that a promise is enough.

Unlike the bilateral contract, the consideration in a unilateral contract is a promise given in exchange for performance. For example, a seller under a listing agreement promises to pay a specified commission in exchange for the broker's performance in bringing forth a ready, willing, and able purchaser.

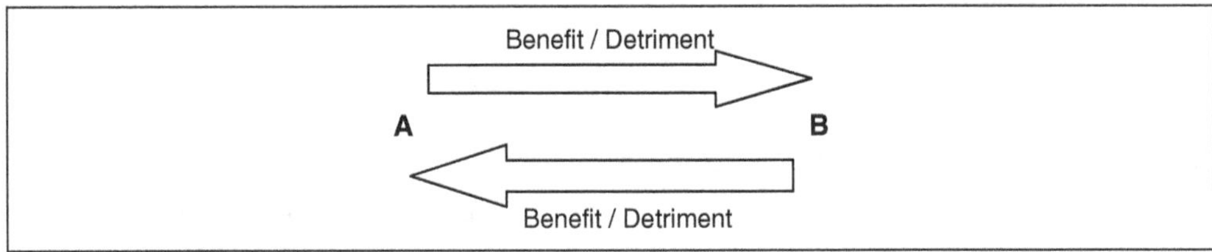

FIGURE 3-1 Mutual Benefit and Detriment in Consideration
Source: © 2021 Mbition LLC

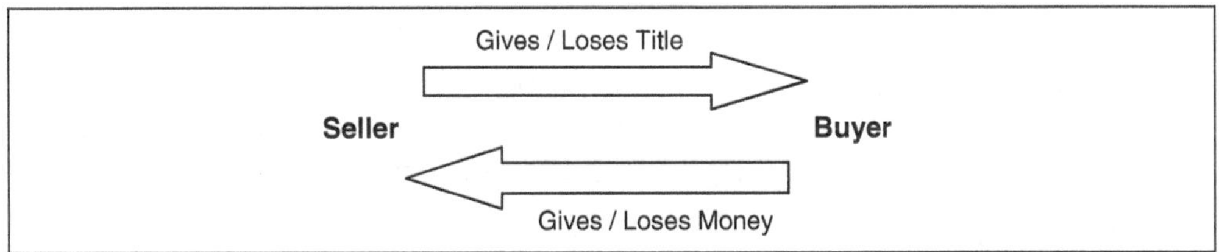

FIGURE 3-2 Exchange of Promises in a Real Estate Sales Contract
Source: © 2021 Mbition LLC

Money as Consideration

Another type of consideration used to form a valid contract is **pecuniary consideration** (money). This type of consideration may also be found in real estate transactions, for instance, with options. In a typical option under the promulgated residential sales contract, a prospective purchaser may pay a fixed sum for the option to terminate the contract for the purchase and sale of real estate for any reason within a specified time. For example, Billy Buyer contracts with Sam Seller whereby Billy Buyer pays $50 to Sam Seller for the unrestricted right to terminate the contract within three days. The $50 that is given is sufficient pecuniary consideration to keep the right to terminate open for three days.

In contrast to this pecuniary consideration is earnest money. A common misconception is that earnest money constitutes the consideration that makes a purchase and sale contract valid. Earnest money, however, does not constitute consideration under a purchase and sale contract. Therefore, *there is no requirement that earnest money be given to create a valid contract.* Earnest money under a purchase and sale contract is merely a gesture of the prospective purchaser's good faith and therefore is only used to make the offer more enticing to the seller. For practical purposes, earnest money is usually included.

There are two types of monetary consideration typically seen with real estate transactions. These are nominal consideration and valuable consideration. **Nominal consideration** is consideration that bears no relation to the real value of the contract. In Texas real estate sales, this is typically seen in a standard warranty deed that transfers title to the property from the owner to the new purchaser. For example, the deed might state, "I, Grantor, for and in consideration of 10 and no/100 dollars ($10.00) do grant, sell, and convey unto said Grantee." In contrast, **valuable consideration** is consideration that bears a substantial relation to the real value of the contract. This type of consideration is sufficient to create a valid contract. For example, Frank gives Tina $50 to keep an offer on Whiteacre open for three days. This is sufficient consideration to bind the option.

Gratuitous Consideration

If either party to the transaction intends to make a gift, then there is typically no detriment induced and therefore there is no consideration. This is often referred to as **gratuitous consideration**. Thus, a promise to make a gift, in itself, is insufficient to create a valid contract. For example, Bob promises to convey Blackacre to Sarah as a gift. Sarah is excited about the prospect of owning Blackacre. Nothing more is said between the parties. A valid contract in this instance has not been created because Sarah has given no benefit and suffered no detriment. See figure 3-3.

However, there may be instances where a gratuitous promise may operate as valid consideration. Specifically, a gratuitous promise will be found to be enforceable if it induces the promisee to take detrimental action in reliance on the promise. For example, in the previous scenario where Bob promised to convey Blackacre to Sarah, if Sarah had sold her existing property in reliance on the promise, then the promise

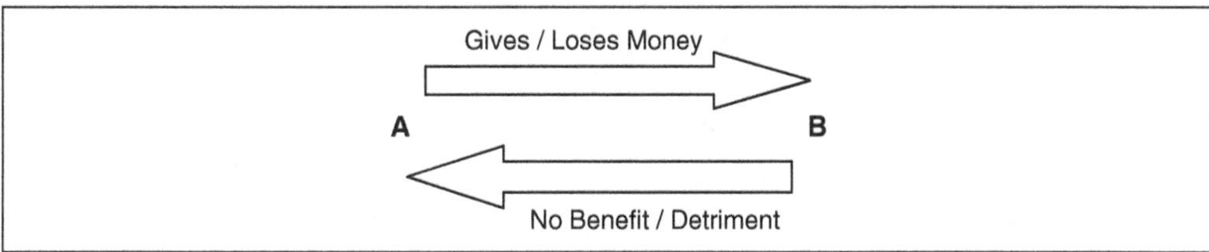

FIGURE 3-3 No Contract with Gratuitous Consideration
Source: © 2021 Mbition LLC

may have been enforced. This form of consideration is very important in those situations where people transfer property to their children or other family members.

Past Consideration

Past consideration refers to an act completed before the contract is created. Past consideration on an old transaction is not consideration on a new transaction and, therefore, cannot create a valid contract. Past consideration is dealt with under three doctrines. These concern a preexisting legal duty, additional consideration, and voidable contracts.

The general rule with regard to a preexisting legal duty is that the promise or performance of a preexisting legal duty does not constitute sufficient consideration for the creation of a subsequent valid contract. A **preexisting legal duty** is a duty a party is already obligated to perform. For example, Ben Builder contracts with Harry Homeowner whereby Ben Builder agrees to build a house on Harry Homeowner's property for $65,000. Ben Builder realizes after he signs the contract that he will not be able to complete the project for any amount below $69,000. Harry Homeowner agrees to the change. After construction of the home, Harry Homeowner pays Ben Builder $65,000. Ben Builder cannot enforce the agreement for the additional $4,000 because he had a preexisting legal duty to construct the house under the old contract. See figure 3-4.

Where additional consideration is combined with the promise or performance of a preexisting legal duty, this is sufficient to create a valid enforceable

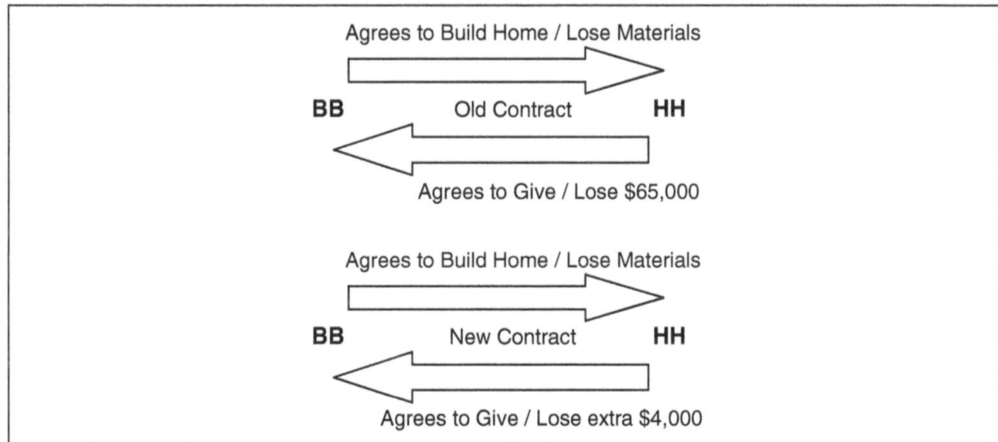

FIGURE 3-4 No Consideration for Preexisting Legal Duty
Source: © 2021 Mbition LLC

agreement. For example, Clarence Contractor contracts with Holly Homeowner to build a home on Holly Homeowner's property for $100,000. Clarence Contractor subsequently finds that he cannot complete the job for less than $105,000. Holly Homeowner agrees, and they modify the agreement. Additional consideration is exchanged to bind this new agreement. Clarence Contractor constructs the home, and Holly Homeowner only pays him $100,000. Clarence may now enforce the agreement for the additional $5,000 even though the agreement involved a preexisting legal duty to construct the house because the new agreement was supported by additional consideration. See figure 3-5.

A voidable contract is a contract that can be voided at the option of one party to the contract. A voidable agreement can be created by a minor. Contracts created by minors are termed voidable because the minor has the option to terminate the contract at any time during his or her period of minority and within a reasonable time after he or she reaches the age of majority with a few exceptions. However, when a voidable agreement is ratified, the new agreement is enforceable without additional consideration. **Ratification** is simply the confirmation of a previous contract. For example, Maggie Minor enters into a contract with Annie Agent in which Annie Agent is to find Maggie Minor a home in exchange for a fee. During Maggie Minor's minority, the contract is voidable at her option. Upon reaching the age of 18, Maggie Minor ratifies the representation agreement. Subsequently, Maggie Minor backs out of the contract, arguing that she has the option to void the contract for a reasonable time after she turns 18. However, the ratified agreement is enforceable even though it relates to a preexisting legal duty and even though it is not supported by additional consideration.

An agreement may be enforceable in some instances without consideration if the facts of the situation indicate that injustice may result. This may arise under the doctrine of **promissory estoppel**. To enforce an agreement without consideration under the doctrine of promissory estoppel, four elements must be

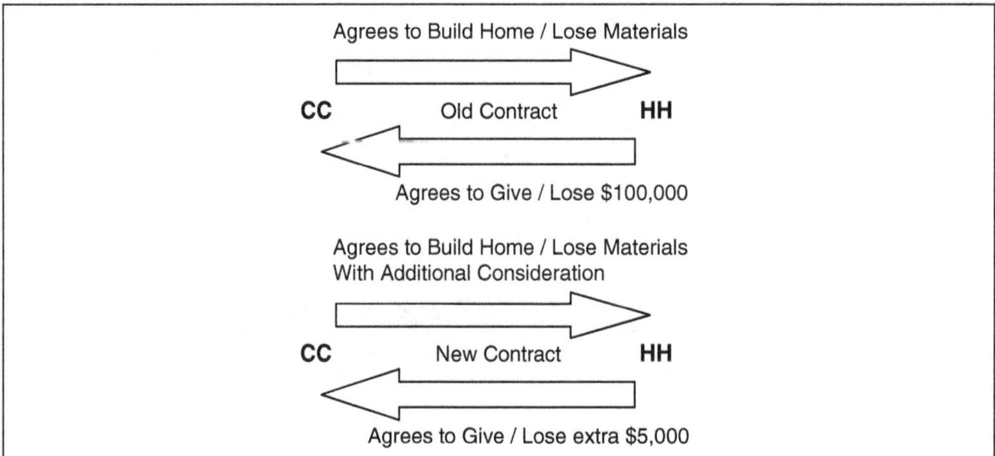

FIGURE 3-5 Preexisting Legal Duty Coupled with Additional Consideration
Source: © 2021 Mbition LLC

established. First, there must be a promise made to the injured party. Second, that promise must be calculated to induce reliance by the injured party. Third, there must be actual reliance on the promise by the injured party. Fourth, some injustice may result if the agreement is not enforced. For example, Owen offers to give Polly Purchaser $10,000 toward a down payment on a new home if she decides to go through with the purchase. Polly Purchaser relies on this promise. Polly Purchaser closes the transaction with $10,000 from her savings. Owen in this case is responsible for the $10,000 he promised to contribute to the closing.

Capacity of the Parties

Another essential element to the validity of a contract is the legal capacity of the parties involved. The purpose for requiring parties to the contract to be legally competent centers around the notion that we as a society should protect individuals who may not be capable of understanding the nature of a contractual relationship. However, given the ambiguity involved in some transactions, it is difficult to determine during a transaction whether a party is incompetent, and it is equally difficult to determine at trial whether or not a party was incompetent at the time of the transaction in question. This difficulty with hindsight can be a detriment because a party cannot be assured of enforcement in some instances. This lack of clarity regarding capacity is reflected in the typical listing and buyer representation agreements that contain provisions attesting to the capacity of the individual.

Minors

There are several classes of individuals who lack the capacity to contract. The first class incapable of contracting is minors. **Minors** can be defined as individuals (1) who are under the age of 18, (2) who have never been married, and (3) who have not had their disability of minority removed by a court order. A contract entered into by a minor is voidable at the option of the minor. In other words, the minor at any time during his or her minority or within a reasonable time after majority may terminate the contract without liability for breach of the contract. For example, Pam Purchaser goes to a brokerage office to solicit help in purchasing a new home. Pam Purchaser talks with Amy Agent, and they enter into a Buyer Representation Agreement. Five days after the contract is signed, Pam Purchaser decides that she is no longer interested in seeking help for the purchase of a home and would rather look for a home on her own. Since Pam Purchaser has backed out of the contract without a legal excuse, Amy Agent sues Pam Purchaser for breach of contract. Pam Purchaser's defense is that she was a minor when she entered into the contract, and she is still a minor, and therefore, she has the right to walk away from the contract. Since the contract was voidable at Pam Purchaser's option due to her minority, Amy Agent will not be able to enforce the contract against Pam Purchaser, and therefore, Pam Purchaser will win. However, even though a contract is voidable at the minor's option, the minor may not disaffirm the obligations under a contract and still retain the benefits. For example, Julie Minor enters into a contract for the purchase of an unimproved lot that she agrees to pay for through financing for one year. If Julie Minor decides to walk away from this agreement during her minority, she cannot keep the property.

Necessaries

There are two major exceptions to the ability of the minor to disaffirm a contract. The first exception involves contracts for necessaries. **Necessaries** are defined as "board, lodging, wearing apparel, medicine, medical attendance, and education." If a contract for necessaries is involved, then the contract can be enforced against the minor. Purchase and sale agreements are considered contracts for necessaries. Although, few minors will have the financial capacity to purchase real estate. But a license holder will want to take extreme caution when working for or with a minor if the opportunity arises because employment agreements are not considered contracts for necessaries.

Misrepresentation

The second exception to the voidability of a minor's contract involves misrepresentation by the minor of the minor's age. A **misrepresentation** is an untrue statement of material fact. Unfortunately, before an individual can raise this exception, he or she must show that he or she was actually misled by the minor and that the misrepresentation induced the making of the contract. Since the general practice in brokerage offices is to require completion of an intake sheet, this document can be used to establish the misrepresentation.

The misrepresentation can be made in writing, verbally, or by conduct. However, the mere fact that the other party believed that he or she was dealing with an adult is insufficient to invoke this exception unless the facts are sufficient to raise the issue of promissory estoppel, discussed earlier.

Mentally Incapacitated Parties

The second class of individuals incapable of contracting is mentally incapacitated parties. A person is considered mentally incapacitated where he or she is incapable of reasoning or acting with discretion in his or her personal affairs. **Mental capacity** refers to the ability of a person to understand the nature and effect of the acts in which he or she is engaged and the business that he or she is transacting. When a mentally incapacitated individual enters into a contract, the contract is voidable at the option of the incapacitated individual. This is often difficult to determine because there is no public record available of mentally incapacitated people if no formal hearing has taken place. If the individual has been judicially declared incompetent, the contract is void. This is easier to determine because this information is typically public record. There are two types of individuals referred to as mentally incapacitated. The first group is the mentally infirm. A **mentally infirm** individual is a person of weak mental health.

The second group of individuals who may be referred to as mentally incapacitated are intoxicated individuals. An **intoxicated individual** is a person who is under the influence of an intoxicant. The intoxicant can consist of alcohol, illicit drugs, prescription medication, or over-the-counter medication. If a person enters into a contract when he or she is intoxicated enough to be deprived of his or her understanding, the contract may be voided by him or her, even though the intoxication was voluntary and not brought about by the acts of the other party.

Guardianships

In some cases, rather than dealing directly with a minor or incapacitated individual, a license holder may deal directly with a guardian acting on behalf of the minor or incapacitated individual. A **guardianship** is a legal arrangement whereby one person, the guardian, is given the legal right and duty to care for another, the ward, and the ward's property.

A guardianship for a minor may be created by a will or other written document of the minor's parent which appoints a guardian to act on behalf of the minor. Where no will or written document dictates the guardianship for a minor or where a guardianship for an incapacitated individual is involved, the guardianship will be created by a court and is established because the ward is unable to legally act on his or her own behalf. In Texas, when a guardianship is created by a court, the appointed guardian is issued certified **Letters of Guardianship**. If an individual claiming to be a guardian attempts to list the property of another, the license holder must get proof of the guardian's authority by requesting a certified copy of these Letters of Guardianship from the guardian before the license holder lists the property and must include this information in the transaction file. Once the guardian has established his or her authority, the guardian may be indicated in all of the necessary documentation as "_______________ (Name of guardian), guardian of ___________________ (Name of ward), ward."

Powers of Attorney

A **power of attorney** is a written instrument whereby one person, the principal, appoints another, the attorney in fact, as his or her agent and gives the agent authority to perform certain acts on behalf of the principal. The powers conferred under the power of attorney can be either general or special. A general power of attorney gives the attorney in fact full power to handle the principal's assets. A special power of attorney gives the attorney in fact limited power to handle the principal's assets. This is typically done in a list form. The key thing a listing agent must remember is to make sure he or she knows up front that the person is acting under a power of attorney. Furthermore, the license holder must read the power of attorney to make sure it authorizes the actions of the attorney in fact. If the actions are authorized the license holder must get a copy of the power of attorney for his or her file; a photocopy will suffice.

In addition, there may be times when the license holder's client requests the license holder to act on the client's behalf if the client happens to be out of town, for example. In this type of a situation, the license holder should be careful not to make any type of final decision on behalf of the client without written authorization to act as an attorney in fact on behalf of the client. The employment agreements typically used with clients in real estate sales transactions do not function as powers of attorney. Without this authorization, if the client decides he or she doesn't like the decisions the license holder made on his or her behalf, the client can always argue that the license holder had no authorization and breached his or her fiduciary duty to the client. The more practical approach to handling matters of out-of-town clients is to get a fax number from them and fax the document to them for their signatures.

In Texas, a real estate license holder may actually encounter two types of powers of attorney. The first is simply referred to as a power of attorney. This power of attorney is only effective while the principal is alive and competent. The second type of power of attorney is referred to as a durable power of attorney. The authority under this **durable power of attorney** continues while the principal is alive and even if the principal becomes incompetent. The attorney in fact under the power of attorney may be indicated in all necessary documentation as "______________ (name of principal) by ________________________ (name of attorney in fact) as agent." The Texas statutory form for the durable power of attorney is in figure 3-6.[2]

Legality

The last essential element of a contract to discuss in this chapter is legality. When parties enter into a contract, the contract must be legal. This applies to legality in the terms as well as legality in the purpose and performance of the contract. Therefore, in real estate sales transactions, the general rule has developed that a contract for the purchase and sale of real property or any interest in real property that violates, or furthers the violation of, law or public policy is illegal. If an illegal contract is involved, the contract is void and unenforceable. Furthermore, the parties to the illegal contract cannot recover from each other under the contract. Therefore, if one party to the illegal contract fails to perform, the non-defaulting party cannot recover either damages or specific performance in a court of law. There are several instances in which a real estate contract has been found illegal. Certain illegal acts or provisions may arise where there is a contravention of public policy, a contravention of law, an unlawful intent of the parties, fraud, or deception.

---

[2] Tex. Est. Code § 752.051.

STATUTORY DURABLE POWER OF ATTORNEY

NOTICE: THE POWERS GRANTED BY THIS DOCUMENT ARE BROAD AND SWEEPING. THEY ARE EXPLAINED IN THE DURABLE POWER OF ATTORNEY ACT, SUBTITLE P, TITLE 2, ESTATES CODE. IF YOU HAVE ANY QUESTIONS ABOUT THESE POWERS, OBTAIN COMPETENT LEGAL ADVICE. THIS DOCUMENT DOES NOT AUTHORIZE ANYONE TO MAKE MEDICAL AND OTHER HEALTH-CARE DECISIONS FOR YOU. YOU MAY REVOKE THIS POWER OF ATTORNEY IF YOU LATER WISH TO DO SO. IF YOU WANT YOUR AGENT TO HAVE THE AUTHORITY TO SIGN HOME EQUITY LOAN DOCUMENTS ON YOUR BEHALF, THIS POWER OF ATTORNEY MUST BE SIGNED BY YOU AT THE OFFICE OF THE LENDER, AN ATTORNEY AT LAW, OR A TITLE COMPANY.

You should select someone you trust to serve as your agent. Unless you specify otherwise, generally the agent's authority will continue until: (1) you die or revoke the power of attorney;(2) your agent resigns, is removed by court order, or is unable to act for you; or (3) a guardian is appointed for your estate.

I, __________ (insert your name and address), appoint __________ (insert the name and address of the person appointed) as my agent to act for me in any lawful way with respect to all of the following powers that I have initialed below. (YOU MAY APPOINT CO-AGENTS. UNLESS YOU PROVIDE OTHERWISE, CO-AGENTS MAY ACT INDEPENDENTLY.)

TO GRANT ALL OF THE FOLLOWING POWERS, INITIAL THE LINE IN FRONT OF (O) AND IGNORE THE LINES IN FRONT OF THE OTHER POWERS LISTED IN (A) THROUGH (N).

TO GRANT A POWER, YOU MUST INITIAL THE LINE IN FRONT OF THE POWER YOU ARE GRANTING.

TO WITHHOLD A POWER, DO NOT INITIAL THE LINE IN FRONT OF THE POWER. YOU MAY, BUT DO NOT NEED TO, CROSS OUT EACH POWER WITHHELD.

____ (A) Real property transactions;
____ (B) Tangible personal property transactions;
____ (C) Stock and bond transactions;
____ (D) Commodity and option transactions;
____ (E) Banking and other financial institution transactions;

FIGURE 3-6 Statutory Durable Power of Attorney
Source: © 2021 Mbition LLC

_____ (F) Business operating transactions;
_____ (G) Insurance and annuity transactions;
_____ (H) Estate, trust, and other beneficiary transactions;
_____ (I) Claims and litigation;
_____ (J) Personal and family maintenance;
_____ (K) Benefits from social security, Medicare, Medicaid, or other governmental programs or civil or military service;
_____ (L) Retirement plan transactions;
_____ (M) Tax matters;
_____ (N) Digital assets and the content of an electronic communication;
_____ (O) ALL OF THE POWERS LISTED IN (A) THROUGH (N). YOU DO NOT HAVE TO INITIAL THE LINE IN FRONT OF ANY OTHER POWER IF YOU INITIAL LINE (O).

SPECIAL INSTRUCTIONS:

Special instructions applicable to agent compensation (initial in front of one of the following sentences to have it apply; if no selection is made, each agent will be entitled to compensation that is reasonable under the circumstances):

_____ My agent is entitled to reimbursement of reasonable expenses incurred on my behalf and to compensation that is reasonable under the circumstances.

_____ My agent is entitled to reimbursement of reasonable expenses incurred on my behalf but shall receive no compensation for serving as my agent.

Special instructions applicable to co-agents (if you have appointed co-agents to act, initial in front of one of the following sentences to have it apply; if no selection is made, each agent will be entitled to act independently):

_____ Each of my co-agents may act independently for me.

_____ My co-agents may act for me only if the co-agents act jointly.

_____ My co-agents may act for me only if a majority of the co-agents act jointly.

Special instructions applicable to gifts (initial in front of the following sentence to have it apply):
_____ I grant my agent the power to apply my property to make gifts outright to or for the benefit of a person, including by the exercise of a presently exercisable

FIGURE 3-6 (Continued)

general power of appointment held by me, except that the amount of a gift to an individual may not exceed the amount of annual exclusions allowed from the federal gift tax for the calendar year of the gift.
ON THE FOLLOWING LINES YOU MAY GIVE SPECIAL INSTRUCTIONS LIMITING OR EXTENDING THE POWERS GRANTED TO YOUR AGENT.

____
____
____
____
____
____
____
____
____

UNLESS YOU DIRECT OTHERWISE BELOW, THIS POWER OF ATTORNEY IS EFFECTIVE IMMEDIATELY AND WILL CONTINUE UNTIL IT TERMINATES.

CHOOSE ONE OF THE FOLLOWING ALTERNATIVES BY CROSSING OUT THE ALTERNATIVE NOT CHOSEN:

(A) This power of attorney is not affected by my subsequent disability or incapacity.
(B) This power of attorney becomes effective upon my disability or incapacity.

YOU SHOULD CHOOSE ALTERNATIVE (A) IF THIS POWER OF ATTORNEY IS TO BECOME EFFECTIVE ON THE DATE IT IS EXECUTED.

IF NEITHER (A) NOR (B) IS CROSSED OUT, IT WILL BE ASSUMED THAT YOU CHOSE ALTERNATIVE (A).

If Alternative (B) is chosen and a definition of my disability or incapacity is not contained in this power of attorney, I shall be considered disabled or incapacitated for purposes of this power of attorney if a physician certifies in writing at a date later than the date this power of attorney is executed that, based on the physician's medical examination of me, I am mentally incapable of managing my financial affairs. I authorize the physician who examines me for this purpose to disclose my physical or mental condition to another person for purposes of this power of attorney. A third party who accepts this power of attorney is fully protected from any action taken under this power of attorney

FIGURE 3-6 (Continued)

that is based on the determination made by a physician of my disability or incapacity.

I agree that any third party who receives a copy of this document may act under it. Termination of this durable power of attorney is not effective as to a third party until the third party has actual knowledge of the termination. I agree to indemnify the third party for any claims that arise against the third party because of reliance on this power of attorney. The meaning and effect of this durable power of attorney is determined by Texas law.

If any agent named by me dies, becomes incapacitated, resigns, refuses to act, or is removed by court order, or if my marriage to an agent named by me is dissolved by a court decree of divorce or annulment or is declared void by a court (unless I provided in this document that the dissolution or declaration does not terminate the agent's authority to act under this power of attorney), I name the following (each to act alone and successively, in the order named) as successor(s) to that agent: ___________.

Signed this ______ day of ___________, ______________

____

(your signature)

State of _________________________
County of ________________________

This document was acknowledged before me on ____________(date) by ___________________________

(name of principal)

____

(signature of notarial officer)

(Seal, if any, of notary) ____

(printed name)

My commission expires: ___________

FIGURE 3-6 (Continued)

IMPORTANT INFORMATION FOR AGENT

Agent's Duties
When you accept the authority granted under this power of attorney, you establish a "fiduciary" relationship with the principal. This is a special legal relationship that imposes on you legal duties that continue until you resign or the power of attorney is terminated, suspended, or revoked by the principal or by operation of law. A fiduciary duty generally includes the duty to:

(1) act in good faith;
(2) do nothing beyond the authority granted in this power of attorney;
(3) act loyally for the principal's benefit;
(4) avoid conflicts that would impair your ability to act in the principal's best interest; and
(5) disclose your identity as an agent when you act for the principal by writing or printing the name of the principal and signing your own name as "agent" in the following manner:

(Principal's Name) by (Your Signature) as Agent

In addition, the Durable Power of Attorney Act (Subtitle P, Title 2, Estates Code) requires you to:

(1) maintain records of each action taken or decision made on behalf of the principal;
(2) maintain all records until delivered to the principal, released by the principal, or discharged by a court; and
(3) if requested by the principal, provide an accounting to the principal that, unless otherwise directed by the principal or otherwise provided in the Special Instructions, must include:
(A) the property belonging to the principal that has come to your knowledge or into your possession;
(B) each action taken or decision made by you as agent;
(C) a complete account of receipts, disbursements, and other actions of you as agent that includes the source and nature of each receipt, disbursement, or action, with receipts of principal and income shown separately;
(D) a listing of all property over which you have exercised control that includes an adequate description of each asset and the asset's current value, if known to you;

FIGURE 3-6 (Continued)

(E) the cash balance on hand and the name and location of the depository at which the cash balance is kept;
(F) each known liability;
(G) any other information and facts known to you as necessary for a full and definite understanding of the exact condition of the property belonging to the principal; and
(H) all documentation regarding the principal's property.

Termination of Agent's Authority

You must stop acting on behalf of the principal if you learn of any event that terminates or suspends this power of attorney or your authority under this power of attorney. An event that terminates this power of attorney or your authority to act under this power of attorney includes:

(1) the principal's death;
(2) the principal's revocation of this power of attorney or your authority;
(3) the occurrence of a termination event stated in this power of attorney;
(4) if you are married to the principal, the dissolution of your marriage by a court decree of divorce or annulment or declaration that your marriage is void, unless otherwise provided in this power of attorney;
(5) the appointment and qualification of a permanent guardian of the principal's estate unless a court order provides otherwise; or
(6) if ordered by a court, your removal as agent (attorney in fact) under this power of attorney. An event that suspends this power of attorney or your authority to act under this power of attorney is the appointment and qualification of a temporary guardian unless a court order provides otherwise.

Liability of Agent

The authority granted to you under this power of attorney is specified in the Durable Power of Attorney Act (Subtitle P, Title 2, Estates Code). If you violate the Durable Power of Attorney Act or act beyond the authority granted, you may be liable for any damages caused by the violation or subject to prosecution for misapplication of property by a fiduciary under Chapter 32 of the Texas Penal Code.

THE AGENT, BY ACCEPTING OR ACTING UNDER THE APPOINTMENT, ASSUMES THE FIDUCIARY AND OTHER LEGAL RESPONSIBILITIES OF AN AGENT.

FIGURE 3-6 (Continued)

Contravention of Public Policy

One of the most fundamental rules of the law of contracts is that a contract that violates public policy is void and unenforceable. A contract that violates public policy is defined as a contract that is contrary to the best interests of the public or the public good. The best interests of the public and the public good are determined by the spirit of the law as well as by the express law itself. Typically, a contract that is vicious even though the contractual intentions were innocent will be declared invalid. In real estate transactions, there are specific provisions that are void as against public policy.

For example, Texas Property Code § 5.026 provides that discriminatory provisions are void as against public policy. The law states that "if a restriction that affects real property, or a provision in a deed that conveys real property or an interest in real property, whether express or incorporated by reference, prohibits the use by or the sale, lease, or transfer to a person because of race, color, religion, or national origin, the provision or restriction is void."

Contravention of Constitution, Statute, or Ordinance

A contract cannot violate the law. Therefore, as a general matter, if a contract is made in violation of an express constitutional, statutory, or ordinance provision, the contract will be deemed void and unenforceable. In addition, if the performance of the contract will result in the violation of any law, then the contract is void and unenforceable. *This is the case even where the parties did not know the law.* A particularly important consideration here is zoning.

Unlawful Intent of the Parties

Contracts may be found void and unenforceable where the subject matter of the contract is intended to be used for an unlawful purpose. However, contracts that are apparently valid on their face will not always be found unenforceable simply because one of the parties to the contract intended, under the contract, to effect an illegal purpose or perform an illegal act. This situation may arise in a real estate sales situation where the real property itself is to be used for an illegal purpose.

Frequently, one of the parties to an otherwise valid real estate contract will acquire knowledge that another party to the transaction intends to use the real property for an unlawful purpose. This knowledge, however, is not sufficient to invalidate the contract where it appears that this intent did not constitute any part of the agreement between the parties and that the party possessing the knowledge did not subsequently agree to participate in the other party's unlawful acts. On the other hand, if one of the parties to the real estate sales agreement not only knows that the other party intends to use the real property illegally, but also actively aids the other's unlawful acts, he or she will not be entitled to enforce the contract. This principle will apply where one party sells property to another under a real estate sales contract intended to materially aid the purchaser in breaking the law.

Contracts Involving Fraud or Deception of Third Parties

Contracts that are intended to deceive third parties or even the public are void as against public policy and are unenforceable in a court at law. This general rule applies to contracts that take advantage of a confidential relationship existing between the parties to the contract. This is the type of deception that might exist where a real estate license holder has breached his or her fiduciary duty to his or her client. In addition, this rule applies to real estate conveyances made in fraud of existing creditors. This may occur where one party sells his or her real estate to a third party to prevent a creditor from obtaining the property. Moreover, contracts that deceive third parties implicate Texas common law fraud, statutory real estate fraud provisions, and the Texas Deceptive Trade Practices Consumer Protection Act.

EXPRESS OR IMPLIED CONTRACTS

Contracts may take various forms. Because of their variety, contracts may be classified according to several different methods. An **express contract** is a contract created by an expression of the parties. This expression may be either verbal or written. Because of the difficulty in proving the existence of a verbal contract, it is beneficial to all parties that the contract be written. In the real estate industry, it is preferred that *all* contracts be in writing. Some examples of express written contracts include residential sales contracts, listing agreements, buyer representation agreements, leases, and property management agreements. In Texas, a commission agreement, as well as a real estate sales contract, must be in writing to be enforceable. This will all be discussed in more detail in a later chapter.

An **implied contract** is a contract that is not created by any expression of the parties, but is inferred from the circumstances of the transaction. When implied contracts are involved, it may be very difficult to determine the parties' true intent. For example, Jane comments to her friend Larry that she really needs help understanding her math class. Larry tells Jane that he is a math tutor and normally charges $10 per hour to help students with their math. Jane asks Larry to meet her after class to review her math homework. Is there an employment agreement? If there is, then for how long and at what rate of payment? There are just too many "loose ends" in this scenario for the parties to be protected.

Traditionally in real estate, contracts may be implied from the circumstances because of the custom of the industry. The most common example is in a standard exclusive listing agreement where there is no mention of marketing the property for sale, however, it is presumed that the property will be marketed because there would be no other way to sell it.

An area of concern with implied contracts in the real estate industry arises in implied employment cases, particularly those involving the creation of undisclosed dual agency relationships. In these situations, the buyer implies from the circumstances that the seller's agent is acting on behalf of the buyer. For example, if an agent that works exclusively for the seller fails to give the buyer an agency disclosure notice indicating the agent's representative status and further offers to talk to the mortgage company on behalf of the buyer to aid the buyer in obtaining financing, then this may lead the buyer to believe—that is, it may be implied—that the agent is acting on the buyer's behalf.

Generally, a license holder can work *with* a buyer as a customer and must be careful not to impliedly work *for* the buyer as a client without informed consent from both parties. This example hopefully demonstrates the importance of getting the relationships, rights, and responsibilities clearly defined in writing early on in the transaction. An exemplary document containing such information is the Texas Real Estate Commission form titled "Information About Brokerage Services," which will be discussed in a later chapter.

UNILATERAL OR BILATERAL CONTRACTS

All contracts require at least two parties. However, when only one party to the contract has made a promise, only that party can be bound by the contract. Thus, if one party to the contract makes the promise, then the other party must accept by performance. This type of contract is termed a **unilateral contract** because of this one-sided promise. A unilateral contract is more familiar in reward situations. For example, an owner posts at the local fire station a sign that offers a $10 reward for the return of a lost dog. When a second party accepts the contract by performing, that is, returning the dog to the owner, the owner is bound to pay the $10 reward to the accepting party. If the second party decided not to look for the dog, there would be no negative consequences of the failure to perform.

In the real estate industry, a unilateral contract is exemplified by an option contract. An **option contract** in the context of a real estate transaction might be seen as an agreement between the buyer and seller. In this agreement, the seller accepts a certain option fee from the buyer. In exchange, the buyer will be allowed to terminate the sales contract for any reason by the end of the preestablished option period. The paragraph dealing with the option fee in the standard real estate sales contract will be discussed in more detail in a later chapter.

In addition, the commission agreement established between a real estate broker and his or her client is an example of a unilateral contract. A listing agreement is one example of a commission agreement that creates an employment relationship between a broker and a seller. Under this agreement, the seller promises to pay a commission to the broker in exchange for the broker's performance in finding a ready, willing, and able purchaser for the seller's property. In this arrangement, if the broker fails to find a ready, willing, and able purchaser during the term of the listing agreement, the broker has not breached the contract, but is simply not entitled to the commission.

In a **bilateral contract**, one party to the contract makes a promise in exchange for a promise by the second contracting party. This is the most common type of contract. Therefore, most of this text will focus on this contract. In real estate transactions, the residential sales contract entered into between the buyer and the seller is an example of a bilateral contract. In these contracts, the seller makes a promise to sell the house, and the buyer makes a promise to pay the money.

VALID, VOID, VOIDABLE, AND UNENFORCEABLE CONTRACTS

A **valid contract** is a contract that has all of the essential elements of a contract and is, therefore, enforceable in a court of law. For example, if two competent parties mutually agree to a legal written real estate sales contract that is supported by consideration, a valid contract is formed. Keep in mind that a contract may be valid and still be unenforceable. An **unenforceable contract** is a contract which for some reason cannot be enforced. A valid contract may be incapable of enforcement where the four-year statute of limitations has lapsed.

A **void contract** is a contract that does not exist under the law; that is, the contract has failed to include all of the essential elements necessary to the creation of a valid contract. This type of contract is unenforceable. A common situation involving void contracts involves illegal contracts. A **voidable contract** is a valid contract, but one that may be legally avoided at the option of one of the parties. The most common situation involving voidable contracts concerns contracts created by minors.

EXECUTED OR EXECUTORY CONTRACTS

An **executed contract** is a contract that has been completely performed by the parties. In most contract situations, an executed contract is merely a contract in which the parties have performed all the formalities under the contract and signed the contract. It is a contract that takes effect immediately or a contract that conveys an immediate right. With the purchase and sale of real estate, the contract is only considered closed and fully executed when the seller has conveyed the title to the buyer and the buyer has paid the purchase price. Several transactions in the real estate industry involve immediately executed contracts. These include property management contracts and leases.

Most contracts concerning the purchase and sale of real estate are executory rather than executed because the purchaser has not yet paid the purchase price nor has the seller conveyed title at the time the sales contract is signed. An **executory contract** is a contract that has not been completed. In real estate sales transactions, the contract signed by both parties regarding the purchase and sale of the property is an executory contract because title to the property does not pass until closing takes place. The period of time between the time that the real estate sales contract is signed and the time when closing takes place is referred to as the **executory period**. See figure 3-7.

The length of this period varies depending on financing approval, title searches, surveys, appraisals, inspections, and environmental assessments. Therefore, the likelihood for loss during this period is high. See figure 3-8.

Several problems can occur during the executory period, which creates an area of concern. Because the parties are essentially in limbo during this executory period, the law dictates special rules that are applicable. These special rules apply when there is a death, destruction of the premises, or a lawsuit involving the seller while the parties are waiting to close a real estate transaction.

One concern during the executory period is what happens if there is a death of one of the parties to the contract.[3] When a party dies, the real estate transaction grinds to a halt until the rights and/or title of the parties are resolved in a probate court. A representative of the deceased party will carry out the real estate transaction. It is important to note that if the seller dies before closing, title to the real estate will not be clear until a probate proceeding has occurred.

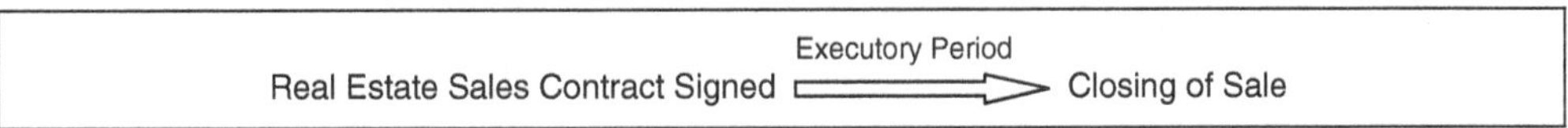

FIGURE 3-7 Executory Period
Source: © 2021 Mbition LLC

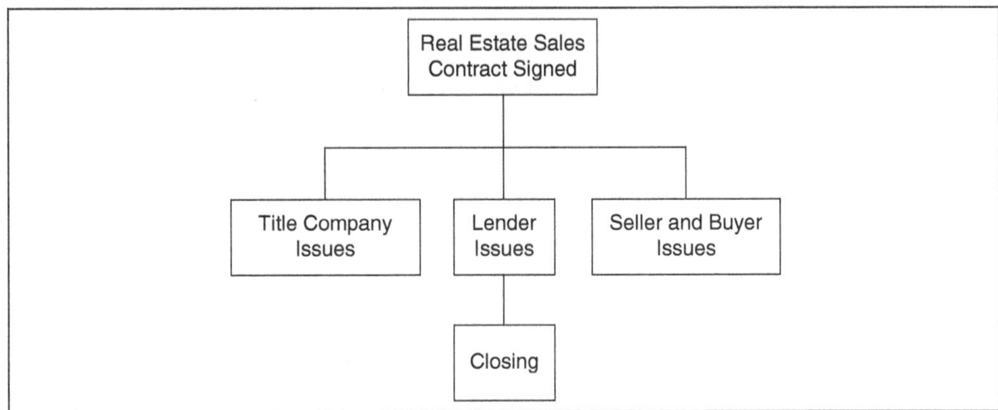

FIGURE 3-8 Concerns During the Executory Period
Source: © 2021 Mbition LLC

[3] See Parson v. Wolfe, 676 S.W.2d 689 (Tex. App.- Amarillo 1984).

A second concern during the executory period is loss or destruction of the property that is the subject of the contract. For loss or destruction to the property during the executory period, Texas has enacted the **Uniform Vendor and Purchaser Risk Act**. This law states that the risk of the loss is on the seller *unless* the buyer is in possession. The reason for this is that the seller is in a better position to protect and insure the property. The pertinent provisions of the Uniform Vendor and Purchaser Risk Act are as follows:

> (b) If, when neither the legal title nor the possession of the subject matter of the contract has been transferred, all or a material part of the property is destroyed without fault of the purchaser or is taken by eminent domain, the vendor may not enforce the contract, and the purchaser is entitled to recover any portion of the contract price paid.
>
> (c) If, when either the legal title or the possession of the subject matter of the contract has been transferred, all or any part of the property is destroyed without fault of the vendor or is taken by eminent domain, the purchaser is not relieved from the duty to pay the contract price, nor is the purchaser entitled to recover any portion of the price already paid.[4]

Paragraph 14 of the promulgated residential sales contract relates to casualty loss on the premises. This paragraph provides that if the property is destroyed during the executory period, the seller is responsible for the loss. If any part of the property is destroyed by fire or casualty loss after the effective date of the contract, the seller must restore the property to its previous condition by the closing date. If the damage is too extensive and the seller is unable to repair the property due to factors beyond his or her control, then the buyer can either terminate the contract and have the earnest money refunded, extend the closing date up to 15 days, or accept the property as is with an assignment of the insurance proceeds if this is permitted by the insurance carrier. If the buyer is in possession of the property under a Buyer's Temporary Residential Lease and the casualty loss is caused by the buyer, matters could get complicated.

The Uniform Vendor and Purchaser Risk Act can be of great importance during a real estate sales transaction, particularly where the prospective purchaser takes possession of the premises before closing under a Buyer's Temporary Residential Lease (TREC 16-5). It may also occur where a seller stays in possession of the premises after closing under a Seller's Temporary Residential Lease (TREC 15-5). In both of these situations, insurance coverage for a tenant in possession is a must for the owner. Most insurance companies do not include this coverage in their standard homeowner's policies. These examples show the importance of

[4] Texas Property Code § 5.007.

a license holder understanding the implications of possession by a buyer *before* closing or of a seller *after* closing. Problems unique to these scenarios *can* arise.

Another concern during the executory period involves seller lawsuits. The five most common lawsuits that arise are divorces, foreclosures, bankruptcies, condemnation (eminent domain), and convictions. All of these will affect the seller's real estate. If a lawsuit involves the seller's real estate, then a lis pendens is typically seen in the county deed records. A **lis pendens** is a notice of pending suit. The general purpose of a lis pendens is to put third parties on notice of the facts and issues involved in the lawsuit affecting a particular parcel of land. Once the lis pendens is on file, the rights of the parties to the suit will not be varied during the pendency of the suit. If the particular parcel of land is the subject of a real estate sales contract or is conveyed during the pendency of a suit, it will not necessarily be prohibited. However, the prospective purchaser steps into the shoes of the seller and acquires whatever interest he or she has after the termination of the suit. If the seller wins, then the conveyance will continue. If the seller loses, the prospective purchaser may walk away with nothing. The use of the lis pendens will apply whenever the real estate is involved in a lawsuit. In addition, certain special rules apply to bankruptcy proceedings.

When a voluntary or involuntary bankruptcy occurs during the pendency of a real estate sales contract, federal law provides that the trustee in bankruptcy may assume or reject any executory contract or unexpired lease of the debtor.[5] If the trustee does not assume or reject an executory contract or an unexpired lease of residential real property within 60 days after the debtor files a petition in bankruptcy, the contract or lease is deemed rejected.[6] In other words, there is no more contract.

Discussion Questions

1. What is consideration and why is it necessary to create a valid contract?
2. What types of consideration are sufficient to create a valid contract? Give an example of each.
3. What types of consideration are not sufficient to create a valid contract? Give an example of each.
4. What are the essential elements to a valid contract?
5. What is the distinction between an express contract and an implied contract?
6. What is the distinction between a bilateral contract and a unilateral contract? What is an example of each of these contracts?

---

[5] 11 U.S.C. § 365(a).

[6] 11 U.S.C. § 365(d)(1).

7. Why is the executory period of a contract so long? What are the risks involved during the executory period?
8. What is the distinction between a void contract and a voidable contract?
9. What is the Uniform Vendor and Purchaser Risk Act?
10. Who constitutes a minor in Texas?
11. What is the general rule regarding the enforceability of minor contracts? What are the exceptions to the rule? Give an example of both the rule and the exceptions.
12. What is the general rule concerning the enforceability of contracts entered into by mentally infirm individuals?
13. When might a guardianship be created?
14. When might a power of attorney be used in a real estate transaction? What is the advantage of working with a durable power of attorney?
15. List some instances where a contract may be found to be illegal.

CHAPTER

4

OWNERSHIP RIGHTS AND LIMITATIONS

KEY TERMS

defeasible fee
easement appurtenant
easement in gross
eminent domain
encumbrance
escheat
estate
family homestead
fee simple absolute
freehold estate
future freehold estates
life estate
life estate pur autre vie
non-freehold estate
police power
present freehold estates
remainder
reversion
rural use
single-adult homestead
surface water
urban use
wetlands

INTERESTS IN REAL ESTATE

There are several interests that can exist simultaneously in real estate. One interest in real estate involves government powers, more specifically the police power, eminent domain, taxation, and escheat. Another interest in real estate is the estate held to the land. Estates in land can include freehold estates, such as fee simple, defeasible fees, life estates, remainders, and reversions. Estates in land can also include statutory estates, such as homestead, or nonfreehold estates, such as those seen with leaseholds. Encumbrances are another interest that can exist in real estate. Encumbrances, or claims against the property, include liens, restrictions, encroachments, easements, and leases. Finally, water rights and mineral rights are two additional interests that can exist in real estate.

GOVERNMENT POWERS

Ownership rights to real estate can be limited by certain government powers. There are four government powers that concern real estate. These powers are the police power, eminent domain, taxation, and escheat. **Police power** is the power of the government to make laws that control land use for the health, safety, and welfare of the people. These powers exist at the federal, state, and local level. Land use at the federal level is regulated by agencies such as the Department of Housing and Urban Development, the Federal Housing Administration, and the Environmental Protection Agency.

State police power comes from the 10th Amendment to the Constitution, which provides that "powers not delegated to the United States by the Constitution, nor prohibited by it to the states, are reserved to the states respectively, or to the people." In Texas, various aspects of land use are regulated by agencies such as the General Land Office, the Texas Water Development Board, and the Texas Commission on Environmental Quality (TCEQ). Locally land use can be controlled by county or city government. Larger counties, for example, may regulate subdivision platting requirements or set forth greater requirements than the TCEQ for septic tank installation. Regulation of land use by city government takes place through zoning.

Zoning permits a city to regulate (1) the height, number of stories, and size of buildings and other structures; (2) the percentage of a lot that may be occupied; (3) the size of yards, courts, and other open spaces; (4) population density; (5) the location and use of buildings, other structures, and land for business, industrial, residential, or other purposes; and (6) the pumping, extraction, and use of groundwater by persons other than retail public utilities for the purpose of preventing the use or contact with groundwater that presents an actual or potential threat to human health.[1] If the place is designated as an area of historical, cultural, or architectural importance and significance, the city may regulate the construction, reconstruction, alteration, or razing of buildings and other structures.[2] The bulk of buildings may also be regulated.[3]

Eminent domain refers to the power of the government to take private property for public use for just compensation. However, Texas law imposes certain limitations on the government's right to physically take property under eminent domain. For instance, private property may not be taken through the use of eminent domain if the taking: (1) confers a private benefit on a particular private party through the use of the property; (2) is for a public use that is merely a pretext to confer a private benefit on a particular private party; (3) is for economic development purposes, unless the economic development is a secondary

[1] Texas Local Government Code § 211.003(a).
[2] Texas Local Government Code § 211.003(b).
[3] Texas Local Government Code § 211.003(c).

purpose resulting from municipal community development or municipal urban renewal activities to eliminate an existing affirmative harm on society from slum or blighted areas; or (4) is not for a public use.[4]

The just compensation to be paid to the property owner is based on the value of the property at the time of the taking. To protect the property owner, a bona fide offer of compensation to the owner for the property requires a written appraisal.[5] Groundwater rights can also be acquired in this manner.[6]

The power of eminent domain can be particularly problematic if the government tries to exercise this power during the executory period of a residential sales contract. If it does, the provisions of the Uniform Vendor and Purchaser Risk Act apply. In short, the property owner cannot enforce the contract with the prospective purchaser.

Another power the government has over real property is the power of **taxation**, which can be enforced through a lien. A property (ad valorem) tax lien is a lien on real property to secure payment of property taxes. On January 1 of each year, a tax lien attaches to real property to secure the payment of all taxes, penalties, and interest ultimately imposed for the year on the property, whether or not the taxes are imposed in the year the lien attaches.[7] Property tax bills are considered delinquent if not paid by February 1 of the following year.[8] At any time after the property tax becomes delinquent, the taxing authority may file suit to foreclose the lien securing payment of the tax, to enforce personal liability for the tax, or both.[9]

In a real estate transaction, the seller must be prepared to show that there are no delinquent taxes at closing. This information can be obtained by the title company acting as escrow agent for the transaction. The county taxing authority is not required to file a property tax lien in the county deed records so delinquent tax information must be obtained directly from the tax office.[10] Since taxes cover the entire year, the taxes will be prorated through the closing date. If the taxes are not paid at or prior to closing, the buyer will have to pay all taxes for the current year as new owner of the property.

Escheat occurs when there are no heirs to receive property upon the death of the property owner, such as can occur when a person dies without a will, or intestate, in Texas. Therefore, title to the property will vest to the state of Texas.[11] Additional laws that apply when a person dies intestate will be covered in a later chapter.

---

[4] Tex. Gov't Code § 2206.001.
[5] Tex. Prop. Code § 21.0113.
[6] Tex. Prop. Code § 21.0121.
[7] Tex. Tax Code § 32.01(a).
[8] Tex. Tax Code § 31.02.
[9] Tex. Tax Code § 33.41(a).
[10] Tex. Prop. Code § 51.008.
[11] Tex. Prop. Code § 71.001.

ESTATES IN LAND

In General

Ownership rights to real estate may also be limited based on the estate held by the owners. An **estate** is an interest that one or more persons hold in land. An estate may be classified as freehold or non-freehold. A **non-freehold**, or leasehold, estate is an estate of fixed duration. Non-freehold estates do not involve ownership rights and are typically created in lease agreements. Leases will be discussed in later chapter. **Freehold estates**, on the other hand, are estates of indefinite duration and are ownership rights that can be conveyed voluntarily by deed or by will. Deeds and wills will be discussed in more detail in a later chapter.

Dividing Ownership Based on Time of Possession

Freehold estates may be classified as either present estates or future estates, depending on when the grantee has the right to possess the premises. See figure 4-1. **Present freehold estates** are simply freehold estates that have a present right of possession. There are three specific types of present freehold estates. The first is the fee simple absolute. The **fee simple absolute** is the largest estate that may be conveyed. This estate is considered the default estate in Texas and is the estate conveyed by default in the Texas Real Estate Commission promulgated real estate sales contracts. When a conveyance of this estate is made, the grantor effectively grants 100% of the surface, subsurface, and air rights to the grantee. The typical way that a grant of a fee simple absolute is made is by using any words that show an intent to convey full property rights. For example, "Grantor deeds Tract X to Jesse."

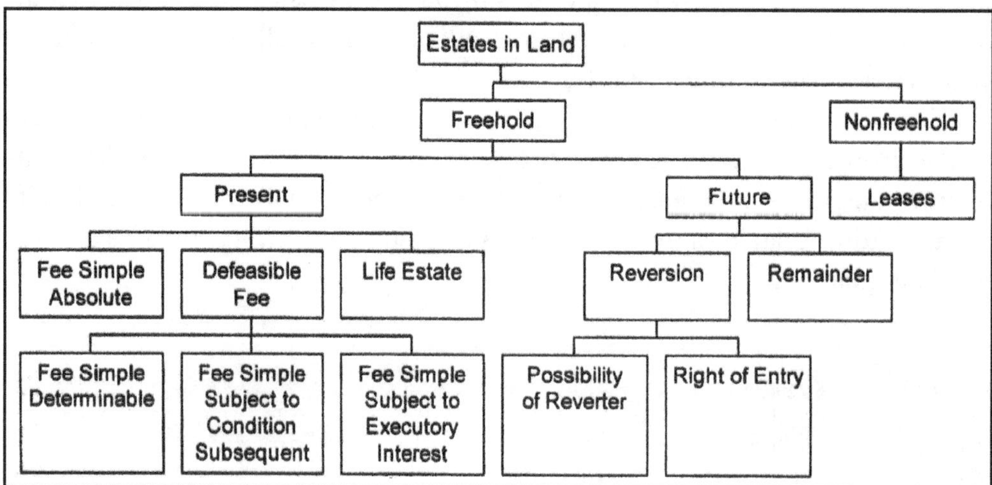

FIGURE 4-1 Estates in Land
Source: © 2021 Mbition LLC

A second type of present freehold estate is referred to as a defeasible fee. A **defeasible fee** is a fee simple absolute that can be defeated by the happening of some event. There are three types of defeasible fee estates used. The first is a fee simple determinable. The fee simple determinable is an estate that will terminate upon the happening of some event. Since there is the possibility that the event will occur, the grantor holds a possibility of reverter, which is a type of future freehold estate. If the event does occur, the estate automatically terminates and reverts to the original grantor thereby creating a fee simple absolute back in the grantor. Special language such as "while" or "so long as" is commonly used to create this type of interest. For example, "Grantor deeds Tract X to Robert so long as the premises are used as a farm."

Oil and gas leases in Texas are not true leases, but instead are fee simple determinable estates. An oil and gas lease typically provides that the petroleum company owns the oil, gas, and other minerals "so long as" there is production. There are additional provisions contained in these leases that continue the lease even when there is cessation of production. Only after continued cessation will the lease actually terminate and the mineral estate revert back to the grantor.

Another type of defeasible fee is the fee simple subject to a condition subsequent. This fee is an estate that will terminate upon the happening of some event. This estate is very similar to the fee simple determinable; however, the future estate held by the grantor is a right of entry. In addition, if the event does occur, the estate does not automatically terminate. The grantor merely has the right to reenter the premises to claim possession. Where the interest is reclaimed, the original grantor again takes a fee simple absolute to the property. Special language such as "if," "but if," or "on condition that" is used to create the fee simple subject to a condition subsequent. For example, "Grantor deeds Tract X to Jennifer on the condition that no alcohol is sold on the premises."

The last type of defeasible fee is the fee simple subject to an executory interest. This fee is an estate that will terminate upon the happening of some event; however, the future estate is held by a third party rather than the original grantor. This future interest in the third party is referred to as an executory interest. If the event occurs and the fee terminates, it will automatically terminate in this designated third party, thereby creating a fee simple absolute in the third party. Language typically used to create a fee simple determinable or a fee simple subject to a condition subsequent is sufficient to create this estate. For example, "Grantor deeds Tract X to Abigail so long as the premises are used as a farm, if not, then to Beth."

The third type of present freehold estate often conveyed in a deed is a life estate. A **life estate** is an estate measured by a life or lives in being. The life estate may be one of two types. The first is a regular life estate. A regular life estate is a life estate measured by the life of the grantee. For example, Mike conveys

"To Bob for life." This conveyance creates a life estate in Bob measured by Bob's life. In this situation, if Bob dies, the property would revert to Mike in the form of a fee simple absolute. The property would not pass to Bob's estate upon Bob's death since Bob's rights and Bob's estate's rights terminate upon the death of Bob. If Mike predeceases Bob, then upon Bob's death the property would pass to Mike's estate. The second type of life estate is a life estate pur autre vie. The **life estate pur autre vie** is a life estate measured by the life of another. For example, Mike conveys "To Bob, for the life of Annie." This conveyance creates a life estate pur autre vie in Bob measured by the life of Annie. If Annie dies before Bob, the property will revert to Mike.

A **future freehold estate** is a freehold estate that has a future right of possession. The two primary types of future freehold estates are the reversion and the remainder. A **reversion** refers to a future estate that returns to the original grantor after the termination of the present freehold estate. This is the default future estate and is typically seen as the future interest associated with a life estate. Two special classes of reversions are respectively, the possibility of reverter, which exists as the future estate of the fee simple determinable estate, and the right of entry, which exists as the future estate of the fee simple subject to a condition subsequent estate.

The second type of future freehold estate is the remainder. A **remainder** is a future estate that transfers to a third party, not the original grantor, after the termination of the present estate. A remainder may be either vested (complete) or contingent (conditional) depending on the type of conveyance made to the third party.

Vested remainders are established without satisfying any conditions and can be (1) indefeasibly vested, (2) vested subject to total divestment, or (3) vested subject to open. Indefeasibly vested remainders simply terminate in a third party. For example, "Grantor deeds Tract X to Sam for life, then to Bob." In this example, when Sam dies, the interest passes to Bob as a fee simple absolute. Vested remainders subject to total divestment are remainders that terminate in a third party, but which can be divested. For example, "Grantor deeds Tract X to Leo for life, then to Dawn if Dawn survives Leo." In this example, as long as Dawn is still alive when Leo dies then Dawn will take the interest as a fee simple absolute. If Dawn is no longer alive, the interest will pass to the grantor or the grantor's estate. Vested remainders subject to open terminate in an open class of individuals. For example, "Grantor deeds Tract X to Aaron for life, then to Aaron's heirs." In this example, Aaron's heirs cannot be determined until after Aaron's death. The heirs will take a fee simple absolute.

The contingent remainder, in contrast to the vested remainders, requires some condition precedent be satisfied before the interest will pass. For example, "Grantor deeds Tract X to Amy for life, then to Ben if Ben survives Amy, otherwise to Chris." In this example, Chris holds a contingent remainder because his interest depends on the divestment of Ben's vested remainder.

ENCUMBRANCES

Ownership rights can also be affected by encumbrances on the property. An **encumbrance** is an interest in property that diminishes its value, but does not prohibit the owner from disposing of the property. Encumbrances can include liens, restrictions, encroachments, easements, and leases. Restrictions and easements will be discussed below while the remaining encumbrances will be discussed later in the text.

Restrictions

Restrictions that limit the use an owner can make of his or her real property are generally in the form of deed restrictions or homeowners association requirements. Deed restrictions are limitations imposed in the deed that is conveyed from the seller to the buyer that restrict how the buyer uses the property. Deed restrictions were common before subdivisions were created as they were a way for the seller of the property to limit the buyer's use of the property to "residential use" for the benefit of the neighbors. Once the deed restriction is conveyed, it runs with the land to all subsequent owners.[12] Those who receive a benefit from the restriction also have the right to enforce it.[13]

Restrictions are also created for subdivisions typically in a declaration of covenants, conditions, and restrictions. The declaration can include very simple restrictions, such as limiting use of the property to residential use and limiting fence height, to very detailed restrictions, such as limiting paint color to only neutrals and limiting the type of roofing material.

Once subdivision restrictions are created and recorded in the county deed records, they run with the land to all subsequent owners. In addition, those who receive the benefit of the restrictions also have the right to enforce them.[14] Although in most cases the homeowners association will enforce the restrictions.

Easements

In General

Easements are non-possessory interests that can be held in real property. An easement is the right of one person to use another person's real property for a specific purpose.[15] There are two types of easements used in Texas—the easement in gross and the easement appurtenant.

---

[12] Nicholls v. Barnett, 374 S.W.2d 770 (Tex. Civ. App. 1964).

[13] Ortiz v. Jeter, 479 S.W.2d 752 (Tex. Civ. App. 1972).

[14] Giles v. Cardenas, 697 S.W.2d 422 (Tex. App. 1985).

[15] See Hubert v. Davis, 170 S.W.3d 706, 710 (Tex. App.-Tyler 2005).

An **easement in gross** is personal and attaches to the individual grantee rather than to a tract of land.[16] Because these easements are personal, they are generally not permitted to be assigned or transferred. However, easements in gross can be made assignable with an express assignment provision in the easement documentation.[17] This type of easement is used to provide a right of way for entities, such as utility companies, to use the property.

An **easement appurtenant**, on the other hand, is an easement designed to benefit another tract of land, rather than an individual. There are two estates involved in the easement appurtenant—the servient estate and the dominant estate. The servient estate is the tract of land on which the easement is imposed whereas the dominant estate is the tract of land benefited by the easement.[18] An easement appurtenant passes with the property unless otherwise indicated.[19] Since this easement involves two estates, the easement terminates if the dominant and servient estate are merged into one owner. Other ways by which an easement can terminate include by written agreement of the parties, abandonment of the easement coupled with the intent to abandon, or failure of the easement's purpose.

Creation

An easement can be created by an express grant, by reservation, by the purchase of land with reference to a map or plat showing abutting roads or streets, by implication, by necessity, by estoppel, or by prescription.[20] For the first three types of easements, the existence of an easement is easily discoverable from the property survey and/or the title search because the easement right is filed in the deed records. For an easement created by an express grant, the owner of the property on which the easement is to be created conveys the easement right. No particular words are necessary as long as the language shows an intent to grant an easement.[21] For example, to create an express easement appurtenant the conveyance might read, "I, Fred Jones, deed an easement across my property Tract A, specifically the eastern-most path from the cattle gate to County Road 15, to the owner of Tract B." In addition, an express easement in gross might read, "I, Fred Jones, deed an easement across my property Tract A for ABC Utilities to erect utility poles."

An easement created by reservation is the opposite of the easement by express grant. With an easement by reservation, the owner of the property on which the easement is to be created conveys the underlying property, but reserves in himself or another an easement across the property. For example, the reservation of an

---

[16] See Shipp v. Stoker, 923 S.W.2d 100, 103 (Tex. App.–Texarkana 1996).

[17] See Farmer's Marine Copper Works, Inc. v. City of Galveston, 757 S.W.2d 148, 151 (Tex. App.–Houston [1 Dist.] 1988).

[18] See Allen v. Allen, 280 S.W.3d 366, 381 (Tex. App.–Amarillo 2008).

[19] See Holmstrom v. Lee, 26 S.W.3d 526, 531 (Tex. App.–Austin 2000).

[20] See Thompson v. Clayton, 346 S.W.3d 650, 654 (Tex. App.–El Paso 2009); Koonce v. Brite Estate, 663 S.W.2d 451, 452 (Tex. 1984); and Mitchell v. Castellaw, 246 S.W.2d 163, 165 (Tex. 1952).

[21] See Hubert v. Davis, 170 S.W.3d 706, 711 (Tex. App.–Tyler 2005).

easement appurtenant might read, "I, Fred Jones, deed Tract A to Bob Garcia, but expressly reserve an easement across Tract A." An easement in gross might read, "ABC Construction deeds Tract A to Fred Jones, but expressly reserves an easement across the property for XYZ Utilities to erect utility poles."

Easements created by the purchase of land with reference to a map or plat showing abutting roads or streets are often seen in subdivisions. During the subdivision planning, utility easements are indicated on the subdivision plat that is filed in the county records.

The remaining four types of easements—those created by implication, by necessity, by estoppel, or by prescription—are more difficult to discover because these easements arise by operation of law without any documentation. These easements can complicate real estate transactions because a prospective purchaser is deemed to have knowledge of an easement affecting the property if the easement would have been disclosed by a reasonably careful inspection of the premises, or if the person had knowledge of facts sufficient to put a prudent buyer on inquiry.[22] Since the determination of each of these easements is a legal question, they will only be discussed briefly below.

An easement by implication is an easement that has already been in use, but the grant was never reduced to writing. To create an implied easement there must be (1) unity of ownership between the dominant and servient estates; (2) apparent use of the easement at the time the dominant estate was granted; (3) continuous use of the easement, so that the parties must have intended its use to pass by grant with the dominant estate; and (4) reasonable necessity of the easement to the use and enjoyment of the dominant estate.[23] Unity of ownership requires a showing that prior to the severance of the two estates, the grantor owned the dominant and servient estate as a unit or single tract.[24]

The easement by necessity may be created when the dominant estate holder has no other means of accessing a roadway. The elements needed to establish an easement by necessity are: (1) unity of ownership prior to separation; (2) access must be a necessity and not a mere convenience; and (3) the necessity must exist at the time of severance of the two estates.[25] The easement by necessity terminates when there is no longer a necessity.

An easement by estoppel is created verbally. In order to establish the easement by estoppel, there must be a showing that (1) a representation was communicated to the promisee, (2) it must have been believed, and (3) there must have been reliance upon the communication.[26]

Last, is the easement by prescription, which is an easement created by adverse possession. In order for a person to establish an easement by prescription, he

---

[22] See Motel Enterprises, Inc. v. Nobani, 784 S.W.2d 545, 548 (Tex. App.–Houston [1 Dist.] 1990).

[23] See Goodenberger v. Ellis, 343 S.W.3d 536, 542 (Tex. App.–Dallas 2011).

[24] See Akers v. Stevenson, 54 S.W.3d 880, 882 (Tex. App.–Beaumont 2001).

[25] See Peacock v. Schroeder, 846 S.W.2d 905, 910 (Tex. App.–San Antonio 1993).

[26] See Exxon Corp. v. Schutzmaier, 537 S.W.2d 282, 285 (Tex. Civ. App. 1976).

must show that his use of the land was: (1) open and notorious, (2) adverse to the owner's claim of right, (3) exclusive, (4) uninterrupted, and (5) continuous for a period of 10 years.[27]

WATER RIGHTS

Ownership rights can also be limited when the seller vertically divides the land into portions. As discussed earlier, a property owner typically owns 100% of his or her land surface, 100% of the underlying subsurface, and certain limited air rights. In certain instances, a property owner may sever one portion of the property from another. This is typically seen where a property owner severs the surface estate from the subsurface estate. When this division takes place, water rights can be carved out.

There are separate laws that govern water rights in Texas. These laws differ depending on whether the water concerned is groundwater or surface water. **Groundwater** is defined as "water percolating below the surface of the earth."[28] It is real property of the landowner.[29] The owner has the right to drill for and produce the groundwater below the surface of real property, without causing waste or malicious drainage of other property or negligently causing subsidence.[30] Under this rule of capture, the landowner is permitted to pump as much groundwater as he or she can even if it accidently depletes the reserves from neighboring landowners.[31] A local groundwater conservation district may however put restrictions on this right to drill.[32]

In contrast, **surface water** in Texas includes "water of the ordinary flow, underflow, and tides of every flowing river, natural stream, and lake, and of every bay or arm of the Gulf of Mexico, and the storm water, floodwater, and rainwater of every river, natural stream, canyon, ravine, depression, and watershed in the state."[33] This water is owned by the state of Texas. However, these waters are held in trust for the benefit of the public.[34] This statute effectively eliminated riparian water rights to surface water in Texas and expressly states that the statute does not recognize any riparian right from title that passed out of the State of Texas after July 1, 1895.[35] These riparian rights traditionally gave the landowner the right to make reasonable use of a body of water that bordered his or her property. The Texas Water Rights Adjudication Act required that any claims of riparian rights

---

[27] See McClung v. Ayers, 352 S.W.3d 723, 727 (Tex. App.–Texarkana 2011).
[28] Tex. Water Code § 35.002(5).
[29] Tex. Water Code § 36.002(a).
[30] Tex. Water Code § 36.002(b).
[31] See City of Del Rio v. Clayton Sam Colt Hamilton Trust, 269 S.W.3d 613, 617 (Tex. App.–San Antonio 2008).
[32] Tex. Water Code § 36.002(d).
[33] Tex. Water Code § 11.021(a).
[34] Tex. Water Code § 11.0235(a).
[35] Tex. Water Code § 11.001(b).

be filed with TCEQ by September 1, 1969, and authorized TCEQ to adjudicate claims for surface water rights that would be in the public's best interest.[36]

State-owned surface water can be appropriated, stored, or diverted for: (1) domestic and municipal uses, including water for sustaining human life and the life of domestic animals; (2) agricultural uses and industrial uses, meaning processes designed to convert materials of a lower order of value into forms having greater usability and commercial value, including the development of power by means other than hydroelectric; (3) mining and recovery of minerals; (4) hydroelectric power; (5) navigation; (6) recreation and pleasure; (7) public parks; (8) game preserves; or (9) any other beneficial use.[37] However, in order to appropriate these waters, an individual must apply for and obtain a permit.[38] Given the number of farm and ranch properties in Texas, a permit is not required for a dam or reservoir with normal storage of not more than 200 acre-feet of water for non-commercial domestic and livestock purposes.[39] A larger tank capacity is permitted as long as the landowner can demonstrate that the larger capacity was not held on average for any 12-month period.[40] However, diverting or impounding the natural flow of surface waters, or permitting a diversion or impounding by him to continue, in a manner that damages another's property by the overflow of the water diverted or impounded is prohibited.[41]

MINERAL RIGHTS

Mineral rights can be effectively severed from the subsurface estate by making an oil, gas, and/or mineral grant in a deed or will. A "mineral" is defined as "oil, gas, uranium, sulphur, lignite, coal, and any other substance that is ordinarily and naturally considered a mineral in this state, regardless of the depth at which [it] is found."[42] In a mineral grant, the property owner conveys all or part of the subsurface estate, or mineral estate, to the grantee. The property owner keeps all or part of his or her surface estate. For example, "Fred conveys title to the surface of Tract X to Fred and title to the subsurface of Tract X to Jim." In addition, a severance of the surface from the subsurface can be accomplished by the use of a mineral reservation in a deed. Where a mineral reservation is involved, the property owner conveys all or part of the surface estate to the grantee, but reserves in himself or herself the remaining subsurface estate. For example, "Fred conveys title to the surface of Tract X to Jim and reserves title to the subsurface of Tract X."

---

36 Tex. Water Code § 11.302 and § 11.303.
37 Tex. Water Code § 11.023.
38 Tex. Water Code § 11.0235(c).
39 Tex. Water Code § 11.142(a).
40 Tex. Water Code § 11.142(a).
41 Tex. Water Code § 11.086.
42 Tex. Prop. Code § 75.001(a)(1).

ENVIRONMENTAL ISSUES

There are several environmental laws both at the federal and state level that impact real property. The Environmental Protection Agency (EPA) implements federal rules and regulations concerning environmental issues and administers various federal statutes whereas the Texas Commission on Environmental Quality (TCEQ), formerly the Texas Natural Resources Conservation Commission (TNRCC), implements environmental rules and regulations specific to Texas.

In Texas, air quality is governed by the federal Clean Air Act and the Texas Clean Air Act. The federal Clean Air Act (42 U.S.C. § 7401 et seq.) regulates air emissions from stationary and mobile sources. This law authorizes the EPA to establish National Ambient Air Quality Standards (NAAQS) to protect public health and public welfare and to regulate emissions of hazardous air pollutants. The Texas Clean Air Act (Tex. Health and Safety Code § 382.001 et seq.) implements the federal programs established by the federal Clean Air Act and includes additional provisions to address some Texas-specific issues. There is currently no requirement for disclosing the air quality in a particular area; however, a list of current non-attainment counties for all criteria pollutants can be found on the EPA's Green Book website.

The Clean Water Act (33 U.S.C. § 1251 et seq.) establishes the basic structure for regulating discharges of pollutants into the waters of the United States. As a result, the EPA has implemented pollution control programs such as setting wastewater standards for industry. In addition, the Act establishes the basic structure for regulating quality standards for surface waters so the EPA has also developed national water quality criteria recommendations for pollutants in surface waters. At the Texas level, these water quality standards are regulated by the TCEQ.[43] This chapter of the Water Code also governs leaking underground and aboveground storage tanks that may pollute groundwater and surface water resources.[44]

The Clean Water Act makes it unlawful to discharge any pollutant from a point source into navigable waters, unless a permit is obtained. These navigable waters are the "waters of the United States, including the territorial seas."[45] A pollutant is "dredged spoil, solid waste, incinerator residue, sewage, garbage, sewage sludge, munitions, chemical wastes, biological materials, radioactive materials, heat, wrecked or discarded equipment, rock, sand, cellar dirt and industrial, municipal, and agricultural waste discharged into water."[46] A point source is defined as "any discernible, confined and discrete conveyance, including but not limited to any pipe, ditch, channel, tunnel, conduit, well, discrete fissure, container, rolling stock, concentrated animal feeding operation, or vessel or other floating craft,

[43] Tex. Water Code Ch. 26.
[44] Tex. Water Code § 26.341.
[45] 33 U.S.C. § 1362(7).
[46] 33 U.S.C. § 1362(6).

from which pollutants are or may be discharged. This term does not include agricultural stormwater discharges and return flows from irrigated agriculture."[47] However, residential homes that are connected to a municipal waste system, use a septic system, or do not have a surface discharge do not need a permit. If the discharge goes directly to surface water, such as can occur with industrial facilities, then a permit must be obtained.

Texas protects its water resources under chapter 26 of the Texas Water Code. According to the Code, "no person may discharge any pollutant, sewage, municipal waste, recreational waste, agricultural waste, or industrial waste from any point source into any water in the state" of Texas without a permit.[48] This law is much broader than the federal Clean Water Act because it is not limited to navigable waters or even surface water. "Water" or "water in the state" under the Texas Water Code means "groundwater, percolating or otherwise, lakes, bays, ponds, impounding reservoirs, springs, rivers, streams, creeks, estuaries, wetlands, marshes, inlets, canals, the Gulf of Mexico, inside the territorial limits of the state, and all other bodies of surface water, natural or artificial, inland or coastal, fresh or salt, navigable or nonnavigable, and including the beds and banks of all watercourses and bodies of surface water, that are wholly or partially inside or bordering the state or inside the jurisdiction of the state."[49] Even the definition for a pollutant is broader than that of the federal component. "Pollutant" means dredged soil, solid waste, incinerator residue, sewage, garbage, sewage sludge, filter backwash, munitions, chemical wastes, biological materials, radioactive materials, heat, wrecked or discarded equipment, rock, sand, cellar dirt, and industrial, municipal, and agricultural waste discharged into any water in the state.[50] A "pollutant" includes runoff water from irrigation associated with an animal feeding operation that is located near a water reservoir obtaining water from an impaired state water resource, but not runoff from irrigation or rainwater from other cultivated or uncultivated rangeland, pastureland, and farmland that is not owned or controlled by an operator of an animal feeding operation on which agricultural waste is applied.[51] Similar to the federal Clean Water Act, a point source is "any discernible, confined and discrete conveyance, including but not limited to any pipe, ditch, channel, tunnel, conduit, well, discrete fissure, container, rolling stock, concentrated animal feeding operation, or vessel or other floating craft, from which pollutants or wastes are or may be discharged into or adjacent to any water in the state."[52] As a result of this broader language, residential homes that use a septic system, for example, must make sure they comply with this law and the rules and regulations of the TCEQ.

---

[47] 33 U.S.C. § 1362(14).

[48] Tex. Water Code § 26.121.

[49] Tex. Water Code § 26.001(5).

[50] Tex. Water Code § 26.001(13).

[51] Tex. Water Code § 26.001(13) and § 26.502.

[52] Tex. Water Code § 26.001(21).

Several environmental laws are implicated when hazards are found on the property. The Comprehensive Environmental Response, Compensation, and Liability Act (CERCLA) (42 U.S.C. § 9601 et seq.) provides a fund to clean up uncontrolled or abandoned hazardous-waste sites as well as accidents, spills, and other emergency releases of pollutants and contaminants into the environment. This statute gives the EPA power to seek out those parties responsible for any release and obtain their cooperation in the cleanup. The Resource Conservation and Recovery Act (RCRA) (42 U.S.C. § 6901 et seq.) gives the EPA the authority to control the generation, transportation, treatment, storage, and disposal of hazardous waste. This statute also addresses management of non-hazardous solid wastes. Authority under this statute extends to environmental problems that could result from underground tanks storing petroleum and other hazardous substances.[53] Hazardous waste is additionally addressed by the Texas Solid Waste Disposal Act (Tex. Health and Safety Code § 361.001 et seq.) and the Texas Comprehensive Municipal Solid Waste Management, Resource Recovery, and Conservation Act (Tex. Health and Safety Code § 363.001 et seq.) At the federal level, the Toxic Substances Control Act (15 U.S.C. § 2601 et seq.) addresses the production, importation, use, and disposal of specific chemicals such as asbestos, indoor radon, and lead-based paint. The Texas Asbestos Health Protection Act (Tex. Occ. Code § 1954.001 et seq.) provides some additional protection at the state level concerning asbestos.

In addition, a seller, including a developer, of unimproved real property that is to be used for residential purposes must provide to the buyer a written notice disclosing the location of a transportation pipeline, including a pipeline for the transportation of natural gas, natural gas liquids, synthetic gas, liquefied petroleum gas, petroleum or a petroleum product, or a hazardous substance.[54] The notice must state the information to the best of the seller's belief and knowledge as of the date the notice is completed and signed by the seller. If the information required to be disclosed is not known to the seller, the seller must indicate that fact in the notice.[55] This notice must be delivered to the buyer on or before the effective date of an executory contract. If a contract is signed without the seller providing the notice, the buyer may terminate the contract for any reason not later than the seventh day after the effective date of the contract.[56] The seller is not required to give the notice if: (1) the seller is obligated to furnish a title insurance commitment to the buyer prior to closing; and (2) the buyer is entitled to terminate the contract if the buyer's objections to title as permitted by the contract are not cured by the seller prior to closing.[57]

---

[53] 42 U.S.C. § 6991.

[54] Tex. Prop. Code § 5.013(a).

[55] Tex. Prop. Code § 5.013(b).

[56] Tex. Prop. Code § 5.013(c).

[57] Tex. Prop. Code § 5.013(f).

At the federal level threatened and endangered species are governed by the Endangered Species Act.[58] This Act was enacted because of concern that several species of fish, wildlife, and plants in the United States were rendered extinct because of economic growth and development. The statute permits the creation of a list of endangered or threatened species that must be protected and specifies the requirements for conservation of the species as well as its habitat. A list is also provided at the state level by the Texas Parks and Wildlife Department, the agency responsible for monitoring threatened and endangered plants and animals in Texas. If endangered or threatened species are found on the property, then the conservation provisions at the federal or state level will apply. This can substantially limit the buyer's ability to use the property as intended.

Wetlands, on the other hand, are governed by the Clean Water Act. The Clean Water Act was implemented to eliminate the discharge of pollutants into the navigable waters of the United States.[59] The Act however does allow the discharge of dredged or fill material into these waters if the person obtains a permit from the Corp of Engineers. This type of discharge is typically done for commercial development, dam projects, and highway development. The permit can be very difficult to obtain if there is a wetlands on the property. A **wetlands** is defined as "those areas that are inundated or saturated by surface or ground water at a frequency and duration sufficient to support, and that under normal circumstances do support, a prevalence of vegetation typically adapted for life in saturated soil conditions. Wetlands generally include swamps, marshes, bogs and similar areas."[60] If a wetlands is found on the property, then the permitting procedure of the Clean Water Act would apply to any buyer seeking to fill a portion of the wetlands for construction. There is no guarantee that the permit will be granted and, if denied, can substantially limit the buyer's ability to use the property as intended. Farming operations, on the other hand, are generally exempt from the permitting requirements.[61]

At the Texas level, wetlands are governed by the Wetlands Act (Tex. Water Code § 11.501 et seq.). This Act provides a more detailed definition for wetlands. Specifically, wetlands means an area (including a swamp, marsh, bog, prairie pothole, or similar area) having a predominance of hydric soils that are inundated or saturated by surface or groundwater at a frequency and duration sufficient to support and that under normal circumstances supports the growth and regeneration of hydrophytic vegetation.[62] Wetlands in Texas do not include "irrigated acreage used as farmland; man-made wetlands of less than one acre; or man-made wetlands not constructed with wetland creation as a stated objective."[63] Hydric

[58] 16 U.S.C. § 1531.
[59] 33 U.S.C. § 1251.
[60] 40 C.F.R. § 230.3(o)(3)(iv).
[61] 40 C.F.R. § 232.3.
[62] Tex. Water Code § 11.502(1).
[63] Tex. Water Code § 11.502(4).

soil is "soil that, in its undrained condition, is saturated, flooded, or ponded long enough during a growing season to develop an anaerobic condition that supports the growth and regeneration of hydrophytic vegetation."[64] Hydrophytic vegetation "means a plant growing in water or a substrate that is at least periodically deficient in oxygen during a growing season as a result of excessive water content."[65]

HOMESTEAD

In General

Homestead law involves another important right in property. It creates both a benefit to the owner of the property as well as a right of possession for a non-owner living on the premises. However, the homestead right cannot be conveyed.

Homestead law in Texas is governed by the Texas Constitution.[66] Under the Texas Constitution, there is a family homestead exemption and a single-adult homestead exemption. In order to create a **family homestead**, the requirements of a family must be satisfied. In order to create a family, (1) two or more persons must (2) live together, (3) with some moral or legal obligation, and (4) there must be some dependence on the head of the family for support. The **single-adult homestead** is created by a single adult. A single adult is defined as a party who is at least 18 years of age, or a person with the disability of minority removed by a court and who is not married or the constituent of a family.

The Homestead Exemption

Once established, the homestead right exempts the property from forced sale by general creditors. However, there are seven exceptions to this rule. The property can be sold to satisfy a debt for (1) purchase money on the property, (2) property taxes, (3) permanent and valuable improvements on the property, (4) preexisting debts, (5) federal tax liens, (6) home equity liens, and (7) reverse mortgages.[67]

Term of Homestead

Once a homestead right is established, typically by intent and occupancy, it continues until people die or the homestead is abandoned. If there is a divorce and there are no children in the family, the homestead is abandoned as a matter of law. Where there are minor children in the homestead, the divorce does not terminate the family homestead. Where the family homestead is abandoned, it is possible for the family homestead to become a single-adult homestead.

---

[64] Tex. Water Code § 11.502(2).

[65] Tex. Water Code § 11.502(3).

[66] Tex. Const. Art. 16 § 50.

[67] Tex. Prop. Code § 41.001.

Extent of Exemption

To establish a homestead right, a person must use the property as a family or single adult. For use, one must distinguish between an urban use and a rural use. An **urban use** is a use of the property located in an urban area. A homestead is considered to be urban if, at the time the designation is made, the property is: (1) located within the limits of a municipality or its extraterritorial jurisdiction or a platted subdivision; and (2) served by police protection, paid or volunteer fire protection, and at least three of the following services provided by a municipality or under contract to a municipality: (A) electric; (B) natural gas; (C) sewer; (D) storm sewer; and (E) water.[68]

A residence for urban homestead purposes is where the person lives and any other contiguous tracts. The property can be used for home and business purposes, but only an individual can claim the exemption. The use is limited to 10 acres. Improvements on the urban homestead are entirely exempt, subject to the previously mentioned exceptions.[69]

It is also possible for a person to establish a **rural use** homestead. The general rule for rural homesteads is that one cannot have a rural homestead in a built-up, urbanized area. This homestead is limited to 200 acres for a family homestead. A single-adult homestead is limited to 100 acres. The rural use homestead can be noncontiguous. Improvements on the rural homestead are exempt, subject to the previously mentioned exceptions.[70]

Conveyancing the Homestead

According to the Texas Family Code, a husband and wife must join in a conveyance of a family homestead regardless of the nature of title to the property.[71] Whether the homestead is the separate property of either spouse or community property, neither spouse may sell, convey, or encumber it without the joinder of the other spouse unless otherwise provided by law. One common situation arises where the husband wants to sell the property and the wife refuses to consent. The husband signs all the necessary paperwork to transfer title, and the wife moves away with the husband after closing. In Texas, since the wife did not sign the conveyance instruments, the husband's attempt to sell the property is voidable at the wife's option. As long as the deed is voidable, the purchaser cannot take possession. The deed ceases to be voidable if the homestead is abandoned, the non-consenting spouse waives his or her homestead right, or the non-consenting spouse dies.

---

[68] Tex. Prop. Code § 41.002(c).
[69] Tex. Prop. Code § 41.002(a).
[70] Tex. Prop. Code § 41.002(b).
[71] Tex. Fam. Code § 5.001.

The importance of these issues for real estate professionals is that once a person or persons begins residency, the homestead right attaches regardless of whether the property is separate or community. This means if one spouse attempts to list property that may be his or her separate property and that person is married, the fact that the other spouse is living on the property is sufficient to raise a red flag that the property is a family homestead. Once this is determined, the signature of both parties is required on all conveyancing documents.

Discussion Questions

1. What is the homestead law and what are the exceptions to this law?
2. Why is it important to know whether property is homestead when listing the property for sale?
3. Explain the government power of eminent domain.
4. Explain the differences between freehold estates and non-freehold estates.
5. Describe three types of present freehold estates and identify which one conveys the most rights.
6. Explain the differences between reversions and remainders.
7. What are the two general types of easements that can created? Give an example of each type.

CHAPTER

5

CONTRACTS USED IN REAL ESTATE

KEY TERMS

accord
breach of contract
buyer agency
Buyer Representation Agreement
Buyer's Temporary Residential Lease
contract for deed
discharge
exclusive agency listing
exclusive right to sell listing
frustration of purpose
general agency
gross lease
ground lease
impossibility of performance
independent contractor
Information About Brokerage Services
lease
lease purchase agreement
listing agreement
modification
multiple listing service
mutual rescission
net lease
net listing
novation
open listing
percentage lease
personal services contracts
Release of Earnest Money
right of first refusal
satisfaction
seller agency
Seller's Disclosure Notice
Seller's Temporary Residential Lease
special agency
sponsoring broker
substitution
tenancy at sufferance
tenancy at will
tenancy for years
tenancy from period to period
Termination of Listing Agreement

REAL ESTATE CONTRACTS

For the real estate industry, contracts are of great importance because several types of transactions are possible, and the terms of the contracts can vary for each situation. There are contracts that deal with the license holder's agency representation of his or her client. There are independent contractor agreements between sales agents and their sponsoring brokers. There are contracts that deal with specific real estate transactions. Some of these transactions may involve commercial property, resi-

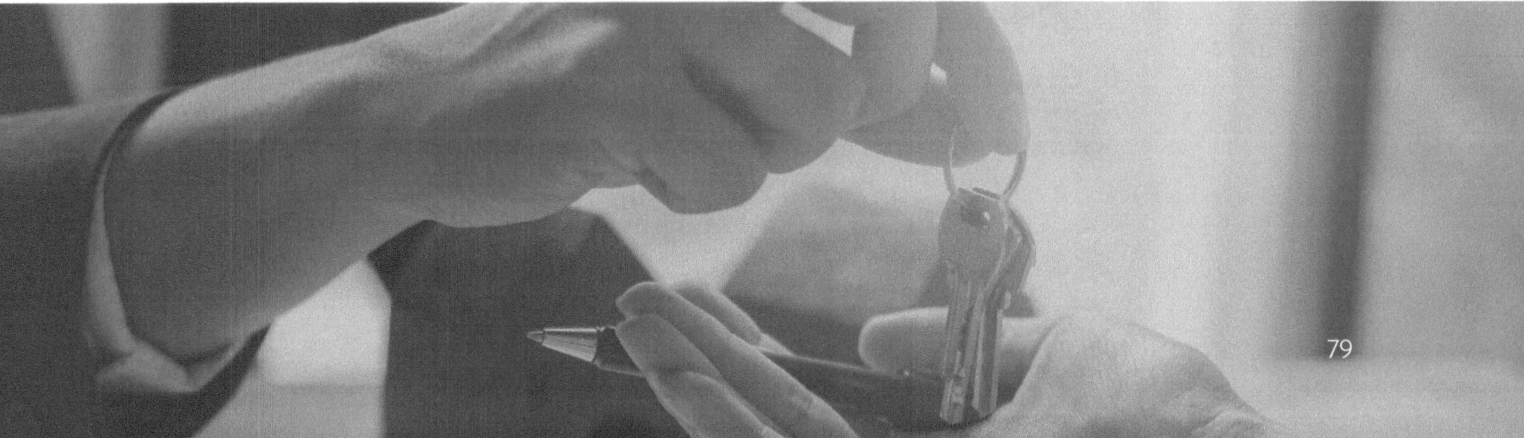

dential property, unimproved property, farm and ranch property, new home construction property, and property under management, to name a few. The terms of the transaction may vary depending, for instance, on the type of financing involved. There are loan contracts involved when a prospective purchaser needs financing for the real estate purchase. There are also lease contracts that can be created between the owner of the property and a tenant. To say there are many different documents in real estate because there are so many situations would be *very* accurate. Learning all the documents takes time, training, and practice.

CONTRACT LAW

A contract sets out the terms and conditions of the agreement between the parties. In contracts for the sale and purchase of real estate, for example, the terms specify what the property owner is selling and what is not included in the sale. There are also provisions that relate to the sales price and the financing involved, as well as which party is to pay specific fees at closing. Of great importance are the provisions for termination of the contract and remedies for breach of the contract.

Once a valid contract is established, certain rights and liabilities arise from the contract. For instance, a party to the contract may elect to assign or delegate his or her rights or liabilities under a contract. This might occur in the context of an assumption transaction. A party to the contract also has the right to amend or terminate the contract. In addition, there may be circumstances under which a party to the contract seeks to discharge his or her performance under that contract. The most common instance of this in real estate sales contracts is when the buyer fails to obtain financing. Obviously, if a buyer can't get financing, he or she can't go through with the transaction. Promulgated residential sales contracts allow the contract to terminate so no further performance is required from the buyer.

The last area of concern for the parties is breach of contract. Breach of contract comes about where one party to the contract fails to perform as indicated in the contract without some legal excuse. The remedies available to the non-defaulting party for such a breach under promulgated residential sales contracts include, for example, monetary damages, specific performance, and rescission with earnest money. There is a great deal to learn about contracts. This is especially true with contracts in the area of real estate.

DISCHARGE OF CONTRACTS

In General

It sometimes can be difficult to distinguish between a discharge of the contract and a breach. **Discharge** is the termination of an obligation under a contract with a valid excuse. Therefore, the primary means by which a contract can be discharged is by performance. In other words, a contract will be discharged when all parties to the contract have performed their obligations. The most obvious example involves a real estate sales transaction where the seller transfers the title and keys to the property to the purchaser and the purchaser transfers the money to the seller at closing.

In contrast, a **breach of contract** can occur when a party to the contract fails to perform as indicated in the contract without a valid excuse. For example, Maria Seller and Richard Purchaser enter into a contract for the purchase and sale of Maria Seller's property. The transaction is scheduled to close on June 15. Richard Purchaser fails to show up at the closing. Maria Seller has grounds for breach of contract against Richard Purchaser for this failure. If one party to a contract has breached the contract, then the remaining parties to the contract are discharged from performance under the contract. In other words, Maria Seller does not have to transfer the title. Additional legal excuses that will discharge a party's obligation to perform under a contract include lapse of time, modification, failure of condition (discussed in a later chapter), impossibility or frustration of purpose, and agreement of the parties.

Discharge by Lapse of Time

A contract may also be discharged when there has been a lapse of time. Lapse of time under a contract may involve two situations. First, if there is a specific date and time indicated in the contract whereby the contract is to terminate, the contract lapses on that specified date and time. For example, Sally Seller and Betty Broker enter into a written contract whereby Betty Broker is to find a purchaser for Sally Seller's home, and in exchange, she is to be paid a 7% commission. The contract indicates that the contract terminates at midnight on July 18. Betty Broker fails to find a buyer for Sally Seller's house by midnight on July 18; therefore, the contract is terminated and the parties to the contract are discharged.

The second situation that may arise with discharge by lapse of time is when there is no time indicated in the contract. If no time is indicated in the contract, then the contract will terminate within a reasonable time. The definition of what constitutes reasonable time is uncertain before performance is due and is only defined in a lawsuit for breach of contract. For example, Beth Buyer and Bob Builder enter into a contract whereby Bob Builder is to build a home for Beth Buyer in exchange for a fee for his services. In the discussion of the contract, nothing is mentioned regarding the time for completion of this agreement. Further, the completion date is not indicated in writing. Nine months later, Beth Buyer is frustrated with Bob Builder's failure to construct a home for her to purchase, so she calls him up and explains her dismay. Bob Builder informs Beth Buyer that they have a contract and that he will sue her for breach of contract for backing out. Beth Buyer walks away from the contract, and Bob Builder sues her for breach of contract. Beth Buyer has the unfortunate obligation of arguing that the contract terminated because nine months is an unreasonable amount of time under the contract; therefore, the contract lapsed. It is then up to the jury to determine what they believe to be a reasonable time. To avoid this situation there should be well-defined deadlines in all contracts.

Discharge by Modification

Another way the parties to a contract may be discharged under the contract is by modification of the contract. **Modification** refers to the amendment of the contract. When the original contract is modified by agreement of the parties, the terms of the original contract that were modified are discharged. The original contract; however, is not entirely discharged. For example, Mike Seller and Susan Buyer enter into a contract for the purchase and sale of Mike Seller's property. In the contract, it is indicated that the transaction will involve seller financing. Subsequently, Susan Buyer receives $100,000 from a deceased relative, and she wants to use this money to purchase the property outright. The parties agree to modify the contract to involve a cash sale rather than seller financing. The original terms of the contract are still in force; the only change to the contract is to the terms regarding the cash sale. All terms with regard to the seller financing are discharged. When issues like financing changes occur, it is best to get a modification agreement written out and signed by the parties.

Discharge by Impossibility or Frustration of Purpose

Another way a party to the contract may be discharged from the contract is when it has become impossible to perform or the purpose underlying the contract has been frustrated. Under the doctrine of **impossibility of performance**, one party's duty to perform under the contract is discharged when, without any fault of that party, it becomes impossible to perform.

Surprisingly, death or insanity of a party to a contract does not automatically make a contract impossible to perform so those circumstances will not normally discharge the party to the contract without a provision in the contract to the contrary. Death or incapacity of a party to the contract may discharge that party where the contract is personal to that party, in the absence of a contrary contractual provision. These contracts are often referred to as **personal services contracts**. For example, a contractor and a purchaser enter into a new home construction contract whereby the contractor is to build a house for the purchaser in Apple Hills subdivision. Subsequently, the contractor dies. In the absence of a contrary contractual provision, the contractor as well as the contractor's estate will be discharged from the contract because the contract called for the personal services of the contractor. Under this same reasoning, if the contractor subsequently had been judicially declared insane, the contractor would have been discharged from his or her obligation under the contract.

However, when the contract does not call for personal services to be performed, the death or insanity of a party will not discharge his or her obligations to perform under the contract, in the absence of a contractual provision to the contrary. In the case of a death of a party to the contract, the obligation to perform will pass to the deceased party's estate. For example, a seller and a prospective purchaser enter into a contract for the purchase and sale of the seller's 100-acre ranch. Subsequently, the seller dies. The death of the seller does not discharge the obligation to perform under the contract; the obligation merely passes to the seller's estate. This situation occurs in the absence of a contrary contractual provision.

In the case of insanity of a party to the contract, the party would not be discharged under the contract. The obligation would pass to a guardian appointed by the court or an attorney in fact under a durable power of attorney, in the absence of a contrary contractual provision.

Frustration of purpose may also operate to discharge the contract. With **frustration of purpose**, nothing has happened to impede performance, but the purpose has been frustrated in some way by the happening of an event. To establish that the purpose under the contract has been frustrated, four elements must be shown. First, there must have been a supervening act. Second, this supervening act must have been unforeseeable at the time the contract was entered into. Third, the purpose or object of the contract was known and recognized by both parties at the time they entered into the contract. Fourth, the supervening act totally destroys the purpose of the contract.

Because the doctrine of frustration of purpose creates a risk of undermining the contract and there may be no certainty that the contract can be enforced, frustration of purpose has become an unpopular defense. The most common time that frustration of purpose arises in a real estate contract is when there has been some supervening illegality. This may occur when a new law is enacted after the making of the contract. For example, a seller and a prospective purchaser enter into a contract for the purchase and sale of the seller's bar and grill in Texas. Subsequently, the Texas legislature passes a law prohibiting the sale of alcohol. The purpose under the contract has become frustrated because of this new legislation; therefore, the contract is discharged.

Discharge by Agreement of the Parties

Mutual Rescission

A contract can be discharged by the mutual agreement of the parties to that contract. This mutual agreement to cancel has also been referred to as **mutual rescission.** In real estate sales transactions, mutual rescission may arise between the parties when both parties realize that for some reason the transaction will not close. For example, a seller and a prospective purchaser enter into a contract for the purchase and sale of the seller's property. Financing is obtained by the purchaser, and the deal is set to close in one week. The purchaser subsequently contacts the seller's agent and indicates that he or she cannot go through with the closing in one week because his or her oldest child has just been diagnosed with a terminal disease, and with all of the medical bills, it will be impossible for the purchaser to make the payments on the new home. Ordinarily, this type of situation would give rise to a breach of contract claim by the seller against the purchaser if the purchaser failed to perform. In addition, there is no legal excuse for the buyer to back out of the deal because of the medical problems of the child. All conditions have been satisfied, so there is no legal excuse based on condition. Further, nothing has happened to the object of the purchase, that is, the house; therefore, performance is possible. Since there is no supervening illegality and the courts frown on the use of the frustration of purpose doctrine, there is no excuse there. The only hope for the purchaser to back out of this contract without legal liability is by mutual agreement of the parties. Obviously, the decision to let the buyer back out of this contract will be solely on the seller.

If mutual rescission is involved, it is of great importance that if the seller agrees to let the purchaser walk away from the transaction without liability that the parties to the contract sign some sort of release of contract form. For example, a common form used to accomplish this purpose is the **Release of Earnest Money** form, which is contained in figure 5-1.

This form dictates that the parties are released of all liability under the contract and indicates who is to receive the earnest money upon termination of the contract. Since this document directly affects the legal rights of the parties, it is important to note that the parties to the contract do have the right to seek legal counsel before proceeding to release.

Substitution and Novation

Sometimes when both parties to the contract cancel the contract, a change of one party for a new party is made. A **substitution** changes one party for another under the contract, but the party who is substituted is still liable under the contract. If the new party fails to perform as promised, both the new party and the original party will be responsible for the damages. A second method for changing the parties to the contract involves a novation. The notion of a novation is of great importance because a **novation** substitutes a new party for an original party to the contract and completely releases the original party to the contract from all liability under that contract. For example, Tom Seller and Bob Buyer enter into a contract for the purchase and sale of Tom Seller's property. Four days before closing, Bob Buyer realizes that he will not be able to go to closing, but requests a novation under the contract. Tom Seller agrees and there is a substitution of Sally Buyer for Bob Buyer in the transaction. Sally Buyer fails to appear at closing. Tom Seller can no longer seek performance under the contract from Bob Buyer by virtue of the novation.

TEXAS ASSOCIATION OF REALTORS®

RELEASE OF EARNEST MONEY

RELEASE OF EARNEST MONEY BETWEEN THE UNDERSIGNED BUYER AND SELLER CONCERNING THE PROPERTY AT

____

NOTICE: This form provides for the release of the parties, brokers, and title companies from all liability under the contract (not just for disbursement of earnest money). Do not sign this form if it is not your intention to release all the persons signing this form from all liability under the contract. READ THIS RELEASE CAREFULLY. If you do not understand the effect of this release, consult your attorney BEFORE signing.

A. The undersigned Buyer and Seller release each other, any broker, title company, and escrow agent from any and all liability under the aforementioned contract.

B. The undersigned direct ______________________ (escrow agent) to disburse the earnest money as follows:

$__________ to__________________

$__________ to__________________

$__________ to__________________

$__________ to__________________

Buyer Date	Seller Date
Buyer Date	Seller Date
Address:	Address:
Other/Cooperating Broker	Listing/Principal Broker
By ______ Date	By ______ Date
Address:	Address:

(TAR-1904) 2-6-02 Page 1 of 1

FIGURE 5-1 Release of Earnest Money
Source: Reprinted with permission of Texas Association of REALTORS®

Note further that a novation requires the consent of *all parties* to the contract. However, this consent can be either express, as by written or oral words, or implied, as by the conduct of the parties, for instance, where there is an acceptance of performance by the new party to the contract. If consent to the novation is not obtained, then the original party to the contract is still liable for damages under the contract. For example, June Seller and Frank Buyer enter into a contract for the purchase and sale of June Seller's home. All conditions under the contract are satisfied, and the parties are set to close in five days. Subsequently,

Frank Buyer does not want to close the deal, but offers a substitution of himself for Jack Buyer under the contract. June Seller does not agree to the substitution. On the day of closing, Frank Buyer does not show up and neither does Jack Buyer. June Seller can still recover against Frank Buyer for breach of the contract by failure to perform under the contract.

Accord and Satisfaction

Accord and satisfaction may sometimes arise to discharge a party's performance under a contract. An **accord** is an executory agreement to accept performance in future satisfaction of a contractual duty. **Satisfaction** is the time when the accord is fully performed. When accord and satisfaction are involved, the party's original contractual duties are suspended for a limited time after the accord is created, and both the original contractual duties and the accord duties are discharged when the accord is satisfied or completely performed. If the party fails to satisfy the accord, the injured party may recover under either the old contract or the new accord. For example, Tony Contractor owes his friend Harry Homeowner $400. Both parties agree that Tony Contractor will construct a gazebo on Harry Homeowner's property within the next 15 days in full satisfaction of the $400 debt. Four days later, Harry Homeowner realizes he needs the $400 in cash and seeks to sue Tony Contractor on the debt. In this instance, Harry Homeowner will not be able to sue on the underlying debt because the accord, the agreement to accept performance to satisfy the debt, suspends the operation of the underlying debt. Unfortunately, Tony Contractor will have to wait until he is damaged under the accord contract before he may raise the accord as an argument against the original contractual obligation. In other words, he must wait until he is both sued and a judgment is returned against him, before he may argue that the accord suspends the debt. However, if Tony Contractor fails to construct the gazebo within the 15-day time frame, Harry Homeowner can seek recovery under the original contract for $400 or under the new contract for construction of the gazebo because there has been no satisfaction.

CONTRACTS USED IN THE REAL ESTATE BUSINESS

There are several categories of contracts used in the real estate business, including promulgated sales contracts, employment agreements, and leases. The first category includes the promulgated sales contracts from the Texas Real Estate Commission. The most common of these promulgated sales contracts is the One- to Four-Family Residential Contract (Resale) (TREC 20-14) (herein referred to as the "promulgated residential sales contract"). This contract will be discussed in greater detail in the next chapter. The remaining contracts (herein referred to as the "promulgated sales contracts") include:

- Unimproved Property Contract (TREC 9-13)
- New Home Contract (Incomplete Construction) (TREC 23-15)

- New Home Contract (Completed Construction) (TREC 24-15)
- Farm and Ranch Contract (TREC 25-12)
- Residential Condominium Contract (Resale) (TREC 30-13)

In addition to the promulgated sales contracts, license holders use employment contracts in several different situations. One of the most common examples is the employment agreements between brokers and sales agents that define the terms of the relationship in the brokerage and the respective rights and liabilities. These agreements are independent contractor agreements. The type of relationship created in the independent contractor agreement is a general agency, where the broker is the principal and the salesperson is the agent. A **general agency** is an agency whereby the agent is given authorization to conduct several transactions. Because of the nature of this type of agency, the principal is responsible for all acts of the agent performed within the scope of the agency. This means the broker's responsibility covers all acts of the sales agent related to real estate, but only in the area of real estate. Actions not within the scope of the real estate transaction are not the broker's responsibility.[1]

There are also employment agreements between brokers and their clients. These employment agreements are quite important in the real estate business because they define the terms of the relationship. The contracts establish an agency relationship between the parties, or a **special agency**. That is, the agreement establishes the license holder as the agent and the client, either the seller or the buyer, as the principal. In a special agency, the agent is given authorization for only limited situations. Therefore, the principal is not responsible for the acts of the agent. An exception exists when the agent relies on information supplied to him or her from the principal. For example, a real estate broker may rely on information given by a seller in a Seller's Disclosure Notice. Under this relationship, the agent owes certain fiduciary duties to the principal, and in turn, the principal owes certain duties to the agent.

The majority of real estate situations involve employment contracts between brokers and sellers. This agency relationship is a **seller agency**, and the contracts involved are listing agreements. However, there are also situations where employment agreements are created between brokers and purchasers. This relationship is a buyer agency and the agreements are buyer representation agreements. See figure 5-2.

Independent Contractor Agreements

In Texas, there are two types of real estate licenses. There is the broker license and the sales agent license. Under the two-license system, a sales agent candidate can not sit for the licensing exam unless he or she has been "sponsored" by a broker.

[1] See Ebby Halliday Real Estate, Inc. v. Murnan, 916 S.W.2d 585 (Tex. App.–Fort Worth 1996).

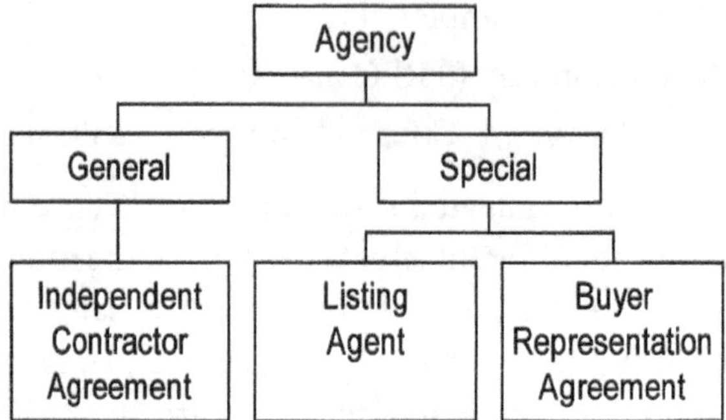

FIGURE 5-2 Employment Contracts and Agency Relationships
Source: © 2021 Mbition LLC

This **sponsoring broker** will be the broker that the new sales agent works with once he or she passes the exam and becomes licensed. The real estate sales agent in Texas cannot practice his or her trade, nor accept a fee, without a sponsoring broker.

The typical business arrangement between real estate sales agents and their sponsoring brokers is that of an **independent contractor**. Under Texas law, independent contractor status turns on whether the employer exercised any type of control over the employee. If there is no control by the employer, then the employee functions as an independent contractor. Essentially, where there is no control, the contractor is responsible for his or her own actions, expenses, fees, and other miscellaneous business overhead. The employer is not responsible for anything. In these arrangements, the parties can contract either verbally or in writing.

However, independent contractor status is somewhat different for real estate professionals. Since Texas law requires all sales agents to be sponsored by a broker, the sales agents can only act in the name of the broker under a general agency scheme. Thus, this agency relationship holds the broker responsible for the acts of the sales agents as if the sales agents were actually employees. The way that the Real Estate License Act is drafted requires the broker to monitor the salesperson's activity; therefore, there is some degree of control. Where there is some degree of control, there is a lesser likelihood of obtaining independent contractor status.

Fortunately for real estate professionals, section 3508 of the Internal Revenue Code provides for independent contractor status regardless of control. This provision, however, requires that (1) there be a written independent contractor agreement that contains the words, "the individual will not be treated as an employee with respect to such services for federal tax purposes," (2) the individual have a real estate license, and (3) the amount paid to the individual be based on production (commission) rather than the number of hours worked.[2]

[2] 26 U.S.C. § 3508.

LISTING AGREEMENTS

In General

An agency relationship can be created in writing, by oral agreement, or by the conduct of the parties. The preferred means of creating the agency relationship is in writing. In Texas, the written agency relationship between a seller and broker is a **listing agreement**. There are four types of listing agreements in Texas. These include the exclusive right to sell listing, the exclusive agency listing, the open listing, and the net listing.

An **exclusive right to sell listing** gives the broker the authority to sell the property, but entitles the broker to a commission regardless of whether the broker or the property owner sells the property during the term of the listing. This is the most common type of listing used in Texas real estate sales. The exclusivity of the relationship means that the seller cannot hire another broker during the listing period. The broker will also benefit because since he or she is entitled to payment, the broker does not have to be concerned about the money and effort spent on advertising and showing the listed property.

An **exclusive agency listing** is a listing where the broker is entitled to a commission only if he or she sells the property during the listing period. The owner does not owe a commission if he or she sells the property during that time. This type of agency is more advantageous to the seller than to the broker. The broker is still entitled to exclusivity; however, if the broker fails to find a buyer and the seller does find a buyer; the broker does not get paid. This does not create as much incentive for the broker to find a buyer because so much money and effort might be spent trying to sell the listing with no guarantee of payment to cover the expenses.

An **open listing** is a listing where the seller can go to several different brokers to list the property and the first broker that sells it gets the commission. As with the exclusive agency listing, if the owner sells the property, he or she does not have to pay a commission. While this type of listing allows the seller greater flexibility in selling his or her property, there is no guarantee to the broker that he or she will get paid. Thus, the broker in these agreements will not work as hard or expend as much money marketing the listing.

A **net listing** is a listing in which the broker's commission is any amount above the agreed on sales price. However, section 535.16 of the rules of the Texas Real Estate Commission cautions against the use of such listings because of the dangers associated with the broker putting his or her interests above the interests of the client.[3]

Regardless of the type of listing agreement used, the license holder will likely use a multiple listing service to market the property. The **multiple listing service** (MLS) is a system, usually available through a local board of REALTORS®, that

[3] 22 T.A.C. § 535.16.

disseminates a broker's information on listed properties to other member brokers and through which participants offer cooperation on transactions as well as specific compensation. A multiple listing service profile sheet is typically made available by the MLS operator for use by participants to indicate all the details of the particular listed property. This information is then compiled and entered into the multiple listing service for other participants to view and potentially cooperate in the sale for a shared commission.

Required Elements of a Listing Agreement

A listing agreement must contain all of the essential elements of a contract to be valid. There must be mutual assent between the parties in the form of an offer and acceptance. There must also be some type of consideration. Typically, this consideration will be in the form of a promise in exchange for performance. For example, in a standard exclusive right to sell listing agreement, the seller promises to pay the broker a specified commission if the broker performs by finding the seller a ready, willing, and able purchaser. There must be capacity of the parties, and there must be legality. In addition, the Texas Occupations Code requires that a commission agreement be in writing and signed by the party to be charged in order to be enforceable.[4]

The completion of a standard listing agreement may vary depending on the form used. The real estate trade associations are the organizations that typically draft these agreements. These associations are composed of real estate professionals and affiliate members. The forms created by these associations are not consumer-friendly; instead the forms are designed to protect the real estate professional and are considered broker-friendly. Forms created by these associations are for members only. Each listing agreement may have specialized language; however, the language of Exclusive Right to Sell Listing Agreement in figure 5-3 is illustrative.

Exclusive Right to Sell Listing Agreement

There are many paragraphs in the sample listing agreement that are similar to the promulgated sales contracts; however, there are also several provisions that are drafted to protect the broker. An explanation for many of the paragraphs is provided below.

Paragraph 1: Parties

This paragraph includes the parties' names. Similar to the promulgated sales contracts, care should be used to include the parties' complete legal names. Also note that only a broker, rather than a salesperson, is a party to the listing agreement. The grant of exclusivity to the broker is provided in this paragraph.

---

[4] See Tex. Occ. Code § 1101.806; Texas Builders v. Keller, 928 S.W.2d 479 (Tex. 1996).

RESIDENTIAL REAL ESTATE LISTING AGREEMENT EXCLUSIVE RIGHT TO SELL

1. **PARTIES:** The parties to this agreement (this Listing) are:

Seller: ____
____
Address: ____
City, State, Zip: ____
Phone: ______________________ Fax: ______________________
E-Mail: ____

Broker: ____
Address: ____
City, State, Zip: ____
Phone: ______________________ Fax: ______________________
E-Mail: ____

Seller appoints Broker as Seller's sole and exclusive real estate agent and grants to Broker the exclusive right to sell the Property.

2. **PROPERTY:** "Property" means the land, improvements, and accessories described below, except for any described exclusions.

A. Land: Lot ______________________, Block ____________, ______________________
______________________ Addition, City of ______________________,
in ______________________ County, Texas known as ______________________
____ (address/zip code),
or as described on attached exhibit. *(If Property is a condominium, attach Condominium Addendum.)*

B. Improvements: The house, garage and all other fixtures and improvements attached to the above-described real property, including without limitation, the following **permanently installed and built-in items, if any:** all equipment and appliances, valances, screens, shutters, awnings, wall-to-wall carpeting, mirrors, ceiling fans, attic fans, mail boxes, television antennas and satellite dish system and equipment, mounts and brackets for televisions and speakers, heating and air-conditioning units, security and fire detection equipment, wiring, plumbing and lighting fixtures, chandeliers, water softener system, kitchen equipment, garage door openers, cleaning equipment, shrubbery, landscaping, outdoor cooking equipment, and all other property owned by Seller and attached to the above-described real property.

C. Accessories: The following described related accessories, if any: window air conditioning units, stove, fireplace screens, curtains and rods, blinds, window shades, draperies and rods, door keys, mailbox keys, above-ground pool, swimming pool equipment and maintenance accessories, artificial fireplace logs, and controls for: (i) satellite dish systems, (ii) garage doors, (iii) entry gates, and (iv) other improvements and accessories.

(TAR-1101) 01-01-14 Initialed for Identification by Broker/Associate ________ and Seller ________, ________ Page 1 of 10

FIGURE 5-3 Exclusive Right to Sell Listing Agreement
Source: Reprinted with permission of Texas Association of REALTORS®

Residential Listing concerning____

D. Exclusions: The following improvements and accessories will be retained by Seller and must be removed prior to delivery of possession: ____
____.

E. Owners' Association: The property ❑ is ❑ is not subject to mandatory membership in a property owners' association.

3. **LISTING PRICE:** Seller instructs Broker to market the Property at the following price: $__________ (Listing Price). Seller agrees to sell the Property for the Listing Price or any other price acceptable to Seller. Seller will pay all typical closing costs charged to sellers of residential real estate in Texas (seller's typical closing costs are those set forth in the residential contract forms promulgated by the Texas Real Estate Commission).

4. **TERM:**

A. This Listing begins on ______________ and ends at 11:59 p.m. on ______________.

B. If Seller enters into a binding written contract to sell the Property before the date this Listing begins and the contract is binding on the date this Listing begins, this Listing will not commence and will be void.

5. **BROKER COMPENSATION:**

A. When earned and payable, Seller will pay Broker:

❑ (1) ________% of the sales price.

❑ (2) ____.

B. Earned: Broker's compensation is earned when any one of the following occurs during this Listing:
(1) Seller sells, exchanges, options, agrees to sell, agrees to exchange, or agrees to option the Property to anyone at any price on any terms;
(2) Broker individually or in cooperation with another broker procures a buyer ready, willing, and able to buy the Property at the Listing Price or at any other price acceptable to Seller; or
(3) Seller breaches this Listing.

C. Payable: Once earned, Broker's compensation is payable either during this Listing or after it ends at the earlier of:
(1) the closing and funding of any sale or exchange of all or part of the Property;
(2) Seller's refusal to sell the Property after Broker's compensation has been earned;
(3) Seller's breach of this Listing; or
(4) at such time as otherwise set forth in this Listing.

Broker's compensation is not payable if a sale of the Property does not close or fund as a result of: (i) Seller's failure, without fault of Seller, to deliver to a buyer a deed or a title policy as required by the contract to sell; (ii) loss of ownership due to foreclosure or other legal proceeding; or (iii) Seller's failure to restore the Property, as a result of a casualty loss, to its previous condition by the closing date set forth in a contract for the sale of the Property.

D. Other Compensation:

(1) Breach by Buyer Under a Contract: If Seller collects earnest money, the sales price, or damages by suit, compromise, settlement, or otherwise from a buyer who breaches a contract for the sale of the Property entered into during this Listing, Seller will pay Broker, after deducting attorney's fees

(TAR-1101) 01-01-14 Initialed for Identification by Broker/Associate________ and Seller________, ________ Page 2 of 10

FIGURE 5-3 (Continued)

Residential Listing concerning____

and collection expenses, an amount equal to the lesser of one-half of the amount collected after deductions or the amount of the Broker's Compensation stated in Paragraph 5A. Any amount paid under this Paragraph 5D(1) is in addition to any amount that Broker may be entitled to receive for subsequently selling the Property.

(2) Service Providers: If Broker refers Seller or a prospective buyer to a service provider (for example, mover, cable company, telecommunications provider, utility, or contractor) Broker may receive a fee from the service provider for the referral. Any referral fee Broker receives under this Paragraph 5D(2) is in addition to any other compensation Broker may receive under this Listing.

(3) Other Fees and/or Reimbursable Expenses: ____
____
____.

E. Protection Period:

(1) "Protection period" means that time starting the day after this Listing ends and continuing for ______ days. "Sell" means any transfer of any fee simple interest in the Property whether by oral or written agreement or option.

(2) Not later than 10 days after this Listing ends, Broker may send Seller written notice specifying the names of persons whose attention was called to the Property during this Listing. If Seller agrees to sell the Property during the protection period to a person named in the notice or to a relative of a person named in the notice, Seller will pay Broker, upon the closing of the sale, the amount Broker would have been entitled to receive if this Listing were still in effect.

(3) This Paragraph 5E survives termination of this Listing. This Paragraph 5E will not apply if:
(a) Seller agrees to sell the Property during the protection period;
(b) the Property is exclusively listed with another broker who is a member of the Texas Association of REALTORS® at the time the sale is negotiated; and
(c) Seller is obligated to pay the other broker a fee for the sale.

F. County: All amounts payable to Broker are to be paid in cash in ______________________________ ______________________________ County, Texas.

G. Escrow Authorization: Seller authorizes, and Broker may so instruct, any escrow or closing agent authorized to close a transaction for the purchase or acquisition of the Property to collect and disburse to Broker all amounts payable to Broker under this Listing.

6. LISTING SERVICES:

❑ A. Broker will file this Listing with one or more Multiple Listing Services (MLS) by the earlier of the time required by MLS rules or 5 days after the date this Listing begins. Seller authorizes Broker to submit information about this Listing and the sale of the Property to the MLS.

Notice: MLS rules require Broker to accurately and timely submit all information the MLS requires for participation including sold data. MLS rules may require that the information be submitted to the MLS throughout the time the Listing is in effect. Subscribers to the MLS may use the information for market evaluation or appraisal purposes. Subscribers are other brokers and other real estate professionals such as appraisers and may include the appraisal district. Any information filed with the MLS becomes the property of the MLS for all purposes. **Submission of information to MLS ensures that persons who use and benefit from the MLS also contribute information.**

(TAR-1101) 01-01-14 Initialed for Identification by Broker/Associate________ and Seller________, ________ Page 3 of 10

FIGURE 5-3 (Continued)

Residential Listing concerning____

❑ B. Seller instructs Broker not to file this Listing with one or more Multiple Listing Service (MLS) until ___ days after the date this Listing begins for the following purpose(s): ____.

(NOTE: Do not check if prohibited by Multiple Listing Service(s).)

❑ C. Broker will not file this Listing with a Multiple Listing Service (MLS) or any other listing service.

Notice: Seller acknowledges and understands that if this option is checked: (1) Seller's Property will not be included in the MLS database available to real estate agents and brokers from other real estate offices who subscribe to and participate in the MLS, and their buyer clients may not be aware that Seller's Property is offered for sale; (2) Seller's Property will not be included in the MLS's download to various real estate Internet sites that are used by the public to search for property listings; and (3) real estate agents, brokers, and members of the public may be unaware of the terms and conditions under which Seller is marketing the Property.

7. ACCESS TO THE PROPERTY:

A. Authorizing Access: Authorizing access to the Property means giving permission to another person to enter the Property, disclosing to the other person any security codes necessary to enter the Property, and lending a key to the other person to enter the Property, directly or through a keybox. To facilitate the showing and sale of the Property, Seller instructs Broker to:
(1) access the Property at reasonable times;
(2) authorize other brokers, their associates, inspectors, appraisers, and contractors to access the Property at reasonable times; and
(3) duplicate keys to facilitate convenient and efficient showings of the Property.

B. Scheduling Companies: Broker may engage the following companies to schedule appointments and to authorize others to access the Property: ____.

C. Keybox: **A keybox is a locked container placed on the Property that holds a key to the Property. A keybox makes it more convenient for brokers, their associates, inspectors, appraisers, and contractors to show, inspect, or repair the Property. The keybox is opened by a special combination, key, or programmed device so that authorized persons may enter the Property, even in Seller's absence. Using a keybox will probably increase the number of showings, but involves risks (for example, unauthorized entry, theft, property damage, or personal injury). Neither the Association of REALTORS® nor MLS requires the use of a keybox.**

(1) Broker ❑ is ❑ is not authorized to place a keybox on the Property.

(2) If a tenant occupies the Property at any time during this Listing, Seller will furnish Broker a written statement (for example, TAR No. 1411), signed by all tenants, authorizing the use of a keybox or Broker may remove the keybox from the Property.

D. Liability and Indemnification: When authorizing access to the Property, Broker, other brokers, their associates, any keybox provider, or any scheduling company are not responsible for personal injury or property loss to Seller or any other person. Seller assumes all risk of any loss, damage, or injury. **Except for a loss caused by Broker, Seller will indemnify and hold Broker harmless from any claim for personal injury, property damage, or other loss.**

8. COOPERATION WITH OTHER BROKERS: Broker will allow other brokers to show the Property to prospective buyers. Broker will offer to pay the other broker a fee as described below if the other broker procures a buyer that purchases the Property.

FIGURE 5-3 (Continued)

Residential Listing concerning____

A. MLS Participants: If the other broker is a participant in the MLS in which this Listing is filed, Broker will offer to pay the other broker:
(1) if the other broker represents the buyer: ______% of the sales price or $_______________; and
(2) if the other broker is a subagent: ______% of the sales price or $_______________.

B. Non-MLS Brokers: If the other broker is not a participant in the MLS in which this Listing is filed, Broker will offer to pay the other broker:
(1) if the other broker represents the buyer: ______% of the sales price or $_______________; and
(2) if the other broker is a subagent: ______% of the sales price or $_______________.

9. INTERMEDIARY: *(Check A or B only.)*

❑ A. Intermediary Status: Broker may show the Property to interested prospective buyers who Broker represents. If a prospective buyer who Broker represents offers to buy the Property, Seller authorizes Broker to act as an intermediary and Broker will notify Seller that Broker will service the parties in accordance with one of the following alternatives.

(1) If a prospective buyer who Broker represents is serviced by an associate other than the associate servicing Seller under this Listing, Broker may notify Seller that Broker will: (a) appoint the associate then servicing Seller to communicate with, carry out instructions of, and provide opinions and advice during negotiations to Seller; and (b) appoint the associate then servicing the prospective buyer to the prospective buyer for the same purpose.

(2) If a prospective buyer who Broker represents is serviced by the same associate who is servicing Seller, Broker may notify Seller that Broker will: (a) appoint another associate to communicate with, carry out instructions of, and provide opinions and advice during negotiations to the prospective buyer; and (b) appoint the associate servicing the Seller under this Listing to the Seller for the same purpose.

(3) Broker may notify Seller that Broker will make no appointments as described under this Paragraph 9A and, in such an event, the associate servicing the parties will act solely as Broker's intermediary representative, who may facilitate the transaction but will not render opinions or advice during negotiations to either party.

❑ B. No Intermediary Status: Seller agrees that Broker will not show the Property to prospective buyers who Broker represents.

Notice: **If Broker acts as an intermediary under Paragraph 9A, Broker and Broker's associates:**
- **may not disclose to the prospective buyer that Seller will accept a price less than the asking price unless otherwise instructed in a separate writing by Seller;**
- **may not disclose to Seller that the prospective buyer will pay a price greater than the price submitted in a written offer to Seller unless otherwise instructed in a separate writing by the prospective buyer;**
- **may not disclose any confidential information or any information Seller or the prospective buyer specifically instructs Broker in writing not to disclose unless otherwise instructed in a separate writing by the respective party or required to disclose the information by the Real Estate License Act or a court order or if the information materially relates to the condition of the property;**
- **may not treat a party to the transaction dishonestly; and**
- **may not violate the Real Estate License Act.**

(TAR-1101) 01-01-14 Initialed for Identification by Broker/Associate________ and Seller________, ________ Page 5 of 10

FIGURE 5-3 (Continued)

Residential Listing concerning____

10. CONFIDENTIAL INFORMATION: During this Listing or after it ends, Broker may not knowingly disclose information obtained in confidence from Seller except as authorized by Seller or required by law. Broker may not disclose to Seller any confidential information regarding any other person Broker represents or previously represented except as required by law.

11. BROKER'S AUTHORITY:

A. Broker will use reasonable efforts and act diligently to market the Property for sale, procure a buyer, and negotiate the sale of the Property.

B. Broker is authorized to display this Listing on the Internet without limitation unless one of the following is checked:

❑ (1) Seller does not want this Listing to be displayed on the Internet.
❑ (2) Seller does not want the address of the Property to be displayed on the Internet.

Notice: Seller understands and acknowledges that, if box 11B(1) is selected, consumers who conduct searches for listings on the Internet will not see information about this Listing in response to their search.

C. Broker is authorized to market the Property with the following financing options:

❑ (1) Conventional
❑ (2) VA
❑ (3) FHA
❑ (4) Cash
❑ (5) Texas Veterans Land Program
❑ (6) Owner Financing
❑ (7) Other

D. In addition to other authority granted by this Listing, Broker may:
(1) advertise the Property by means and methods as Broker determines, including but not limited to creating and placing advertisements with interior and exterior photographic and audio-visual images of the Property and related information in any media and the Internet;
(2) place a "For Sale" sign on the Property and remove all other signs offering the Property for sale or lease;
(3) furnish comparative marketing and sales information about other properties to prospective buyers;
(4) disseminate information about the Property to other brokers and to prospective buyers, including applicable disclosures or notices that Seller is required to make under law or a contract;
(5) obtain information from any holder of a note secured by a lien on the Property;
(6) accept and deposit earnest money in trust in accordance with a contract for the sale of the Property;
(7) disclose the sales price and terms of sale to other brokers, appraisers, or other real estate professionals;
(8) in response to inquiries from prospective buyers and other brokers, disclose whether the Seller is considering more than one offer (Broker will not disclose the terms of any competing offer unless specifically instructed by Seller);
(9) advertise, during or after this Listing ends, that Broker "sold" the Property; and
(10) place information about this Listing, the Property, and a transaction for the Property on an electronic transaction platform (typically an Internet-based system where professionals related to the transaction such as title companies, lenders, and others may receive, view, and input information).

E. Broker is not authorized to execute any document in the name of or on behalf of Seller concerning the Property.

FIGURE 5-3 (Continued)

Residential Listing concerning______________________

12. SELLER'S REPRESENTATIONS: Except as provided by Paragraph 15, Seller represents that:

A. Seller has fee simple title to and peaceable possession of the Property and all its improvements and fixtures, unless rented, and the legal capacity to convey the Property;
B. Seller is not bound by a listing agreement with another broker for the sale, exchange, or lease of the Property that is or will be in effect during this Listing;
C. any pool or spa and any required enclosures, fences, gates, and latches comply with all applicable laws and ordinances;
D. no person or entity has any right to purchase, lease, or acquire the Property by an option, right of refusal, or other agreement;
E. Seller is current and not delinquent on all loans and all other financial obligations related to the Property, including but not limited to mortgages, home equity loans, home improvement loans, homeowner association fees, and taxes, except______________________;
F. Seller is not aware of any liens or other encumbrances against the Property, except______________________;
G. the Property is not subject to the jurisdiction of any court;
H. all information relating to the Property Seller provides to Broker is true and correct to the best of Seller's knowledge; and
I. the name of any employer, relocation company, or other entity that provides benefits to Seller when selling the Property is: ______________________.

13. SELLER'S ADDITIONAL PROMISES: Seller agrees to:

A. cooperate with Broker to facilitate the showing, marketing, and sale of the Property;
B. not rent or lease the Property during this Listing without Broker's prior written approval;
C. not negotiate with any prospective buyer who may contact Seller directly, but refer all prospective buyers to Broker;
D. not enter into a listing agreement with another broker for the sale, exchange, lease, or management of the Property to become effective during this Listing without Broker's prior written approval;
E. maintain any pool and all required enclosures in compliance with all applicable laws and ordinances;
F. provide Broker with copies of any leases or rental agreements pertaining to the Property and advise Broker of tenants moving in or out of the Property;
G. complete any disclosures or notices required by law or a contract to sell the Property; and
H. amend any applicable notices and disclosures if any material change occurs during this Listing.

14. LIMITATION OF LIABILITY:

A. If the Property is or becomes vacant during this Listing, Seller must notify Seller's casualty insurance company and request a "vacancy clause" to cover the Property. Broker is not responsible for the security of the Property nor for inspecting the Property on any periodic basis.

B. **Broker is not responsible or liable in any manner for personal injury to any person or for loss or damage to any person's real or personal property resulting from any act or omission not caused by Broker's negligence, including but not limited to injuries or damages caused by:**
(1) other brokers, their associates, inspectors, appraisers, and contractors who are authorized to access the Property;
(2) other brokers or their associates who may have information about the Property on their websites;
(3) acts of third parties (for example, vandalism or theft);
(4) freezing water pipes;
(5) a dangerous condition on the Property;
(6) the Property's non-compliance with any law or ordinance; or
(7) Seller, negligently or otherwise.

(TAR-1101) 01-01-14 Initialed for Identification by Broker/Associate________ and Seller________, ________ Page 7 of 10

Residential Listing concerning______________________

C. **Seller agrees to protect, defend, indemnify, and hold Broker harmless from any damage, costs, attorney's fees, and expenses that:**
(1) are caused by Seller, negligently or otherwise;
(2) arise from Seller's failure to disclose any material or relevant information about the Property; or
(3) are caused by Seller giving incorrect information to any person.

15. SPECIAL PROVISIONS:

16. DEFAULT: If Seller breaches this Listing, Seller is in default and will be liable to Broker for the amount of the Broker's compensation specified in Paragraph 5A and any other compensation Broker is entitled to receive under this Listing. If a sales price is not determinable in the event of an exchange or breach of this Listing, the Listing Price will be the sales price for purposes of computing compensation. If Broker breaches this Listing, Broker is in default and Seller may exercise any remedy at law.

17. MEDIATION: The parties agree to negotiate in good faith in an effort to resolve any dispute related to this Listing that may arise between the parties. If the dispute cannot be resolved by negotiation, the dispute will be submitted to mediation. The parties to the dispute will choose a mutually acceptable mediator and will share the cost of mediation equally.

18. ATTORNEY'S FEES: If Seller or Broker is a prevailing party in any legal proceeding brought as a result of a dispute under this Listing or any transaction related to or contemplated by this Listing, such party will be entitled to recover from the non-prevailing party all costs of such proceeding and reasonable attorney's fees.

19. ADDENDA AND OTHER DOCUMENTS: Addenda that are part of this Listing and other documents that Seller may need to provide are:

- ☒ A. Information About Brokerage Services;
- ☐ B. Seller Disclosure Notice (§5.008, Texas Property Code);
- ☐ C. Addendum for Seller's Disclosure of Information on Lead-Based Paint and Lead-Based Paint Hazards (required if Property was built before 1978);
- ☐ D. Residential Real Property Affidavit (T-47 Affidavit; related to existing survey);
- ☐ E. MUD, Water District, or Statutory Tax District Disclosure Notice (Chapter 49, Texas Water Code);
- ☐ F. Request for Information from an Owners' Association;
- ☐ G. Request for Mortgage Information;
- ☐ H. Information about Mineral Clauses in Contract Forms;
- ☐ I. Information about On-Site Sewer Facility;
- ☐ J. Information about Property Insurance for a Buyer or Seller;
- ☐ K. Information about Special Flood Hazard Areas;
- ☐ L. Condominium Addendum to Listing;
- ☐ M. Keybox Authorization by Tenant;
- ☐ N. Seller's Authorization to Release and Advertise Certain Information; and
- ☐ O. ______________________.

(TAR-1101) 01-01-14 Initialed for Identification by Broker/Associate________ and Seller________, ________ Page 8 of 10

FIGURE 5-3 (Continued)

Residential Listing concerning____

20. AGREEMENT OF PARTIES:

A. Entire Agreement: This Listing is the entire agreement of the parties and may not be changed except by written agreement.

B. Assignability: Neither party may assign this Listing without the written consent of the other party.

C. Binding Effect: Seller's obligation to pay Broker earned compensation is binding upon Seller and Seller's heirs, administrators, executors, successors, and permitted assignees.

D. Joint and Several: All Sellers executing this Listing are jointly and severally liable for the performance of all its terms.

E. Governing Law: Texas law governs the interpretation, validity, performance, and enforcement of this Listing.

F. Severability: If a court finds any clause in this Listing invalid or unenforceable, the remainder of this Listing will not be affected and all other provisions of this Listing will remain valid and enforceable.

G. Notices: Notices between the parties must be in writing and are effective when sent to the receiving party's address, fax, or e-mail address specified in Paragraph 1.

21. ADDITIONAL NOTICES:

A. Broker's compensation or the sharing of compensation between brokers is not fixed, controlled, recommended, suggested, or maintained by the Association of REALTORS®, MLS, or any listing service.

B. In accordance with fair housing laws and the National Association of REALTORS® Code of Ethics, Broker's services must be provided and the Property must be shown and made available to all persons without regard to race, color, religion, national origin, sex, disability, familial status, sexual orientation, or gender identity. Local ordinances may provide for additional protected classes (for example, creed, status as a student, marital status, or age).

C. Broker advises Seller to contact any mortgage lender or other lien holder to obtain information regarding payoff amounts for any existing mortgages or liens on the Property.

D. Broker advises Seller to review the information Broker submits to an MLS or other listing service.

E. Broker advises Seller to remove or secure jewelry, prescription drugs, other valuables, firearms and any other weapons.

F. Statutes or ordinances may regulate certain items on the Property (for example, swimming pools and septic systems). Non-compliance with the statutes or ordinances may delay a transaction and may result in fines, penalties, and liability to Seller.

G. If the Property was built before 1978, Federal law requires the Seller to: (1) provide the buyer with the federally approved pamphlet on lead poisoning prevention; (2) disclose the presence of any known lead-based paint or lead-based paint hazards in the Property; (3) deliver all records and reports to the buyer related to such paint or hazards; and (4) provide the buyer a period up to 10 days to have the Property inspected for such paint or hazards.

(TAR-1101) 01-01-14 Initialed for Identification by Broker/Associate________ and Seller________, ________ Page 9 of 10

H. Broker cannot give legal advice. READ THIS LISTING CAREFULLY. If you do not understand the effect of this Listing, consult an attorney BEFORE signing.

Broker's Printed Name License No.	Seller's Printed Name
❑ Broker's Signature Date ❑ Broker's Associate's Signature, as an authorized agent of Broker	Seller's Signature Date
Broker's Associate's Printed Name, if applicable	Seller's Printed Name
	Seller's Signature Date

(TAR-1101) 01-01-14 Page 10 of 10

FIGURE 5-3 (Continued)

Paragraph 3: Listing Price

In paragraph 3, the seller indicates his or her listing price for the property. Often individuals are not sure what to ask for as a listing price. One method of determining a possible listing price is by the formula indicated in figure 5-4.

Paragraph 4: Term

This paragraph indicates both a beginning date and a termination date. The parties can always agree to an extension if necessary. Note if the seller enters into a sales contract before the beginning of the listing agreement, the listing is void. This occurs in those instances where the parties postdate the commencement of this listing agreement to allow for "beautification" of the property before marketing.

Paragraph 5: Broker's Fee

The broker's fee is specified in paragraph 5. The specific commission or amount is also indicated in paragraph 5A, as well as when the amount is earned and payable. This paragraph provides that if the prospective buyer breaches the sales contract and the seller gets earnest money as liquidated damages, the broker is entitled to half, but not to exceed the amount in 5A. If there is a collection of damages from the prospective buyer for breach of contract, the broker is entitled to half after attorney's fees, not to exceed the amount in 5A.

Paragraph 5E provides for a protection period after the term of the contract. This paragraph applies when the seller closes a real estate transaction on the property with a buyer after the term of the contract, but when the broker had brought the property to the attention of the buyer. This paragraph would allow the broker to seek a commission on the deal if certain conditions were met. However, the paragraph does not apply where another Texas licensed broker represents the seller.

The employment agreements between the brokers and their clients are the only documents used to provide details about the payment of brokers' fees. This

Sample Calculation to Establish List Price

An owner desires a net of \$80,000 from the sale of his home, the seller will pay the broker a 7% commission, and closing costs are expected to be \$2,000. What should the list price be?

Sales Price – Loan Amount – Commission – Closing Costs = Net Proceeds

Sales Price		Loan Amount		Commission		Closing Costs		Net Proceeds
X	–	0	–	(X)(0.07)	–	\$2,000	=	\$80,000
						0.93X	=	\$82,000
						X	=	\$88,172

FIGURE 5-4 Sample Calculation to Establish List Price
Source: © 2021 Mbition LLC

is clarified in the promulgated sales contracts. Although, an agreement concerning the sharing of commissions between brokers is indicated on the last page of the promulgated residential sales contract under "Broker Information." Paragraph 5G of the listing agreement further provides authorization for the use of an escrow agent for closing and for the escrow agent to pay the broker's commission based on the percentages reflected in the promulgated sales contract.

However, there are specific rules that govern commissions. Under the Rules of the Texas Real Estate Commission, "a salesperson may not receive a commission or other fee except with the written consent of the salesperson's sponsoring broker or the broker who sponsored the salesperson when the salesperson became entitled to the commission or other valuable consideration."[5] A sample calculation of broker and salesperson commission is contained in figure 5-5.

In addition, a real estate salesperson may pay a commission to another person as long as it is made with the written consent of the salesperson's sponsoring broker.[6] There are instances where a broker will authorize the escrow agent to pay the commission to the salesperson directly. This is not a problem. However, a growing problem exists with what are often referred to as "undisclosed builder bonuses," where a builder pays certain amounts directly to the salesperson involved in the real estate transaction without the knowledge and consent of the salesperson's sponsoring broker.

There are also specific provisions of the Real Estate License Act that govern commissions. "A licensed broker may not compensate a person directly or indirectly for performing an act of a broker unless the person is a license holder or a real estate broker licensed in another state who does not conduct in this state any of the negotiations for which the commission or other compensation is paid."[7]

Broker and Salesperson Commission

Barney the broker has a listing agreement with Sammy the seller for 8% commission on the sale of seller's home. The home is sold for $100,000. The broker is entitled to the following commission:

$100,000 x 0.08 = $8,000

The salesperson who took the listing and got the home sold works with Barney Broker under an independent contractor agreement to receive 60% on all sales. The salesperson is entitled to:

0.60 x $8,000 = $4,800

This will leave the broker with:

$8,000 - $4,800 = $3,200

FIGURE 5-5 Broker and Salesperson Commission
Source: © 2021 Mbition LLC

[5] 22 T.A.C. § 535.3.
[6] 22 T.A.C. § 535.3.
[7] Tex. Occ. Code § 1101.651(a).

This provision applies any time there is no licensure, which includes times when a broker or salesperson has a suspended or revoked license, as well as instances where the broker or salesperson is practicing with an inactive status license.

Paragraph 6: Listing Services

This paragraph gives an option of whether the seller wants the property listed with a multiple listing service. Obviously, it is to the seller's advantage to have the property listed in this system; however, it is still his or her choice.

Paragraph 7: Access to the Property

Provisions regarding access to the property are indicated in paragraph 7. This paragraph makes clear what type of authorization the broker has to access the property as well as any listed companies. Of importance is the provision concerning a keybox and whether or not the seller authorizes a keybox to be placed on the property. The two common types of keyboxes are electronic and combination. Note that if a tenant is in possession of the premises, then possession is exclusive and the seller has no right to authorize access to the premises. Therefore, if a tenant is in possession, his or her consent must be obtained for a keybox. An indemnification clause is provided to hold the broker harmless for use of the keybox.

Paragraph 8: Cooperation with Other Brokers

Paragraph 8 allows the broker to cooperate with other brokers in getting the property sold. This paragraph also provides for how any commission will be shared.

Paragraph 9: Intermediary

Paragraph 9 indicates whether or not the seller authorizes the broker to act as an intermediary. A real estate license holder who attempts to represent both parties to a real estate transaction acts as a dual agent without paperwork to the contrary. Since the license holder is agent to both parties, he or she owes the same fiduciary duties to both parties. Because the seller is seeking the highest price possible for his or her property and the purchaser is seeking the lowest price, there is an inherent conflict that may arise under a dual agency situation.

On January 1, 1996, intermediary representation became effective in Texas to help alleviate some of the problems with dual agency. Under the intermediary status, the real estate broker acts as an intermediary. The intermediary is a neutral third party to the actual transaction, rather than a representative of either party.

Paragraph 10: Confidential Information

This paragraph provides that the broker must not knowingly disclose confidences of the seller, EVER! Keep in mind once they are clients they are ALWAYS clients. Confidences should never be disclosed unless authorized by the client or by law.

Paragraph 11: Broker's Authority

Paragraph 11 indicates the broker's authority concerning the real estate transaction. Most of this paragraph is self-explanatory, but there are a few things to keep in mind. First, there may be laws that prohibit the placing of a "For Sale" sign on the property. These laws often exist as homeowners association restrictions. Check the subdivision before placing a sign. Next, notice that the broker does not have authorization to execute documents on the seller's behalf. A power of attorney is required for such an action. Powers of attorney were discussed in greater detail in an earlier chapter.

Paragraph 12: Seller's Representations

Paragraph 12 encompasses several different issues. In paragraph 12A, the seller represents that he or she has fee simple title to the property. Fee simple title is 100% ownership. This concept was discussed earlier. Furthermore, this paragraph indicates that the seller has the legal capacity to convey the property. This provision is an attempt to deal with the gray areas of capacity discussed in an earlier chapter. Paragraph 12B is necessary to create the exclusivity of the listing agreement.

Paragraph 12D is necessary so there are no surprises, such as the right of first refusal. There is no sense in wasting time marketing the property if someone else has a prior right or option to buy that has not been exercised.

Paragraph 12E is necessary because if there are any delinquencies under the mortgage instrument, then the property may be subject to a foreclosure either presently or during the executory period. This information must be known. The problems that can occur were discussed in an earlier chapter. These same problems can occur if the property is subject to the jurisdiction of the court as referenced in paragraph 12F. The remaining paragraphs are self-explanatory.

Paragraph 14: Limitation of Liability

This paragraph provides a basic indemnification provision that holds the broker harmless from non-negligent activities. Keep in mind that if the seller has vacated the premises, there is no requirement for a license holder to stand watch over the seller's property. The seller can get insurance from an insurance carrier to cover potential loss during vacancy.

Paragraph 16: Default

This paragraph provides for the remedies when either the broker or seller breaches the contract.

BUYER AGENCY AGREEMENT

In General

The **buyer representation agreement** creates an agency relationship between the real estate broker and the buyer in a real estate sales transaction. In Texas, the most commonly used buyer representation agreement is the exclusive right to purchase representation agreement. A sample buyer representation agreement is contained in figure 5-6.

This agreement entitles the real estate broker to a commission regardless of whether the broker finds real estate for the purchaser to purchase or whether the

RESIDENTIAL BUYER/TENANT REPRESENTATION AGREEMENT

1. **PARTIES:** The parties to this agreement are:

   Client: ______________________________

   Address: ______________________________
   City, State, Zip: ______________________________
   Phone: ______________________________ Fax: ______________
   E-Mail: ______________________________

   Broker: ______________________________

   Address: ______________________________
   City, State, Zip: ______________________________
   Phone: ______________________________ Fax: ______________
   E-Mail: ______________________________

2. **APPOINTMENT:** Client grants to Broker the exclusive right to act as Client's real estate agent for the purpose of acquiring property in the market area.

3. **DEFINITIONS:**
   A. *"Acquire"* means to purchase or lease.
   B. *"Closing"* in a sale transaction means the date legal title to a property is conveyed to a purchaser of property under a contract to buy. "Closing" in a lease transaction means the date a landlord and tenant enter into a binding lease of a property.
   C. *"Market area"* means that area in the State of Texas within the perimeter boundaries of the following areas: ______________________________.
   D. *"Property"* means any interest in real estate including but not limited to properties listed in a multiple listing service or other listing services, properties for sale by owners, and properties for sale by builders.

4. **TERM:** This agreement commences on ______________________________ and ends at 11:59 p.m. on ______________________________.

5. **BROKER'S OBLIGATIONS:** Broker will: (a) use Broker's best efforts to assist Client in acquiring property in the market area; (b) assist Client in negotiating the acquisition of property in the market area; and (c) comply with other provisions of this agreement.

6. **CLIENT'S OBLIGATIONS:** Client will: (a) work exclusively through Broker in acquiring property in the market area and negotiate the acquisition of property in the market area only through Broker; (b) inform other brokers, salespersons, sellers, and landlords with whom Client may have contact that Broker exclusively represents Client for the purpose of acquiring property in the market area and refer all such persons to Broker; and (c) comply with other provisions of this agreement.

(TAR-1501) 1-1-14 Initialed for Identification by Broker/Associate ________ and Client ________, ________ Page 1 of 5

FIGURE 5-6 Buyer Representation Agreement
Source: Reprinted with permission from Texas Association of REALTORS®

Buyer/Tenant Representation Agreement between ____________________

7. REPRESENTATIONS:

A. Each person signing this agreement represents that the person has the legal capacity and authority to bind the respective party to this agreement.

B. Client represents that Client is not now a party to another buyer or tenant representation agreement with another broker for the acquisition of property in the market area

C. Client represents that all information relating to Client's ability to acquire property in the market area Client gives to Broker is true and correct.

D. Name any employer, relocation company, or other entity that will provide benefits to Client when acquiring property in the market area: ____________________.

8. INTERMEDIARY: *(Check A or B only.)*

❑ A. Intermediary Status: Client desires to see Broker's listings. If Client wishes to acquire one of Broker's listings, Client authorizes Broker to act as an intermediary and Broker will notify Client that Broker will service the parties in accordance with one of the following alternatives.

1) If the owner of the property is serviced by an associate other than the associate servicing Client under this agreement, Broker may notify Client that Broker will: (a) appoint the associate then servicing the owner to communicate with, carry out instructions of, and provide opinions and advice during negotiations to the owner; and (b) appoint the associate then servicing Client to the Client for the same purpose.

2) If the owner of the property is serviced by the same associate who is servicing Client, Broker may notify Client that Broker will: (a) appoint another associate to communicate with, carry out instructions of, and provide opinions and advice during negotiations to Client; and (b) appoint the associate servicing the owner under the listing to the owner for the same purpose.

3) Broker may notify Client that Broker will make no appointments as described under this Paragraph 8A and, in such an event, the associate servicing the parties will act solely as Broker's intermediary representative, who may facilitate the transaction but will not render opinions or advice during negotiations to either party.

❑ B. No Intermediary Status: Client does not wish to be shown or acquire any of Broker's listings.

Notice: If Broker acts as an intermediary under Paragraph 8A, Broker and Broker's associates:

- **may not disclose to Client that the seller or landlord will accept a price less than the asking price unless otherwise instructed in a separate writing by the seller or landlord;**
- **may not disclose to the seller or landlord that Client will pay a price greater than the price submitted in a written offer to the seller or landlord unless otherwise instructed in a separate writing by Client;**
- **may not disclose any confidential information or any information a seller or landlord or Client specifically instructs Broker in writing not to disclose unless otherwise instructed in a separate writing by the respective party or required to disclose the information by the Real Estate License Act or a court order or if the information materially relates to the condition of the property;**
- **shall treat all parties to the transaction honestly; and**
- **shall comply with the Real Estate License Act.**

9. COMPETING CLIENTS: Client acknowledges that Broker may represent other prospective buyers or tenants who may seek to acquire properties that may be of interest to Client. Client agrees that Broker may, during the term of this agreement and after it ends, represent such other prospects, show the other prospects the same properties that Broker shows to Client, and act as a real estate broker for such other prospects in negotiating the acquisition of properties that Client may seek to acquire.

10. CONFIDENTIAL INFORMATION:

A. During the term of this agreement or after its termination, Broker may not knowingly disclose information obtained in confidence from Client except as authorized by Client or required by law. Broker may not disclose to Client any information obtained in confidence regarding any other

(TAR-1501) 1-1-14 Initialed for Identification by Broker/Associate ________ and Client ________, ________ Page 2 of 5

FIGURE 5-6 (Continued)

Buyer/Tenant Representation Agreement between ______________________________

person Broker represents or may have represented except as required by law.

B. Unless otherwise agreed or required by law, a seller or the seller's agent is not obliged to keep the existence of an offer or its terms confidential. If a listing agent receives multiple offers, the listing agent is obliged to treat the competing buyers fairly.

11. BROKER'S FEES:

A. Commission: The parties agree that Broker will receive a commission calculated as follows: (1) ____% of the gross sales price if Client agrees to purchase property in the market area; and (2) if Client agrees to lease property in the market area a fee equal to *(check only one box)*: ❑________% of one month's rent or ❑______% of all rents to be paid over the term of the lease.

B. Source of Commission Payment: Broker will seek to obtain payment of the commission specified in Paragraph 11A first from the seller, landlord, or their agents. **If such persons refuse or fail to pay Broker the amount specified, Client will pay Broker the amount specified less any amounts Broker receives from such persons.**

C. Earned and Payable: A person is not obligated to pay Broker a commission until such time as Broker's commission is *earned and payable*. Broker's commission is *earned* when: (1) Client enters into a contract to buy or lease property in the market area; or (2) Client breaches this agreement. Broker's commission is *payable*, either during the term of this agreement or after it ends, upon the earlier of: (1) the closing of the transaction to acquire the property; (2) Client's breach of a contract to buy or lease a property in the market area; or (3) Client's breach of this agreement. If Client acquires more than one property under this agreement, Broker's commissions for each property acquired are earned as each property is acquired and are payable at the closing of each acquisition.

D. Additional Compensation: If a seller, landlord, or their agents offer compensation in excess of the amount stated in Paragraph 11A (including but not limited to marketing incentives or bonuses to cooperating brokers) Broker may retain the additional compensation in addition to the specified commission. Client is not obligated to pay any such additional compensation to Broker.

E. Acquisition of Broker's Listing: Notwithstanding any provision to the contrary, if Client acquires a property listed by Broker, Broker will be paid in accordance with the terms of Broker's listing agreement with the owner and Client will have no obligation to pay Broker.

F. In addition to the commission specified under Paragraph 11A, Broker is entitled to the following fees.
   1) Construction: If Client uses Broker's services to procure or negotiate the construction of improvements to property that Client owns or may acquire, Client ensures that Broker will receive from Client or the contractor(s) at the time the construction is substantially complete a fee equal to:______________________________.
   2) Service Providers: If Broker refers Client or any party to a transaction contemplated by this agreement to a service provider (for example, mover, cable company, telecommunications provider, utility, or contractor) Broker may receive a fee from the service provider for the referral.
   3) Other:______________________________
   ____
   ______________________________.

G. Protection Period: "Protection period" means that time starting the day after this agreement ends and continuing for _____ days. Not later than 10 days after this agreement ends, Broker may send Client written notice identifying the properties called to Client's attention during this agreement. If Client or a relative of Client agrees to acquire a property identified in the notice during the protection period, Client will pay Broker, upon closing, the amount Broker would have been entitled to receive if

FIGURE 5-6 (Continued)

this agreement were still in effect. This Paragraph 11G survives termination of this agreement. This Paragraph 11G will not apply if Client is, during the protection period, bound under a representation agreement with another broker who is a member of the Texas Association of REALTORS® at the time the acquisition is negotiated and the other broker is paid a fee for negotiating the transaction.

H. Escrow Authorization: Client authorizes, and Broker may so instruct, any escrow or closing agent authorized to close a transaction for the acquisition of property contemplated by this agreement to collect and disburse to Broker all amounts payable to Broker.

I. County: Amounts payable to Broker are to be paid in cash in ________________ County, Texas.

12. **MEDIATION**: The parties agree to negotiate in good faith in an effort to resolve any dispute that may arise related to this agreement or any transaction related to or contemplated by this agreement. If the dispute cannot be resolved by negotiation, the parties will submit the dispute to mediation before resorting to arbitration or litigation and will equally share the costs of a mutually acceptable mediator.

13. **DEFAULT**: If either party fails to comply with this agreement or makes a false representation in this agreement, the non-complying party is in default. If Client is in default, Client will be liable for the amount of compensation that Broker would have received under this agreement if Client was not in default. If Broker is in default, Client may exercise any remedy at law.

14. **ATTORNEY'S FEES**: If Client or Broker is a prevailing party in any legal proceeding brought as a result of a dispute under this agreement or any transaction related to this agreement, such party will be entitled to recover from the non-prevailing party all costs of such proceeding and reasonable attorney's fees.

15. **LIMITATION OF LIABILITY: Neither Broker nor any other broker, or their associates, is responsible or liable for any person's personal injuries or for any loss or damage to any person's property that is not caused by Broker. Client will hold broker, any other broker, and their associates, harmless from any such injuries or losses. Client will indemnify Broker against any claims for injury or damage that Client may cause to others or their property.**

16. **ADDENDA:** Addenda and other related documents which are part of this agreement are:

- ☑ Information About Brokerage Services
- ☐ Protecting Your Home from Mold
- ☐ Information Concerning Property Insurance
- ☐ General Information and Notice to a Buyer
- ☐ Protect Your Family from Lead in Your Home
- ☐ Information about Special Flood Hazard Areas
- ☐ For Your Protection: Get a Home Inspection
- ☐ ____________________

17. **SPECIAL PROVISIONS:**

18. **ADDITIONAL NOTICES:**

A. **Broker's fees and the sharing of fees between brokers are not fixed, controlled, recommended, suggested, or maintained by the Association of REALTORS® or any listing service.**

B. **In accordance with fair housing laws and the National Association of REALTORS® Code of Ethics, Broker's services must be provided without regard to race, color, religion, national origin, sex, disability, familial status, sexual orientation, or gender identity. Local ordinances may provide for additional protected classes (for example, creed, status as a student, marital status, or age).**

C. **Broker is not a property inspector, surveyor, engineer, environmental assessor, or compliance inspector. Client should seek experts to render such services in any acquisition.**

D. **If Client purchases property, Client should have an abstract covering the property examined by an attorney of Client's selection, or Client should be furnished with or obtain a title policy.**

E. **Buyer may purchase a residential service contract. Buyer should review such service contract or the scope of coverage, exclusions, and limitations. The purchase of a residential service contract is optional. There are several residential service companies operating in Texas.**

CONSULT AN ATTORNEY: Broker cannot give legal advice. This is a legally binding agreement. READ IT CAREFULLY. If you do not understand the effect of this agreement, consult your attorney BEFORE signing.

Broker's Printed Name — License No.	Client's Printed Name
☐ Broker's Signature — Date ☐ Broker's Associate's Signature, as an authorized agent of Broker	Client's Signature — Date
Broker's Associate's Printed Name, if applicable	Client's Printed Name
	Client's Signature — Date

FIGURE 5-6 (Continued)

purchaser finds his or her own property. The same basic rules that existed for the listing agreement, such as the writing requirement, apply to buyer representation agreements.[8] In addition, the same elements necessary to the creation of a contract are required.

The buyer representation agreement is very similar to the listing agreement. The key thing to keep in mind with this agreement is that everything in the buyer representation agreement centers on the market area that is established early on in the contract. In addition, the broker's fees are generally different in the buyer representation agreement than in the listing agreement. In many cases, the buyer's broker will seek compensation first from the seller's broker. If the seller's broker refuses to pay or only partially pays the buyer broker's commission, then the buyer is still responsible to pay the buyer's broker's fee indicated in the contract. The calculation of the split of commissions is indicated in figure 5-7.

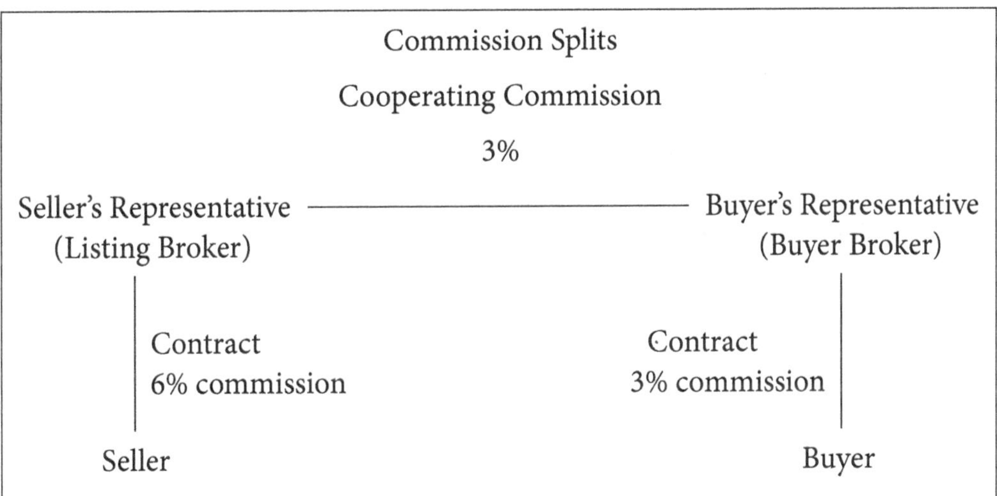

Seller representative will pay Buyer representative 3%, therefore Seller representative takes remaining 3% and Buyer is not responsible for any difference.

If cooperating commission is any less than 3% (the amount in the underlying buyer representative agreement), the buyer will be responsible to pay the difference in commission.

FIGURE 5-7 Commission Splits
Source: © 2021 Mbition LLC

[8] Trammell Crow Co. No. 60 v. Harkinson, 944 S.W.2d 631 (Tex. 1997).

Furthermore, buyer representatives must be concerned with competing buyers. Therefore, the typical buyer representation agreement notifies the buyer that the broker does represent other buyer clients and that occasionally two buyers are interested in the same piece of property.

Unfortunately, all too often buyers working with buyer agents expect the buyer agents to perform functions that are not within their expertise. Most buyer representation agreements advise the buyer that the broker is not qualified to perform certain services, such as inspections or surveys, and therefore the buyer should seek out and hire the appropriate professional.

Agency Disclosure Form

An important addendum to both the listing agreement and buyer representation agreement is an agency disclosure form. The real estate license holder is required to furnish a party in a real estate transaction a written agency disclosure notice at the time of the first substantive communication.[9] A sample agency disclosure form that complies with the Texas Real Estate License Act is the "**Information About Brokerage Services**" form contained in figure 5-8. Where a client is involved, this signed notice becomes attached to the employment contract. Where a customer is involved, this signed notice becomes part of the transaction file.

The license holder is required to furnish the written agency disclosure notice except in certain limited circumstances. The license holder is not required to provide the notice if:

(1) the proposed transaction is for a residential lease for less than one year and a sale is not being considered; or

(2) the license holder meets with a party who the license holder knows is represented by another license holder; or

(3) the communication occurs at a property that is held open for any prospective buyer or tenant and the communication concerns that property.[10]

Termination of Real Estate Employment Agreements

Once an agency relationship has been created either through a listing agreement or a buyer representation agreement, there are several ways the relationship can be terminated other than by expiration of time under the agreement. Termination of the agreement can be by mutual agreement of the parties, revocation by the client, renunciation by the real estate agent, a supervening illegality, or completion of the objective under the agency contract, to name a few. A form commonly used by the parties to terminate the listing agreement by mutual agreement is the **Termination of Listing Agreement** form by the Texas Association of REALTORS® shown in figure 5-9.

---

[9] Tex. Occ. Code § 1101.558(b-1).

[10] Tex. Occ. Code § 1101.558(c).

11-2-2015

Information About Brokerage Services

Texas law requires all real estate license holders to give the following information about brokerage services to prospective buyers, tenants, sellers and landlords.

TYPES OF REAL ESTATE LICENSE HOLDERS:

- **A BROKER** is responsible for all brokerage activities, including acts performed by sales agents sponsored by the broker.
- **A SALES AGENT** must be sponsored by a broker and works with clients on behalf of the broker.

A BROKER'S MINIMUM DUTIES REQUIRED BY LAW (A client is the person or party that the broker represents):

- Put the interests of the client above all others, including the broker's own interests;
- Inform the client of any material information about the property or transaction received by the broker;
- Answer the client's questions and present any offer to or counter-offer from the client; and
- Treat all parties to a real estate transaction honestly and fairly.

A LICENSE HOLDER CAN REPRESENT A PARTY IN A REAL ESTATE TRANSACTION:

AS AGENT FOR OWNER (SELLER/LANDLORD): The broker becomes the property owner's agent through an agreement with the owner, usually in a written listing to sell or property management agreement. An owner's agent must perform the broker's minimum duties above and must inform the owner of any material information about the property or transaction known by the agent, including information disclosed to the agent or subagent by the buyer or buyer's agent.

AS AGENT FOR BUYER/TENANT: The broker becomes the buyer/tenant's agent by agreeing to represent the buyer, usually through a written representation agreement. A buyer's agent must perform the broker's minimum duties above and must inform the buyer of any material information about the property or transaction known by the agent, including information disclosed to the agent by the seller or seller's agent.

AS AGENT FOR BOTH - INTERMEDIARY: To act as an intermediary between the parties the broker must first obtain the written agreement of *each party* to the transaction. The written agreement must state who will pay the broker and, in conspicuous bold or underlined print, set forth the broker's obligations as an intermediary. A broker who acts as an intermediary:

- Must treat all parties to the transaction impartially and fairly;
- May, with the parties' written consent, appoint a different license holder associated with the broker to each party (owner and buyer) to communicate with, provide opinions and advice to, and carry out the instructions of each party to the transaction.
- Must not, unless specifically authorized in writing to do so by the party, disclose:
  - that the owner will accept a price less than the written asking price;
  - that the buyer/tenant will pay a price greater than the price submitted in a written offer; and
  - any confidential information or any other information that a party specifically instructs the broker in writing not to disclose, unless required to do so by law.

AS SUBAGENT: A license holder acts as a subagent when aiding a buyer in a transaction without an agreement to represent the buyer. A subagent can assist the buyer but does not represent the buyer and must place the interests of the owner first.

TO AVOID DISPUTES, ALL AGREEMENTS BETWEEN YOU AND A BROKER SHOULD BE IN WRITING AND CLEARLY ESTABLISH:

- The broker's duties and responsibilities to you, and your obligations under the representation agreement.
- Who will pay the broker for services provided to you, when payment will be made and how the payment will be calculated.

LICENSE HOLDER CONTACT INFORMATION: This notice is being provided for information purposes. It does not create an obligation for you to use the broker's services. Please acknowledge receipt of this notice below and retain a copy for your records.

Licensed Broker /Broker Firm Name or Primary Assumed Business Name	License No.	Email	Phone
Designated Broker of Firm	License No.	Email	Phone
Licensed Supervisor of Sales Agent/ Associate	License No.	Email	Phone
Sales Agent/Associate's Name	License No.	Email	Phone

Buyer/Tenant/Seller/Landlord Initials   Date

Regulated by the Texas Real Estate Commission   **Information available at www.trec.texas.gov**

IABS 1-0

FIGURE 5-8 Information About Brokerage Services
Source: Reprinted with permission of Texas Real Estate Commission

TERMINATION OF LISTING

TERMINATION OF LISTING BETWEEN THE UNDERSIGNED PARTIES CONCERNING THE PROPERTY LOCATED AT

____

A. Definitions: "Owner" means the seller or landlord of the above-referenced Property. "Listing" means the above-referenced listing agreement.

B. Representation: Owner represents that there are currently no negotiations pending or contemplated with anyone for the sale, lease, or exchange of the Property.

C. Termination Date: The parties terminate the Listing at 11:59 p.m. on ______________.

D. Termination Fees:

(1) Upon execution of this termination agreement, Owner will pay Broker a fee of $__________ for services rendered through the termination date.

(2) If Owner agrees to sell or lease the Property on or before ______________, by oral or written agreement or option, Owner will pay Broker at the time the Property is sold or leased a fee equal to *(check all that apply)*:

❑ (a) ______% of the sales price if Owner sells the Property.
❑ (b) ______% of the gross rent over the term of the lease if Owner leases the Property.
❑ (c) ____
____.

(3) The fees specified in Paragraph D(2) are payable only if Owner agrees to sell or lease the Property to: *(Check one box only)*

❑ (a) anyone.
❑ (b) ____
____
____.

E. Release: Except for the promises and representation in this document, Owner and Broker release each other from **all** obligations under or related to the Listing (including but not limited to the protection period clause which will no longer apply).

Broker's (Company's) Printed Name	License No.	Seller or Landlord	Date
By: Broker's Associate's Signature	Date	Seller or Landlord	Date

(TAR-1410) 4-14-06 Page 1 of 1

FIGURE 5-9 Termination of Listing Agreement
Source: Reprinted with permission of Texas Association of REALTORS®

LEASING REAL ESTATE

One of the benefits derived from the bundle of rights associated with real estate ownership is the right to transfer possession to the real estate. Possession to real estate is transferred by way of a lease. A **lease** is a written or oral agreement between a landlord and tenant that establishes or modifies the terms, conditions, rules, or other provisions regarding the use and occupancy of a dwelling.[11] The landlord is the owner, lessor, or sublessor of the dwelling. The landlord is not the same as the manager or the landlord's agent unless otherwise indicated in the lease.[12] The tenant is the person authorized by the lease to occupy the dwelling to the exclusion of others and who is obligated under the lease to pay rent.[13] The tenant may also be referred to as the lessee.

In real estate sales it is important to know whether a lease exists on the property or whether an owner is contemplating a lease, as the property cannot be sold until termination of the tenancy. For example, paragraph 10B of the promulgated residential sales contract clarifies that the seller may not execute any leases without the buyer's consent. If a lease already exists on the property, the seller has seven days to deliver a copy of the lease to the buyer.

LEASEHOLD ESTATES

As mentioned in an earlier chapter, the lease arrangement between the landlord and tenant is a non-freehold estate, often referred to as a leasehold estate or tenancy. There are four types of leasehold estates (tenancies) recognized in Texas. These are the tenancy for years, the tenancy from period to period, the tenancy at will, and the tenancy at sufferance.

The **tenancy for years** is a tenancy with a fixed duration. The duration does not need to be in terms of years, but may be for any specific time period with a fixed termination date. However, if the term of the tenancy is for longer than one year, the Statute of Frauds requires the lease for that tenancy to be in writing to be enforceable. A tenancy for years automatically terminates at the end of the duration; therefore, no notice of termination is required.[14]

The **tenancy from period to period** is a tenancy without a fixed duration. Instead, the tenancy rolls over from some specific period to the next. This might be a week-to-week, month-to-month, or year-to-year tenancy. The lease generally specifies the amount of notice required to either renew or terminate the lease. In many cases, this is one-term notice. In the absence of such a provision, a month-to-month tenancy, for example, requires one-month's notice.[15]

---

[11] Tex. Prop. Code § 92.001(3).

[12] Tex. Prop. Code § 92.001(2).

[13] Tex. Prop. Code § 92.001(6).

[14] Carrasco v. Stewart, 224 S.W.3d 363, 368 (Tex. App.–El Paso 2006).

[15] Struve v. Park Place Apartments, 923 S.W.2d 50, 52 (Tex. App.–Tyler 1995).

The **tenancy at will** is a tenancy for an indefinite and uncertain length of time and might be tied to a specific event. For example, the parties might create a tenancy to last "only until the property is sold." The tenancy at will can be terminated at the will of either of the parties.[16]

The last tenancy is the **tenancy at sufferance**. A tenancy at sufferance is created when a tenant remains in possession of the premises after termination of the lease.[17] With this type of tenancy, the landlord can treat the tenant holding over as either a trespasser or as a tenant holding under the terms of the original lease.[18] Most leases specify what will happen to a tenant who maintains possession after lease termination and may even provide for the creation of a "new tenancy."

LEASE AGREEMENTS

Lease agreements can take many forms depending on the transaction. Broadly, there can be both residential as well as commercial tenancies. And a residential tenancy can refer specifically to an apartment tenancy or to a tenancy in any other residential dwelling owned by the landlord. Common lease agreements are not drafted by the Texas Real Estate Commission, but are generally drafted by attorneys for the property owners. Although, a uniform Apartment Lease Contract used for apartment tenancies is available from the Texas Apartment Association (TAA) for its members.

The general rule of thumb concerning lease agreements is that the agreement between the parties controls the relationship. If the agreement does not speak to an issue between the parties, then the Texas Property Code will apply. Commercial tenancies are addressed in chapter 93 of the Texas Property Code, whereas residential tenancies are addressed in chapter 92. The rights and responsibilities of the parties are different in each of these tenancies with the residential tenancy provisions providing more protection for the tenant. Many of the statutory provisions that protect tenants in Texas are included in the TAA's Apartment Lease Contract. A discussion of some common lease provisions is provided below.

Security Deposit

The landlord will require that the tenant deposit a security deposit to ensure compliance with the lease agreement. The amount of the deposit will be specified in the contract. At the end of the lease, the landlord may deduct from the security deposit any damages and charges for which the tenant is legally liable under the lease or as a result of breaching the lease.[19] However, the landlord may not retain

---

[16] Providence Land Services, LLC v. Jones, 353 S.W.3d 538, 542 (Tex. App.–Eastland 2011).

[17] Bockelmann v. Marynick, 788 S.W.2d 569, 571 (Tex. 1990).

[18] Bockelmann v. Marynick, 788 S.W.2d 569, 571 (Tex. 1990).

[19] Tex. Prop. Code § 92.104(a); 93.006(a).

any portion of the security deposit to cover normal wear and tear.[20] Normal wear and tear is defined as "deterioration that results from the intended use of the dwelling or commercial premises including, breakage or malfunction due to age or deteriorated condition, but the term does not include deterioration that results from negligence, carelessness, accident, or abuse of the premises, equipment, or chattels by the tenant, . . . , or by a guest or invitee of the tenant."[21] If the landlord does retain a portion of the security deposit, the landlord must give the tenant the balance of the security deposit, if any, along with a written description and itemized list of all deductions. The description and itemized list of deductions is not required however if: (1) the tenant owes rent when the tenant surrenders possession of the premises; and (2) there is no controversy concerning the amount of rent owed.[22]

A landlord is required to refund a security deposit to the tenant on or before the 30th day after the tenant surrenders the premises for residential tenancies and on or before the 60th day for commercial tenancies.[23] However, the landlord is not obligated to return the tenant's security deposit or give the tenant a written description of damages and charges until the tenant gives the landlord a written statement of the tenant's forwarding address for sending the refund.[24] However, the tenant does not forfeit the right to the refund merely for failing to give the forwarding address.[25]

The tenant cannot withhold payment of the last month's rent on grounds that the security deposit is security for the unpaid rent.[26] If the tenant does so, he or she is liable to the landlord for three times the rent wrongfully withheld and the landlord's attorney's fees for the lawsuit to recover the rent.[27] The landlord can also be held liable for failing to return the security deposit or by failing to give the requisite written description and itemization of deductions by the requisite deadline. Failure of the landlord to return the security deposit can result in liability of $100, three times the portion of the deposit withheld, and the tenant's reasonable attorney's fees to bring suit.[28] The landlord's failure to provide the written description and itemization of deductions can result in forfeiture of the right to withhold any of the security deposit or to bring suit against the tenant for damages to the premises and liability for attorney's fees.[29]

---

[20] Tex. Prop. Code § 92.104(b); 93.006(b).
[21] Tex. Prop. Code § 92.001(4); 93.006(b).
[22] Tex. Prop. Code § 92.104(c); 93.006(c).
[23] Tex. Prop. Code § 92.103(a); 93.005(a).
[24] Tex. Prop. Code § 92.107(a); 93.009(a).
[25] Tex. Prop. Code § 92.107(b); 93.009(b).
[26] Tex. Prop. Code § 92.108(a); 93.010(a).
[27] Tex. Prop. Code § 92.108(b); 93.010(b).
[28] Tex. Prop. Code § 92.109(a); 93.011(a).
[29] Tex. Prop. Code § 92.109(b); 93.011(b).

Rent

The amount of rent is also a common provision in the lease. This provision typically includes the due date for payment as well as where the payment is to be delivered. For residential tenancies, the typical rent is a fixed amount per month payable in advance. The rent terms for a commercial tenancy, on the other hand, can vary.

If a tenant fails to pay rent to the landlord, then the tenant is in default and all remedies specified in the lease agreement will apply. Many lease agreements will, however, simply make reference to existing Texas law. The most common remedy sought by the landlord is the eviction lawsuit, sometimes referred to as a forcible entry and detainer action. The primary objective of this suit is for the landlord to regain possession of the premises. However, the landlord can also request unpaid rent. The landlord must give a tenant at least three days' written notice to vacate the premises before the landlord files a forcible detainer suit, unless the parties have contracted for a shorter or longer notice period in a written lease or agreement.[30] The eviction proceeding is filed in the Texas justice courts, which have exclusive jurisdiction over these actions.[31] At the end of the proceeding, a writ of possession will be issued that authorizes the landlord to regain possession.

The landlord may change the door locks of a tenant delinquent in paying a portion of the rent.[32] However, the tenant must be given notice of where he or she can pick up a replacement key. For residential tenancies, the tenant is entitled to receive a replacement key at any hour regardless of whether the tenant pays rent.[33] However, for commercial tenancies, the replacement key can only be obtained during the landlord's business hours and only if the tenant pays the delinquent rent.[34] If the landlord refuses to give the tenant the key to the premises, the tenant has the right to bring an action to regain the premises. If the tenant is successful, the court will issue a writ of reentry allowing the tenant to regain possession.[35] The type of rent paid under the lease agreement also dictates the type of lease involved between the parties.

TYPES OF LEASES

In Texas, the type of lease agreement between the parties depends on the type of rent paid. There are several types of leases in Texas. These include the gross lease, ground lease, percentage lease, and net lease.

The **gross lease** is a lease for a flat sum of rent. From this amount, the landlord will generally pay all expenses associated with the property, such as taxes, water,

---

[30] Tex. Prop. Code § 24.005.
[31] Tex. Prop. Code § 24.004.
[32] Tex. Prop. Code § 92.0081(b); 93.002(c).
[33] Tex. Prop. Code § 92.0081(c).
[34] Tex. Prop. Code § 93.002(f).
[35] Tex. Prop. Code § 92.009; 93.003.

utilities, insurance, and the like. Gross leases are commonly used when leasing apartments, leasehold condominiums, and commercial office space. Similar to the **gross lease** is the ground lease. A ground lease is a lease for a flat sum of rent, but the rent is paid to the landlord for vacant land. The purpose of the lease is to permit the tenant to construct a building on the site. The ground lease is often a long-term lease and generally used for the construction of large commercial buildings.

The **percentage lease** is a lease for a small base rent with an additional rent payment based on a percentage of gross profits on the premises. Percentage leases are often used when the location of the property is important. Therefore, these types of leases are often associated with shopping centers.

The last type of lease is the net lease. The **net lease** requires the tenant to pay not only rent, but also the expenses of the property. There are different types of net leases depending on the types of expense the tenant is required to pay. A net lease alone generally implies that the tenant is only required to pay property taxes in addition to the rent. However, a double net lease requires that the tenant not only pay property taxes, but also insurance. The triple net lease, on the other hand, requires that the tenant not only pay property taxes and insurance, but also maintenance on the property.

TEMPORARY LEASES

An area of concern involves temporary leases associated with promulgated residential sales contracts. This specifically refers to the use of one of the TREC promulgated contracts with either the Buyer's Temporary Residential Lease or the Seller's Temporary Residential Lease.

The **Seller's Temporary Residential Lease** is a promulgated addendum used when the seller is to remain in possession of the premises after closing. See figure 5-10. Notice this form can not be used where the seller occupies the premises for longer than 90 days after closing. Under longer time periods, the parties should consult with an attorney for the preparation of a more detailed lease. This addendum can be used with any of the current promulgated sales contract forms.

The lease form is rather simple if you have ever been a party to an apartment lease. Keep in mind that the owner of the property is the landlord and the party in possession, without title, is the tenant. Under this lease, closing has already occurred and title has already passed to the buyer. Therefore, the buyer is the landlord. The seller would merely be in possession as the tenant. The terms specified in the lease are negotiable between the parties so there are any number of possibilities. It is important that this form be read before it is ever used in a transaction to consider the number of problems that can occur with such a lease. It is important the parties understand the risks involved in such a lease. The parties should contact their insurance agents before closing occurs.

PROMULGATED BY THE TEXAS REAL ESTATE COMMISSION (TREC) 12-05-11
(NOTICE: For use only when SELLER occupies the property for no more than 90 days AFTER the closing)

SELLER'S TEMPORARY RESIDENTIAL LEASE

1. **PARTIES:** The parties to this Lease are______________________________ (Landlord) and ______________________________(Tenant).
2. **LEASE:** Landlord leases to Tenant the Property described in the Contract between Landlord as Buyer and Tenant as Seller known as ______________________________(address).
3. **TERM:** The term of this Lease commences on the date the sale covered by the Contract is closed and funded and terminates ________________, unless terminated earlier by reason of other provisions.
4. **RENTAL:** Tenant shall pay to Landlord as rental $__________ per day (excluding the day of closing and funding) with the full amount of rental for the term of the Lease to be paid at the time of funding of the sale. Tenant will not be entitled to a refund of rental if this Lease terminates early due to Tenant's default or voluntary surrender of the Property.
5. **DEPOSIT:** Tenant shall pay to Landlord at the time of funding of the sale $____________as a deposit to secure performance of this Lease by Tenant. Landlord may use the deposit to satisfy Tenant's obligations under this Lease. Landlord shall refund any unused portion of the deposit to Tenant with an itemized list of all deductions from the deposit within 30 days after Tenant (a) surrenders possession of the Property and (b) provides Landlord written notice of Tenant's forwarding address.
6. **UTILITIES:** Tenant shall pay all utility charges except ______________________________ which Landlord shall pay.
7. **USE OF PROPERTY:** Tenant may use the Property only for residential purposes. Tenant may not assign this Lease or sublet any part of the Property.
8. **PETS:** Tenant may not keep pets on the Property except ______________________________.
9. **CONDITION OF PROPERTY:** Tenant accepts the Property in its present condition and state of repair at the commencement of the Lease. Upon termination, Tenant shall surrender the Property to Landlord in the condition required under the Contract, except normal wear and tear and any casualty loss.
10. **ALTERATIONS:** Tenant may not alter the Property or install improvements or fixtures without the prior written consent of the Landlord. Any improvements or fixtures placed on the Property during the Lease become the Property of Landlord.
11. **SPECIAL PROVISIONS:**
12. **INSPECTIONS:** Landlord may enter at reasonable times to inspect the Property. Tenant shall provide Landlord door keys and access codes to allow access to the Property during the term of Lease.
13. **LAWS:** Tenant shall comply with all applicable laws, restrictions, ordinances, rules and regulations with respect to the Property.
14. **REPAIRS AND MAINTENANCE:** Except as otherwise provided in this Lease, Tenant shall bear all expense of repairing and maintaining the Property, including but not limited to the yard, trees and shrubs, unless otherwise required by the Texas Property Code. Tenant shall promptly repair at Tenant's expense any damage to the Property caused directly or indirectly by any act or omission of the Tenant or any person other than the Landlord, Landlord's agents or invitees.

Initialed for identification by Landlord ______ and Tenant__________ TREC NO. 15-5

FIGURE 5-10 Seller's Temporary Residential Lease
Source: Reprinted with permission of Texas Real Estate Commission

Seller's Temporary Residential Lease ______________________ Page 2 of 2 12-05-11
(Address of Property)

15. INDEMNITY: Tenant indemnifies Landlord from the claims of all third parties for injury or damage to the person or property of such third party arising from the use or occupancy of the Property by Tenant. This indemnification includes attorney's fees, costs and expenses incurred by Landlord.

16. INSURANCE: Landlord and Tenant shall each maintain such insurance on the contents and Property as each party may deem appropriate during the term of this Lease. NOTE: CONSULT YOUR INSURANCE AGENT; POSSESSION OF THE PROPERTY BY SELLER AS TENANT MAY CHANGE INSURANCE POLICY COVERAGE.

17. DEFAULT: If Tenant fails to perform or observe any provision of this Lease and fails, within 24 hours after notice by Landlord, to commence and diligently pursue to remedy such failure, Tenant will be in default.

18. TERMINATION: This Lease terminates upon expiration of the term specified in Paragraph 3 or upon Tenant's default under this Lease.

19. HOLDING OVER: Tenant shall surrender possession of the Property upon termination of this Lease. Any possession by Tenant after termination creates a tenancy at sufferance and will not operate to renew or extend this Lease. Tenant shall pay $______ per day during the period of any possession after termination as damages, in addition to any other remedies to which Landlord is entitled.

20. ATTORNEY'S FEES: The prevailing party in any legal proceeding brought under or with respect to this Lease is entitled to recover from the non-prevailing party all costs of such proceeding and reasonable attorney's fees.

21. SMOKE ALARMS: The Texas Property Code requires Landlord to install smoke alarms in certain locations within the Property at Landlord's expense. Tenant expressly waives Landlord's duty to inspect and repair smoke alarms.

22. SECURITY DEVICES: The requirements of the Texas Property Code relating to security devices do not apply to a residential lease for a term of 90 days or less.

23. CONSULT YOUR ATTORNEY: Real estate licensees cannot give legal advice. This Lease is intended to be legally binding. READ IT CAREFULLY. If you do not understand the effect of this Lease, consult your attorney BEFORE signing.

24. NOTICES: All notices from one party to the other must be in writing and are effective when mailed to, hand-delivered at, or transmitted by facsimile or electronic transmission as follows:

To Landlord: ______________________	**To Tenant:** ______________________
______________________	______________________
______________________	______________________
______________________	______________________
Telephone: ( ) ______________	Telephone: ( ) ______________
Facsimile: ( ) ______________	Facsimile: ( ) ______________
E-mail: ______________________	E-mail: ______________________

______________________	______________________
Landlord	Tenant
______________________	______________________
Landlord	Tenant

TREC
TEXAS REAL ESTATE COMMISSION

TREC NO. 15-5

FIGURE 5-10 (Continued)

The **Buyer's Temporary Residential Lease** is a promulgated addendum used when the buyer is to take possession of the premises prior to the closing date. See figure 5-11. It is important to remember that this form can only be used for tenancies of not more than 90 days. If a longer tenancy is contemplated or subsequently arises, a standard residential lease should be used. This addendum can be used with any of the current promulgated sales contract forms. This lease is almost identical to the Seller's Temporary Residential Lease. In this form, the seller is still the title holder and is, therefore, the landlord. The buyer would merely be in possession as a tenant. Again, the parties should talk with their insurance agents before entering a temporary lease. The termination date of this lease is different.

The termination can be (a) upon the closing and funding of the sale, (b) termination of the sales contract prior to closing, (c) the tenant's default under the lease, or (d) the tenant's default under the sales contract. Caution should be used in allowing a prospective buyer to take possession of the seller's property before the prospective buyer has proven his or her ability to proceed with the sale, for instance, by qualifying for a loan. If the prospective buyer fails to qualify for the loan, there may be difficulty in getting the prospective buyer to leave. An eviction procedure may be necessary, which would tie up the ultimate sale of the seller's property for a period of time.

DISCHARGE OF LEASES

Once a lease agreement is created, there are a number of ways the lease can terminate. A lease can terminate by its own terms. For example, a tenancy for years simply expires at the end of the contract period.[36] In addition, a valid foreclosure of a landlord's interest in property terminates any lease agreement.[37] The tenant may also surrender the property thereby terminating the lease. Surrender of the lease may occur by operation of law when the tenant abandons the premises and the landlord reenters the property.[38] Furthermore, the lease can be terminated by mutual agreement of the parties.[39]

OPTIONS

Option contracts are also very common in real estate sales transactions. When the prospective purchaser enters into a contract, he or she will not know what repairs are necessary for the property. As a result, the purchaser may elect to pay an option fee for the right to terminate the contract for any reason within a specified number of days after the contract is signed. Paragraph 23 of the promulgated

[36] Carrasco v. Stewart, 224 S.W.3d 363, 368 (Tex. App.–El Paso 2006).
[37] Coinmach Corp. v. Aspenwood Apartment Corp., 417 S.W.3d 909, 915 (Tex. 2013).
[38] Cavalcade Oil Corp. v. Samuel, 746 S.W.2d 842, 844 (Tex. App.–El Paso 1988).
[39] Moser Co. v. Awalt Indus. Properties, Inc., 584 S.W.2d 902, 906 (Tex. Civ. App. 1979).

PROMULGATED BY THE TEXAS REAL ESTATE COMMISSION (TREC) 12-05-11

(NOTICE: For use only when BUYER occupies the property for no more than 90 days PRIOR the closing)

TREC
TEXAS REAL ESTATE COMMISSION

BUYER'S TEMPORARY RESIDENTIAL LEASE

1. **PARTIES:** The parties to this Lease are______________________________ (Landlord) and ______________________________(Tenant).
2. **LEASE:** Landlord leases to Tenant the Property described in the Contract between Landlord as Seller and Tenant as Buyer known as ______________________________(address).
3. **TERM:** The term of this Lease commences ____________________ and terminates as specified in Paragraph 18.
4. **RENTAL:** Rental will be $____________ per day. Upon commencement of this Lease, Tenant shall pay to Landlord the full amount of rental of $ ____________ for the anticipated term of the Lease (commencement date to the Closing Date specified in Paragraph 9 of the Contract). If the actual term of this Lease differs from the anticipated term, any additional rent or reimbursement will be paid at closing. No portion of the rental will be applied to payment of any items covered by the Contract.
5. **DEPOSIT:** Tenant has paid to Landlord $________________ as a deposit to secure performance of this Lease by Tenant. If this Lease is terminated before the Closing Date, Landlord may use the deposit to satisfy Tenant's obligations under this Lease. Landlord shall refund to Tenant any unused portion of the deposit together with an itemized list of all deductions from the deposit within 30 days after Tenant (a) surrenders possession of the Property and (b) provides Landlord written notice of Tenant's forwarding address. If this Lease is terminated by the closing and funding of the sale of the Property, the deposit will be refunded to Tenant at closing and funding.
   NOTICE: The deposit must be in addition to the earnest money under the Contract.
6. **UTILITIES:** Tenant shall pay all utility connections, deposits and charges except ______________________________, which Landlord shall pay.
7. **USE OF PROPERTY:** Tenant may use the Property only for residential purposes. Tenant may not assign this Lease or sublet any part of the Property.
8. **PETS:** Tenant may not keep pets on the Property except ________________________.
9. **CONDITION OF PROPERTY:** Tenant accepts the Property in its present condition and state of repair, but Landlord shall make all repairs and improvements required by the Contract. If this Lease is terminated prior to closing, Tenant shall surrender possession of the Property to Landlord in its present condition, as improved by Landlord, except normal wear and tear and any casualty loss.
10. **ALTERATIONS:** Tenant may not: (a) make any holes or drive nails into the woodwork, floors, walls or ceilings (b) alter, paint or decorate the Property or (c) install improvements or fixtures without the prior written consent of Landlord. Any improvements or fixtures placed on the Property during the Lease become a part of the Property.
11. **SPECIAL PROVISIONS:**
12. **INSPECTIONS:** Landlord may enter at reasonable times to inspect, replace, repair or complete the improvements. Tenant shall provide Landlord door keys and access codes to allow access to the Property during the term of the Lease.
13. **LAWS:** Tenant shall comply with all applicable laws, restrictions, ordinances, rules and regulations with respect to the Property.
14. **REPAIRS AND MAINTENANCE:** Except as otherwise provided in this Lease, Tenant shall bear all expense of repairing, replacing and maintaining the Property, including but not limited to the yard, trees, shrubs, and all equipment and appliances, unless otherwise required by the Texas Property Code. Tenant shall promptly repair at Tenant's expense any damage to the Property caused directly or indirectly by any act or omission of the Tenant or any person other than the Landlord, Landlord's agents or invitees.

Initialed for identification by Landlord ______ and Tenant________ TREC NO. 16-5

FIGURE 5-11 Buyer's Temporary Residential Lease
Source: Reprinted with permission of Texas Real Estate Commission

Buyer's Temporary Residential Lease____ Page 2 of 2 12-05-11
(Address of Property)

15.INDEMNITY: Tenant indemnifies Landlord from the claims of all third parties for injury or damage to the person or property of such third party arising from the use or occupancy of the Property by Tenant. This indemnification includes attorney's fees, costs and expenses incurred by Landlord.

16.INSURANCE: Landlord and Tenant shall each maintain such insurance on the contents and Property as each party may deem appropriate during the term of this Lease. NOTE: CONSULT YOUR INSURANCE AGENT; POSSESSION OF THE PROPERTY BY BUYER AS TENANT MAY CHANGE INSURANCE POLICY COVERAGE.

17.DEFAULT: If Tenant fails to perform or observe any provision of this Lease and fails, within 24 hours after notice by Landlord, to commence and diligently pursue to remedy such failure, Tenant will be in default.

18.TERMINATION: This Lease terminates upon (a) closing and funding of the sale under the Contract, (b) termination of the Contract prior to closing, (c) Tenant's default under this Lease, or (d) Tenant's default under the Contract, whichever occurs first. Upon termination other than by closing and funding of the sale, Tenant shall surrender possession of the property.

19.HOLDING OVER: Any possession by Tenant after termination creates a tenancy at sufferance and will not operate to renew or extend this Lease. Tenant shall pay $_______ per day during the period of any possession after termination as damages, in addition to any other remedies to which Landlord is entitled.

20.ATTORNEY'S FEES: The prevailing party in any legal proceeding brought under or with respect to this Lease is entitled to recover from the non-prevailing party all costs of such proceeding and reasonable attorney's fees.

21.SMOKE ALARMS: The Texas Property Code requires Landlord to install smoke alarms in certain locations within the Property at Landlord's expense. Tenant expressly waives Landlord's duty to inspect and repair smoke alarms.

22.SECURITY DEVICES: The requirements of the Texas Property Code relating to security devices do not apply to a residential lease for a term of 90 days or less.

23.CONSULT YOUR ATTORNEY: Real estate licensees cannot give legal advice. This Lease is intended to be legally binding. READ IT CAREFULLY. If you do not understand the effect of this Lease, consult your attorney BEFORE signing.

24.NOTICES: All notices from one party to the other must be in writing and are effective when mailed to, hand-delivered at, or transmitted by facsimile or electronic transmission as follows:

To Landlord: ______________________	**To Tenant:** ______________________
______________________	______________________
______________________	______________________
______________________	______________________
Telephone: ( ) ______________	Telephone: ( ) ______________
Facsimile: ( ) ______________	Facsimile: ( ) ______________
E-mail: ______________________	E-mail: ______________________

______________________	______________________
Landlord	Tenant
______________________	______________________
Landlord	Tenant

TREC
TEXAS REAL ESTATE COMMISSION

The form of this contract has been approved by the Texas Real Estate Commission. TREC forms are intended for use only by trained real estate licensees. No representation is made as to the legal validity or adequacy of any provision in any specific transactions. It is not intended for complex transactions. Texas Real Estate Commission, P.O. Box 12188, Austin, TX 78711-2188, 512-936-3000 (http://www.trec.texas.gov) TREC NO. 16-5. This form replaces TREC NO. 16-4.

TREC NO. 16-5

FIGURE 5-11 (Continued)

residential sales contract concerns an option and an option fee. The fee is to be paid to the seller, not the escrow agent as is the case for earnest money. Once the contract is executed the buyer may have the property inspected. If the buyer wants certain repairs made, then he or she can negotiate repairs with the seller prior to the termination of the option period. If the seller refuses, then the buyer can terminate the contract if he or she chooses by the end of the option period or stay in the contract through closing. If the buyer elects to terminate the contract, the option fee will not be refunded, but the earnest money will be refunded. To terminate the contract under this paragraph, the buyer should use a Notice of Termination of Contract form to terminate the contract. If the Notice of Termination of Contract is faxed, then some type of return receipt should be used to ensure the seller's receipt of the termination. If the seller agrees, then the parties should amend the contract before the end of the option period. The parties should use the Amendment form for this purpose. See figure 5-12 for a chart of options available under this paragraph. The option fee may or may not be credited at closing.

CONTRACT FOR DEED

Another type of contract, which looks to a lay observer like a lease, is the contract for deed. The **contract for deed**, or installment land contract, is a creative financing technique usually seen with people who cannot obtain traditional financing, for instance, because they have a bad debt, can't make a down payment, or won't qualify for a loan. In a contract for deed situation, the seller promises to convey

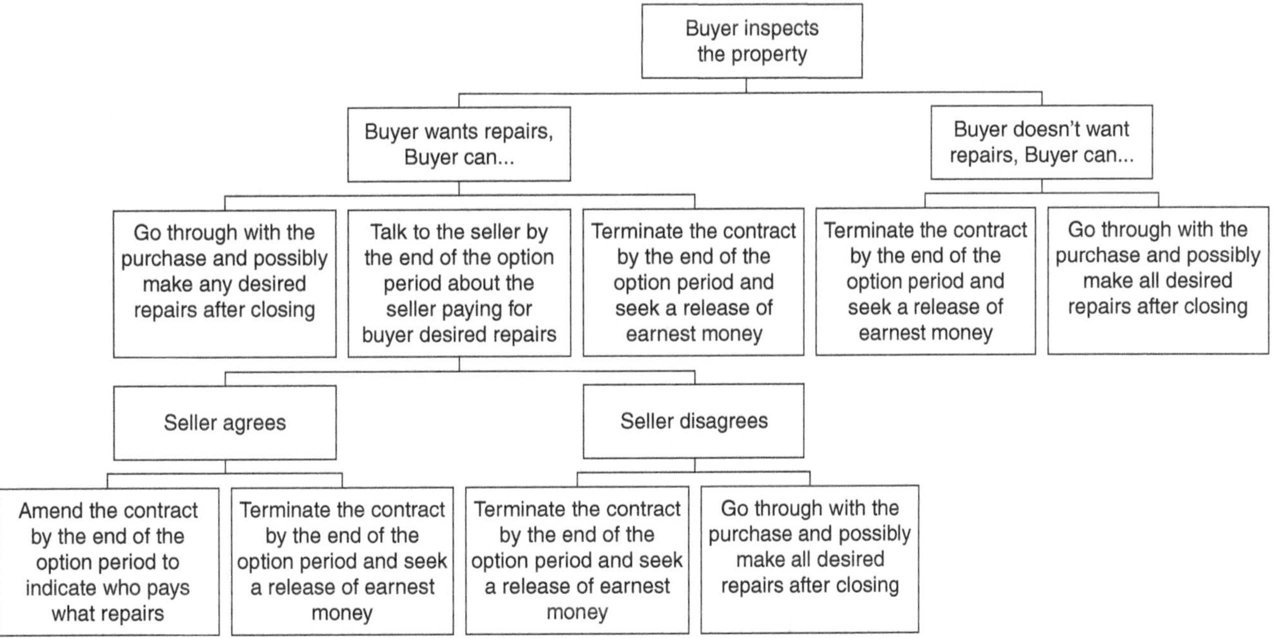

FIGURE 5-12 Options Available under Paragraph 23
Source: © 2021 Mbition LLC

title, in the form of a deed, to the buyer once the purchase price is paid. This purchase price is paid in several installments usually over several years. Because of the complex nature of a contract for deed, the parties should speak with a lawyer to determine their rights and liabilities before proceeding with this type of financing. Typically when dealing with a contract for deed, the lawyer involved will instruct that the promulgated contract form be used as a template for all of the general information concerning the sale.

Once the contract is signed, there will be a primary executory period between the signing of the contract and the first closing. After this first closing, the buyer takes possession and assumes responsibility to pay taxes and insurance. If the buyer defaults, the seller can keep all payments already made, but the court normally finds that forfeiture clauses are invalid. If the buyer defaults and the seller throws the buyer off of the property, the buyer does have certain statutory remedies.

A seller may enforce a forfeiture of interest and the acceleration of the indebtedness of a purchaser in default under an executory contract for conveyance of real property used or to be used as the purchaser's residence only after notifying the purchaser of the seller's intent to enforce the forfeiture and acceleration and the expiration of the following periods: (1) if the purchaser has paid less than 10% of the purchase price, 15 days after the date notice is given; (2) if the purchaser has paid 10% or more but less than 20% of the purchase price, 30 days after the date notice is given; and (3) if the purchaser has paid 20% or more of the purchase price, 60 days after the date notice is given.[40]

If both parties perform according to the contract for deed, when the full payment is made by the buyer, the buyer is entitled to the title. The title is transferred to the buyer at a second closing. This time period between the first closing and this second closing is often referred to as a secondary executory period. In a contract for deed situation, this secondary executory period can be quite long, sometimes as long as 15 years. As mentioned previously, any time an executory period is involved, there is a greater likelihood that problems will arise that may affect the purchaser's rights.

LEASE PURCHASE AGREEMENTS

Leases that mention the possibility of a purchase are also common contracts. The first is a **lease purchase agreement**. With a lease purchase agreement, the landlord gives the tenant the right, up front, to purchase the property at a later date with specific terms. This is also referred to as an option to purchase. If the tenant validly exercises the purchase option before it terminates, the option will be converted into a contract of purchase and sale.[41] A percentage of the rent already paid is often applied toward the down payment.

---

[40] Tex. Prop. Code § 5.061.

[41] Moosavideen v. Garrett, 300 S.W.3d 791, 801 (Tex. App.–Houston [1st Dist.] 2008).

The second agreement that falls within this category is a right of first refusal. The right of first refusal does not give the tenant an up-front right to purchase the property. Instead, the **right of first refusal** gives the tenant the right to make the first offer to purchase the property. This generally includes the right to receive notice if the landlord receives an offer to purchase the property and the right to match or better the offer. There is no requirement that the landlord accept the tenant's offer.

Discussion Questions

1. What exactly is a discharge of a contract?
2. Discuss the various means by which a contract can be discharged. Give an example of each as it relates to the real estate profession.
3. What is a breach of contract and how might a breach of contract occur in a real estate transaction?
4. What are the various promulgated contract forms utilized in Texas and in what transactions are these contracts used?
5. Richard Vega and Angela Vega, a married couple enter the brokerage office of John Cal, Co. to list their property located at 844 Sandstone, Ban, Texas 78111 at Lot 16, Block 58, ncb 1706, Village Plaza Subdivision, Bass County, Texas. The property is a single-family, detached home. They do not want the satellite dish included in the sale of the property, but they would like the sofa and coffee table included in the sale. There is no homeowners association. They want to list the property at $100,000 and they will accept all types of financing except for assumptions. The term of the listing agreement is 90 days with an option to terminate after 30 days. The protection period is 45 days. The multiple listing service for the area is the Banc Board of REALTORS®. The seller authorizes intermediary representation and will pay a 6% commission. The sellers authorize a keybox to be placed on the premises and they wish to be informed of all backup offers. The listing associate is Fred Vivian. In this scenario, what type of representation is involved? What type of documentation would be used to create an enforceable commission agreement? Complete a sample commission agreement using the facts provided.
6. Jessica Sonya and Pete Plaza enter into a buyer's representation agreement with Grand Realty Inc. to find them a house between Loop 411 and I-619 in Via, Texas. The term of the agreement is 60 days with a 30-day protection period. The fee is to be paid by the seller at 2.5% and a refundable retainer to be paid by the buyer of $500. Intermediary status is not authorized but the broker does represent both buyers and sellers. The buyer's associate is Johnny Matthias. What type of representation is involved in this situation?

What type of documentation would be used to create an enforceable commission agreement? Complete a sample commission agreement using the facts provided.

7. Michael Smith and Mickey Lee, a married couple, enter the brokerage office of Lynn Wynn Realty to list their property located at 1314 Fifteen Road, Yellow, Texas 78000 at Lot 17, Block 18, ncb 1920, Callen subdivision, Submarine County, Texas. The property is a garden home. The house is located in a subdivision that requires mandatory membership in the homeowners association. They want to list the property at $90,000 and they will accept only offers involving third-party financing. The term of the listing is six months with an option to terminate after two months. The protection period is 60 days. The MLS for the area is the Yellow Board of REALTORS®. The sellers authorize intermediary status and negotiate a 7.5% commission. The sellers authorize a keybox to be placed on the property and they wish to be informed of all backup offers. The listing agent is Bob Market. What type of relationship is involved? Complete the necessary form. Vickie Anne goes to Lynn Wynn Realty to look for a house to purchase. What procedure would be involved if the buyer is interested in looking at one of the broker's listings and in proposing an offer on one of the broker's listings? What procedure is involved if the buyer wants the listing broker to represent her in the negotiations?
8. In June 2005, Eric Brown marries Kate Chambers. In September 2005 they enter into a real estate sales contract with Victor Graves, a single man to purchase Mr. Graves' five-acre lot. The property is located in a rural community in Kendall County, Texas described in volume 202, page 176 of the deed records of Kendall County, Texas, said tract being more particularly described in exhibit A. After the contract paperwork is sent to the title company, the title company contacts the Browns' representative to find out in which county Eric and Kate were married because they can't find a marriage license on record. Subsequently the Browns' representative finds out that the Browns are common law married. The real estate transaction closes four weeks later and title is transferred to the Browns by general warranty deed. The Browns financed the real estate transaction with FHA financing. The deed and deed of trust for the transaction were recorded in the deed records for Kendall County.

After the purchase, the Browns notice that the area is growing considerably and they hear rumor that a major highway may be constructed next to their property. Acting on this rumor, they file the necessary paperwork to convert the zoning of the property from residential to commercial. Once the zoning change was approved, they began construction of a small business center on the property. The new center was to cover approximately two-thirds of the property with the remaining area to be for parking. Six units would be constructed within the center and each unit was to be constructed with its own electrical connections.

To set up the electrical connections, the Browns granted an easement to Golfland utility company to access the lines. The easement was recorded in the deed records of Kendall County even though one of the units fell within Kerr County. The construction on the new business center was completed in May 2006. After construction and after a heated argument with his wife about how to lease the units, Eric Brown hired Acme Management Company to handle the leasing of the units at the center.

In July 2006, Acme Management Company found a tenant for Unit C. The lease granted possession to "Miller's Muffins, a partnership composed of Frank Miller and Frank Miller, Jr." for one year for $500 per month. In October 2006, Acme Management Company found a tenant for Unit B. The lease granted possession to "Mike Hudson d/b/a Hudson's Huffy Shop" for one year for $200 per month plus 3% of gross sales. Because the tenant in Unit B was a sole proprietor, Acme Management Company required that Mike Hudson's wife, Emily, sign the lease as well. However, the tenant in Unit B requests that the landlord not lease to another bike shop.

Acme Management Company is only able to find the two tenants for all of the units and at the end of their contract the company demands a higher fee. Kate Brown subsequently becomes frustrated with Acme Management Company and decides to go shopping to help ease her pain. As a result she runs up credit card bills in excess of $50,000 and can no longer make the minimum payments on the cards. The creditors file suit against her to collect the money owed and receive a judgment against her.

With the stress involved with the business center and his wife's judgment, Eric Brown has a heart attack and dies. Unfortunately he never had the opportunity to make a will since he was so busy. Eric is survived by his wife, Kate, and their two children, Kathy and Amy.

a) What is the most current TREC form used for a standard residential real estate transaction?
b) Is the property owned by the Browns community or separate property?
c) What document might the title company require to confirm that the Browns are married?
d) If after six months Eric became bored with the property, could he have sold the property without his wife's permission?
e) What elements are necessary to establish a common law marriage in the state of Texas?
f) What authority has been given to Acme Management Company for leasing the units?
g) Is the power of attorney from Eric Brown valid without his wife's signature?
h) What type of interest is held by Golfland utility company?
i) What type of legal entity is the tenant in Unit C?

j) What type of legal entity is the tenant in Unit B?
k) What type of lease was given to the tenant in Unit C?
l) What type of lease was given to the tenant in Unit B?
m) What is the purpose of the request by the tenant of Unit B that the landlord not lease to other bike shops?
n) What law do you look to in Texas to determine if property is non-exempt?

9. In November 1990, the Montague Vista apartment complex was constructed in San Antonio, Texas. When the apartment complex was constructed, it was considered to be one of the most upscale apartment complexes in the city providing limited access gates, 24-hour security monitoring, athletic facilities, and covered parking. The units within the complex included several 525-square-foot one-bedroom apartments, 800-square-foot one-bedroom apartments, 1200-square-foot two-bedroom apartments, 1500-square-foot two-bedroom apartments, and 1800-square-foot three-bedroom apartments.

In April 2007 the Montague Vista apartment complex was purchased by the BCG Real Estate Group. After the purchase the BCG Real Estate Group took steps to begin the conversion of the Montague Vista apartment complex into condominium units. Before the conversion, the complex consisted of 8 buildings with 36 units each. The final condominium complex was to only contain 6 buildings with 36 units each. The 72 tenants in the buildings to be demolished were given written notice that their leases would not be renewed at their termination. The remaining tenants in the 216 units were given the option to purchase their existing units before the new construction began at a reduced purchase price. If a decision to purchase was made after construction, then market value at time of completion would be charged. Of the tenants in the 216 units, tenants in 54 of the units elected to purchase before construction. Tenants in 141 of the units elected to terminate their leases at the end of their term. Tenants in 21 of the units elected to wait until completion of construction to make a decision.

May Summers was one of the tenants that elected to purchase her one-bedroom unit before construction began. Ms. Summers' lease was scheduled to terminate in June 2007; however, construction was not to begin until October 2007. Because of this BCG Real Estate Group elected to extend her existing lease month to month until construction was complete. In December 2007 construction was completed on building 4 and Ms. Summer's unit 402. In January 2008, Ms. Summers finalized the paperwork to close on the purchase of her new condominium. At closing she received a special warranty deed granting the condominium unit and all common elements from BCG Real Estate Group to May E. Summers, a single woman. In March 2008, Ms. Summers marries Don Smith. Mr. Smith moves into the condominium with his new wife. After about two weeks they realize that the one-bedroom unit is too small for them both, so they both decide to sell it. Unfortunately after about a month, they both get frustrated trying to do FOR SALE BY OWNER, so they give up their sales attempts. In April 2008, both May and Don decide to find a house to buy. Since May makes $500 per month payments to the bank for the mortgage on the condominium, she and Don elect to have Don's daughter from a previous marriage, Angela Smith, move into the condominium and pay rent in the amount of $600 per month to May and Don. Since Angela is family, Don and May do not have her sign a written lease, but they verbally agree that the term will be for one year. May and Don subsequently purchase a house located at 111 East Hampton, more specifically described as Lot 4, Block 10 in the South Subdivision from Walter Miller, a single man. They purchase the property as community property with rights of survivorship.

Frank Miller and his wife, Mary, also elected to purchase their two-bedroom unit prior to construction. Construction on building 3 was completed in November 2007 and BCG Real Estate Group conveyed a special warranty deed to them concerning their unit, 308, and the common elements of the condominium. The deed also included a deed restriction that unit 308 was to be used for residential purposes only. In January 2008, the Millers conveyed the condominium to their children in a way that would allow the Millers to live on the property until they died and the property would automatically pass to the children at that time. The Millers conveyed as follows:

"Frank Miller and wife, Mary Miller, a married couple, convey Montague Vista Condominiums Unit No. 308, and the space encompassed by the boundaries thereof, located in Building 3; parking space No. 308A and the space encompassed by the boundaries thereof, located in Building 3; and an undivided .956% ownership interest in and to the common elements of the Condominium Project known as Montague Vista Condominiums to Frank Miller and wife Mary Miller, a married couple, for life and then to Andy Miller and James Miller."

a) Is condominium unit 402 owned by May Summers community property or separate property?
b) What might be required from Don Smith before May Summers can list condominium unit 402 for sale?
c) What type of interest did BCG Real Estate Group have in condominium unit 402 before the conveyance to May Summers?
d) What type of interest did May Summers receive from BCG Real Estate Group in her special warranty deed?
e) What is the tenancy created between May, Don, and Angela concerning unit 402 referred to as?
f) Is there any requirement that the lease between May, Don, and Angela be in writing?
g) If Angela stops paying rent to May and Don, what type of lawsuit can May and Don bring against her?

h) In what court would a forcible entry and detainer action be brought?
i) If the eviction is successful, what document would be issued by the court to give possession back to May and Don?
j) Is the property located at 111 East Hampton community property or separate property between May and Don?
k) Are there automatic rights of survivorship between May and Don concerning the property located at 111 East Hampton if one of them dies?
l) What type of interest did Frank and Mary Miller have in unit 308 before they sold it?
m) What type of interest did Frank and Mary Miller have in unit 308 after they sold it?
n) What type of interest did Andy and James Miller have in unit 308 after Frank and Mary Miller conveyed it?

CHAPTER

6

THE SALES CONTRACT

KEY TERMS

acceptance
Addendum for "Backup" Contract
anticipatory repudiation
backup offer
benefit of the bargain damages
client
communication
counteroffer
customer
damages
destruction of the subject matter
direct communication
direct revocation
expression of intent
general breach of contract
good faith
illegality
imputed communication
indirect communication
indirect revocation
inquiry
invitation to offer
lapse of time
letters of intent
liquidated damages
merger
mitigation of damages
multiple offers
mutual assent
net proceeds
offer
offeree
offeror
pre-contractual liability
promissory estoppel
rejection
rescission
restitution
revocation
Seller's Disclosure Notice
specific performance
Statute of Frauds
substantial performance
time is of the essence

This chapter looks at various aspects associated with the promulgated sales contracts. The steps involved in making an offer and accepting it will be explored along with details of the most commonly used promulgated sales contract, the TREC 20-14. Specific attention will be paid to financing information, disclosures, conveyancing of the property, the parties' signatures, the Statute of Frauds writing requirement, what constitutes default under the contract, and remedies for breach.

OFFER AND ACCEPTANCE

The Offer

Mutual assent involves an offer by one party and an acceptance by the other. Both the offer and acceptance are essential to the creation of a valid contract. An **offer** is a proposal to act or perform communicated by one party to another with the intent that the proposal be accepted to form a contract. In this situation, the person proposing the offer is referred to as the **offeror,** and the person to whom the offer is communicated is the **offeree**. In the typical real estate sales transaction, the buyer, as offeror, makes a written offer to the seller, as offeree, for the purchase of the seller's property. The offer is commonly prepared on an applicable TREC promulgated sales contract form, which will depend on the type of property involved. The offer must then be communicated to the seller.

Communication of the Offer

In order for the offer to be effective, it must be communicated to the offeree. **Communication** is the act of transmitting information. A communication can be either direct or indirect. A **direct communication** is made directly to the intended party. For instance, the offeror in a real estate sales transaction might communicate his or her offer directly to the offeree by telephone. In contrast, an **indirect communication** is a communication made indirectly to the intended party by way of a third party or third-party device. For example, an offeror uses an indirect means of communication when he or she leaves an offer in the form of a message with a third party receptionist or voice mail.

In real estate sales transactions, communication of the offer to the offeree is very important. However, in most of these transactions, communication will be made either directly or indirectly to a representative of the offeree. When a representative is involved, a special type of indirect communication applies. This indirect communication is referred to as imputed communication. **Imputed communication**, often referred to as imputed notice, is a concept whereby communication to an agent is considered communication to his or her principal. That is, communication to a real estate license holder is considered communication to his or her client. In this regard, a **client** is a person or entity who has contracted with the real estate license holder for professional services and advice. This concept of imputed notice, however, does not apply to customers involved in a real estate transaction. For purposes of discussion, a **customer** is a person who is working with a real estate license holder, as volunteer, to the extent necessary to complete the transaction, but he or she has not specifically contracted with the license holder for professional services or advice.

For example, Amy Agent represents Sally Seller in a real estate transaction. Peggy Purchaser goes to Amy Agent's office to see what homes fit her budget. Peggy chooses Sally's house. Peggy Purchaser is notified that Amy Agent only acts as a subagent of the seller. Peggy sees the home and loves it, so she proposes an offer to Sally to purchase the home for $60,000. Peggy's communication to the seller's agent will be imputed to the seller. However, let's say Sally proposes a counteroffer back to Peggy; this is done via a communication to the seller's subagent, Amy Agent. Amy is working with Peggy, as a customer, so the offer will not be imputed to Peggy. Amy must tell Peggy of the counteroffer.

Requirements and Manner of an Offer

In order for an offer to be valid, it must not be subject to any conditions. In addition, the offer must sufficiently identify the real estate concerned. The identification must be made by a proper legal description. A street address is insufficient. The offeror must also state the price and any other essential terms. These requirements are met where the offeror uses a promulgated sales contract form.

When an offer is created, it may take one of two forms. The offer may be made verbally. However, there is the problem of establishing that the verbal offer existed as well as its terms. In addition there may be a requirement that the contract be in writing. This issue will be discussed later in this chapter. It is always preferred that the offer be proposed in writing so that its existence is clear as well as its terms. As previously mentioned, in many real estate sales transactions, the offer is typically proposed on a standard TREC promulgated sales contract form. The buyer will initial each page of the offer and sign the signature page, but the final acceptance date will be left blank. See figure 6-1. This is an important point in time for the license holder to correctly convey the wishes of the principals on

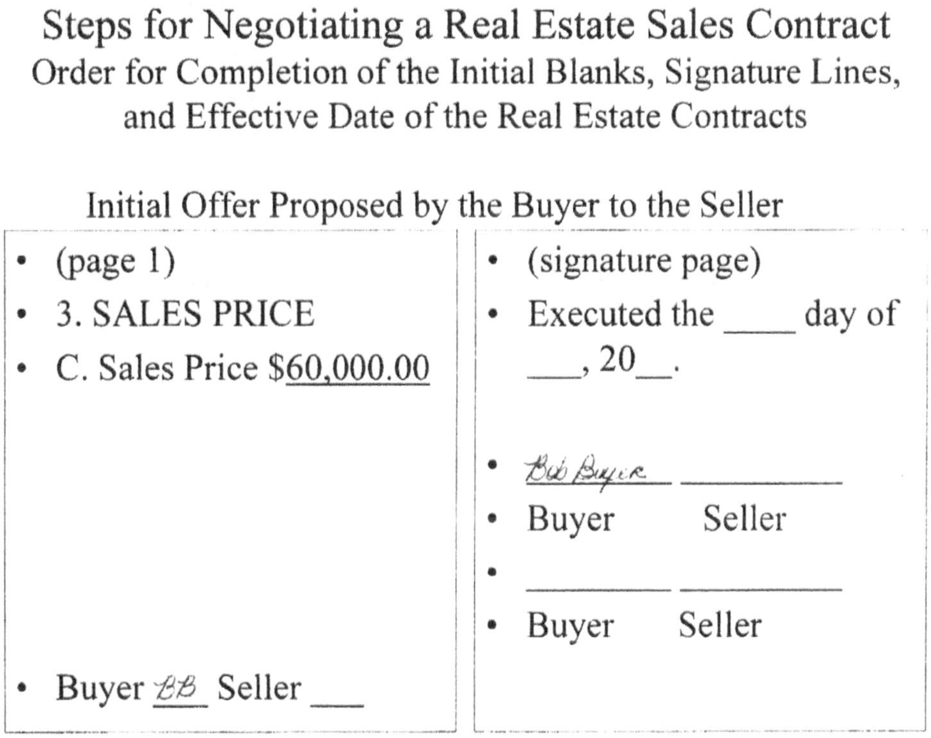

Steps for Negotiating a Real Estate Sales Contract
Order for Completion of the Initial Blanks, Signature Lines, and Effective Date of the Real Estate Contracts

Initial Offer Proposed by the Buyer to the Seller

• (page 1) • 3. SALES PRICE • C. Sales Price $60,000.00 • Buyer BB Seller ___	• (signature page) • Executed the ____ day of ___, 20__. • Bob Buyer ________ • Buyer Seller • ________ ________ • Buyer Seller

FIGURE 6-1 Proposing the Offer
Source: © 2021 Mbition LLC

the contract. It is easy to get excited and make an error by forgetting to include a key element or failing to state the parties' desires clearly.

Presentation of an Offer

In real estate sales transactions, the offer will typically be communicated by the prospective purchaser, in writing, to the seller. In these situations, certain tactics on behalf of the real estate license holder can prove helpful in the offering procedure. When it is time to communicate the offer, it is best for a buyer's representative to present it in person. However, this may not always be possible. Thus, many presentations occur by facsimile or email. Few are conducted by postal mail because of the delays involved.

Once the offer has been communicated to the seller's representative, the seller's representative should review the offer and indicate the overall situation to the seller. This phase is usually referred to as presentment of the offer. See figure 6-2. The seller's interest is the bottom line, which is what his or her net proceeds will be from the sale if the indicated offer is used. **Net proceeds** are the amount of proceeds left after closing expenses and indebtedness have been paid. See figures 6-3 and 6-4.

Distinguished from Non-Offers

There are several types of communications that may appear to be, but are not, offers. These communications may arise as expressions of intention, invitations to offer, and inquiries.

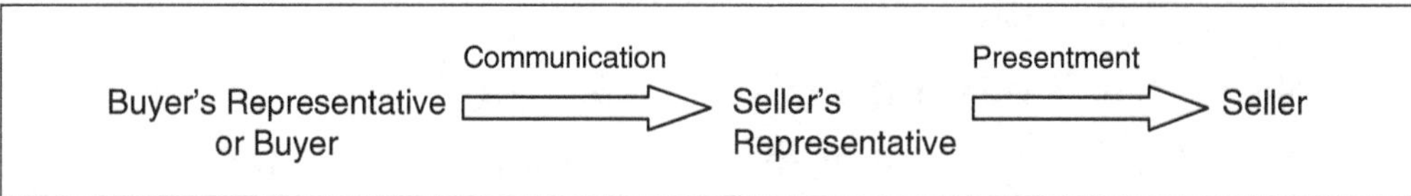

FIGURE 6-2 Communication and Presentment
Source: © 2021 Mbition LLC

Net Proceeds = Total Proceeds – Loan Balance – Closing Costs – Broker Commission

FIGURE 6-3 Calculation of Net Proceeds
Source: © 2021 Mbition LLC

Sample Calculation of Net Proceeds

What would the seller net from the sale of his home for $100,000 if the existing lien of $80,000 must be paid, the broker's fee of 5% of the sales price must be paid, and the closing costs of $2,000 must be paid?

$100,000 – $80,000 – $100,000 (0.05) – $2,000 = $13,000

FIGURE 6-4 Sample Calculation of Net Proceeds
Source: © 2021 Mbition LLC

Expression of Intention

An expression of intent is not an offer. An **expression of intent** refers to a statement made by a person in which the person seeks to accomplish a specific goal. For example, Sam Seller is sitting in a coffee shop with his pal, Fred Friend. Sam tells Fred, "I am going to sell my house for $127,500." This statement is merely an expression of the seller's intent and not an offer to his friend.

In the real estate industry, particularly in commercial transactions, parties to negotiations often use **letters of intent** to express their intent with regard to matters involved in the transaction. The general rule is that these letters do not constitute offers; however, in negotiations one must be careful not to include any promises on which another party may rely. If the other party does rely on these promises, it could convert a mere expression of intent into an offer.

Invitations to Offer Distinguished from Inquiries

An **invitation to offer** simply invites parties to make offers on a particular piece of property. An invitation to offer may begin negotiations on the sale or rental of real property. An **inquiry** is a question proposed concerning a piece of property with the intent that an answer be forthcoming, but neither an invitation to offer nor an inquiry constitutes an offer. For example, Betty Buyer calls Sally Seller and asks, "Will you sell me your ranch in Blanco County for $400,000?" This statement is not an offer, but merely an inquiry with the expectation that there will be either a "yes" or "no" response. If Sally Seller responds, "I am trying to sell my ranch, but I cannot sell for any less than $657,000," this statement is not an offer to sell at $657,000, but merely an invitation for Betty Buyer to make an offer of not less than $657,000.

Multiple Offers

In a typical real estate sales transaction, the license holder, acting as agent for the seller, has a duty to disclose all information to the seller. This information includes all offers that the license holder receives. However, one of the most common problems facing real estate professionals concerns multiple offers. **Multiple offers** may be implicated in a situation where the seller receives several offers simultaneously concerning a parcel of real estate. If the seller and prospective purchaser are in the midst of negotiations, the seller's agent still owes the seller the duty to present all offers, unless otherwise instructed, until the seller and prospective buyer have agreed in writing on all aspects of the negotiations. Once the offer is communicated to the seller, it is up to the seller to determine what should be done with the pending offers as well as the newly submitted offer. In these cases, the seller has the option of rejecting all of the offers, accepting one of the offers and rejecting the others, or proposing a counteroffer to one and rejecting the others. However, in no instance should the license holder allow the seller to submit a counteroffer on all pending offers. This would leave all prospective purchasers open to accept the counteroffers, which would create several contracts for the sale of only one piece of property. Many local REALTOR® boards will have some guidelines on how to handle multiple offers. Likewise a brokerage firm may have internal policies on this issue or use a standard "Seller's Invitation to Buyer to Submit New Offer" form, such as the one used by the Texas Association of REALTORS®. Once a sales contract is formed, however, the submission of additional offers is dictated by contract. The promulgated residential sales contract provides for backup offers, which will be discussed later.

One problem that may arise with multiple offers is when an agent of the seller fails to present an offer to the seller for a period of time while waiting for a better offer. One way to keep a license holder, or the license holder's client, from sitting on an offer is to limit the time for acceptance of the offer. For example, an offer might state, "This offer will terminate at 5:00 p.m. on Friday, May 27, unless acceptance is received by that time." On the date and time indicated, the offer will terminate. Whether there is a termination clause or not, the license holder has a duty of disclosure to his or her principal of *all* offers as promptly as possible once received. Sitting on an offer can be a serious breach of fiduciary duty.

Backup Offers and Contracts

An issue that arises with regard to this duty of presenting all offers concerns backup offers. A **backup offer** is a second offer presented during the pendency of a contract. Typically backup offers arise when the property owner has a pending contract for the sale and purchase of the real estate. During the executory period of this contract, the seller receives another offer from a prospective buyer on the property. In this instance, the seller may elect to enter into negotiations on this "backup offer" in hopes of creating a "backup" contract in case the pending contract fails to close. If terms on the backup offer are agreed upon and the parties enter into a contract, it is of *utmost importance* in Texas that the real estate license holder attach an **Addendum for "Backup" Contract** (TREC 11-7) to the completed promulgated sales contract form. This addendum states that the backup contract does not take effect until the termination of the pending sales contract. The issue of whether or not to even present backup offers once the property is under contract is addressed in some of the listing agreements as well as in the real estate sales contracts. A license holder should discuss this topic carefully when the listing is taken.

Termination of the Offer

There are some instances where an offeror changes his or her mind and would like to terminate the offer. There are several methods available whereby the offeror can terminate his or her offer.

Revocation by the Offeror

The offeror can terminate the offer by simply revoking it. **Revocation** refers to the act by the offeror of withdrawing the offer. The revocation or withdrawal of the offer by the offeror can be either direct or indirect. A **direct revocation** is the more common type of revocation and involves a statement made by the offeror or the offeror's representative to the offeree or the offeree's representative indicating the desire to withdraw the offer. An **indirect revocation** by an offeror is a revocation whereby the offeror says or does something that indicates a desire to withdraw the offer and that is known by the offeree. In both cases, however, the revocation must be communicated to the offeree. The same rules for communication apply. In addition, the offeror has the right to revoke any time before the offeree accepts. Once the offeree accepts, a contract is formed. The only way to terminate at that point is either by discharge or breach of the contract.

The general rule is that an acceptance of an offer by the offeree is effective upon dispatch of the acceptance; however, a revocation of an offer by the offeror is not effective until it is received by the offeree. For example, Ollie Buyer makes an offer to Sally Seller on June 1 to purchase her property for $100,000. Sally Seller receives the offer on June 5 and is so excited about the offer that she immediately dispatches an acceptance that same day. On June 6, Ollie Buyer mails a revocation to Sally Seller that is not received until June 8. Sally Seller's acceptance is received by Ollie on June 9. In this case, since Sally Seller's acceptance was dispatched before she received Ollie Buyer's revocation, a valid contract was formed. This is why fax and email communication can be useful.

This example is a great reminder that information between principals needs to be conveyed as soon as possible. Technology has made these responses quicker and easier, but sometimes the option of a fax, for example, is not available. The information should start flowing between the parties as soon as possible. However, this does not imply rushing or pressing the consumer to make a hasty decision.

Rejection by the Offeree

The second means by which an offer can be terminated is by rejection by the offeree. **Rejection** refers to the refusal by the offeree to accept the terms of the offer. Rejection by the offeree is typically express, that is, by words, either written or verbal. For example, Bob Buyer proposes an offer to Sylvia Seller to purchase her home for $40,000. Sylvia Seller sends back a letter that states, "I reject your offer of $40,000." In another example, Barbara Buyer proposes an offer to Sal Seller to purchase his lot for $25,000. Sal Seller calls Barbara Buyer and says, "I reject your offer of $25,000 for my lot."

Often, the rejection is not quite so clear. Many real estate license holders fail to notify the other party that their client has rejected the offer. With the risk that there will not be a communication of rejection, it is wise to put in a specific termination date for the offer. With this clarification, a license holder and his or her client won't have to be sitting around twiddling their thumbs wondering if a response is forthcoming. Once the pending offer is terminated, the buyer can propose another offer on another property.

There may be times, however, where rather than giving an outright rejection to the offer, the offeree makes a counteroffer. A **counteroffer** is a proposal made by the offeree that relates to the same matter as the original offer, but proposes a substitute for portions of the original proposal. Where a counteroffer is made, the original offer is rejected, and a new offer is put up for negotiation by the offeree. Counteroffers are typically proposed on the same sales contract on which the offeror proposed his or her offer. The change is indicated on the form, the offeree initials the change and includes a date and time for the change. The date and time are particularly important when the negotiation occurs via fax. Correction fluid should not be used to indicate a change. In addition, the offeree initials all of the remaining pages of the agreement and signs the document. For example, the prospective purchaser dispatches an offer to the seller to purchase her home for $100,000. The seller is not willing to accept any less than the listing price of $150,000 so she crosses out the $100,000, writes in $150,000, and initials, dates, and writes the time next to the change. The seller's act of crossing out the $100,000 provision operates as a rejection, and the addition of the $150,000 provision operates as a new offer proposed for negotiation.

The parties may make several counteroffers before an agreement is reached. Keep in mind that *each* counteroffer represents a new proposal with the previous proposal now void. For example, it is important to remind the seller that crossing out the buyer's request that a dining table be part of the sale makes the entire offer from the buyer ancient history. Even if the seller later has a change of heart and says (or writes), "Okay the table will stay," the buyer is no longer obligated to honor the original proposal. Help the principals see the *true risk* in making changes to an offer.

One practice to avoid is the submission of an unsigned counteroffer. Such offers may be relied upon by the other party and may subject the offeree to liability for failed negotiations. A better practice to utilize when an offeree does not want to get tied into any particular negotiations is to simply reject the offer outright and invite the offeror to propose a new offer consistent with certain delineated terms. This would be done on a separate form so as not to be confused with a counteroffer. As mentioned earlier, the TAR form "Seller's Invitation to Buyer to Submit New Offer" can be used for this purpose.

Lapse of Time

The third way an offer can be terminated is by lapse of time. This can be the **lapse of time** specified in the offer itself. For example, Billy Buyer makes an offer to Samantha Seller on a promulgated residential sales contract form to purchase Samantha Seller's condominium for $83,000. In the form, Billy Buyer indicates "This offer will terminate by 5:00 p.m. on Friday, June 15, unless an acceptance is received by that time." In this case, if Samantha Seller fails to accept by 5:00 p.m. on Friday, June 15, the offer terminates by lapse of time.

In proposing an offer for the purchase or sale of real estate, it is a good idea to put some limitation on the time for acceptance. This forces the offeree to make a decision as to whether or not to accept, and it prevents the offeree from sitting on the offer too long in the hope of receiving a higher or better offer. In addition, it helps to alleviate problems associated with the other party's failure to communicate a rejection. This concept applies equally to counteroffers.

Where no time is specified in the offer, the offer will terminate within a reasonable time. For example, Becky Buyer makes an offer to Sid Seller on a promulgated residential sales contract form to purchase Sid Seller's house for $67,000. In the form, Becky Buyer fails to indicate when the offer will terminate. In this case, if Sid Seller fails to accept the offer within a reasonable time, the offer will terminate by lapse of time. What is a reasonable time leaves some room for problems in that one person may feel two days is enough time and another may think two months is not enough time.

An important concept that has an impact on issues of lapsed time is "time is of the essence" provisions. A **time is of the essence** provision requires that all times indicated under a contract be interpreted exactly. In the absence of this language, it is presumed that certain delays will be allowed. In fact, there are automatic extensions for certain situations outlined in the promulgated sales contracts. "Time is of the essence" provisions are more common in commercial real estate transactions. But "time is of the essence" provisions in residential real estate sales transactions can be found in the sales contracts such as the One- to Four-Family Residential Contract (Resale) (TREC 20-14), the Addendum for Sale of Other Property by Buyer (TREC 10-6), the Addendum for Backup Contract (TREC 11-7), the Short Sale Addendum (TREC 45-1), and the Third Party Financing Addendum (TREC 40-7).

Destruction of the Subject Matter

The fourth way an offer can terminate before it is accepted is by **destruction of the subject matter** indicated in the offer. Destruction of the subject matter refers to the partial or complete loss of the property due to some Act of God or a governmental taking. For example, Ben Buyer makes an offer to Shelby Seller to purchase her home for $85,000. Subsequently, the home burns down. Since the subject matter of the offer has been destroyed, the offer for the purchase of that home is terminated. In the event of partial damage, other options exist. Repair of the property or lowering the price have all been used as solutions to this particular problem.

Death or Insanity of the Offeror

An offer also can be terminated before acceptance by the subsequent death or insanity of the offeror. For example, Beth Buyer makes an offer to Sam Seller to purchase his lake front condominium for $250,000. Two days later, Beth Buyer dies and the offer has not been accepted. In this case, the offer terminates upon the death of Beth Buyer.

Illegality of the Subject Matter

The last way in which an offer can terminate is by subsequent illegality. **Illegality** refers to that which is contrary to the principles of law, morals, or public policy. For example, Bob Buyer makes an offer to Samantha Seller to purchase her bar for $500,000. Subsequently, the Texas legislature passes a law prohibiting the sale of alcohol. Since the offer has not been accepted in this instance, the illegality will terminate the offer.

Keep in mind in all the situations where an offer can be terminated, acceptance had not yet occurred.

The Acceptance

As mentioned earlier, acceptance is an essential element to the creation of a valid contract. **Acceptance** is an action taken by the offeree upon receipt of the offer that manifests his or her agreement to the terms of the offer by the means indicated in the offer. For example, a seller of real estate receives an offer from a prospective purchaser. The offer contains terms preferred by the seller. Since the terms are acceptable, the seller may choose to accept the offer by signing the documents. Once the offer is accepted by the offeree, a contract is formed. This agreement of the parties in the form of the offer and acceptance is often referred to as mutual assent or the "meeting of the minds."

Who May Accept the Offer

In order to accept an offer, the offer must first be communicated. Communication refers to the act of transmitting information to another. As was the case for offers, communication of an acceptance can be either direct or indirect. Furthermore, the only person who may accept an offer is the party to whom the offer is communicated. In a real estate transaction, an offer is communicated to the seller through the listing broker. The broker has no authority to accept the offer, unless he or she is accepting on behalf of the seller under a duly authorized power of attorney.

Validity of Acceptance

In order for the acceptance of an offer to be valid, it must be identical to the offer. Any attempt to vary the terms of the original offer may constitute a counteroffer and, therefore, a rejection of the original offer. In addition, the acceptance cannot be conditioned on the happening of an event.

Manner of Acceptance

Written Versus Verbal Acceptance

There are several ways an acceptance can be given, unless the offeror indicates a preference. While an acceptance can be given verbally, the preferred manner of acceptance by an offeree is an acceptance in writing. With the acceptance in writing, there is less likelihood that one of the parties to the transaction will refute the acceptance. Furthermore, since the acceptance forms the contract, it is a good idea to make a copy of both the offer and the acceptance before the acceptance is communicated to the offeror. There may also be important considerations to make in view of the Statute of Frauds writing requirement.

Silence

The general rule is that silence does not constitute acceptance. However, if an offeree takes benefits indicated in the offer without verbal or written acceptance, then silence may be sufficient to constitute an acceptance. It is important to remember that in order to show the party's assent to an agreement by silence, proof must be established that the party heard and fully understood what was said. This is especially important to remember when dealing with a person who does not understand the English language or when dealing with a visually or hearing impaired person. It should be evident that silence is *not* a safe way to demonstrate a meeting of the minds. Get the offers and counteroffers in writing or run the risk of problems.

Pre-Contractual Liability

Liability for Failed Negotiations

The general rule is that parties are free to negotiate without worrying about precontractual liability. **Precontractual liability** is liability that arises due to failed negotiations between the parties before a contract is formed. Preliminary discussions between the parties to a prospective real estate sale do not typically give rise to enforceable rights or duties until a contract is formed. If an agreement is reached between the parties and reduced to writing, all prior negotiations are merged into the writing. The term **merger** refers to the termination of one contract by its inclusion into another. There are, however, three exceptions where a party to the precontractual negotiations may be liable for failed negotiations. These exceptions include instances involving restitution, promissory estoppel, and good faith.

Restitution

Restitution is one exception by which an injured party to failed negotiations can recover. **Restitution** is an equitable remedy under which an injured party is restored to his or her original position before the injury occurred and placed in the position that he or she would have been in had the injury not occurred. Restitution arises when the party at fault receives a benefit from the injured party under such circumstances that the party at fault ought to compensate the injured party for the benefit received. In this case, the law will imply a promise by the party at fault to pay the reasonable value of benefits received to the injured party. There is no enforcement of the promise, just a return of the benefit conferred. For example, an attorney provides legal services for a client with the expectation of being paid. If the client doesn't pay, then restitution may be an adequate remedy for the attorney to recover his or her fee. However, real estate license holders should be careful providing services for a client without a written contract. In Texas, if the client fails to pay and there is no written contract, the right to a commission cannot be enforced.

Promissory Estoppel

Where parties to a negotiation fail to reach any agreement, one party to the contract may be responsible to the other parties where promissory estoppel can be established. **Promissory estoppel** is a doctrine that arises when a party to a contract relies on a promise of another party to the contract, and injustice would result if the injured party was not able to recover. Promissory estoppel will allow recovery by the injured party if four elements are satisfied. First, there must have been a promise made to the injured party by the party at fault. Second, the party at fault should reasonably have expected action or forbearance in reliance on that promise by the injured party. Third, there is actual reliance on the promise by the injured party. Fourth, injustice can only be avoided by enforcing the promise.

Good Faith

Preliminary negotiations and agreements to enter into a binding contract in the future are not contracts. Parties, however, may agree to negotiate in good faith, and this agreement may constitute a binding contract. **Good faith** refers to an honest intention to contract and the absence of the intent to defraud. The test to determine whether there is a contract in this instance consists of three factors. First, the parties must have shown their intention to be bound by the agreement to negotiate in good faith. Second, the terms of the agreement must be sufficiently definite to be enforced. Third, there must be consideration. Agreements to negotiate in good faith are common in commercial real estate transactions.

A clear perspective of what constitutes an agreement is essential for the license holder. For *any* party to a real estate transaction to think "a deal" has been made means *all* parties should have the same understanding.

THE DOCUMENT

As mentioned above, negotiation for a real estate transaction typically occurs on the promulgated sales contract form. Although there are several different

2-12-18

TREC
TEXAS REAL ESTATE COMMISSION

PROMULGATED BY THE TEXAS REAL ESTATE COMMISSION (TREC)

ONE TO FOUR FAMILY RESIDENTIAL CONTRACT (RESALE)

NOTICE: Not For Use For Condominium Transactions

1. PARTIES: The parties to this contract are ____________________ (Seller) and ____________________ (Buyer). Seller agrees to sell and convey to Buyer and Buyer agrees to buy from Seller the Property defined below.

2. PROPERTY: The land, improvements and accessories are collectively referred to as the "Property".

A. LAND: Lot __________ Block __________, ____________________ Addition, City of ____________________, County of ____________________, Texas, known as ____________________ (address/zip code), or as described on attached exhibit.

B. IMPROVEMENTS: The house, garage and all other fixtures and improvements attached to the above-described real property, including without limitation, the following **permanently installed and built-in items,** if any: all equipment and appliances, valances, screens, shutters, awnings, wall-to-wall carpeting, mirrors, ceiling fans, attic fans, mail boxes, television antennas, mounts and brackets for televisions and speakers, heating and air-conditioning units, security and fire detection equipment, wiring, plumbing and lighting fixtures, chandeliers, water softener system, kitchen equipment, garage door openers, cleaning equipment, shrubbery, landscaping, outdoor cooking equipment, and all other property owned by Seller and attached to the above described real property.

C. ACCESSORIES: The following described related accessories, if any: window air conditioning units, stove, fireplace screens, curtains and rods, blinds, window shades, draperies and rods, door keys, mailbox keys, above ground pool, swimming pool equipment and maintenance accessories, artificial fireplace logs, and controls for: (i) garage doors, (ii) entry gates, and (iii) other improvements and accessories.

D. EXCLUSIONS: The following improvements and accessories will be retained by Seller and must be removed prior to delivery of possession: ____________________.

E. RESERVATIONS: Any reservation for oil, gas, or other minerals, water, timber, or other interests is made in accordance with an attached addendum.

3. SALES PRICE:

A. Cash portion of Sales Price payable by Buyer at closing .... $__________

B. Sum of all financing described in the attached: ❑ Third Party Financing Addendum, ❑ Loan Assumption Addendum, ❑ Seller Financing Addendum .... $__________

C. Sales Price (Sum of A and B).. $__________

4. LICENSE HOLDER DISCLOSURE: Texas law requires a real estate license holder who is a party to a transaction or acting on behalf of a spouse, parent, child, business entity in which the license holder owns more than 10%, or a trust for which the license holder acts as a trustee or of which the license holder or the license holder's spouse, parent or child is a beneficiary, to notify the other party in writing before entering into a contract of sale. Disclose if applicable: ____________________.

5. EARNEST MONEY: Within 3 days after the Effective Date, Buyer must deliver $__________ as earnest money to ____________________, as escrow agent, at ____________________ (address). Buyer shall deliver additional earnest money of $__________ to escrow agent within _____ days after the Effective Date of this contract. If Buyer fails to deliver the earnest money within the time required, Seller may terminate this contract or exercise Seller's remedies under Paragraph 15, or both, by providing notice to Buyer before Buyer delivers the earnest money. If the last day to deliver the earnest money falls on a Saturday, Sunday, or legal holiday, the time to deliver the earnest money is extended until the end of the next day that is not a Saturday, Sunday, or legal holiday. **Time is of the essence for this paragraph.**

6. TITLE POLICY AND SURVEY:

A. TITLE POLICY: Seller shall furnish to Buyer at ❑ Seller's ❑ Buyer's expense an owner policy of title insurance (Title Policy) issued by ____________________ (Title Company) in the amount of the Sales Price, dated at or after closing, insuring Buyer against loss under the provisions of the Title Policy, subject to the promulgated exclusions (including existing building and zoning ordinances) and the following exceptions:

(1) Restrictive covenants common to the platted subdivision in which the Property is located.

(2) The standard printed exception for standby fees, taxes and assessments.

Initialed for identification by Buyer______ ______ and Seller ______ ______ TREC NO. 20-14

FIGURE 6-5 One to Four Family Residential Contract (TREC 20-14)

Source: Reprinted with permission of Texas Real Estate Commission

Contract Concerning ____ Page 2 of 10 2-12-18
(Address of Property)

(3) Liens created as part of the financing described in Paragraph 3.
(4) Utility easements created by the dedication deed or plat of the subdivision in which the Property is located.
(5) Reservations or exceptions otherwise permitted by this contract or as may be approved by Buyer in writing.
(6) The standard printed exception as to marital rights.
(7) The standard printed exception as to waters, tidelands, beaches, streams, and related matters.
(8) The standard printed exception as to discrepancies, conflicts, shortages in area or boundary lines, encroachments or protrusions, or overlapping improvements:
❑(i) will not be amended or deleted from the title policy; or
❑(ii) will be amended to read, "shortages in area" at the expense of ❑Buyer ❑Seller.
(9) The exception or exclusion regarding minerals approved by the Texas Department of Insurance.

B. COMMITMENT: Within 20 days after the Title Company receives a copy of this contract, Seller shall furnish to Buyer a commitment for title insurance (Commitment) and, at Buyer's expense, legible copies of restrictive covenants and documents evidencing exceptions in the Commitment (Exception Documents) other than the standard printed exceptions. Seller authorizes the Title Company to deliver the Commitment and Exception Documents to Buyer at Buyer's address shown in Paragraph 21. If the Commitment and Exception Documents are not delivered to Buyer within the specified time, the time for delivery will be automatically extended up to 15 days or 3 days before the Closing Date, whichever is earlier. If the Commitment and Exception Documents are not delivered within the time required, Buyer may terminate this contract and the earnest money will be refunded to Buyer.

C. SURVEY: The survey must be made by a registered professional land surveyor acceptable to the Title Company and Buyer's lender(s). (Check one box only)
❑(1) Within _______ days after the Effective Date of this contract, Seller shall furnish to Buyer and Title Company Seller's existing survey of the Property and a Residential Real Property Affidavit promulgated by the Texas Department of Insurance (T-47 Affidavit). **If Seller fails to furnish the existing survey or affidavit within the time prescribed, Buyer shall obtain a new survey at Seller's expense no later than 3 days prior to Closing Date.** If the existing survey or affidavit is not acceptable to Title Company or Buyer's lender(s), Buyer shall obtain a new survey at ❑Seller's ❑Buyer's expense no later than 3 days prior to Closing Date.
❑(2) Within ________ days after the Effective Date of this contract, Buyer shall obtain a new survey at Buyer's expense. Buyer is deemed to receive the survey on the date of actual receipt or the date specified in this paragraph, whichever is earlier.
❑(3) Within ________ days after the Effective Date of this contract, Seller, at Seller's expense shall furnish a new survey to Buyer.

D. OBJECTIONS: Buyer may object in writing to defects, exceptions, or encumbrances to title: disclosed on the survey other than items 6A(1) through (7) above; disclosed in the Commitment other than items 6A(1) through (9) above; or which prohibit the following use or activity: ____.
Buyer must object the earlier of (i) the Closing Date or (ii) ______ days after Buyer receives the Commitment, Exception Documents, and the survey. Buyer's failure to object within the time allowed will constitute a waiver of Buyer's right to object; except that the requirements in Schedule C of the Commitment are not waived by Buyer. Provided Seller is not obligated to incur any expense, Seller shall cure any timely objections of Buyer or any third party lender within 15 days after Seller receives the objections (Cure Period) and the Closing Date will be extended as necessary. If objections are not cured within the Cure Period, Buyer may, by delivering notice to Seller within 5 days after the end of the Cure Period: (i) terminate this contract and the earnest money will be refunded to Buyer; or (ii) waive the objections. If Buyer does not terminate within the time required, Buyer shall be deemed to have waived the objections. If the Commitment or Survey is revised or any new Exception Document(s) is delivered, Buyer may object to any new matter revealed in the revised Commitment or Survey or new Exception Document(s) within the same time stated in this paragraph to make objections beginning when the revised Commitment, Survey, or Exception Document(s) is delivered to Buyer.

E. TITLE NOTICES:
(1) ABSTRACT OR TITLE POLICY: Broker advises Buyer to have an abstract of title covering the Property examined by an attorney of Buyer's selection, or Buyer should be furnished with or obtain a Title Policy. If a Title Policy is furnished, the Commitment should be promptly reviewed by an attorney of Buyer's choice due to the time limitations on Buyer's right to object.
(2) MEMBERSHIP IN PROPERTY OWNERS ASSOCIATION(S): The Property ❑is ❑is not

Initialed for identification by Buyer______ ______ and Seller _______ ______ TREC NO. 20-14

FIGURE 6-5 (Continued)

Contract Concerning ____ Page 3 of 10 2-12-18
(Address of Property)

subject to mandatory membership in a property owners association(s). If the Property is subject to mandatory membership in a property owners association(s), Seller notifies Buyer under §5.012, Texas Property Code, that, as a purchaser of property in the residential community identified in Paragraph 2A in which the Property is located, you are obligated to be a member of the property owners association(s). Restrictive covenants governing the use and occupancy of the Property and all dedicatory instruments governing the establishment, maintenance, or operation of this residential community have been or will be recorded in the Real Property Records of the county in which the Property is located. Copies of the restrictive covenants and dedicatory instruments may be obtained from the county clerk. **You are obligated to pay assessments to the property owners association(s). The amount of the assessments is subject to change. Your failure to pay the assessments could result in enforcement of the association's lien on and the foreclosure of the Property.**

Section 207.003, Property Code, entitles an owner to receive copies of any document that governs the establishment, maintenance, or operation of a subdivision, including, but not limited to, restrictions, bylaws, rules and regulations, and a resale certificate from a property owners' association. A resale certificate contains information including, but not limited to, statements specifying the amount and frequency of regular assessments and the style and cause number of lawsuits to which the property owners' association is a party, other than lawsuits relating to unpaid ad valorem taxes of an individual member of the association. These documents must be made available to you by the property owners' association or the association's agent on your request.

If Buyer is concerned about these matters, the TREC promulgated Addendum for Property Subject to Mandatory Membership in a Property Owners Association(s) should be used.

(3) STATUTORY TAX DISTRICTS: If the Property is situated in a utility or other statutorily created district providing water, sewer, drainage, or flood control facilities and services, Chapter 49, Texas Water Code, requires Seller to deliver and Buyer to sign the statutory notice relating to the tax rate, bonded indebtedness, or standby fee of the district prior to final execution of this contract.

(4) TIDE WATERS: If the Property abuts the tidally influenced waters of the state, §33.135, Texas Natural Resources Code, requires a notice regarding coastal area property to be included in the contract. An addendum containing the notice promulgated by TREC or required by the parties must be used.

(5) ANNEXATION: If the Property is located outside the limits of a municipality, Seller notifies Buyer under §5.011, Texas Property Code, that the Property may now or later be included in the extraterritorial jurisdiction of a municipality and may now or later be subject to annexation by the municipality. Each municipality maintains a map that depicts its boundaries and extraterritorial jurisdiction. To determine if the Property is located within a municipality's extraterritorial jurisdiction or is likely to be located within a municipality's extraterritorial jurisdiction, contact all municipalities located in the general proximity of the Property for further information.

(6) PROPERTY LOCATED IN A CERTIFICATED SERVICE AREA OF A UTILITY SERVICE PROVIDER: Notice required by §13.257, Water Code: The real property, described in Paragraph 2, that you are about to purchase may be located in a certificated water or sewer service area, which is authorized by law to provide water or sewer service to the properties in the certificated area. If your property is located in a certificated area there may be special costs or charges that you will be required to pay before you can receive water or sewer service. There may be a period required to construct lines or other facilities necessary to provide water or sewer service to your property. You are advised to determine if the property is in a certificated area and contact the utility service provider to determine the cost that you will be required to pay and the period, if any, that is required to provide water or sewer service to your property. The undersigned Buyer hereby acknowledges receipt of the foregoing notice at or before the execution of a binding contract for the purchase of the real property described in Paragraph 2 or at closing of purchase of the real property.

(7) PUBLIC IMPROVEMENT DISTRICTS: If the Property is in a public improvement district, §5.014, Property Code, requires Seller to notify Buyer as follows: As a purchaser of this parcel of real property you are obligated to pay an assessment to a municipality or county for an improvement project undertaken by a public improvement district under Chapter 372, Local Government Code. The assessment may be due annually or in periodic installments. More information concerning the amount of the assessment and the due dates of that assessment may be obtained from the municipality or county levying the assessment. The amount of the assessments is subject to change. Your failure to pay the assessments could result in a lien on and the foreclosure of your property.

(8) TRANSFER FEES: If the Property is subject to a private transfer fee obligation, §5.205, Property Code, requires Seller to notify Buyer as follows: The private transfer fee

Initialed for identification by Buyer______ ______ and Seller _______ ______ TREC NO. 20-14

FIGURE 6-5 (Continued)

Contract Concerning ____ Page 4 of 10 2-12-18
(Address of Property)

obligation may be governed by Chapter 5, Subchapter G of the Texas Property Code.

(9) PROPANE GAS SYSTEM SERVICE AREA: If the Property is located in a propane gas system service area owned by a distribution system retailer, Seller must give Buyer written notice as required by §141.010, Texas Utilities Code. An addendum containing the notice approved by TREC or required by the parties should be used.

(10) NOTICE OF WATER LEVEL FLUCTUATIONS: If the Property adjoins an impoundment of water, including a reservoir or lake, constructed and maintained under Chapter 11, Water Code, that has a storage capacity of at least 5,000 acre-feet at the impoundment's normal operating level, Seller hereby notifies Buyer: "The water level of the impoundment of water adjoining the Property fluctuates for various reasons, including as a result of: (1) an entity lawfully exercising its right to use the water stored in the impoundment; or (2) drought or flood conditions."

7.PROPERTY CONDITION:

A. ACCESS, INSPECTIONS AND UTILITIES: Seller shall permit Buyer and Buyer's agents access to the Property at reasonable times. Buyer may have the Property inspected by inspectors selected by Buyer and licensed by TREC or otherwise permitted by law to make inspections. Any hydrostatic testing must be separately authorized by Seller in writing. Seller at Seller's expense shall immediately cause existing utilities to be turned on and shall keep the utilities on during the time this contract is in effect.

B. SELLER'S DISCLOSURE NOTICE PURSUANT TO §5.008, TEXAS PROPERTY CODE (Notice): (Check one box only)

❑ (1) Buyer has received the Notice.

❑ (2) Buyer has not received the Notice. Within _______ days after the Effective Date of this contract, Seller shall deliver the Notice to Buyer. If Buyer does not receive the Notice, Buyer may terminate this contract at any time prior to the closing and the earnest money will be refunded to Buyer. If Seller delivers the Notice, Buyer may terminate this contract for any reason within 7 days after Buyer receives the Notice or prior to the closing, whichever first occurs, and the earnest money will be refunded to Buyer.

❑ (3)The Seller is not required to furnish the notice under the Texas Property Code.

C. SELLER'S DISCLOSURE OF LEAD-BASED PAINT AND LEAD-BASED PAINT HAZARDS is required by Federal law for a residential dwelling constructed prior to 1978.

D. ACCEPTANCE OF PROPERTY CONDITION: "As Is" means the present condition of the Property with any and all defects and without warranty except for the warranties of title and the warranties in this contract. Buyer's agreement to accept the Property As Is under Paragraph 7D(1) or (2) does not preclude Buyer from inspecting the Property under Paragraph 7A, from negotiating repairs or treatments in a subsequent amendment, or from terminating this contract during the Option Period, if any.

(Check one box only)

❑ (1) Buyer accepts the Property As Is.

❑ (2) Buyer accepts the Property As Is provided Seller, at Seller's expense, shall complete the following specific repairs and treatments: _______________________________________.
____.
(Do not insert general phrases, such as "subject to inspections" that do not identify specific repairs and treatments.)

E. LENDER REQUIRED REPAIRS AND TREATMENTS: Unless otherwise agreed in writing, neither party is obligated to pay for lender required repairs, which includes treatment for wood destroying insects. If the parties do not agree to pay for the lender required repairs or treatments, this contract will terminate and the earnest money will be refunded to Buyer. If the cost of lender required repairs and treatments exceeds 5% of the Sales Price, Buyer may terminate this contract and the earnest money will be refunded to Buyer.

F. COMPLETION OF REPAIRS AND TREATMENTS: Unless otherwise agreed in writing: (i) Seller shall complete all agreed repairs and treatments prior to the Closing Date; and (ii) all required permits must be obtained, and repairs and treatments must be performed by persons who are licensed to provide such repairs or treatments or, if no license is required by law, are commercially engaged in the trade of providing such repairs or treatments. At Buyer's election, any transferable warranties received by Seller with respect to the repairs and treatments will be transferred to Buyer at Buyer's expense. If Seller fails to complete any agreed repairs and treatments prior to the Closing Date, Buyer may exercise remedies under Paragraph 15 or extend the Closing Date up to 5 days if necessary for Seller to complete the repairs and treatments.

G. ENVIRONMENTAL MATTERS: Buyer is advised that the presence of wetlands, toxic substances, including asbestos and wastes or other environmental hazards, or the presence of a threatened or endangered species or its habitat may affect Buyer's intended use of the Property. If Buyer is concerned about these matters, an addendum promulgated by TREC or required by the parties should be used.

Initialed for identification by Buyer______ ______ and Seller ______ ______ TREC NO. 20-14

FIGURE 6-5 (Continued)

Contract Concerning ____ Page 5 of 10 2-12-18
(Address of Property)

H. RESIDENTIAL SERVICE CONTRACTS: Buyer may purchase a residential service contract from a residential service company licensed by TREC. If Buyer purchases a residential service contract, Seller shall reimburse Buyer at closing for the cost of the residential service contract in an amount not exceeding $_______________. Buyer should review any residential service contract for the scope of coverage, exclusions and limitations. **The purchase of a residential service contract is optional. Similar coverage may be purchased from various companies authorized to do business in Texas.**

8. BROKERS' FEES: All obligations of the parties for payment of brokers' fees are contained in separate written agreements.

9. CLOSING:

A. The closing of the sale will be on or before ______________________, 20____, or within 7 days after objections made under Paragraph 6D have been cured or waived, whichever date is later (Closing Date). If either party fails to close the sale by the Closing Date, the non-defaulting party may exercise the remedies contained in Paragraph 15.

B. At closing:

(1) Seller shall execute and deliver a general warranty deed conveying title to the Property to Buyer and showing no additional exceptions to those permitted in Paragraph 6 and furnish tax statements or certificates showing no delinquent taxes on the Property.

(2) Buyer shall pay the Sales Price in good funds acceptable to the escrow agent.

(3) Seller and Buyer shall execute and deliver any notices, statements, certificates, affidavits, releases, loan documents and other documents reasonably required for the closing of the sale and the issuance of the Title Policy.

(4) There will be no liens, assessments, or security interests against the Property which will not be satisfied out of the sales proceeds unless securing the payment of any loans assumed by Buyer and assumed loans will not be in default.

(5)If the Property is subject to a residential lease, Seller shall transfer security deposits (as defined under §92.102, Property Code), if any, to Buyer. In such an event, Buyer shall deliver to the tenant a signed statement acknowledging that the Buyer has acquired the Property and is responsible for the return of the security deposit, and specifying the exact dollar amount of the security deposit.

10. POSSESSION:

A. Buyer's Possession: Seller shall deliver to Buyer possession of the Property in its present or required condition, ordinary wear and tear excepted: ❑upon closing and funding ❑according to a temporary residential lease form promulgated by TREC or other written lease required by the parties. Any possession by Buyer prior to closing or by Seller after closing which is not authorized by a written lease will establish a tenancy at sufferance relationship between the parties. **Consult your insurance agent prior to change of ownership and possession because insurance coverage may be limited or terminated. The absence of a written lease or appropriate insurance coverage may expose the parties to economic loss.**

B. Leases:

(1)After the Effective Date, Seller may not execute any lease (including but not limited to mineral leases) or convey any interest in the Property without Buyer's written consent.

(2) If the Property is subject to any lease to which Seller is a party, Seller shall deliver to Buyer copies of the lease(s) and any move-in condition form signed by the tenant within 7 days after the Effective Date of the contract.

11. SPECIAL PROVISIONS: (Insert only factual statements and business details applicable to the sale. TREC rules prohibit license holders from adding factual statements or business details for which a contract addendum, lease or other form has been promulgated by TREC for mandatory use.)

12. SETTLEMENT AND OTHER EXPENSES:

A. The following expenses must be paid at or prior to closing:

(1) Expenses payable by Seller (Seller's Expenses):

(a) Releases of existing liens, including prepayment penalties and recording fees; release of Seller's loan liability; tax statements or certificates; preparation of deed; one-half of escrow fee; and other expenses payable by Seller under this contract.

(b) Seller shall also pay an amount not to exceed $_____________ to be applied in the following order: Buyer's Expenses which Buyer is prohibited from paying by FHA, VA, Texas Veterans Land Board or other governmental loan programs, and then to other Buyer's Expenses as allowed by the lender.

Initialed for identification by Buyer______ ______ and Seller _______ ______ TREC NO. 20-14

FIGURE 6-5 (Continued)

(2) Expenses payable by Buyer (Buyer's Expenses): Appraisal fees; loan application fees; origination charges; credit reports; preparation of loan documents; interest on the notes from date of disbursement to one month prior to dates of first monthly payments; recording fees; copies of easements and restrictions; loan title policy with endorsements required by lender; loan-related inspection fees; photos; amortization schedules; one-half of escrow fee; all prepaid items, including required premiums for flood and hazard insurance, reserve deposits for insurance, ad valorem taxes and special governmental assessments; final compliance inspection; courier fee; repair inspection; underwriting fee; wire transfer fee; expenses incident to any loan; Private Mortgage Insurance Premium (PMI), VA Loan Funding Fee, or FHA Mortgage Insurance Premium (MIP) as required by the lender; and other expenses payable by Buyer under this contract.

B. If any expense exceeds an amount expressly stated in this contract for such expense to be paid by a party, that party may terminate this contract unless the other party agrees to pay such excess. Buyer may not pay charges and fees expressly prohibited by FHA, VA, Texas Veterans Land Board or other governmental loan program regulations.

13. PRORATIONS: Taxes for the current year, interest, maintenance fees, assessments, dues and rents will be prorated through the Closing Date. The tax proration may be calculated taking into consideration any change in exemptions that will affect the current year's taxes. If taxes for the current year vary from the amount prorated at closing, the parties shall adjust the prorations when tax statements for the current year are available. If taxes are not paid at or prior to closing, Buyer shall pay taxes for the current year.

14. CASUALTY LOSS: If any part of the Property is damaged or destroyed by fire or other casualty after the Effective Date of this contract, Seller shall restore the Property to its previous condition as soon as reasonably possible, but in any event by the Closing Date. If Seller fails to do so due to factors beyond Seller's control, Buyer may (a) terminate this contract and the earnest money will be refunded to Buyer (b) extend the time for performance up to 15 days and the Closing Date will be extended as necessary or (c) accept the Property in its damaged condition with an assignment of insurance proceeds, if permitted by Seller's insurance carrier, and receive credit from Seller at closing in the amount of the deductible under the insurance policy. Seller's obligations under this paragraph are independent of any other obligations of Seller under this contract.

15. DEFAULT: If Buyer fails to comply with this contract, Buyer will be in default, and Seller may (a) enforce specific performance, seek such other relief as may be provided by law, or both, or (b) terminate this contract and receive the earnest money as liquidated damages, thereby releasing both parties from this contract. If Seller fails to comply with this contract, Seller will be in default and Buyer may (a) enforce specific performance, seek such other relief as may be provided by law, or both, or (b) terminate this contract and receive the earnest money, thereby releasing both parties from this contract.

16. MEDIATION: It is the policy of the State of Texas to encourage resolution of disputes through alternative dispute resolution procedures such as mediation. Any dispute between Seller and Buyer related to this contract which is not resolved through informal discussion will be submitted to a mutually acceptable mediation service or provider. The parties to the mediation shall bear the mediation costs equally. This paragraph does not preclude a party from seeking equitable relief from a court of competent jurisdiction.

17. ATTORNEY'S FEES: A Buyer, Seller, Listing Broker, Other Broker, or escrow agent who prevails in any legal proceeding related to this contract is entitled to recover reasonable attorney's fees and all costs of such proceeding.

18. ESCROW:

A. ESCROW: The escrow agent is not (i) a party to this contract and does not have liability for the performance or nonperformance of any party to this contract, (ii) liable for interest on the earnest money and (iii) liable for the loss of any earnest money caused by the failure of any financial institution in which the earnest money has been deposited unless the financial institution is acting as escrow agent.

B. EXPENSES: At closing, the earnest money must be applied first to any cash down payment, then to Buyer's Expenses and any excess refunded to Buyer. If no closing occurs, escrow agent may: (i) require a written release of liability of the escrow agent from all parties, (ii) require payment of unpaid expenses incurred on behalf of a party, and (iii) only deduct from the earnest money the amount of unpaid expenses incurred on behalf of the party receiving the earnest money.

C. DEMAND: Upon termination of this contract, either party or the escrow agent may send a release of earnest money to each party and the parties shall execute counterparts of the release and deliver same to the escrow agent. If either party fails to execute the release, either party may make a written demand to the escrow agent for the earnest money. If only one party makes written demand for the earnest money, escrow agent shall promptly

FIGURE 6-5 (Continued)

Contract Concerning ______________________________ Page 7 of 10 2-12-18
(Address of Property)

provide a copy of the demand to the other party. If escrow agent does not receive written objection to the demand from the other party within 15 days, escrow agent may disburse the earnest money to the party making demand reduced by the amount of unpaid expenses incurred on behalf of the party receiving the earnest money and escrow agent may pay the same to the creditors. If escrow agent complies with the provisions of this paragraph, each party hereby releases escrow agent from all adverse claims related to the disbursal of the earnest money.

D. DAMAGES: Any party who wrongfully fails or refuses to sign a release acceptable to the escrow agent within 7 days of receipt of the request will be liable to the other party for (i) damages; (ii) the earnest money; (iii) reasonable attorney's fees; and (iv) all costs of suit.

E. NOTICES: Escrow agent's notices will be effective when sent in compliance with Paragraph 21. Notice of objection to the demand will be deemed effective upon receipt by escrow agent.

19. REPRESENTATIONS: All covenants, representations and warranties in this contract survive closing. If any representation of Seller in this contract is untrue on the Closing Date, Seller will be in default. Unless expressly prohibited by written agreement, Seller may continue to show the Property and receive, negotiate and accept back up offers.

20. FEDERAL TAX REQUIREMENTS: If Seller is a "foreign person," as defined by Internal Revenue Code and its regulations, or if Seller fails to deliver an affidavit or a certificate of non-foreign status to Buyer that Seller is not a "foreign person," then Buyer shall withhold from the sales proceeds an amount sufficient to comply with applicable tax law and deliver the same to the Internal Revenue Service together with appropriate tax forms. Internal Revenue Service regulations require filing written reports if currency in excess of specified amounts is received in the transaction.

21. NOTICES: All notices from one party to the other must be in writing and are effective when mailed to, hand-delivered at, or transmitted by fax or electronic transmission as follows:

To Buyer at: ______________________	**To Seller at:** ______________________
______________________	______________________
Phone: ( ) ______________	Phone: ( ) ______________
Fax: ( ) ______________	Fax: ( ) ______________
E-mail: ______________	E-mail: ______________

22. AGREEMENT OF PARTIES: This contract contains the entire agreement of the parties and cannot be changed except by their written agreement. Addenda which are a part of this contract are (Check all applicable boxes):

- ❑ Third Party Financing Addendum
- ❑ Seller Financing Addendum
- ❑ Addendum for Property Subject to Mandatory Membership in a Property Owners Association
- ❑ Buyer's Temporary Residential Lease
- ❑ Loan Assumption Addendum
- ❑ Addendum for Sale of Other Property by Buyer
- ❑ Addendum for Reservation of Oil, Gas and Other Minerals
- ❑ Addendum for "Back-Up" Contract
- ❑ Addendum for Coastal Area Property
- ❑ Addendum for Authorizing Hydrostatic Testing
- ❑ Addendum Concerning Right to Terminate Due to Lender's Appraisal
- ❑ Environmental Assessment, Threatened or Endangered Species and Wetlands Addendum
- ❑ Seller's Temporary Residential Lease
- ❑ Short Sale Addendum
- ❑ Addendum for Property Located Seaward of the Gulf Intracoastal Waterway
- ❑ Addendum for Seller's Disclosure of Information on Lead-based Paint and Lead-based Paint Hazards as Required by Federal Law
- ❑ Addendum for Property in a Propane Gas System Service Area
- ❑ Other (list): ______________________

Initialed for identification by Buyer______ ______ and Seller _______ ______ TREC NO. 20-14

FIGURE 6-5 (Continued)

23. TERMINATION OPTION: For nominal consideration, the receipt of which is hereby acknowledged by Seller, and Buyer's agreement to pay Seller $________________ (Option Fee) within 3 days after the Effective Date of this contract, Seller grants Buyer the unrestricted right to terminate this contract by giving notice of termination to Seller within _______ days after the Effective Date of this contract (Option Period). Notices under this paragraph must be given by 5:00 p.m. (local time where the Property is located) by the date specified. If no dollar amount is stated as the Option Fee or if Buyer fails to pay the Option Fee to Seller within the time prescribed, this paragraph will not be a part of this contract and Buyer shall not have the unrestricted right to terminate this contract. If Buyer gives notice of termination within the time prescribed, the Option Fee will not be refunded; however, any earnest money will be refunded to Buyer. The Option Fee ❑will ❑will not be credited to the Sales Price at closing. **Time is of the essence for this paragraph and strict compliance with the time for performance is required.**

24. CONSULT AN ATTORNEY BEFORE SIGNING: TREC rules prohibit real estate license holders from giving legal advice. READ THIS CONTRACT CAREFULLY.

Buyer's Attorney is: ______________________	Seller's Attorney is: ______________________
______________________	______________________
Phone: ( ) ______________________	Phone: ( ) ______________________
Fax: ( ) ______________________	Fax: ( ) ______________________
E-mail: ______________________	E-mail: ______________________

EXECUTED the ______day of ______________________, 20____ (Effective Date).
(BROKER: FILL IN THE DATE OF FINAL ACCEPTANCE.)

______________________ Buyer	______________________ Seller
______________________ Buyer	______________________ Seller

TREC
TEXAS REAL ESTATE COMMISSION

The form of this contract has been approved by the Texas Real Estate Commission. TREC forms are intended for use only by trained real estate license holders. No representation is made as to the legal validity or adequacy of any provision in any specific transactions. It is not intended for complex transactions. Texas Real Estate Commission, P.O. Box 12188, Austin, TX 78711-2188, (512) 936-3000 (http://www.trec.texas.gov) TREC NO. 20-14. This form replaces TREC NO. 20-13.

FIGURE 6-5 (Continued)

Contract Concerning ______________________________ Page 9 of 10 2-12-18
(Address of Property)

BROKER INFORMATION
(Print name(s) only. Do not sign)

Other Broker Firm — License No.	Listing Broker Firm — License No.
represents ❑ Buyer only as Buyer's agent ❑ Seller as Listing Broker's subagent	represents ❑ Seller and Buyer as an intermediary ❑ Seller only as Seller's agent
Associate's Name — License No.	Listing Associate's Name — License No.
Associate's Email Address — Phone	Listing Associate's Email Address — Phone
Licensed Supervisor of Associate — License No.	Licensed Supervisor of Listing Associate — License No.
Other Broker's Address — Phone	Listing Broker's Office Address — Phone
City — State — Zip	City — State — Zip
	Selling Associate's Name — License No.
	Selling Associate's Email Address — Phone
	Licensed Supervisor of Selling Associate — License No.
	Selling Associate's Office Address
	City — State — Zip

Listing Broker has agreed to pay Other Broker ______________________ of the total sales price when the Listing Broker's fee is received. Escrow agent is authorized and directed to pay Other Broker from Listing Broker's fee at closing.

TREC NO. 20-14

FIGURE 6-5 (Continued)

OPTION FEE RECEIPT

Receipt of $______________ (Option Fee) in the form of ______________________________
is acknowledged.

Seller or Listing Broker ______________ Date ______________

EARNEST MONEY RECEIPT

Receipt of $______________ Earnest Money in the form of ______________________________
is acknowledged.

Escrow Agent Received by ______________ Email Address Date/Time ______________

Address ______________ Phone ______________

City State Zip ______________ Fax ______________

CONTRACT RECEIPT

Receipt of the Contract is acknowledged.

Escrow Agent Received by ______________ Email Address Date ______________

Address ______________ Phone ______________

City State Zip ______________ Fax ______________

ADDITIONAL EARNEST MONEY RECEIPT

Receipt of $______________ additional Earnest Money in the form of ______________________________
is acknowledged.

Escrow Agent Received by ______________ Email Address Date/Time ______________

Address ______________ Phone ______________

City State Zip ______________ Fax ______________

TREC NO. 20-14

FIGURE 6-5 (Continued)

promulgated sales contract forms, the most commonly used form is the One to Four Family Residential Contract (TREC 20-14), shown in figure 6-5. Therefore, the remainder of this chapter will highlight key paragraphs within this contract. Contract examples utilizing this form are provided in the appendix.

FINANCING INFORMATION

The sales price indicated in paragraph 3 of form 20-14 takes into account the down payment to be presented at closing and the financed amount discussed in more detail in the appropriate addenda. It is important to note that with regard to the down payment that this amount is not necessarily going to be the same amount as the earnest money. If the deal goes through to closing, the earnest money, if any, will be applied first to the down payment. In most cases, there are no set guidelines as to what amounts are used for the down payment and the financed amount. However, there are preset amounts established for FHA transactions. Paragraph 3, however, is essentially the same in all of the promulgated residential sales contract forms.

Eight payment methods are anticipated by the promulgated residential sales contract. These include all cash, seller financing, assumption, third-party conventional financing, VA financing, FHA financing, USDA-guaranteed financing, and reverse mortgage financing. For an all-cash transaction, paragraph 3B will not be used. A seller financing transaction will utilize the Seller Financing Addendum and the appropriate box will be marked in paragraph 3B. An assumption transaction will utilize the Loan Assumption Addendum and the appropriate box will be marked in paragraph 3B. And the Third Party Financing Addendum will be used for the remaining five financing options with the appropriate box marked accordingly.

DISCLOSURES

Seller's Disclosure Notice

One of the most important disclosures found in the promulgated residential sales contract relates to the Seller's Disclosure Notice. A **Seller's Disclosure Notice** is a typical addendum attached to the listing agreement rather than the sales contract. Within the Seller's Disclosure Notice the seller indicates everything he or she knows about the property and represents that the document was completed to the best of his or her knowledge. The Texas Property Code requires a seller of residential real property that consists of no more than one dwelling unit in Texas to give the buyer written notice of the property condition.[1] A sample seller disclosure notice form from the Texas Real Estate Commission is in figure 6-6.

The seller must complete this notice in its entirely. It is important that the seller's handwriting be the only one on the disclosure provisions because the agent is

[1] Tex. Prop. Code § 5.008(a).

8-7-2017

APPROVED BY THE TEXAS REAL ESTATE COMMISSION (TREC)

EQUAL HOUSING OPPORTUNITY

SELLER'S DISCLOSURE NOTICE

CONCERNING THE PROPERTY AT____
(Street Address and City)

THIS NOTICE IS A DISCLOSURE OF SELLER'S KNOWLEDGE OF THE CONDITION OF THE PROPERTY AS OF THE DATE SIGNED BY SELLER AND IS NOT A SUBSTITUTE FOR ANY INSPECTIONS OR WARRANTIES THE PURCHASER MAY WISH TO OBTAIN. IT IS NOT A WARRANTY OF ANY KIND BY SELLER OR SELLER'S AGENTS.

Seller ☐ is ☐ is not occupying the Property. If unoccupied, how long since Seller has occupied the Property? ________

1. The Property has the items checked below [Write Yes (Y), No (N), or Unknown (U)]:

____Range	____Oven	____Microwave
____Dishwasher	____Trash Compactor	____Disposal
____Washer/Dryer Hookups	____Window Screens	____Rain Gutters
____Security System	____Fire Detection Equipment	____Intercom System
	____Smoke Detector	
	____Smoke Detector-Hearing Impaired	
	____Carbon Monoxide Alarm	
	____Emergency Escape Ladder(s)	
____TV Antenna	____Cable TV Wiring	____Satellite Dish
____Ceiling Fan(s)	____Attic Fan(s)	____Exhaust Fan(s)
____Central A/C	____Central Heating	____Wall/Window Air Conditioning
____Plumbing System	____Septic System	____Public Sewer System
____Patio/Decking	____Outdoor Grill	____Fences
____Pool	____Sauna	____Spa ____Hot Tub
____Pool Equipment	____Pool Heater	____Automatic Lawn Sprinkler System
____Fireplace(s) & Chimney (Wood burning)		____Fireplace(s) & Chimney (Mock)
____Natural Gas Lines		____Gas Fixtures
____Liquid Propane Gas	____LP Community (Captive)	____LP on Property
Garage: ____Attached	____Not Attached	____Carport
Garage Door Opener(s):	____Electronic	____Control(s)
Water Heater:	____Gas	____Electric
Water Supply: ____City	____Well ____MUD	____Co-op

Roof Type:______________________________ Age:__________________ (approx.)

Are you (Seller) aware of any of the above items that are not in working condition, that have known defects, or that are in need of repair? ☐ Yes ☐ No ☐ Unknown. If yes, then describe. (Attach additional sheets if necessary):____________

____

____

____

TREC No. OP-H

FIGURE 6-6 Seller's Disclosure Notice

Seller's Disclosure Notice Concerning the Property at ______________________ Page 2 8-7-2017
(Street Address and City)

2. Does the property have working smoke detectors installed in accordance with the smoke detector requirements of Chapter 766, Health and Safety Code? ☐ Yes ☐ No ☐ Unknown. If the answer to this question is no or unknown, explain (Attach additional sheets if necessary): ______________________

* Chapter 766 of the Health and Safety Code requires one-family or two-family dwellings to have working smoke detectors installed in accordance with the requirements of the building code in effect in the area in which the dwelling is located, including performance, location, and power source requirements. If you do not know the building code requirements in effect in your area, you may check unknown above or contact your local building official for more information. A buyer may require a seller to install smoke detectors for the hearing impaired if: (1) the buyer or a member of the buyer's family who will reside in the dwelling is hearing impaired; (2) the buyer gives the seller written evidence of the hearing impairment from a licensed physician; and (3) within 10 days after the effective date, the buyer makes a written request for the seller to install smoke detectors for the hearing impaired and specifies the locations for the installation. The parties may agree who will bear the cost of installing the smoke detectors and which brand of smoke detectors to install.

3. Are you (Seller) aware of any known defects/malfunctions in any of the following? Write Yes (Y) if you are aware, write No (N) if you are not aware.

____Interior Walls	____Ceilings	____Floors
____Exterior Walls	____Doors	____Windows
____Roof	____Foundation/Slab(s)	____Sidewalks
____Walls/Fences	____Driveways	____Intercom System
____Plumbing/Sewers/Septics	____Electrical Systems	____Lighting Fixtures

____Other Structural Components (Describe): ______________________

If the answer to any of the above is yes, explain. (Attach additional sheets if necessary): ______________________

4. Are you (Seller) aware of any of the following conditions? Write Yes (Y) if you are aware, write No (N) if you are not aware.

____Active Termites (includes wood destroying insects)	____Previous Structural or Roof Repair
____Termite or Wood Rot Damage Needing Repair	____Hazardous or Toxic Waste
____Previous Termite Damage	____Asbestos Components
____Previous Termite Treatment	____Urea-formaldehyde Insulation
____Previous Flooding	____Radon Gas
____Improper Drainage	____Lead Based Paint
____Water Penetration	____Aluminum Wiring
____Located in 100-Year Floodplain	____Previous Fires
____Present Flood Insurance Coverage	____Unplatted Easements
____Landfill, Settling, Soil Movement, Fault Lines	____Subsurface Structure or Pits
____Single Blockable Main Drain in Pool/Hot Tub/Spa*	____Previous Use of Premises for Manufacture of Methamphetamine

If the answer to any of the above is yes, explain. (Attach additional sheets if necessary): ______________________

* A single blockable main drain may cause a suction entrapment hazard for an individual.

TREC No. OP-H

FIGURE 6-6 (Continued)

Seller's Disclosure Notice Concerning the Property at ______________________________ Page 2 8-7-2017
(Street Address and City)

2. Does the property have working smoke detectors installed in accordance with the smoke detector requirements of Chapter 766, Health and Safety Code? ☐ Yes ☐ No ☐ Unknown. If the answer to this question is no or unknown, explain (Attach additional sheets if necessary): ______________________________

* Chapter 766 of the Health and Safety Code requires one-family or two-family dwellings to have working smoke detectors installed in accordance with the requirements of the building code in effect in the area in which the dwelling is located, including performance, location, and power source requirements. If you do not know the building code requirements in effect in your area, you may check unknown above or contact your local building official for more information. A buyer may require a seller to install smoke detectors for the hearing impaired if: (1) the buyer or a member of the buyer's family who will reside in the dwelling is hearing impaired; (2) the buyer gives the seller written evidence of the hearing impairment from a licensed physician; and (3) within 10 days after the effective date, the buyer makes a written request for the seller to install smoke detectors for the hearing impaired and specifies the locations for the installation. The parties may agree who will bear the cost of installing the smoke detectors and which brand of smoke detectors to install.

3. Are you (Seller) aware of any known defects/malfunctions in any of the following? Write Yes (Y) if you are aware, write No (N) if you are not aware.

_____Interior Walls	_____Ceilings	_____Floors
_____Exterior Walls	_____Doors	_____Windows
_____Roof	_____Foundation/Slab(s)	_____Sidewalks
_____Walls/Fences	_____Driveways	_____Intercom System
_____Plumbing/Sewers/Septics	_____Electrical Systems	_____Lighting Fixtures

_____Other Structural Components (Describe): ______________________________

If the answer to any of the above is yes, explain. (Attach additional sheets if necessary): ______________________________

4. Are you (Seller) aware of any of the following conditions? Write Yes (Y) if you are aware, write No (N) if you are not aware.

_____Active Termites (includes wood destroying insects)	_____Previous Structural or Roof Repair
_____Termite or Wood Rot Damage Needing Repair	_____Hazardous or Toxic Waste
_____Previous Termite Damage	_____Asbestos Components
_____Previous Termite Treatment	_____Urea-formaldehyde Insulation
_____Previous Flooding	_____Radon Gas
_____Improper Drainage	_____Lead Based Paint
_____Water Penetration	_____Aluminum Wiring
_____Located in 100-Year Floodplain	_____Previous Fires
_____Present Flood Insurance Coverage	_____Unplatted Easements
_____Landfill, Settling, Soil Movement, Fault Lines	_____Subsurface Structure or Pits
_____Single Blockable Main Drain in Pool/Hot Tub/Spa*	_____Previous Use of Premises for Manufacture of Methamphetamine

If the answer to any of the above is yes, explain. (Attach additional sheets if necessary): ______________________________

* A single blockable main drain may cause a suction entrapment hazard for an individual.

TREC No. OP-H

FIGURE 6-6 (Continued)

entitled to rely on any statements made by the seller in the notice, and the agent may be indemnified for any loss he or she may experience in reliance on the disclosure.

This notice must be delivered to the buyer on or before the effective date of the contract, which would be indicated in paragraph 7B(1) of the promulgated residential sales contract. Certain remedies are provided to a prospective purchaser in the real estate sales contract who does not receive this notice. More specifically, according to paragraph 7B(2) within a specified number of days after the effective date of the contract, the seller must deliver the notice to the buyer. If the buyer does not receive the notice, the buyer may terminate the contract at any time prior to the closing and the earnest money will be refunded to the buyer. If the seller does deliver the notice, the buyer may terminate the contract for any reason within seven days after the buyer receives the notice or prior to the closing, whichever first occurs, and the earnest money will be refunded to the buyer.

Neither the seller nor the seller's agent, however, has a duty to disclose information related to whether a death occurred on the premises by natural causes, suicide, or an accident unrelated to the condition of the property. Furthermore, neither the seller nor the seller's agent has a duty to disclose whether a previous occupant of the premises had, may have had, has, or may have AIDS, HIV-related illnesses, or HIV infection.[2]

There are also instances where the seller is not required to provide a seller disclosure notice. These instances apply to transfers (1) pursuant to a court order or foreclosure sale; (2) by a trustee in bankruptcy; (3) to a mortgagee by a mortgagor or successor in interest, or to a beneficiary of a deed of trust by a trustor or successor in interest; (4) by a mortgagee or a beneficiary under a deed of trust who has acquired the real property at a sale conducted pursuant to a power of sale under a deed of trust or a sale pursuant to a court ordered foreclosure or has acquired the real property by a deed in lieu of foreclosure; (5) by a fiduciary in the course of the administration of a decedent's estate, guardianship, conservatorship, or trust; (6) from one co-owner to one or more other co-owners; (7) made to a spouse or to a person or persons in the lineal line of consanguinity of one or more of the transferors; (8) between spouses resulting from a decree of dissolution of marriage or a decree of legal separation or from a property settlement agreement incident to such decree; (9) to or from any governmental entity; (10) of a new residence of not more than one dwelling unit which has not previously been occupied for residential purposes; and (11) transfers of real property where the value of any dwelling does not exceed five percent (5%) of the value of the property.[3] If the seller falls under one of these exceptions, the seller would indicate such in paragraph 7B(3) of the promulgated residential sales contract.

---

[2] Tex. Prop. Code § 5.008(c).

[3] Tex. Prop. Code § 5.008(e).

Miscellaneous Disclosures

There are also several miscellaneous disclosures and notices provided in the contract. Several notices are provided in paragraph 6E. Paragraph 6E(1) advises the purchaser to have an abstract of title reviewed by an attorney of the purchaser's choice or to obtain an owner's policy of title insurance. According to the Texas Occupations Code, this notice must be given in writing when an offer to purchase is signed.[4] Failure to give this notice can result in loss of commission to the broker.[5] Therefore, many brokers choose to have the buyer sign a form similar to the TREC Notice to Prospective Buyer (TREC OP-C). See figure 6-7.

Paragraph 6E(2) provides information on whether the property is or is not subject to mandatory membership in a property owners association. Notice is given that assessments are mandatory and failure to pay such assessments can result in a lien on and the foreclosure of the property. In addition, paragraph 6E(3) notifies the buyer that the seller is required to deliver for signature a statutory notice related to the tax rate, bonded indebtedness, or standby fee for a property located in a utility or other statutorily created district providing water, sewer, drainage, or flood control facilities and services under the Texas Water Code. This type of disclosure is typically seen with a municipal utility district (MUD).

Paragraph 6E(4) notifies the buyer that section 33.135 of the Texas Natural Resources Code requires that a notice regarding coastal area property be included as part of the contract. The Addendum for Coastal Area Property has been promulgated for this purpose. Paragraph 6E(5) is a general notice concerning possible annexation of the property subject to the contract. If a buyer is concerned, he or she can contact all municipalities in the area for information.

Paragraph 6E(6) applies any time the seller is selling unimproved property in a statutorily created district. The buyer is obligated to determine whether the property is located within a certificated service area and, if so, to contact the utility provider directly about costs. In addition, paragraph 6E(7) applies any time the property is subject to a municipality assessment for improvements. The buyer is provided notice and has the opportunity to contact the municipality for the amount of the assessment. Failure to pay the assessment can result in a lien on the property and ultimate foreclosure.

Paragraph 6E(8) concerns the transfer fee notification provided for by the Texas Property Code. Paragraph 6E(9) applies any time the property is located in a propane gas system service area owned by a distribution system retailer. The TREC Addendum for Property in a Propane Gas System Service Area (TREC 47-0) is used to provide the requisite notice to the buyer.

---

[4] Tex. Occ. Code § 1101.555.

[5] Tex. Occ. Code § 1101.806.

APPROVED BY THE TEXAS REAL ESTATE COMMISSION 10-10-11

NOTICE TO PROSPECTIVE BUYER

As required by law, I advise you to have the abstract covering the property known as ____ (Address) examined by an attorney of your own selection OR you should be furnished with or obtain a policy of title insurance.

If the property is situated in a Utility District, Chapter 49 of the Texas Water Code requires you to sign and acknowledge the statutory notice from the seller of the property relating to the tax rate, bonded indebtedness or standby fee of the District.

DATED: ______________________, _________.

____
Brokerage Company Name

____
Broker or Sales Associate

I have received a copy of this **NOTICE TO PROSPECTIVE BUYER.**

____
Prospective Buyer

____
Prospective Buyer

This form has been approved by the Texas Real Estate Commission (TREC) for use when a contract of sale has not been promulgated by TREC. The form should be presented before an offer to purchase is signed by the prospective buyer. Texas real Estate Commission, P.O. Box 12188, Austin, Texas 78711-2188, 512-936-3000 (http://www.trec.texas.gov). TREC Notice to Prospective Buyer. OP-C replaces MA-C.

TREC NO. OP-C

FIGURE 6-7 Notice to Prospective Buyer
Source: Reprinted with permission of Texas Real Estate Commission

The notice in paragraph 6E(10) came about as a result of new Texas Property Code section 5.019, which addresses the issue of water level fluctuations. If the seller does not give notice to the buyer before the effective date of the contract, the buyer can terminate the contract for any reason within seven days after receiving the notice from the seller or the information from another person.

In addition to the notices provided in paragraph 6E, there are also general environmental disclosures provided in the contract. For instance, paragraph 7G points out that if the purchaser is concerned about wetlands, toxic substances, or threatened or endangered species on the premises that may affect his or her use of the property, the Environmental Assessment, Threatened or Endangered Species, and Wetlands Addendum should be used. It is noted in paragraph 7C that a lead-based paint disclosure should be attached if the residence was constructed prior to 1978.

Furthermore, disclosures concerning certain federal tax requirements are found in paragraph 20 of the sales contract. More specifically, paragraph 20 provides that if the seller is a foreign person or fails to deliver an affidavit that he or she is not a foreign person, the buyer may withhold the taxes from the sales proceeds and deliver them to the IRS with the appropriate forms. In addition, if cash in excess of $10,000 is received in the transaction, this fact must be reported to the IRS along with the appropriate IRS form. In large cash transactions, it is wise to request that the individual take the funds to the bank and get a cashier's check.

CONVEYANCE OF THE PROPERTY

When the real estate transaction is closed, the seller's property will be conveyed to the buyer by deed. However, the conveyance can only occur if certain issues associated with the property are resolved. The seller should have fee simple absolute title to the entire property. Anything less than fee simple absolute title, if known, should have been brought to the buyer's attention before negotiations. The seller's deed alone may not reflect the entire title interest. This can occur where a separate conveyance is made by the seller, such as conveyance of a mineral estate, after the seller acquired title. Paragraph 10B(1) provides that after the effective date of the contract, the seller may not execute any lease or convey any interest in the property without the buyer's written consent.

In addition, the property cannot be conveyed if there is a third party with a right to purchase or acquire the property by a right of first refusal or other agreement unless there is documentation in place from that third party that he or she does not wish to exercise the right.

The property can be sold if there is a tenant on the premises; however, the buyer will take ownership subject to the lease. Paragraph 10B(2) provides that if the property is subject to a lease the seller must deliver to the buyer copies of the lease and any move-in condition form signed by the tenant within seven days after the effective date of the contract. In addition, paragraph 9B of the sales contract provides that if the property is subject to a lease, the seller must transfer the security deposits to the buyer at closing. The buyer must also deliver to the tenant a signed statement acknowledging that the buyer has acquired the property and is responsible for the return of the security deposit in the appropriate dollar amount.

Furthermore, if there are any liens that cannot be satisfied by the sales proceeds, then the property cannot be conveyed. Paragraph 19 of the sales contract contains the seller's representation that there will be no liens, assessments, or security interests affecting the property that will not be satisfied out of the proceeds of the sale. The seller will be considered in default if the representations are untrue on the closing date because the conveyance will not be possible, unless an assumption transaction is involved. In addition, paragraph 9B requires that the seller show that there are no delinquent taxes on the property at the time of closing.

If all of the issues are resolved as of the closing date, then conveyance of the property will be by warranty deed unless otherwise provided in the contract. Both general and special warranty deeds will be discussed in a later chapter.

SIGNATURES

In many real estate sales transactions, the offer is completed on a promulgated sales contract form by the buyer, and the offer is then communicated to the seller. Once the seller receives the offer, he or she may either reject the offer, counteroffer with new terms, or accept the offer as proposed. If the seller chooses to accept the offer, he or she should indicate the acceptance on the same form on which the offer was proposed by initialing each page, signing the signature page, and including the date of final acceptance. See figure 6-8. He or she should then make a copy and send the final contract back to the buyer. Of course, there may be license holders acting as selling and/or listing agents involved in these communications.

A similar situation that arises more frequently in real estate transactions involves acceptance of a counteroffer. In a real estate sales transaction, the buyer or the buyer's representative proposes an offer to purchase the seller's property to the seller or the seller's representative, if any. This offer is usually prepared on a standard form. Upon receipt of the offer in a counteroffer situation, the seller makes changes to the offer on the same standard form, initials the change and includes the date and time next to the change. Each page is initialed and the signature page is signed, but no final acceptance date is included at this stage. The seller then proposes the new offer back to the buyer or the buyer's representative. With the counteroffer, the seller becomes the offeror and the buyer becomes the offeree. The buyer has the option to reject the offer, counteroffer with new terms, or accept the offer as proposed. If the buyer chooses to accept

Steps for Negotiating a Real Estate Sales Contract
Order for Completion of the Initial Blanks, Signature Lines, and Effective Date of the Real Estate Contracts

Initial Offer Proposed by the Buyer to the Seller

• (page 1) • 3. SALES PRICE • C. Sales Price $60,000.00 • Buyer BB Seller ___	• (signature page) • Executed the ____ day of ___, 20__. • Bob Buyer ________ • Buyer Seller • ________ ________ • Buyer Seller

Seller's Acceptance of the Buyer's Initial Offer

• (page 1) • 3. SALES PRICE • C. Sales Price $60,000.00 • Buyer BB Seller SS	• (signature page) • Executed the 15th day of May, 2014. • Bob Buyer Sam Seller • Buyer Seller • ________ ________ • Buyer Seller

FIGURE 6-8 Accepting an Offer
Source: © 2021 Mbition LLC

the counteroffer, he or she should indicate the acceptance on the same form on which the offer was proposed by including his or her initials next to the change along with the date and time. The final acceptance date will also be included. See figure 6-9. He or she will then make a copy and send the final contract back to the seller.

STATUTE OF FRAUDS

The **Statute of Frauds** arose as an effort to prevent fraud and perjury as to the actual terms of a contract by requiring certain contracts to be in writing and signed by the

Steps for Negotiating a Real Estate Sales Contract
Order for Completion of the Initial Blanks, Signature Lines, and Effective Date of the Real Estate Contracts

Initial Offer Proposed by the Buyer to the Seller

• (page 1) • 3. SALES PRICE • C. Sales Price $60,000.00 • Buyer BB Seller ___	• (signature page) • Executed the ____ day of ____, 20__. • Bob Buyer ________ • Buyer Seller • ________ ________ • Buyer Seller

Seller's Counteroffer of the Buyer's Initial Offer

• (page 1) • 3. SALES PRICE • C. Sales Price ~~$60,000.00~~ SS $65,000.00 5/13/14 8:30am • Buyer BB Seller SS	• (signature page) • Executed the ____ day of ____, 20__. • Bob Buyer Sam Seller • Buyer Seller • ________ ________ • Buyer Seller

Buyer's Acceptance of the Seller's Counteroffer

• (page 1) • 3. SALES PRICE • C. Sales Price ~~$60,000.00~~ BB SS $65,000.00 5/15/14 5/13/14 2:15pm 8:30am • Buyer BB Seller SS	• (signature page) • Executed the 15th day of May, 20 14. • Bob Buyer Sam Seller • Buyer Seller • ________ ________ • Buyer Seller

FIGURE 6-9 Accepting a Counteroffer
Source: © 2021 Mbition LLC

party to be charged or by his or her authorized agent. A document satisfies the Statute of Frauds if it constitutes a memorandum. A memorandum is an instrument in writing that is signed by the party against whom enforcement is sought, or his or her representative. In addition, a memorandum should at least contain an identification of the land by an adequate property description, the price of the property, and a date for performance. The form of the writing, however, is immaterial.

Since the complexities of a real estate transaction make it prone to fraud, the Statute of Frauds is implicated in three types of contracts. This statute provides that contracts for the sale of goods priced at $500 or more, contracts for the sale of land, and contracts that cannot be performed within a year must be in writing to be enforceable in a court of law.

Contracts for the Sale of Goods

For contracts for the sale of goods of $500 or more, the Statute of Frauds requires that the contract be in writing. The pertinent parts of the statute follow:

> Except as otherwise provided in this section a contract for the sale of goods for the price of $500 or more is not enforceable by way of action or defense unless there is some writing sufficient to indicate that a contract for sale has been made between the parties and signed by the party against whom enforcement is sought or by his authorized agent or broker. A writing is not insufficient because it omits or incorrectly states a term agreed upon but the contract is not enforceable under this paragraph beyond the quantity of goods shown in such writing.[6]

For example, Anthony Seller and Grant Buyer enter into a residential real estate sales contract whereby Anthony Seller promises to convey his four-bedroom home to Grant Buyer in exchange for Grant Buyer's promise that he will convey the proceeds in the amount of $105,000. Subsequently, Anthony Seller orally promises to convey all of the furniture in the house to Grant Buyer in exchange for $4,000. The agreement is not reduced to writing. At the closing of the sale, Grant Buyer transfers the sales price to Anthony Seller along with a separate check for the $4,000 they had agreed to under their oral agreement. After the sale has funded, Grant Buyer finds that Anthony Seller failed to leave any of the furniture that had previously been agreed upon. In such a dispute, the oral contract would not be enforceable because of the failure of the parties to satisfy the Statute of Frauds, unless an exception applies.

To prevent violations of the Statute of Frauds where personal goods in excess of $500 are to be transferred in the sale, as well as to prevent the seller from failing to convey the goods, it is wise to reduce all such agreements to writing. A com-

[6] Tex. Bus. & Comm. Code § 2.201(a).

mon means by which a seller may convey personal property is by a separate bill of sale or a Non-realty Items Addendum.

Application to Contracts for the Sale of Land or Interests in Land

The Statute of Frauds also requires that contracts for the sale of land or interests in land be in writing to be enforceable by a court of law. For example, Barry Seller and Merna Buyer orally agree that Barry Seller will convey his home to Merna Buyer on January 10 in exchange for $92,500. Barry Seller fails to comply with the agreement. Merna Buyer attempts to seek relief in court. Under the Statute of Frauds, a contract for the sale of real estate must be in writing to be enforceable. Since the agreement in this case was oral, Merna Buyer will not be able to enforce the agreement unless an exception applies.

The specific provisions of Texas law which mandate this requirement follow:

(a) A promise or agreement described in subsection (b) of this section is not enforceable unless the promise or agreement, or a memorandum of it, is
  (1) in writing; and
  (2) signed by the person to be charged with the promise or agreement or by someone lawfully authorized to sign for him.

(b) Subsection (a) of this section applies to:
  (4) a contract for the sale of real estate;
  (5) a lease of real estate for a term longer than one year;
  (6) an agreement that is not to be performed within one year from the date of making the agreement;
  (7) a promise or agreement to pay a commission for the sale or purchase of:
    (A) an oil or gas mining lease;
    (B) an oil or gas royalty;
    (C) minerals; or
    (D) a mineral interest.[7]

Contracts Not to be Performed within One Year

For contracts that cannot possibly be performed within one year, the Statute of Frauds requires those contracts to be in writing. The specific provisions of this statute follow:

> A conveyance of an estate of inheritance, a freehold, or an estate for more than one year, in land and tenements, must be in writing and must be

[7] Tex. Bus. & Comm. Code § 26.01.

> subscribed and delivered by the conveyor or by the conveyor's agent authorized in writing.[8]

There are enough instances in Texas of individuals orally contracting to purchase real estate that there is a body of law that has developed to provide an exception to the writing requirement of the Statute of Frauds. This exception, known as the **part performance doctrine**, allows for the enforcement of an oral agreement that would normally fall within the provisions of the Statute of Frauds. In order to enforce the oral agreement, several elements must be present. The purchaser must show that (1) there was an oral agreement, (2) partial consideration was paid, (3) the purchaser took possession of the property, and (4) the purchaser made permanent and valuable improvements to the property.[9] In order for the improvements to be considered valuable, they must be substantial and add materially to the value of the property.

DEFAULT AND BREACH OF CONTRACT

In General

Once a contract has been formed, the parties to the contract must perform according to the terms of the agreement. In most situations, it is sufficient if the parties show that they are able, ready, and willing to perform. However there are instances where one party to the contract may fail to perform as promised. Where one party to the contract fails to perform as specified in the contract, either by failing or refusing to perform or merely by failing to perform by the time indicated in the contract, this party is said to have breached the contract. Breach of contract will, therefore, occur any time a party to the contract fails to perform without a legal excuse. Once a party has defaulted on performance under the contract, the non-defaulting party has a difficult decision to make. The breach will not only excuse performance by the non-defaulting party, but it will also entitle the party to recover for any damage he or she may have sustained due to the breach. This party must decide whether he or she wishes to seek enforcement by way of a negotiation process, by way of a lawsuit for breach of contract, or by any means specified in the contract. However, in order to entitle the non-defaulting party to enforce the agreement or recover damages for breach by the defaulting party, or to assert a claim or right under the contract, the non-defaulting party must show that he or she has performed or tendered performance, or that he or she has a legal excuse for not performing or tendering performance.

---

8 Tex. Prop. Code § 5.021.

9 Fandey v. Lee, 880 S.W.2d 164 (Tex. App.–El Paso 1994); Elizondo v. Gomez, 957 S.W.2d 862 (Tex. App.–San Antonio 1997).

Negotiation to prevent a lawsuit is a common and practical way of settling disputes between the parties, particularly in real estate transactions. The negotiation process can be helpful to separate the parties from the problem. In a typical negotiation, the interests of the individuals are identified. The parties may be interested in maintaining a long-term business relationship. They may also be interested in protecting their business reputation. In most cases, the reason the parties seek the negotiation process and even mediation rather than a lawsuit is because the cost of a lawsuit can be high. In addition, the non-defaulting party to the negotiation process may be interested in receiving the benefit of his or her bargain under the contract as well as fair treatment. The parties to a real estate sales transaction automatically agree to have their future disputes handled by some type of mediation if the Texas Real Estate Commission promulgated contract is used.

In many cases, the non-defaulting party may choose to file a lawsuit against the defaulting party for breach of contract. There also may be additional claims against the defaulting party that the non-defaulting party would like to assert, such as an action for fraud.

General and Anticipatory Breach

There are two types of breach of contract that might be applicable in a breach of contract action. The most common type of breach of contract is a general breach of contract. A **general breach of contract** arises where a party to the contract fails to perform on the date and time indicated for performance. For example, the seller and the prospective purchaser enter into a contract for the sale and purchase of the seller's property. The parties are ready to settle the transaction in five days. On the day of closing, the buyer fails to appear to tender performance under the contract. This failure to close is a default under the contract, and the seller in this instance may seek to recover any damages suffered in a breach of contract action against the prospective purchaser.

Breach of contract can also occur by an anticipatory repudiation. **Anticipatory repudiation**, or anticipatory breach, is a breach of contract that occurs before the time for performance is due under the contract. In order to constitute an anticipatory breach, three elements must exist. First, the renunciation must be made before the time for performance is due. Second, the defaulting party must make the renunciation with positive and unconditional words or actions that evidence the party's desire to breach. Third, the words must be unequivocal, that is, understood. For example, Betty Buyer and Sam Seller enter into a contract for the sale and purchase of Sam Seller's home for $65,000. Closing on the property is scheduled in one week. The day before closing, Betty Buyer calls Sam Seller to tell him that she will not be there at closing to present the money. Betty Buyer's anticipation of her breach on the date for performance, the closing date, constitutes a breach of contract in the absence of a valid legal excuse.

REMEDIES

In General

The general rule for recovery of a remedy for breach of contract is to put the non-defaulting party in the position that he or she would have been in had the contract been performed. For example, the promulgated residential sales contract provides for the rights and remedies of each party in the case of default. Paragraph 15 provides that if the buyer defaults under the contract, the seller may (a) enforce specific performance, seek other relief as provided by law, or both or (b) terminate the contract and receive the earnest money as liquidated damages. If the seller defaults under the contract, the buyer may (a) enforce specific performance, seek other relief as provided by law, or both, or (b) terminate the contract and receive the earnest money back.

Damages

In an action for breach of contract, the non-defaulting party may seek damages as a result of the breach. **Damages** are pecuniary compensation that can be recovered in a court of law by a person who has suffered a loss as a result of a breach of contract. However, there are several different ways that damages can be calculated.

The most common way in which damages are calculated in breach of contract actions is by measuring the benefit that the non-defaulting party would have received from the contract. These damages are often referred to as **benefit of the bargain damages.** These types of damages are measured by the difference between the benefit received and the benefit promised under the contract.

Under the theory of **restitution**, the non-defaulting party to a contract can recover for the value of services he or she gave to the non-defaulting party irrespective of whether the non-defaulting party would have lost money on the contract and would have been unable to recover in a suit on the contract. The measure of damages for restitution is the reasonable value of the performance. The reasonable value of the performance is the amount for which such services would have been purchased from one in a similar situation to that of the non-defaulting party at the time and place that the services were rendered. It is important to note, however, that where a non-defaulting party has fully performed under a contract and been refused payment, he or she cannot recover more than the contract price.

Mitigation of Damages

In General

There are a few instances where damage recovery in a breach of contract action will be mitigated. **Mitigation of damages** refers to the principle that an injured party cannot recover damages that could reasonably have been avoided. The first case where there may be a limitation on damages relates to the avoidability by the non-defaulting party as it relates to mitigation of damages. The general rule is that a non-defaulting party under a contract has a duty to mitigate his or her damages. This duty to mitigate damages applies to contracts for the purchase and sale of complete or partial interests in real estate as well as residential and commercial leases.

Substantial Performance

The second situation that arises with regard to avoidability is substantial performance. The majority of states, including Texas, recognize the doctrine of substantial performance. **Substantial performance** is the doctrine that recognizes that performance under a contract that deviates slightly from the terms of the contract will be considered complete performance under the contract less the damages that result from deviation from the contract. Substantial performance limits the damages awarded where the defaulting party has substantially performed under the contract. Damages are measured according to the loss in value rather than the cost to complete the project. This doctrine is limited to those instances where (1) the cost to complete the construction is grossly disproportionate to the loss in value, and (2) the defaulting party acted in good faith.

The issue of substantial performance arises more often in building construction contracts.[10] For example, Phil Purchaser enters into a contract with Blanco Builders for the construction of a new home for $104,000 on the lot that Phil Purchaser recently bought. Blanco Builders subsequently stops building three months later due to a shortage of workers. All that remains to be added to the new home, however, is the carpet. The value of the house at this point in construction is $103,000. Since the builder has substantially performed under the contract, in a suit for breach of contract, damages would be assessed according to the cost of adding the materials necessary to conform the property to the intended contractual specifications.

Specific Performance

The second remedy available to a non-defaulting party in a breach of contract action is specific performance. **Specific performance** is a remedy that requires exact performance by the defaulting party under the contract. For example, with a seller this would mean forcing the seller to go through with closing to transfer title to the property. This remedy is quite common in transactions involving real estate because real property is unique. Specific performance may be used in a transaction in which the seller defaults under the sales contract.

[10] Vance v. My Apartment Steak House of San Antonio, Inc., 677 S.W.2d 480 (Tex. 1984).

For example, seller and prospective purchaser enter into a contract for the purchase and sale of the seller's property. All conditions under the contract are satisfied, and the transaction goes smoothly until closing. However, the seller fails to appear at closing. The failure of the seller to appear at the closing gives the non-defaulting purchaser grounds to bring a lawsuit for breach of contract. In this action, the purchaser may seek to have the seller specifically perform under the contract. In other words, the purchaser may seek to have the seller go through with the closing procedure and transfer the title and keys to the property.

Rescission

The next remedy available to a non-defaulting party where there has been a breach of contract is rescission. **Rescission** is cancellation of the contract. Under the promulgated residential sales contract, where one party has defaulted on performance, the contract may be cancelled allowing the non-defaulting party to recover liquidated damages as indicated in the contract.

Liquidated Damages

Liquidated damages is the sum that a party to a contract agrees to pay if he or she breaches the contract and is used to predict damages if the contract is breached. A contract may include a liquidated damages provision stipulating that a fixed definite sum is to be paid in the event of a breach. In contracts for the purchase and sale of real property in Texas, a liquidated damages provision is commonly used, and the liquidated damages under these contracts are referred to as earnest money.

When a contract is formed between a seller and a prospective purchaser, the prospective purchaser will usually present a specified sum of money as earnest money to the contract. This earnest money *is not mandatory* to the creation of a valid contract for the sale of real estate in Texas, but it is often used. The reason for the use of this sum is quite obviously to act as security for the seller in the contract, but it also acts as a gesture of sincerity by the prospective purchaser that indicates the purchaser's good faith under the contract. Where one party to the contract breaches, the non-defaulting party receives the earnest money as liquidated damages. For example, Sammy Seller and Frank Buyer enter into a contract for the purchase and sale of Sammy Seller's ranch. Frank Buyer presents Sammy Seller with a check for $5,000 as a gesture of his good faith under the contract. At closing, Frank Buyer fails to appear. In this instance, the non-defaulting party, Sammy Seller, can seek the earnest money as liquidated damages under the contract.

Attorney's Fees

Texas courts follow the American Rule concerning the award of attorney's fees. The American Rule states that attorney's fees may be awarded where provided by statute or contract.[11] Promulgated sales contracts as well as agency employment agreements include attorney's fees paragraphs. Specifically, these paragraphs provide that a prevailing party in a legal proceeding can recover reasonable attorney's fees and costs. However, the policy in Texas is to encourage settlement so these contracts also provide for mediation before litigation if a dispute arises. The contract paragraphs provide that the parties can choose a mutually acceptable mediator at the time the dispute arises and share the costs equally. However, the parties can also predesignate a mediator in the special provisions paragraph of the specific contract.

Discussion Questions

1. Who are the two parties typically involved in an offer?
2. How might a prospective buyer communicate an offer to a seller? Give an example of each manner of communication.
3. How should an offer be presented?
4. What are some types of non-offers? Give an example of each type.
5. What are multiple offers and how should they be handled?
6. Discuss backup offers and the means to create a backup contract.
7. Discuss the various means by which an offer may terminate. Give an example of each manner of termination.
8. When is acceptance of an offer typically effective, and what are some exceptions to this rule? Give an example of each situation.
9. Discuss the means by which an offeree can accept an offer.
10. By what manner can the offeree accept an offer? Give an example of each.
11. What is the general rule with regard to pre-contractual liability, and what are the exceptions to the rule? Give an example of each.
12. What is the underlying purpose of the Statute of Frauds?
13. For what circumstances does the Statute of Frauds require a writing? Give an example of each.
14. What are the necessary elements that a writing must contain to satisfy the Statute of Frauds?
15. When does the part performance doctrine apply?
16. What is dispute resolution and what are the underlying purposes and advantages of negotiation?
17. Name the types of breach that may occur between parties and give an example of each.
18. List the various remedies that may be available for a non-defaulting party in a breach of contract action. Give an example of each.

---

[11] Intercontinental Group Partnership v. KB Home Lone Star L.P., 295 S.W.3d 650 (Tex. 2009).

CHAPTER

7 CONTINGENCIES, ADDENDA, AND AMENDMENTS

KEY TERMS

amendment
condition precedent
condition subsequent
parol evidence rule
partially integrated
totally integrated

CONTINGENCIES

In addition to the ways in which one may be discharged from a contract, discussed in an earlier chapter, there may be instances where a party to the contract is discharged from performing under the contract due to a contingency or condition in the contract. The most common types of conditions that exist in a contract include the condition precedent and the condition subsequent.

A contract can be discharged by a condition precedent. A **condition precedent** is a condition that must occur before a party to a contract is obligated to perform under the contract. If the condition never occurs, then the party has no responsibility to perform under the contract. One example of a condition precedent in the real estate industry concerns backup contracts. Under a backup contract, the prospective purchaser is not responsible for performing until the prior contract terminates. The condition occurs in this instance before the party is obligated to perform. If the condition is satisfied, that is the prior contract terminates, then the parties to the contract must be prepared to perform their obligations under the contract. If the condition is not satisfied, the contract will be discharged and the parties will return to the position that they were in before the contract was created.

The second type of condition that can discharge a contract is a **condition subsequent**. A condition subsequent is a condition that exists after the parties enter into a contract that will terminate one of the parties' obligations to perform under the contract. In other words, the contract is in full force until this condition occurs and terminates the obligation to perform. In real estate sales transactions one of the most common conditions subsequent is when the prospective purchaser must sell his or her current residence and collect the proceeds before he or she can go to closing

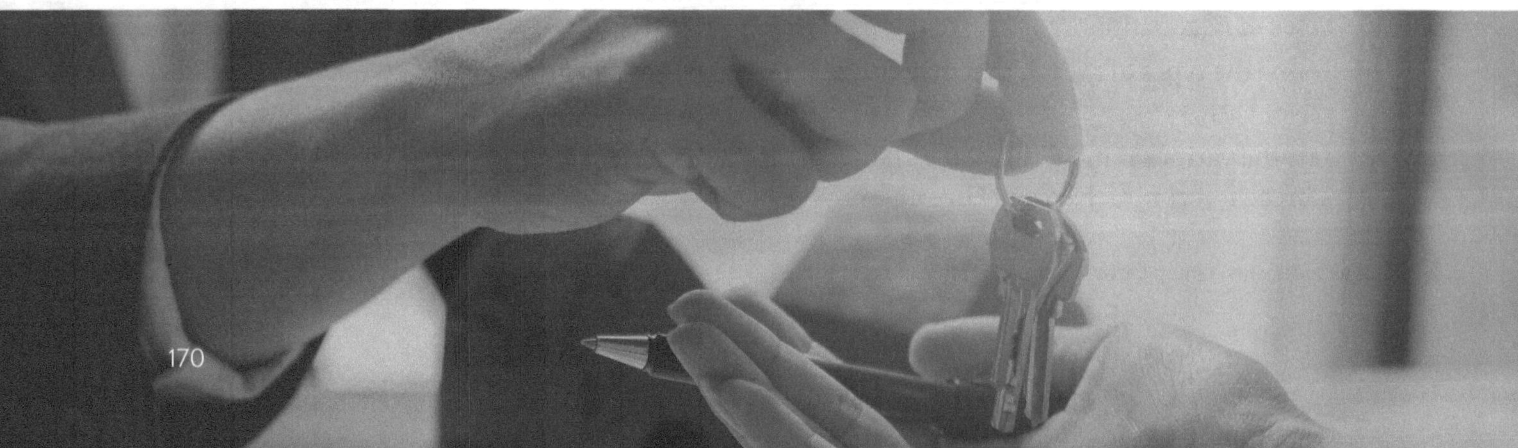

on the current contract. Failure of the prospective purchaser to sell his or her current residence is grounds to discharge the contract, and the parties to the contract are returned to the same position that they were in before they entered into the contract. That is, the contract terminates and the buyer receives his or her earnest money back.

With this contingency, the seller has the right to continue looking for backup offers until the closing date and generally should considering the risk involved. If the seller accepts a backup offer, the seller can require the buyer to waive the contingency concerning the sale of his or her current residence. If the buyer waives the contingency, the buyer is expected to have the proceeds to go forward with closing. If the buyer fails to waive the contingency, the contract will terminate and the earnest money will be refunded. Unfortunately, if the buyer waives the contingency and the buyer's loan or assumption approval is contingent on the buyer's sale of his or her current property, then the buyer is in default under the contract if the current property is not sold by the closing date.

Another example of a condition subsequent that exists in the promulgated residential sales contract is that the contract is contingent on the prospective purchaser obtaining financing. Essentially, failure of the purchaser to obtain financing is grounds to discharge the contract, and the parties return to their status quo.[1] There are two aspects to this that must be considered. The first aspect that must be considered is buyer approval. Buyer approval is considered to have been obtained when the terms of the loan(s) are available and the lender determines that the buyer has satisfied all of the lender's requirements related to the buyer's assets, income, and credit history. If the buyer cannot obtain buyer approval, then the buyer may give written notice to the seller and the contract will terminate and the earnest money will be refunded to the buyer. If the buyer fails to give the requisite notice, then the contingency is removed and the parties move forward with the contract. The second aspect that must be considered is property approval. Property approval is deemed to have been obtained when the property has satisfied the lender's underwriting requirements for the loan, including but not limited to appraisal, insurability, and lender-required repairs. If property approval is not obtained, then the buyer may terminate the contract by giving notice to the seller before closing and the earnest money will be refunded to the buyer.

AMENDMENTS

Mutual amendment is a fair way to correct a written contract to accurately reflect the terms of the intended agreement. However, if one party disputes the amendment of the contract, then in most cases the original written agreement will stand. Therefore, any amendment should not be agreed upon by phone. Instead, the **Amendment** form (TREC 39-8) should be used. See figure 7-1.

---

[1] See R. Conrad Moore & Associates, Inc. v. Lerma, 946 S.W.2d 90 (Tex. App.–El Paso 1997).

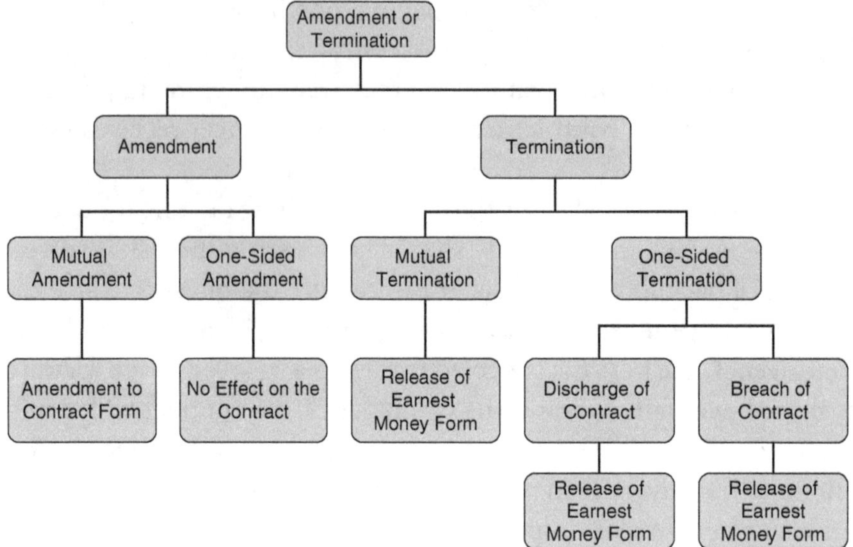

FIGURE 7-1 Amendment or Termination
Source: © 2021 Mbition LLC

The **parol evidence rule** states that terms set forth in writing intended by the parties to be a final expression of their agreement may not be contradicted or modified by evidence of a prior agreement or a contemporaneous oral agreement.[2] Under this rule a contemporaneous oral agreement is simply an oral agreement that takes place simultaneously with the written agreement.

There are three underlying policies to this rule. First, written contracts are more accurate than memory. Since the promulgated residential sales contract is 10 pages long in standard type, it is easy to see how memory could fail to account for all of the terms. The second policy of the parol evidence rule is that written contracts tend to avoid fraud. Obviously, if the parties to a transaction enter into a written contract and each party has a copy, then it is almost impossible for one party to defraud the other. Third, written contracts encourage reliability and precision of the contract terms. This rule is especially important for real estate professionals.

Once there is a final contract between the parties, a court of law will not allow evidence of a prior agreement or a contemporaneous oral agreement to contradict or modify the completed contract. Thus, for the real estate professional it is very important during negotiations, when using the promulgated sales contract forms to propose offers and counteroffers, that each party to the contract indicate next to each change made the initials of the party, the time, and the date. This is particularly important when negotiations occur via fax or email.

When the contract is finally completed on the promulgated sales contract form, it may be wise to indicate, on a clean contract form, the terms of the parties' agreement. Do not discard the original, however. In real estate transactions, the original contract may be required by the escrow agent. However, it is crucial that

[2] Weinacht v. Phillips Coal Co., 673 S.W.2d 677 (Tex. App.–Dallas 1984).

the terms match the agreement of the parties. It is a good idea to have someone else in the office read the documents to make sure that all of the proper provisions have been included as well as have both parties to the contract read the provisions before initialing and signing. Therefore, in the absence of an exception, evidence of the prior agreement would not be admissible in a court of law.

In addition, no oral agreements should accompany the contract because, in most circumstances, evidence concerning this agreement would not be admissible in court to contradict the written contract. This issue comes up with real estate professionals where oral promises are made concerning non-realty items, for instance, a piece of furniture will pass with the sale of the property. Failure to include the promise in a writing as part of the contract may create a problem at closing if the seller decides that he or she would rather keep the piece of furniture. Such an issue, as little as it may seem, has killed many real estate sales.

A couple of instances allow for extrinsic evidence to be considered to supplement the final agreement of the parties. The first is by evidence of course of dealing or usage of trade. For example, in a real estate sales contract, certain provisions may be supplemented according to what the real estate industry standard was at the time that the contract was created. As mentioned in an earlier chapter, marketing techniques are often implied into the listing agreement according to what the industry is doing at the time. The second means to supplement an agreement is by evidence of consistent additional terms unless the court finds the writing to be the complete contract of the parties. A contract that is considered to be the complete agreement of the parties is often referred to as **totally integrated**. To determine whether the contract is totally integrated, the court will look to the intent of the parties as indicated in the contract itself, any collateral agreement, and the circumstances surrounding the making of the contract.

When the agreement is not considered to be the exclusive contract of the parties, the agreement is referred to as **partially integrated**. Extrinsic evidence of another agreement is never allowed to supplement a totally integrated contract, but can be allowed to supplement a partially integrated contract. To alleviate some of the confusion surrounding whether the contract is totally integrated, the promulgated sales contract forms contain a paragraph that states that the contract constitutes the entire agreement of the parties. These contracts are, therefore, totally integrated. But this is another reminder to make certain all aspects of the agreement are reflected on the final written sales contract.

A problem that arises with the parol evidence rule is that it deals only with prior and contemporaneous statements. The rule does not speak to the problem of when the parties seek to prove that the provisions of the contract were modified after the contract was made. A second rule of interpretation deals with this issue.

The requirements of the Statute of Frauds apply to modifications of contracts that fall within the Statute of Frauds. Contracts for the sale of real estate and contracts that cannot be performed within one year must be in writing.

This includes real estate sales contracts and most leases. In these situations, the modification of any of these contracts must be in writing. The Amendment form from TREC should be used to modify a promulgated sales contract. Remember a license holder cannot sue for a commission without a written agreement, so any modifications to the commission agreement must also be in writing.

ADDENDA

In General

The residential sales contract provides for various addenda to the contract to be selected. However, neither the Information about Brokerage Services nor the Seller's Disclosure Notice is included in this list. If a broker is working for a seller, these two documents become attachments to the Listing Agreement. Only the Information About Brokerage Services would be an attachment to the Buyer's Representation Agreement if a broker is working for a buyer. If a broker is only working with an individual as a customer, then the documents are part of the transaction file. Some title companies may request the information to ensure compliance with disclosure laws. A complete discussion of the promulgated addenda is presented below.

Financing Addenda

There are several addenda associated with financing the real estate transaction. For owner financing, the Seller Financing Addendum (TREC 26-7) is used. If an assumption transaction is involved, then the Loan Assumption Addendum (TREC 41-2) should be used. This addendum is often used in association with the Addendum for Release of Liability under Assumed Loan and/or Restoration of Seller's VA Entitlement (TREC 12-3), which allows the seller to seek a release of liability on the underlying loan. Most real estate transactions will likely involve third party financing, which requires use of the Third Party Financing Addendum (TREC 40-7). Numerous types of third party financing are found in this addendum, including third party conventional financing, VA financing, and FHA financing, among others. Each of these addenda is discussed in more detail in a later chapter.

Leasing Addenda

There are two leasing addenda that can be used with the residential sales contract. The Buyer's Temporary Residential Lease (TREC 16-5) is used when the buyer moves into the property before closing, and ownership transfer, takes place. In addition, the Seller's Temporary Residential Lease (TREC 15-5) is used if the seller is to remain in the property after closing. These addenda were discussed in an earlier chapter.

Additional Addenda

Addendum Concerning Right to Terminate Due to Lender's Appraisal (TREC 49-0)

This addendum is used by the buyer to terminate the contract if the lender returns a low appraisal on the subject property. This addendum will be discussed in greater detail in a later chapter.

Short Sale Addendum (TREC 45-1)

The Short Sale Addendum is used during negotiations when the seller must sell the property for less than the total debt remaining on the loan. The Short Sale Addendum is discussed in greater detail in a later chapter.

Addendum for Property Subject to Mandatory Membership in a Property Owners Association (TREC 36-8)

This promulgated addendum permits the buyer to seek information from the seller regarding the presence of mandatory membership in a homeowners association, as well as the association's fees and assessments. See figure 7-2. This addendum can be used with any of the current promulgated sales contract forms where mandatory membership in a homeowners association is involved.

In paragraph A, which deals with the resale certificate, A(1) is the situation where the seller must provide the homeowners association information within a certain specified time. There is a standard TREC resale certificate (TREC 37-5) that can be used to indicate the information requested. A predetermined amount of time is indicated within which the seller must deliver the resale certificate to the buyer. If the buyer does not receive the information, the buyer can terminate the contract and receive his or her earnest money back. Even if the seller delivers the information, the buyer may terminate the contract for any reason within three days after the buyer receives the information and receive his or her earnest money back. Paragraph A(2) puts the burden on the buyer to obtain the subdivision information. Paragraph A(3) is the situation in which the buyer has already received and approved a copy of the resale certificate before signing the contract. This might occur in one of those situations in which the seller had one prepared for a previous prospective purchaser. Paragraph A(4) is the situation in which the buyer does not require delivery of the resale certificate under this addendum, such as if the buyer already lives in the same subdivision where the seller's property is located.

Paragraph B deals with material changes that might occur after the buyer receives the information while paragraph C specifies the amount of transfer fees that the seller and buyer have agreed to pay. Paragraph D requires the buyer to pay any deposits for reserves. And paragraph E is the seller's authorization to the subdivision association to release any updated information to the buyer upon request.

PROMULGATED BY THE TEXAS REAL ESTATE COMMISSION (TREC)

08-18-2014

ADDENDUM FOR PROPERTY SUBJECT TO MANDATORY MEMBERSHIP IN A PROPERTY OWNERS ASSOCIATION

(NOT FOR USE WITH CONDOMINIUMS)

ADDENDUM TO CONTRACT CONCERNING THE PROPERTY AT

____

(Street Address and City)

____

(Name of Property Owners Association, (Association) and Phone Number)

A. SUBDIVISION INFORMATION: "Subdivision Information" means: (i) a current copy of the restrictions applying to the subdivision and bylaws and rules of the Association, and (ii) a resale certificate, all of which are described by Section 207.003 of the Texas Property Code.

(Check only one box):

☐ 1. Within ____________ days after the effective date of the contract, Seller shall obtain, pay for, and deliver the Subdivision Information to the Buyer. If Seller delivers the Subdivision Information, Buyer may terminate the contract within 3 days after Buyer receives the Subdivision Information or prior to closing, whichever occurs first, and the earnest money will be refunded to Buyer. If Buyer does not receive the Subdivision Information, Buyer, as Buyer's sole remedy, may terminate the contract at any time prior to closing and the earnest money will be refunded to Buyer.

☐ 2. Within ____________ days after the effective date of the contract, Buyer shall obtain, pay for, and deliver a copy of the Subdivision Information to the Seller. If Buyer obtains the Subdivision Information within the time required, Buyer may terminate the contract within 3 days after Buyer receives the Subdivision Information or prior to closing, whichever occurs first, and the earnest money will be refunded to Buyer. If Buyer, due to factors beyond Buyer's control, is not able to obtain the Subdivision Information within the time required, Buyer may, as Buyer's sole remedy, terminate the contract within 3 days after the time required or prior to closing, whichever occurs first, and the earnest money will be refunded to Buyer.

☐ 3. Buyer has received and approved the Subdivision Information before signing the contract. Buyer ☐ does ☐ does not require an updated resale certificate. If Buyer requires an updated resale certificate, Seller, at Buyer's expense, shall deliver it to Buyer within 10 days after receiving payment for the updated resale certificate from Buyer. Buyer may terminate this contract and the earnest money will be refunded to Buyer if Seller fails to deliver the updated resale certificate within the time required.

☐ 4. Buyer does not require delivery of the Subdivision Information.

The title company or its agent is authorized to act on behalf of the parties to obtain the Subdivision Information ONLY upon receipt of the required fee for the Subdivision Information from the party obligated to pay.

B. MATERIAL CHANGES. If Seller becomes aware of any material changes in the Subdivision Information, Seller shall promptly give notice to Buyer. Buyer may terminate the contract prior to closing by giving written notice to Seller if: (i) any of the Subdivision Information provided was not true; or (ii) any material adverse change in the Subdivision Information occurs prior to closing, and the earnest money will be refunded to Buyer.

C. FEES: Except as provided by Paragraphs A, D and E, Buyer shall pay any and all Association fees or other charges associated with the transfer of the Property not to exceed $____________ and Seller shall pay any excess.

D. DEPOSITS FOR RESERVES: Buyer shall pay any deposits for reserves required at closing by the Association.

E. AUTHORIZATION: Seller authorizes the Association to release and provide the Subdivision Information and any updated resale certificate if requested by the Buyer, the Title Company, or any broker to this sale. If Buyer does not require the Subdivision Information or an updated resale certificate, and the Title Company requires information from the Association (such as the status of dues, special assessments, violations of covenants and restrictions, and a waiver of any right of first refusal), ☐ Buyer ☐ Seller shall pay the Title Company the cost of obtaining the information prior to the Title Company ordering the information.

NOTICE TO BUYER REGARDING REPAIRS BY THE ASSOCIATION: The Association may have the sole responsibility to make certain repairs to the Property. If you are concerned about the condition of any part of the Property which the Association is required to repair, you should not sign the contract unless you are satisfied that the Association will make the desired repairs.

Buyer	Seller
Buyer	Seller

The form of this addendum has been approved by the Texas Real Estate Commission for use only with similarly approved or promulgated forms of contracts. Such approval relates to this contract form only. TREC forms are intended for use only by trained real estate licensees. No representation is made as to the legal validity or adequacy of any provision in any specific transactions. It is not intended for complex transactions. Texas Real Estate Commission, P.O. Box 12188, Austin, TX 78711-2188, (512) 936-3000 (www.trec.texas.gov) TREC No. 36-8. This form replaces TREC No. 36-7.

TREC NO. 36-8

FIGURE 7-2 Addendum for Property Subject to Mandatory Membership in a Property Owners Association

Source: Reprinted with permission of Texas Real Estate Commission

Environmental Assessment, Threatened or Endangered Species, and Wetlands Addendum (TREC 28-2)

The Environmental Assessment, Threatened or Endangered Species, and Wetlands Addendum permits the buyer, at his or her expense, to seek an environmental assessment report, a report to determine whether there are threatened or endangered species on the property or a report to determine whether there is a wetlands on the property. See figure 7-3. The environmental

PROMULGATED BY THE TEXAS REAL ESTATE COMMISSION (TREC)

12-05-11

ENVIRONMENTAL ASSESSMENT, THREATENED OR ENDANGERED SPECIES, AND WETLANDS ADDENDUM

TO CONTRACT CONCERNING THE PROPERTY AT

____

(Address of Property)

❑ A. ENVIRONMENTAL ASSESSMENT: Buyer, at Buyer's expense, may obtain an environmental assessment report prepared by an environmental specialist.

❑ B. THREATENED OR ENDANGERED SPECIES: Buyer, at Buyer's expense, may obtain a report from a natural resources professional to determine if there are any threatened or endangered species or their habitats as defined by the Texas Parks and Wildlife Department or the U.S. Fish and Wildlife Service.

❑ C. WETLANDS: Buyer, at Buyer's expense, may obtain a report from an environmental specialist to determine if there are wetlands, as defined by federal or state law or regulation.

Within _____days after the effective date of the contract, Buyer may terminate the contract by furnishing Seller a copy of any report noted above that adversely affects the use of the Property and a notice of termination of the contract. Upon termination, the earnest money will be refunded to Buyer.

Buyer	Seller
Buyer	Seller

This form has been approved by the Texas Real Estate Commission for use with similarly approved or promulgated contract forms. Such approval relates to this form only. TREC forms are intended for use only by trained real estate licensees. No representation is made as to the legal validity or adequacy of any provision in any specific transactions. It is not suitable for complex transactions. Texas Real Estate Commission, P.O. Box 12188, Austin, TX 78711-2188, 512-936-3000 (http://www.trec.texas.gov) TREC No. 28-2. This form replaces TREC No. 28-1.

TREC No. 28-2

FIGURE 7-3 Environmental Assessment, Threatened or Endangered Species, and Wetlands Addendum
Source: Reprinted with permission of Texas Real Estate Commission

assessment is designed to determine whether the property is contaminated with a hazardous substance. Concerns about hazards, such as asbestos building materials, mold, and mildew, can be alleviated by obtaining an environmental assessment. The remainder of this addendum is used to determine whether there is a specific species or habitat on the premises. Once the report is complete, the buyer has the option to terminate the contract within a specified amount of time if an adverse report is obtained. However, in order to terminate the contract the buyer must provide the seller with a copy of any adverse report. This addendum can be used with any of the standard promulgated sales contract forms.

Addendum for Sale of Other Property by Buyer (TREC 10-6)

The Addendum for Sale of Other Property by Buyer is a promulgated addendum used to create a condition to the contract that requires that the buyer's current property be sold and the proceeds collected before closing can occur on a pending contract for the purchase of another piece of property. See figure 7-4. This addendum can be used with any of the current promulgated sales contract forms.

Addendum for "Backup" Contract (TREC 11-7)

The Addendum for "Backup" Contract is a promulgated addendum that can be attached to any of the promulgated sales contract forms. See figure 7-5. This addendum is to be used with a backup contract that serves as notice to the purchaser under that contract that the contract is contingent on the termination of a prior contract. If the prior contract terminates before a specified date, then the contingency no longer exists. The specified date indicated is usually long enough to allow for the prospective buyer under the first contract to seek and obtain financing. If the first prospective buyer is not able to get financing, the seller would like a second buyer sitting in the wings ready to go forward with the transaction. However, if the previous contract does not terminate by that date, then the backup contract terminates and the earnest money under that contract is refunded to the prospective buyer.

Condominium Resale Certificate (TREC 32-4)

This promulgated addendum is to be used in transactions involving the sale and purchase of condominiums. See figure 7-6. This addendum allows the purchaser to obtain information as to assessments and fees that may be charged by the condominium association.

Addendum for Coastal Area Property (TREC 33-2)

The Addendum for Coastal Area Property (Authority from Texas Natural Resources Code § 33.135) is a promulgated addendum for use when a person

PROMULGATED BY THE TEXAS REAL ESTATE COMMISSION (TREC)

12-05-11

ADDENDUM FOR SALE OF OTHER PROPERTY BY BUYER

TO CONTRACT CONCERNING THE PROPERTY AT

____
(Address of Property)

A. The contract is contingent upon Buyer's **receipt of the proceeds** from the sale of Buyer's property at____
(Address) on or before ______________________, 20______ (the Contingency). If the Contingency is not satisfied or waived by Buyer by the above date, the contract will terminate automatically and the earnest money will be refunded to Buyer.

NOTICE: The date inserted in this Paragraph should be no later than the Closing Date specified in Paragraph 9 of the contract.

B. If Seller accepts a written offer to sell the Property, Seller shall notify Buyer (1) of such acceptance **AND** (2) that Seller requires Buyer to waive the Contingency. Buyer must waive the Contingency on or before the ______________ day after Seller's notice to Buyer; otherwise the contract will terminate automatically and the earnest money will be refunded to Buyer.

C. Buyer may waive the Contingency only by notifying Seller of the waiver and depositing $__________ with escrow agent as additional earnest money. All notices and waivers must be in writing and are effective when delivered in accordance with the contract.

D. If Buyer waives the Contingency and fails to close and fund solely due to Buyer's non-receipt of proceeds from Buyer's property described in Paragraph A above, Buyer will be in default. If such default occurs, Seller may exercise the remedies specified in Paragraph 15 of the contract.

E. For purposes of this Addendum time is of the essence; strict compliance with the times for performance stated herein is required.

______________________ Buyer	______________________ Seller
______________________ Buyer	______________________ Seller

TREC TEXAS REAL ESTATE COMMISSION

This form has been approved by the Texas Real Estate Commission for use with similarly approved or promulgated contract forms. Such approval relates to this form only. TREC forms are intended for use only by trained real estate licensees. No representation is made as to the legal validity or adequacy of any provision in any specific transactions. It is not suitable for complex transactions. Texas Real Estate Commission, P.O. Box 12188, Austin, TX 78711-2188, 512-936-3000 (http://www.trex.texas.gov) TREC No. 10-6. This form replaces TREC No. 10-5.

TREC No. 10-6

FIGURE 7-4 Addendum for Sale of Other Property by Buyer
Source: Reprinted with permission of Texas Real Estate Commission

PROMULGATED BY THE TEXAS REAL ESTATE COMMISSION (TREC)

12-05-11

ADDENDUM FOR "BACK-UP" CONTRACT

TO CONTRACT CONCERNING THE PROPERTY AT

____
(Address of Property)

A. The contract to which this Addendum is attached (the Back-Up Contract) is binding upon execution by the parties, and the earnest money and any Option Fee must be paid as provided in the Back-Up Contract. The Back-Up Contract is contingent upon the termination of a previous contract (the First Contract) dated ______________________, 20______, for the sale of Property. Except as provided by this Addendum, neither party is required to perform under the Back-Up Contract while it is contingent upon the termination of the First Contract.

B. If the First Contract does not terminate on or before ______________________, 20_____, the Back-Up Contract terminates and the earnest money will be refunded to Buyer. Seller must notify Buyer immediately of the termination of the First Contract. For purposes of performance, the effective date of the Back-Up Contract changes to the date Buyer receives notice of termination of the First Contract (Amended Effective Date).

C. An amendment or modification of the First Contract will not terminate the First Contract.

D. If Buyer has the unrestricted right to terminate the Back-Up Contract, the time for giving notice of termination begins on the effective date of the Back-Up Contract, continues after the Amended Effective Date and ends upon the expiration of Buyer's unrestricted right to terminate the Back-Up Contract.

E. For purposes of this Addendum, time is of the essence. Strict compliance with the times for performance stated herein is required.

______________________	______________________
Buyer	Seller
______________________	______________________
Buyer	Seller

This form has been approved by the Texas Real Estate Commission for use with similarly approved or promulgated contract forms. Such approval relates to this form only. TREC forms are intended for use only by trained real estate licensees. No representation is made as to the legal validity or adequacy of any provision in any specific transactions. It is not suitable for complex transactions. Texas Real Estate Commission, P.O. Box 12188, Austin, TX 78711-2188, 512-936-3000 (http://www.trec.texas.gov) TREC No. 11-7. This form replaces TREC No. 11-6.

TREC No. 11-7

FIGURE 7-5 Addendum for "Backup" Contract
Source: Reprinted with permission of Texas Real Estate Commission

PROMULGATED BY THE TEXAS REAL ESTATE COMMISSION (TREC) 8-17-2015

TREC
TEXAS REAL ESTATE COMMISSION

CONDOMINIUM RESALE CERTIFICATE
(Section 82.157, Texas Property Code)

Condominium Certificate concerning Condominium Unit_____, in Building _______, of _____________ _________________________________,a condominium project, located at _________________ ___________________________________(Address), City of ____________________________, County of ___________________________, Texas, on behalf of the condominium owners' association (the Association) by the Association's governing body (the Board).

A. The Declaration ☐does ☐does not contain a right of first refusal or other restraint that restricts the right to transfer the Unit. If a right of first refusal or other restraint exists, see Section _______of the Declaration.

B. The periodic common expense assessment for the Unit is $__________ per _______________.

C. There ☐ is ☐is not a common expense or special assessment due and unpaid by the Seller to the Association. The total unpaid amount is $____________ and is for ________________________.

D. Other amounts ☐are ☐are not payable by Seller to the Association. The total unpaid amount is $_______________and is for ____.

E. Capital expenditures approved by the Association for the next 12 months are $_____________.

F. Reserves for capital expenditures are $_____________;of this amount $__________________ has been designated for____.

G. The current operating budget and balance sheet of the Association is attached.

H. The amount of unsatisfied judgments against the Association is $ _________________________.

I. There ☐are ☐are not any suits pending against the Association. The nature of the suits is ____.

J. The Association ☐does ☐does not provide insurance coverage for the benefit of unit owners as per the attached summary from the Association's insurance agent.

K. The Board ☐has ☐has no knowledge of alterations or improvements to the Unit or to the limited common elements assigned to the Unit or any portion of the project that violate any provision of the Declaration, by-laws or rules of the Association. Known violations are:_______________ ____.

L. The Board ☐has ☐has not received notice from a governmental authority concerning violations of health or building codes with respect to the Unit, the limited common elements assigned to the Unit, or any other portion of the condominium project. Notices received are: ______________ ____.

M. The remaining term of any leasehold estate that affects the condominium is _______________ and the provisions governing an extension or a renewal of the lease are: _________________ ____ ____.

N. The Association's managing agent is ____
(Name of Agent)

____
(Mailing Address)

______________________________ ______________________________
(Phone) (Fax)

____
(E-mail Address)

TREC NO. 32-4

FIGURE 7-6 Condominium Resale Certificate
Source: Reprinted with permission of Texas Real Estate Commission

____
(Address of Property)

O. Association fees resulting from the transfer of the unit described above:

Description	Paid To	Amount

P. Required contribution, if any, to the capital reserves account $______________.

REQUIRED ATTACHMENTS:

1. Operating Budget
2. Insurance Summary
3. Balance Sheet

NOTICE: The Certificate must be prepared no more than three months before the date it is delivered to Buyer.

____
Name of Association

By: ______________________

Name: ______________________

Title: ______________________

Date: ______________________

Mailing Address: ______________________

E-mail: ______________________

TREC
TEXAS REAL ESTATE COMMISSION

FIGURE 7-6 (Continued)

sells, transfers, or conveys an interest other than a mineral, leasehold, or security interest in real property adjoining and abutting the tidally influenced waters of the state. See figure 7-7. Failure to include the notice is grounds for the purchaser to terminate the contract with a return of the earnest money. Failure to provide this statement prior to closing, either in the executory contract for conveyance or in a separate written statement, constitutes a deceptive act under the Texas Deceptive Trade Practices Consumer Protection Act.[3]

Essentially, this addendum notifies a prospective purchaser that the property may have a natural water boundary that changes with nature. In other words, the water body may either flood or recede, and the property owner would either lose or gain portions of the property. The second paragraph of this addendum is where the seller indicates any knowledge of prior fill on the property. Paragraph 3 is simply a notice that any construction, such as a pier, over state submerged lands usually requires a permit. The fourth paragraph is a notice to the prospective buyer to seek an attorney or other professional regarding the legal effect of the information contained in the addendum.

Addendum for Property Located Seaward of the Gulf Intracoastal Waterway

The Addendum for Property Located Seaward of the Gulf Intracoastal Waterway (Authority from Texas Natural Resources Code § 61.025) (TREC 34-4) is a promulgated addendum for use when a person sells or conveys an interest, other than a mineral, leasehold, or security interest, in real property located seaward of the Gulf Intracoastal Waterway to its southernmost point and then seaward of the longitudinal line also known as 97°, 12′, 19″, which runs southerly to the international boundary from the intersection of the centerline of the Gulf Intracoastal Waterway and the Brownsville Ship Channel. See figure 7-8. Failure to include the notice is grounds for the purchaser to terminate the contract with a return of the earnest money. Failure to provide this statement prior to closing, either in the executory contract for conveyance or in a separate written statement, constitutes a deceptive act under the Texas Deceptive Trade Practices Consumer Protection Act.[4]

This addendum informs the prospective purchaser that he or she may be purchasing a piece of property that contains a public easement. This public easement allows the public the right to access the beach in a predesignated location. The property owner cannot interfere with that public easement in any manner or risk a lawsuit by the state of Texas. The prospective purchaser should determine the rate of shoreline erosion in the vicinity of the property and has the right to seek legal counsel as to his or her legal rights regarding the information contained in this addendum.

---

[3] Tex. Nat. Res. Code § 33.135(d).

[4] Tex. Nat. Res. Code § 61.025(d).

PROMULGATED BY THE TEXAS REAL ESTATE COMMISSION (TREC)

12-05-11

EQUAL HOUSING OPPORTUNITY

ADDENDUM FOR
COASTAL AREA PROPERTY
(SECTION 33.135, TEXAS NATURAL RESOURCES CODE)

TO CONTRACT CONCERNING THE PROPERTY AT

____
(Address of Property)

NOTICE REGARDING COASTAL AREA PROPERTY

1. The real property described in and subject to this contract adjoins and shares a common boundary with the tidally influenced submerged lands of the state. The boundary is subject to change and can be determined accurately only by a survey on the ground made by a licensed state land surveyor in accordance with the original grant from the sovereign. The owner of the property described in this contract may gain or lose portions of the tract because of changes in the boundary.

2. The seller, transferor, or grantor has no knowledge of any prior fill as it relates to the property described in and subject to this contract except:______________________________________
____
____.

3. State law prohibits the use, encumbrance, construction, or placing of any structure in, on, or over state-owned submerged lands below the applicable tide line, without proper permission.

4. The purchaser or grantee is hereby advised to seek the advice of an attorney or other qualified person as to the legal nature and effect of the facts set forth in this notice on the property described in and subject to this contract. Information regarding the location of the applicable tide line as to the property described in and subject to this contract may be obtained from the surveying division of the General Land Office in Austin.

Buyer	Seller
Buyer	Seller

This form has been approved by the Texas Real Estate Commission for use with similarly approved or promulgated contract forms. Such approval relates to this form only. TREC forms are intended for use only by trained real estate licensees. No representation is made as to the legal validity or adequacy of any provision in any specific transactions. It is not suitable for complex transactions. Texas Real Estate Commission, P.O. Box 12188, Austin, TX 78711-2188, 512-936-3000 (http://www.trec.texas.gov) TREC No. 33-2 This form replaces TREC No. 33-1.

TREC No. 33-2

FIGURE 7-7 Addendum for Coastal Area Property
Source: Reprinted with permission of Texas Real Estate Commission

PROMULGATED BY THE TEXAS REAL ESTATE COMMISSION (TREC) 12-05-11

TREC
TEXAS REAL ESTATE COMMISSION

ADDENDUM FOR PROPERTY LOCATED SEAWARD OF THE GULF INTRACOASTAL WATERWAY

(SECTION 61.025, TEXAS NATURAL RESOURCES CODE)

TO CONTRACT CONCERNING THE PROPERTY AT

____
(Address of Property)

DISCLOSURE NOTICE CONCERNING LEGAL AND ECONOMIC RISKS OF PURCHASING COASTAL REAL PROPERTY NEAR A BEACH

WARNING: THE FOLLOWING NOTICE OF POTENTIAL RISKS OF ECONOMIC LOSS TO YOU AS THE PURCHASER OF COASTAL REAL PROPERTY IS REQUIRED BY STATE LAW.

- READ THIS NOTICE CAREFULLY. DO NOT SIGN THIS CONTRACT UNTIL YOU FULLY UNDERSTAND THE RISKS YOU ARE ASSUMING.
- BY PURCHASING THIS PROPERTY, YOU MAY BE ASSUMING ECONOMIC RISKS OVER AND ABOVE THE RISKS INVOLVED IN PURCHASING INLAND REAL PROPERTY.
- IF YOU OWN A STRUCTURE LOCATED ON COASTAL REAL PROPERTY NEAR A GULF COAST BEACH, IT MAY COME TO BE LOCATED ON THE PUBLIC BEACH BECAUSE OF COASTAL EROSION AND STORM EVENTS.
- AS THE OWNER OF A STRUCTURE LOCATED ON THE PUBLIC BEACH, YOU COULD BE SUED BY THE STATE OF TEXAS AND ORDERED TO REMOVE THE STRUCTURE.
- THE COSTS OF REMOVING A STRUCTURE FROM THE PUBLIC BEACH AND ANY OTHER ECONOMIC LOSS INCURRED BECAUSE OF A REMOVAL ORDER WOULD BE SOLELY YOUR RESPONSIBILITY.

The real property described in this contract is located seaward of the Gulf Intracoastal Waterway to its southernmost point and then seaward of the longitudinal line also known as 97 degrees, 12', 19" which runs southerly to the international boundary from the intersection of the centerline of the Gulf Intracoastal Waterway and the Brownsville Ship Channel. If the property is in close proximity to a beach fronting the Gulf of Mexico, the purchaser is hereby advised that the public has acquired a right of use or easement to or over the area of any public beach by prescription, dedication, or presumption, or has retained a right by virtue of continuous right in the public since time immemorial, as recognized in law and custom.

The extreme seaward boundary of natural vegetation that spreads continuously inland customarily marks the landward boundary of the public easement. If there is no clearly marked natural vegetation line, the landward boundary of the easement is as provided by Sections 61.016 and 61.017, Natural Resources Code.

Much of the Gulf of Mexico coastline is eroding at rates of more than five feet per year. Erosion rates for all Texas Gulf property subject to the open beaches act are available from the Texas General Land Office.

State law prohibits any obstruction, barrier, restraint, or interference with the use of the public easement, including the placement of structures seaward of the landward boundary of the easement. OWNERS OF STRUCTURES ERECTED SEAWARD OF THE VEGETATION LINE (OR OTHER APPLICABLE EASEMENT BOUNDARY) OR THAT BECOME SEAWARD OF THE VEGETATION LINE AS A RESULT OF PROCESSES SUCH AS SHORELINE EROSION ARE SUBJECT TO A LAWSUIT BY THE STATE OF TEXAS TO REMOVE THE STRUCTURES.

The purchaser is hereby notified that the purchaser should: (1) determine the rate of shoreline erosion in the vicinity of the real property; and (2) seek the advice of an attorney or other qualified person before executing this contract or instrument of conveyance as to the relevance of these statutes and facts to the value of the property the purchaser is hereby purchasing or contracting to purchase.

______________________	______________________
Buyer	Seller
______________________	______________________
Buyer	Seller

This form has been approved by the Texas Real Estate Commission for use with similarly approved or promulgated contract forms. Such approval relates to this form only. TREC forms are intended for use only by trained real estate licensees. No representation is made as to the legal validity or adequacy of any provision in any specific transactions. It is not suitable for complex transactions. Texas Real Estate Commission, P.O. Box 12188, Austin, TX 78711-2188, 512-936-3000 (http://www.trec.texas.gov) TREC No. 34-4. This form replaces TREC No. 34-3.

TREC No. 34-4

FIGURE 7-8 Addendum for Property Located Seaward of the Gulf Intracoastal Waterway
Source: Reprinted with permission of Texas Real Estate Commission

Subdivision Information, Including Resale Certificate for Property Subject to Mandatory Membership in a Property Owners' Association (TREC 37-5)

This promulgated addendum is used in conjunction with the Addendum for Property Subject to Mandatory Membership in a Property Owners Association. See figure 7-9. This certificate lists the information the purchaser requested in the Addendum. This form may be used with any of the promulgated sales contracts that may involve a mandatory homeowners association.

Notice of Buyer's Termination of Contract (TREC 38-5)

This promulgated addendum is used any time the buyer wishes to terminate the residential real estate sales contract for a specific reason indicated on the form. See figure 7-10. If this notice is provided to the seller by way of fax, the buyer should seek a return receipt to ensure that the seller received the termination.

Amendment (TREC 39-8)

This promulgated addendum is used when the parties to the residential real estate sales contract wish to amend their contract. See figure 7-11. Specific checkboxes are provided in the form to make the process easier.

Addendum for Reservation of Oil, Gas, and Other Minerals (TREC 44-2)

This addendum is used any time the seller of the property is interested in reserving oil, gas, or other mineral interests in the property. See figure 7-12. If no reservation is made, the buyer takes 100% of the subsurface interest.

Addendum for Property in a Propane Gas System Service Area (TREC 47-0)

This addendum is used to provide notice to a prospective purchaser that the property is located in a propane gas system service area owned by a distribution system retailer. This notice is required by section 141.010 of the Texas Utilities Code. See figure 7-13.

Other Mandatory Forms – Lead-Based Paint Addendum

Lead-based paint and lead-based paint hazards became clear with the enactment of the federal Residential Lead-Based Paint Hazard Reduction Act.[5] This law directed the Department of Housing and Urban Development in cooperation with the Environmental Protection Agency to issue regulations requiring disclosure of information on lead-based paint and lead-based paint hazards on certain housing constructed before 1978.

This law was passed because of insurmountable evidence that children six years of age and younger can suffer serious problems if they ingest or inhale

[5] 42 U.S.C. Ch. 63A.

PROMULGATED BY THE TEXAS REAL ESTATE COMMISSION (TREC)

2-10-2014

TREC
TEXAS REAL ESTATE COMMISSION

SUBDIVISION INFORMATION, INCLUDING RESALE CERTIFICATE FOR PROPERTY SUBJECT TO MANDATORY MEMBERSHIP IN A PROPERTY OWNERS' ASSOCIATION

(Chapter 207, Texas Property Code)

Resale Certificate concerning the Property (including any common areas assigned to the Property) located at ______________________________(Street Address), City of ______________________, County of ______________, Texas, prepared by the property owners' association (Association).

A. The Property ❑is ❑ is not subject to a right of first refusal (other than a right of first refusal prohibited by statute) or other restraint contained in the restrictions or restrictive covenants that restricts the owner's right to transfer the owner's property.

B. The current regular assessment for the Property is $______________ per ________.

C. A special assessment for the Property due after this resale certificate is delivered is $_______ payable as follows______________________________ for the following purpose:______________________________.

D. The total of all amounts due and unpaid to the Association that are attributable to the Property is $ ______________ .

E. The capital expenditures approved by the Association for its current fiscal year are $ ______________.

F. The amount of reserves for capital expenditures is $______________.

G. Unsatisfied judgments against the Association total $______________.

H. Other than lawsuits relating to unpaid ad valorem taxes of an individual member of the association, there ❑ are ❑ are not any suits pending in which the Association is a party. The style and cause number of each pending suit is: ______________.

I. The Association's board ❑has actual knowledge ❑has no actual knowledge of conditions on the Property in violation of the restrictions applying to the subdivision or the bylaws or rules of the Association. Known violations are: ______________.

J. The Association ❑has ❑has not received notice from any governmental authority regarding health or building code violations with respect to the Property or any common areas or common facilities owned or leased by the Association. A summary or copy of each notice is attached.

K. The amount of any administrative transfer fee charged by the Association for a change of ownership of property in the subdivision is $__________. Describe all fees associated with the transfer of ownership (include a description of each fee, to whom each fee is payable and the amount of each fee).__________

____

____

TREC NO. 37-5

FIGURE 7-9 Subdivision Information, Including Resale Certificate for Property Subject to Mandatory Membership in a Property Owners' Association

Source: Reprinted with permission of Texas Real Estate Commission

L. The Association's managing agent is ______________________________
(Name of Agent)

____
(Mailing Address)

______________________________ ______________________________
(Telephone Number) (Fax Number)

____
(E-mail Address)

M. The restrictions ☐ do ☐ do not allow foreclosure of the Association's lien on the Property for failure to pay assessments.

REQUIRED ATTACHMENTS:

1. Restrictions
2. Rules
3. Bylaws
4. Current Balance Sheet
5. Current Operating Budget
6. Certificate of Insurance concerning Property and Liability Insurance for Common Areas and Facilities
7. Any Governmental Notices of Health or Housing Code Violations

NOTICE: This Subdivision Information may change at any time.

____
Name of Association

By: ______________________________

Print Name: ______________________________

Title: ______________________________

Date: ______________________________

Mailing Address: ______________________________

E-mail: ______________________________

TREC
TEXAS REAL ESTATE COMMISSION

FIGURE 7-9 (Continued)

11-15-18

PROMULGATED BY THE TEXAS REAL ESTATE COMMISSION (TREC)

NOTICE OF BUYER'S TERMINATION OF CONTRACT

CONCERNING THE CONTRACT FOR THE SALE OF THE PROPERTY AT

____
(Street Address and City)

BETWEEN THE UNDERSIGNED BUYER AND ______________________________
______________________________ (SELLER)

Buyer notifies Seller that the contract is terminated pursuant to the following:

❑(1) The unrestricted right of Buyer to terminate the contract under Paragraph 23 of the contract.

❑(2) Buyer cannot obtain Buyer Approval in accordance with the Third Party Financing Addendum to the contract.

❑(3) The Property does not satisfy Property Approval in accordance with the Third Party Financing Addendum to the contract. Buyer has delivered to Seller lender's written statement setting forth the reason(s) for lender's determination.

❑(4) Buyer elects to terminate under Paragraph A of the Addendum for Property Subject to Mandatory Membership in a Property Owners' Association.

❑(5) Buyer elects to terminate under Paragraph 7B(2) of the contract relating to the Seller's Disclosure Notice.

❑(6) Buyer elects to terminate under Paragraph (3) of the Addendum Concerning Right to Terminate Due to Lender's Appraisal. Buyer has delivered a copy of the Appraisal to Seller.

❑(7) Buyer elects to terminate under Paragraph 6.D. of the contract (6.C. for Residential Condominium Contract) because timely objections were not cured by the end of the Cure Period.

❑(8) Other *(identify the paragraph number of contract or the addendum)*: ______________
____
____
____
____

NOTE: This notice is not an election of remedies. Release of the earnest money is governed by the contract.

CONSULT AN ATTORNEY BEFORE SIGNING: TREC rules prohibit real estate license holders from giving legal advice. READ THIS FORM CAREFULLY.

Buyer	Date	Buyer	Date

This form has been approved by the Texas Real Estate Commission for use with similarly approved or promulgated contract forms. Such approval relates to this form only. TREC forms are intended for use only by trained real estate license holders. No representation is made as to the legal validity or adequacy of any provision in any specific transactions. It is not suitable for complex transactions. Texas Real Estate Commission, P.O. Box 12188, Austin, TX 78711-2188, (512) 936-3000 (http://www.trec.texas.gov) TREC No. 38-6. This form replaces TREC No. 38-5.

TREC No. 38-6

FIGURE 7-10 Notice of Buyer's Termination of Contract
Source: Reprinted with permission of Texas Real Estate Commission

TREC
TEXAS REAL ESTATE COMMISSION

PROMULGATED BY THE TEXAS REAL ESTATE COMMISSION (TREC) 11-2-2015

EQUAL HOUSING OPPORTUNITY

AMENDMENT
TO CONTRACT CONCERNING THE PROPERTY AT

____
(Street Address and City)

Seller and Buyer amend the contract as follows: (check each applicable box)

❑(1) The Sales Price in Paragraph 3 of the contract is:
A. Cash portion of Sales Price payable by Buyer at closing .... $_______________
B. Sum of financing described in the contract .... $_______________
C. Sales Price (Sum of A and B) .... $_______________

❑(2) In addition to any repairs and treatments otherwise required by the contract, Seller, at Seller's expense, shall complete the following repairs and treatments:

❑(3) The date in Paragraph 9 of the contract is changed to ________________________, 20______.

❑(4) The amount in Paragraph 12A(1)(b) of the contract is changed to $ ____________________.

❑(5) The cost of lender required repairs and treatment, as itemized on the attached list, will be paid as follows: $ ______________________ by Seller; $ _______________________ by Buyer.

❑(6) Buyer has paid Seller an additional Option Fee of $ _________________ for an extension of the unrestricted right to terminate the contract on or before 5:00 p.m. on ______________________________, 20________. This additional Option Fee ❑ will ❑ will not be credited to the Sales Price.

❑(7) Buyer waives the unrestricted right to terminate the contract for which the Option Fee was paid.

❑(8) The date for Buyer to give written notice to Seller that Buyer cannot obtain Buyer Approval as set forth in the Third Party Financing Addendum is changed to ________________, 20______.

❑(9) **Other Modifications**: (Insert only factual statements and business details applicable to this sale.)

EXECUTED the ______day of __________________________, 20______ . (BROKER: FILL IN THE DATE OF FINAL ACCEPTANCE.)

______________________ Buyer	______________________ Seller
______________________ Buyer	______________________ Seller

TREC
TEXAS REAL ESTATE COMMISSION

This form has been approved by the Texas Real Estate Commission for use with similarly approved or promulgated contract forms. Such approval relates to this form only. TREC forms are intended for use only by trained real estate license holders . No representation is made as to the legal validity or adequacy of any provision in any specific transactions. It is not intended for complex transactions. Texas Real Estate Commission, P.O. Box 12188, Austin, TX 78711-2188, 512-936-3000 (http://www.trec.texas.gov) TREC No. 39-8. This form replaces TREC No. 39-7.

TREC NO. 39-8

FIGURE 7-11 Amendment
Source: Reprinted with permission of Texas Real Estate Commission

PROMULGATED BY THE TEXAS REAL ESTATE COMMISSION (TREC) 11-18-14

TREC

TEXAS REAL ESTATE COMMISSION

ADDENDUM FOR RESERVATION OF OIL, GAS, AND OTHER MINERALS

ADDENDUM TO CONTRACT CONCERNING THE PROPERTY AT

____

(Street Address and City)

NOTICE: For use ONLY if Seller reserves all or a portion of the Mineral Estate.

A. "Mineral Estate" means all oil, gas, and other minerals in and under and that may be produced from the Property, any royalty under any existing or future mineral lease covering any part of the Property, executive rights (including the right to sign a mineral lease covering any part of the Property), implied rights of ingress and egress, exploration and development rights, production and drilling rights, mineral lease payments, and all related rights and benefits. The Mineral Estate does NOT include water, sand, gravel, limestone, building stone, caliche, surface shale, near-surface lignite, and iron, but DOES include the reasonable use of these surface materials for mining, drilling, exploring, operating, developing, or removing the oil, gas, and other minerals from the Property.

B. *Subject to Section C below,* the Mineral Estate owned by Seller, if any, will be conveyed unless reserved as follows (check one box only):

❑ (1) Seller reserves all of the Mineral Estate owned by Seller.

❑ (2) Seller reserves an undivided ________interest in the Mineral Estate owned by Seller. *NOTE: If Seller does not own all of the Mineral Estate, Seller reserves only this percentage or fraction of Seller's interest.*

C. Seller ❑ does ❑ does *not* reserve and retain implied rights of ingress and egress and of reasonable use of the Property (including surface materials) for mining, drilling, exploring, operating, developing, or removing the oil, gas, and other minerals. *NOTE: Surface rights that may be held by other owners of the Mineral Estate who are not parties to this transaction (including existing mineral lessees) will NOT be affected by Seller's election. Seller's failure to complete Section C will be deemed an election to convey all surface rights described herein.*

D. If Seller does not reserve all of Seller's interest in the Mineral Estate, Seller shall, within 7 days after the Effective Date, provide Buyer with the contact information of any existing mineral lessee known to Seller.

IMPORTANT NOTICE: The Mineral Estate affects important rights, the full extent of which may be unknown to Seller. A full examination of the title to the Property completed by an attorney with expertise in this area is the only proper means for determining title to the Mineral Estate with certainty. In addition, attempts to convey or reserve certain interest out of the Mineral Estate separately from other rights and benefits owned by Seller may have unintended consequences. Precise contract language is essential to preventing disagreements between present and future owners of the Mineral Estate. If Seller or Buyer has any questions about their respective rights and interests in the Mineral Estate and how such rights and interests may be affected by this contract, they are strongly encouraged to consult an attorney with expertise in this area.

CONSULT AN ATTORNEY BEFORE SIGNING: TREC rules prohibit real estate licensees from giving legal advice. READ THIS FORM CAREFULLY.

Buyer	Seller
Buyer	Seller

The form of this addendum has been approved by the Texas Real Estate Commission for use with similarly approved or promulgated contract forms. Such approval relates to this contract form only. TREC forms are intended for use only by trained real estate license holders. No representation is made as to the legal validity or adequacy of any provision in any specific transactions. It is not intended for complex transactions. Texas Real Estate Commission, P.O. Box 12188, Austin, TX 78711-2188, 512-936-3000 (http://www.trec.texas.gov) TREC No. 44-2. This form replaces TREC No. 44-1.

TREC NO. 44-2

FIGURE 7-12 Addendum for Reservation of Oil, Gas, and Other Minerals
Source: Reprinted with permission of Texas Real Estate Commission

PROMULGATED BY THE TEXAS REAL ESTATE COMMISSION (TREC)

2-10-2014

ADDENDUM FOR PROPERTY IN A PROPANE GAS SYSTEM SERVICE AREA

(Section 141.010, Utilities Code)

CONCERNING THE PROPERTY AT ______________________________
(Street Address and City)

NOTICE

The above referenced real property that you are about to purchase may be located in a propane gas system service area, which is authorized by law to provide propane gas service to the properties in the area pursuant to Chapter 141, Utilities Code. If your property is located in a propane gas system service area, there may be special costs or charges that you will be required to pay before you can receive propane gas service. There may be a period required to construct lines or other facilities necessary to provide propane gas service to your property. You are advised to determine if the property is in a propane gas system service area and contact the distribution system retailer to determine the cost that you will be required to pay and the period, if any, that is required to provide propane gas service to your property.

Buyer hereby acknowledges receipt of this notice at or before execution of a binding contract for the purchase of the above referenced real property or at the closing of the real property.

Section 141.010(a), Utilities Code, requires this notice to include a copy of the notice the distribution system retailer is required to record in the real property records. A copy of the recorded notice is attached.

NOTE: Seller can obtain a copy of the required recorded notice from the county clerk's office where the property is located or from the distribution system retailer.

Buyer	Date	Seller	Date
Buyer	Date	Seller	Date

The form of this addendum has been approved by the Texas Real Estate Commission for use only with similarly approved or promulgated forms of contracts. Such approval relates to this contract form only. TREC forms are intended for use only by trained real estate licensees. No representation is made as to the legal validity or adequacy of any provision in any specific transactions. It is not intended for complex transactions. Texas Real Estate Commission, P.O. Box 12188, Austin, TX 78711-2188, (512) 936-3000 (www.trec.texas.gov) TREC No. 47-0.

TREC NO. 47-0

FIGURE 7-13 Addendum for Property in a Propane Gas System Service Area
Source: Reprinted with permission of Texas Real Estate Commission

lead-based paint chips or dust. These problems can include learning disabilities, decreased brain and central nervous system development, and brain damage. In addition, lead-based paint is dangerous to pregnant women as well as women of childbearing age because of the potential risk that the lead poisoning can be passed to a fetus.

A copy of a lead hazard information pamphlet must be provided to any prospective purchaser of a home constructed prior to 1978. In addition, a lead-based paint addendum must be attached to all residential contracts in which the home was constructed prior to 1978. A sample of a lead-based paint addendum (OP_L) is contained in figure 7-14.

Prospective purchasers of pre-1978 homes are often curious as to the means available for testing the home for lead-based paint. There are two primary methods available for lead-based paint testing. The first is paint chip sampling. As its name implies, the method of testing involves an analysis of actual paint chips from the premises. In this type of lead paint testing, the inspector removes various squares of the wall surfaces in each room. Given that this method of testing is highly invasive, the prospective purchaser as well as the seller of the property will not be pleased with the destruction of the home.

The second and more modern means of testing for lead-based paint is X-ray fluorescence. X-ray fluorescence is a non-intrusive technique of testing for lead paint in which an inspector shines a beam of light of a predetermined wavelength onto the walls. If lead is exposed, it will fluoresce. Results can be obtained immediately.

One thing to keep in mind regarding lead-based paint testing is that one should be wary of over-the-counter lead paint testing kits, unless the kit is approved by the Department of Housing and Urban Development or the Texas Department of Health.

Where a real estate license holder is working with a seller of a home constructed prior to 1978, it would be wise to let the seller know of the lead paint disclosure requirements before the home is listed. Since the lead paint notice must be given to any potential purchaser anyway, the seller may choose to get the property inspected up front and use the results of the inspection as a bargaining tool. If the seller gets the inspection and the inspector indicates that there is no lead detected in the home, the seller should request a written certification that the dwelling is "lead-free." The downside, of course, is that if the house tests positive for lead paint, this information must be disclosed to the prospective purchaser in the seller's disclosure notice. However, the seller may choose to remedy the problem and seek a "lead-free" certification upon a second inspection before the property is listed.

The lead-based paint addendum approved by TREC provides a brief warning statement in the first paragraph. This is followed by the seller's disclosure of the presence of lead hazards as well as records and reports available to the seller. Keep in mind if an earlier prospective purchaser had an inspection done and lead was

APPROVED BY THE TEXAS REAL ESTATE COMMISSION 12-05-11

ADDENDUM FOR SELLER'S DISCLOSURE OF INFORMATION ON LEAD-BASED PAINT AND LEAD-BASED PAINT HAZARDS AS REQUIRED BY FEDERAL LAW

CONCERNING THE PROPERTY AT ______________________________
(Street Address and City)

A. LEAD WARNING STATEMENT: "Every purchaser of any interest in residential real property on which a residential dwelling was built prior to 1978 is notified that such property may present exposure to lead from lead-based paint that may place young children at risk of developing lead poisoning. Lead poisoning in young children may produce permanent neurological damage, including learning disabilities, reduced intelligence quotient, behavioral problems, and impaired memory. Lead poisoning also poses a particular risk to pregnant women. The seller of any interest in residential real property is required to provide the buyer with any information on lead-based paint hazards from risk assessments or inspections in the seller's possession and notify the buyer of any known lead-based paint hazards. A risk assessment or inspection for possible lead-paint hazards is recommended prior to purchase."

NOTICE: Inspector must be properly certified as required by federal law.

B. SELLER'S DISCLOSURE:

1. PRESENCE OF LEAD-BASED PAINT AND/OR LEAD-BASED PAINT HAZARDS (check one box only):
   ☐(a) Known lead-based paint and/or lead-based paint hazards are present in the Property (explain): ________________.
   ☐(b) Seller has no actual knowledge of lead-based paint and/or lead-based paint hazards in the Property.
2. RECORDS AND REPORTS AVAILABLE TO SELLER (check one box only):
   ☐(a) Seller has provided the purchaser with all available records and reports pertaining to lead-based paint and/or lead-based paint hazards in the Property (list documents): ________________.
   ☐(b) Seller has no reports or records pertaining to lead-based paint and/or lead-based paint hazards in the Property.

C. BUYER'S RIGHTS (check one box only):

☐1. Buyer waives the opportunity to conduct a risk assessment or inspection of the Property for the presence of lead-based paint or lead-based paint hazards.
☐2. Within ten days after the effective date of this contract, Buyer may have the Property inspected by inspectors selected by Buyer. If lead-based paint or lead-based paint hazards are present, Buyer may terminate this contract by giving Seller written notice within 14 days after the effective date of this contract, and the earnest money will be refunded to Buyer.

D. BUYER'S ACKNOWLEDGMENT (check applicable boxes):

☐1. Buyer has received copies of all information listed above.
☐2. Buyer has received the pamphlet *Protect Your Family from Lead in Your Home*.

E. BROKERS' ACKNOWLEDGMENT: Brokers have informed Seller of Seller's obligations under 42 U.S.C. 4852d to: (a) provide Buyer with the federally approved pamphlet on lead poisoning prevention; (b) complete this addendum; (c) disclose any known lead-based paint and/or lead-based paint hazards in the Property; (d) deliver all records and reports to Buyer pertaining to lead-based paint and/or lead-based paint hazards in the Property; (e) provide Buyer a period of up to 10 days to have the Property inspected; and (f) retain a completed copy of this addendum for at least 3 years following the sale. Brokers are aware of their responsibility to ensure compliance.

F. CERTIFICATION OF ACCURACY: The following persons have reviewed the information above and certify, to the best of their knowledge, that the information they have provided is true and accurate.

Buyer	Date	Seller	Date
Buyer	Date	Seller	Date
Other Broker	Date	Listing Broker	Date

The form of this addendum has been approved by the Texas Real Estate Commission for use only with similarly approved or promulgated forms of contracts. Such approval relates to this contract form only. TREC forms are intended for use only by trained real estate licensees. No representation is made as to the legal validity or adequacy of any provision in any specific transactions. It is not suitable for complex transactions. Texas Real Estate Commission, P.O. Box 12188, Austin, TX 78711-2188, 512-936-3000 (http://www.trec.texas.gov)

TREC NO. OP-L

FIGURE 7-14 Lead-Based Paint Addendum
Source: Reprinted with permission of Texas Real Estate Commission

found, the seller must disclose that information to any subsequent prospective purchasers. The buyer has certain specified rights indicated in paragraph C. The buyer can either waive his or her right to an inspection or he or she can seek an inspection within 10 days of the effective date of the contract. If the buyer detects lead paint or lead paint hazards, he or she can terminate with 14 days' notice.

Paragraphs D and E are the buyer's acknowledgment and the broker's acknowledgment of compliance, respectively. Note that in paragraph F, not only do the buyer and seller sign, but the brokers sign as well. These parties make their signatures to indicate that the information they provided was correct. Any misrepresentation could not only subject the seller to liability, but the broker as well.

Discussion Questions

1. What is the underlying purpose of the parol evidence rule?
2. What is the parol evidence rule and what exactly does it mean?
3. Discuss the various aspects of the parol evidence rule and how it relates to real estate transactions.
4. Identify the types of conditions that can exist in the sales contract and give an example of each.
5. List three promulgated addenda and indicate in what circumstances the addenda are to be used.

CHAPTER

8

FINANCING REAL ESTATE

KEY TERMS

annual percentage rate
assumption
computerized loan origination
conforming loan
debt
deed in lieu of foreclosure
deed of trust
deed of trust to secure assumption
due on sale clause
finance charge
lien theory
loan origination
power of sale clause
private mortgage insurance
promissory note
real estate lien note
security
security interest
seller financing
short sale
title theory
trust clause

MORTGAGE LAW

Financing real estate is an important part of a real estate transaction. Although there may be instances when a buyer can purchase real estate through an all-cash transaction, the majority of buyers must seek financing. Therefore, a discussion of various financing options is quite common. However, financing real estate involves mortgages. Mortgages are a type of encumbrance on property. And as an encumbrance, the mortgage burdens title to the real estate.

More specifically, a mortgage involves the transfer of an interest in the property from the buyer to a lender to secure the loan. In a mortgage, the buyer is referred to as the mortgagor and the lender is referred to as the mortgagee. The mortgage will provide that the buyer make installment payments with interest over the life of the loan. If the buyer defaults, then the lender is entitled to the property title.

There are two theories in the United States concerning mortgages. One of these theories is the title theory. In a **title theory** state, a bank with a mortgage on the property holds title to the property until the underlying debt on the real estate is paid. When the debt is paid, the title is transferred to the owner. In contrast to a title theory state is a lien theory state. In a **lien theory** state, a bank with a mortgage on property merely holds a lien on the property during the term of the debt while the purchaser holds legal title to the property. A lien is a claim on the property for payment of a debt. Texas is a lien theory state.

SECURITY AND DEBT

As part of the mortgage process, the purchaser will enter into an agreement with a lender to create a debt in exchange for a loan to purchase real estate. This **debt** is a specified sum of money the buyer is obligated to pay to the lender as well the lender's right to receive and enforce the payment. In a lien theory state, like Texas, the purchaser pledges the real estate as security or collateral to the lender to secure repayment of the real estate loan. **Security** furnished to the lender is a resource to be used in case the buyer fails in the principal obligation. In other words, this collateral is the lender's protection against the purchaser's default in case the purchaser fails to make payments according to the loan terms. If the purchaser defaults on the loan, then the purchaser can lose title to the property in a foreclosure proceeding.

Being a lien theory state dictates which financing documents are used in Texas. When a real estate purchaser obtains financing from a third-party lender, certain documents are necessary to protect the lender from loss. The two documents involved in a financing situation are the promissory note and the security interest.

PROMISSORY NOTE

The **promissory note** is a written promise by the maker to pay a specified sum at a specified time to a person named in the agreement, the payee. This document is a contract between the lender and the borrower and functions like an IOU. Since this document is merely a contract, it is not typically recorded. In real estate sales transactions, the promissory note is more commonly called a **real estate lien note**. A sample real estate lien note is shown in figure 8-1.

MORTGAGES OR DEEDS OF TRUST

The second document commonly encountered in real estate financing situations is the security interest. A **security interest** is a form of interest in property that provides that the property may be sold if the purchaser defaults on his or her debt for the property as agreed to in the promissory note. The security interest in Texas is referred to as a **deed of trust**. The typical deed of trust used in Texas is shown in figure 8-2. The deed of trust designates a trustee who is empowered to sell the

REAL ESTATE LIEN NOTE

$ _____ *[Loan amount]* __________ *[City]*, __________ County, Texas

__________ *[Date]*

For value received, the undersigned, __________ *[borrower]*, hereafter referred to individually and collectively as "Maker," promises to pay unto the order of __________ *[lender]*, hereafter referred to as "Payee," the sum of $ _____, hereafter referred to as "Principal Amount Borrowed." This sum shall be paid to Payee in lawful and legal tender of the United States of America, together with interest computed and payable as stated below.

PRINCIPAL AMOUNT BORROWED

Pursuant to the Maker's request, Payee has loaned $ _____ to Maker. Maker agrees to repay said sum upon the terms and conditions and at the interest rate stated in this Note.

INTEREST AND INTEREST RATE

1. Interest Rate Prior to Maturity:

(a) Interest shall accrue on the unpaid principal amount borrowed at the rate of __________ percent per annum over __________ *[lender]'s* prime rate, as that prime rate may change from time to time.

(b) The prime rate is defined as the rate charged by __________ for short-term loans to substantial and responsible commercial borrowers.

(c) Payee shall notify Maker from time to time as the prime rate changes.

2. Interest Rate After Maturity:

(a) Interest shall accrue on the unpaid principal at the maximum rate allowed by law, but in no event less than ___% per annum, for any and all monies owed on the principal and interest accruing after the date this Note matures.

(b) Such interest shall be referred to as "interest rate after maturity."

PAYMENT AND MATURITY DATE

1. This Note is due and matures on __________ .

2. This Note shall be due and payable as follows: Maker shall pay to Payee __________ installments payable toward the principal in the amount of $ _____, and __________ installments of interest in an amount as determined by Payee's interest rate.

FIGURE 8-1 Real Estate Lien Note
Source: © 2021 Mbition LLC

3. Principal and interest payments shall be paid to Payee at the address or location specified by Payee on or before the date on which the installments are due.

4. Installments shall commence on __________ , and shall continue on the __________ day of each and every month thereafter until the entire principal and interest is paid in full.

5. Each payment shall be applied first to any accrued interest, late charges, or attorney's fees, if any, and the balance of the payment shall then be applied to reduce the principal.

6. Any check, draft, money order, or other instrument given in payment of all or any this Note may be accepted by Payee and handled in collection in the customary manner, but such payment shall not constitute payment hereunder, or diminish any rights of Payee, except to the extent that actual cash proceeds of such instrument are unconditionally received by Payee.

7. If any installment becomes overdue for more than 10 days, at Payee's option a late charge of $ _____ shall be due in order to defray the expense of handling the delinquent payment. This late charge shall not be considered interest on the Note, but shall be considered a processing and administration fee.

PREPAYMENT

1. Maker at any time subsequent to the execution of this Note, but prior to maturity, shall have the right to prepay this Note in whole or in part at any time and in such amounts as Maker shall so desire.

2. Interest shall immediately cease to accrue as of the date of the prepayment on any amount of the principal that is so prepaid.

3. Any prepayment of the principal shall be credited to the payment of the installments last accruing under this Note.

4. Prepayment of a part of this Note shall not affect the Maker's obligations to continue the regular payments stated in this Note.

SECURITY OR VENDOR'S LIEN

1. For purposes of securing Payee and the payment of this Note when due, Maker hereby pledges, transfers, and delivers to Payee a Vendor's Lien and Security Interest in and to the following described property: __________

2. Payee shall have a first lien on any and all deposits or other sums of Maker that may be credited by or due from Maker to Payee or any Co-maker, signer, endorser, surety or guarantor of this Note, as additional security or collateral for payment of the Note. Payee, at its option, may at any time, without notice and without any liability, retain any or all of any part of any

FIGURE 8-1 (Continued)

such deposits or other sums of Maker, held by Payee, until all sums due and owing on this Note, or any other Note owed by Maker to Payee, have been paid in full, or Payee may apply or set off all or any part of any such deposits or other sums credited by or due from Maker to Payee or against any sums due on this Note in any order of preference that Payee in its sole discretion may choose.

DEFAULT

1. It is agreed that time is of the essence in this Note.

2. If default is made in any part of the principal or interest of this Note as it becomes due and payable upon the performance of any obligation, agreement, or covenant contained in any instrument securing payment of this Note, then in either event, Payee shall have the option to declare the entire unpaid balance of both the principal and accrued interest immediately due and payable without notice, and may foreclose any and all liens securing payments for the same.

3. The failure of Payee to exercise this option shall not constitute a waiver of Payee's right to exercise the option in the event of a subsequent default.

4. It is further agreed that all past due principal and interest shall bear interest from the date it is due until paid, at the maximum lawful rate that the undersigned may legally contract for under the laws of the State of Texas or under applicable federal laws.

5. In any event, all past due principal and interest shall bear an interest rate of at least ___% per year.

ATTORNEY'S FEES

In the event of default by Maker under this Note or under any of the accompanying instruments securing the payment of this Note, or if this Note is placed in the hands of an attorney or agency for collection, regardless of whether suit is filed, or if this Note is collected by suit or legal process including, but not limited to, through the Probate Court or Bankruptcy proceedings, Maker agrees to pay an additional sum equal to ___% of all sums then due, including principal and interest, or reasonable attorney's fees, whichever is higher, as attorney's fees and expenses of collection, or such greater amount as may be reasonable.

WAIVERS

Maker and any and all sureties, guarantors, and endorsers of this Note, and all other parties now or hereafter liable on the Note, severally waive grace, demand, presentment for payment, protest, notice of any kind (including, but not limited to, notice of dishonor, notice of protest, notice of intention to accelerate and notice of acceleration), and diligence in collecting and bringing suit against any party to this Note, further and agree:

FIGURE 8-1 (Continued)

1. To all extensions and partial payments, with or without notice, before or after maturity;

2. To any substitution, exchange, or release of any security now or hereafter given for this Note;

3. To the release of any party primarily or secondarily liable hereon; and,

4. That it will not be necessary for Payee, in order to enforce payment of this Note, to first institute or exhaust Payee's remedies against Maker or any other party liable on this Note or against any security for this Note.

USURY EXCLUSION

1. All agreements between Maker and Payee are expressly limited so that in no contingency or event shall the amount paid or agreed to be paid to Payee for the use, forbearance, or detention of the money to be lent under this Note exceed the maximum amount permissible under the applicable federal and state usury laws.

2. It is therefore the intention of Maker and Payee to conform strictly to the state and federal usury laws applicable to this loan transaction.

3. Therefore, in this Note or in any of the documents securing payment of this Note or otherwise relating to this Note, the aggregate of all interest and any other charges constituting interest under applicable law, contracted for, chargeable, or receivable under this Note or otherwise in connection with this transaction, shall under no circumstance exceed the maximum amount of interest permitted by law.

4. If any interest in excess of the maximum amount permitted by law is charged or collected under this Note or under any of the documents securing payment under or otherwise relating to this Note, then in such event:

a. The provisions of this paragraph shall govern and control;

b. Neither Maker nor Maker's heirs, legal representatives, successors, assigns, or any other party liable for the payment of this note shall be obligated to pay the amount of such interest that is in excess of the maximum permitted by law;

c. Any excess of interest shall be deemed a mistake and is hereby cancelled automatically, and if previously paid shall at the option of Payee of this Note be refunded to Maker or credited to the principal amount of this Note; and

d. The effective rate of interest shall automatically reduce to the maximum lawful contract rate allowed under the applicable usury laws as they may be construed by courts of appropriate jurisdiction. To the extent permitted by law, the determination of the rate of interest shall be made by amortizing, prorating, allocating, and spreading in equal parts during the period of the full stated term of the loan all interest at any time contracted for, charged, or received from Maker in connection with this Note.

PERSONAL LIABILITY

1. This Note shall be the joint and several obligation of all Makers and endorsers, and shall be binding upon them, individually and severally, their heirs, legal representatives, successors, and assigns.

FIGURE 8-1 (Continued)

2. Each Maker and endorser hereby, jointly and severally, waives presentment for payment, demand, protest, and notice, and agrees that exercise of the option to accelerate the maturity of this Note and the time of the payment may be extended from time to time without notice and without releasing any of the parties.

ASSIGNMENT

This Note, and all rights and powers under it, together with the property securing it, if any, may be transferred and assigned by Payee at such time and upon such terms as Payee may deem advisable, and any such assignee shall succeed to all the rights and powers of Payee hereunder.

CONSTRUCTION

This Note shall be governed by and construed under the laws of the State of Texas.

In witness whereof, the undersigned, intending to be legally bound, have executed this Note on this the __________ day of __________, 20_____.

________________________, Maker

Maker's Address:

____

________________________, Payee

Payee's Address:

____

FIGURE 8-1 (Continued)

DEED OF TRUST

The State of Texas
County of ________

This deed of trust is entered into by ______________ of ______________ County, Texas, here (Grantor; whether one or more); ______________, of ______________ County, Texas, here called Trustee; and ______________ of ______________ County, Texas, (Lender).

1. Grantor, to secure payment of the indebtedness described here, and in consideration of the sum of _____________ Dollars (_____) paid by Trustee to Grantor, receipt of which is acknowledged, and for the further consideration, uses, purposes, and trusts provided here, grants, sells, and conveys to Trustee, Trustee's successors, and assigns, the following described real property, situated in ______________ County, Texas: ______________ [legal description of property]; together with all improvements and fixtures now or attached later to or used in connection with the above-described premises, including heating, air conditioning, plumbing, refrigeration, and lighting fixtures and equipment, which are deemed to be fixtures and part of the realty, and are a portion of the security for the indebtedness described here.

2. To have and to hold the property, together with all the rights, privileges, and appurtenances belonging to it, to Trustee, Trustee's successors and assigns, forever. Grantor hereby binds himself and his heirs, executors, administrators, and legal representatives, to warrant and defend the premises to Trustee, Trustee's successors, substitutes, and assigns, forever, against all claims to it.

3. This conveyance is made in trust to secure the payment of the principal sum of ________ Dollars (_____), as evidenced by a promissory note of even date executed by Grantor, payable to the order of _____________, Lender, the terms of which are incorporated here by reference, together with interest at the rate of _______ percent (___%) per annum on the unpaid balance, both interest and principal payable __________ [monthly or quarterly or semiannually or annually] as it accrues at the office of ___________ [lender] in ___________[city], ___________ County, Texas, in ______________ [monthly or quarterly or semiannual or annual] installments of ____________ Dollars (_______) each, including interest, the first such installment to be paid on _______________ [date], successive installments to be paid on __________ [insert due dates of successive periodic installments, such as: the first day of each month thereafter or the first day of January in each year thereafter], and continuing until the principal and interest are fully paid.

4. If Grantor shall promptly pay or cause to be paid the note when due and any other indebtedness secured by it, and keep and perform each and every other covenant, condition, and stipulation here, then this deed of trust shall become null and void and shall be released by Lender at the expense of Grantor.

5. Grantor covenants and agrees as follows:

(a) Title. Grantor warrants that ___________ [he or she] is lawfully seised of the above-described property, that _____________ [he or she] has the right to convey it, and that it is free from encumbrances.

FIGURE 8-2 Deed of Trust
Source: © 2021 Mbition LLC

(b) Payment. Grantor will pay the principal of and interest on the note secured here in accordance with the terms of it.

(c) Taxes. Grantor will pay all taxes and assessments that are or may become due on the property described here before any interest or penalty accrues on it.

(d) Insurance. Grantor will insure the improvements on the property described here, including improvements made in the future, against fire, windstorm, or other hazard as may be reasonably required by Lender, in the amount of not less than ___________ Dollars (_____). Policies of such insurance shall be carried by companies approved by Lender, shall include a mortgage indemnity clause in favor of Lender and shall be in form as Lender may require. All insurance policies shall be delivered to Lender. Renewals of the policies must be delivered to Lender at least ten (10) days prior to the expiration of the policies' renewal. In the event of loss, Lender is authorized to collect the proceeds due under the policies and to apply them at his option either in reduction of the indebtedness secured by it or in restoration or repair of the damaged property.

(e) Prior liens. Grantor agrees that in the event a lien, charge, or encumbrance is claimed or asserted to be prior or superior to the lien of this deed of trust, ______________ [he or she] is immediately to pay off, discharge, or remove the lien, charge, or encumbrance from the property, whether or not it proves in fact to be prior or superior to the lien of this deed of trust.

(f) Occupancy. Grantor will keep the property occupied and if it becomes and remains vacant for more than thirty (30) consecutive days, Lender may at __________ [his or her] option request Trustee to take the possession of it and rent it. Such rental, less the reasonable costs of collection of it, shall be applied as a credit on the indebtedness hereby secured.

(g) Repairs. Grantor (1) will maintain the property in good repair; (2) will not remove or demolish any building or improvement on it; and (3) will not commit, suffer, or permit any waste, impairment, or deterioration of the property.

(h) Future liens. Grantor agrees not to allow to be fixed, or to enter into any contract where there may be fixed on the property any mechanic's lien or other lien without the written consent of Lender.

(i) Condemnation. If the property or any part of it shall be condemned and taken under the power of eminent domain, all damages and awards for the property taken, to the amount then unpaid on the indebtedness hereby secured, shall be paid to Lender, and the amount shall be credited on the indebtedness secured by it and may, at the option of Lender, be applied to the last maturing installments.

(j) Unsecured indebtedness. If any part of the indebtedness described here cannot lawfully be secured by this deed of trust or the lien granted, Grantor agrees that payments shall be applied first to the discharge of that unsecured portion of the indebtedness until it is paid.

FIGURE 8-2 (Continued)

6. In the event that Grantor fails to pay any taxes or assessments or to insure the property as provided above, or should Grantor fail to take the necessary steps to preserve the priority of the lien granted by this deed of trust, then Lender shall have the right, at ____________ [his or her] option, to pay any such taxes or assessments or any necessary insurance premiums, or to remove or defend any suit in relation to the preservation of the priority of the lien granted by this deed of trust. Any sums that may be so paid by Lender shall at once become an indebtedness from Grantor to Lender, shall bear interest from the date of payment of it at __________________ percent (___%) per annum, shall be payable on demand, and shall be a part of the indebtedness secured by it.

7. If default shall be made in any payment, or part of it, under the note or other indebtedness secured by it, or if Grantor shall fail to keep or perform any of the covenants, conditions, or stipulations here, then the described indebtedness, together with all accrued interest on it and all other sums secured by it, shall, at the option of Lender, become at once due and payable without demand or notice. Trustee here, or any substitute Trustee, shall be and is, authorized and empowered, when requested to do so by Lender after such default (which request is hereby conclusively presumed), to sell the property at a public sale at auction held between the hours of 10 o'clock a.m. and 4 o'clock p.m. of the first Tuesday in any month, in the county in which the premises, or any part is situated, after advertisement of the time, place, and terms of the sale and the property to be sold by posting, or causing to be posted, for at least twenty-one (21) consecutive days prior to the date of the sale written notice at the courthouse door of each county in which the property is located. Notice must also be given by filing a copy in the office of the county clerk of each county in which the property is located and by serving written notice of the proposed sale by certified mail on each debtor obligated to pay such debt according to the records of Lender at least 21 days preceding the date of the sale as provided by statute. Grantor authorized and empowers Trustee to sell the premises, together, or in lots or parcels, as Trustee shall deem expedient, and to execute and deliver to the purchaser of the premises deeds of conveyance of it by fee simple title, with covenants of general warranty. The title of such purchaser, when so made by Trustee, Grantor binds _____________ [himself or herself] to warrant and forever defend.

8. In the event of a sale, any one or more of Lenders of the indebtedness then secured by it, or any part of it, shall have the right to become the purchaser in the event that Lender should be the highest bidder, and shall have the right, in lieu of cash payment, to apply the amount bid against the indebtedness owing by Grantor to the owner and Lender of the indebtedness.

9. In the event of a sale of the property, or of any part thereof, under the power granted here, Grantor, Grantor's heirs, executors, administrators, assigns, successors, or any other person holding under them or in possession of the property, shall become a tenant at will or the purchaser at the foreclosure sale, and should such tenant refuse to surrender possession of the property on demand, the purchaser shall be entitled to institute and maintain the statutory action for forcible detainer, and to procure a writ of possession under it.

10. It is expressly agreed that the recitals in the conveyance to the purchaser shall be full evidence of the truth of the matters stated there, and all prerequisites to the sale shall be presumed to have been performed.

FIGURE 8-2 (Continued)

11. Lender, in any event, is authorized here to appoint a substitute Trustee or a successor Trustee to act instead of Trustee named here without other formality than designation of such substitute or successor Trustee in writing. The authority conferred here shall extend to the appointment of other successor and substitute Trustees successively until the indebtedness secured here has been paid in full, or until the property is sold, and each substitute and successor Trustee shall succeed to all the rights and powers of the original Trustee named here.

12. Grantor assigns to Lender all rents on the premises covered here and authorizes Lender (a) to take possession of the premises at any time there shall be a default in the payment of the debt secured here or in the performance of any obligation herein contained, (b) to rent them for Grantor, (c) to deduct from such rents all costs of collection and administration, and (d) to apply the remainder of those rents on the debt secured here.

13. Failure of Lender to exercise an option available under the terms of this instrument or the note secured here shall not constitute a waiver of Lender's rights to exercise the same on any subsequent default.

14. Neither Grantor nor any party liable for the indebtedness secured here shall be required to pay interest in excess of the rate allowed by the laws of the State of Texas. The intention of the parties is to conform strictly to the usury laws now in force, and any contract for interest secured here shall be held to be subject to reduction to the amount allowed under the usury laws as now or later construed by the courts having jurisdiction.

15. The time for payment of all or any part of the indebtedness described here may be extended, or any part of the indebtedness released from the lien created here, without affecting or altering the priority of the lien in favor of any junior encumbrancer or any person acquiring an interest in the property described here, or any part of it. It is the intention of the parties to preserve the priority of this lien against all liens that may be placed on the property, notwithstanding the granting of extensions in the time for payment of the indebtedness secured here or the release from this lien of portions of the property.

16. In the event the proceeds of the indebtedness secured by this deed of trust are used to pay off or discharge any lien or encumbrance on the property described here, Lender shall be subrogated to all such liens or encumbrances and to all of the rights of the persons of those to whom such payments are made.

17. Grantor represents that this deed of trust and the note secured here are given for the following purpose: _____________ [insert brief statement of purpose for note and deed of trust, such as: to secure payment of a vendor's lien].

18. All covenants, agreements, and terms contained here shall bind, and the benefits and advantages shall inure to, the respective heirs, executors, administrators, successors, and assigns of the parties.

FIGURE 8-2 (Continued)

19. Whenever used, the singular number shall include the plural and the plural the singular, and the word "Lender" shall include any payee of the indebtedness secured here or any transferee of it whether by operation of law or otherwise.

Dated_______________ [date]

____
Signatures

____
Acknowledgments

FIGURE 8-2 (Continued)

property in the case of default by the grantor, the debtor, for the benefit of the lender, the beneficiary. Since this document more directly affects the property, this document is the one commonly recorded.

There are two important paragraphs contained within the deed of trust. The first paragraph to consider is the trust clause, contained in paragraph 3 of the provided deed of trust. The **trust clause** specifies that the conveyance under the deed of trust is made in trust to secure payment of the underlying debt in the promissory note. This clause gives the trustee the right to enforce the instrument in case the debtor defaults. The second paragraph to consider is the power of sale clause, contained in paragraph 7 of the provided deed of trust. The **power of sale clause** gives the trustee authority to sell the property at public auction (non-judicial foreclosure) if the debtor defaults. Without this paragraph, the trustee would be required to go to court (judicial foreclosure) to foreclose on the property, which would be a more expensive process.

OWNER FINANCING

A **seller financing** transaction is a transaction in which the seller, rather than a lending institution, finances the transaction. Seller financing can be used in conjunction with third party conventional loans, assumptions, and Texas Veteran's Housing Assistance Program Loans.

For a seller financing transaction, the real estate professional must use the Seller Financing Addendum (TREC 26-7). The Seller Financing Addendum is a promulgated addendum that is to be used in seller financing transactions to specify the details of the financing arrangement between the buyer and the seller. See figure 8-3. This addendum can be used with any of the current promulgated sales contract forms.

Note this form is not to be used for complex transactions, such as contracts for deed. Paragraphs A and B provide for credit documentation and approval, respectively. In paragraph C, the specific requirements of the promissory note between the buyer and seller are expressed. The promissory note is basically the IOU from the buyer to the seller. Since it is a contract between the parties, it is not recorded. The terms vary; however, it is not uncommon for a seller financing transaction to be for a shorter period of time and at a higher interest rate than traditional lender financing.

In paragraph D, the terms of the deed of trust are completed. The deed of trust is the security instrument that will permit the seller to sell the property if the buyer defaults on the loan. Since the deed of trust creates a security interest, it is recorded in the deed records. Notice in D(1)(a) the parties indicate that consent is not required for future transfers. Paragraph D(1)(b) is the situation where consent is required from the seller, which also allows the seller to require the note to be due in full if consent is not obtained.

PROMULGATED BY THE TEXAS REAL ESTATE COMMISSION (TREC) 11-2-2015

SELLER FINANCING ADDENDUM

TO CONTRACT CONCERNING THE PROPERTY AT

____
(Address of Property)

A. **CREDIT DOCUMENTATION.** To establish Buyer's creditworthiness, Buyer shall deliver to Seller within_______days after the effective date of this contract, ❑ credit report ❑ verification of employment, including salary ❑ verification of funds on deposit in financial institutions ❑ current financial statement and ❑ ____. Buyer hereby authorizes any credit reporting agency to furnish copies of Buyer's credit reports to Seller at Buyer's sole expense.

B. **BUYER'S CREDIT APPROVAL.** If the credit documentation described in Paragraph A is not delivered within the specified time, Seller may terminate this contract by notice to Buyer within 7 days after expiration of the time for delivery, and the earnest money will be paid to Seller. If the credit documentation is timely delivered, and Seller determines in Seller's sole discretion that Buyer's credit is unacceptable, Seller may terminate this contract by notice to Buyer within 7 days after expiration of the time for delivery and the earnest money will be refunded to Buyer. If Seller does not terminate this contract, Seller will be deemed to have approved Buyer's creditworthiness.

C. **PROMISSORY NOTE.** The promissory note in the amount of $____________(Note), included in Paragraph 3B of the contract payable by Buyer to the order of Seller will bear interest at the rate of _____% per annum and be payable at the place designated by Seller. Buyer may prepay the Note in whole or in part at any time without penalty. Any prepayments are to be applied to the payment of the installments of principal last maturing and interest will immediately cease on the prepaid principal. The Note will contain a provision for payment of a late fee of 5% of any installment not paid within 10 days of the due date. Matured unpaid amounts will bear interest at the rate of 1½% per month or at the highest lawful rate, whichever is less. The Note will be payable as follows:

❑ (1) In one payment due ______________________________ after the date of the Note with interest payable ❑ at maturity ❑ monthly ❑ quarterly. (check one box only)

❑ (2) In monthly installments of $ ______________ ❑ including interest ❑plus interest (check one box only) beginning ____________________ after the date of the Note and continuing monthly thereafter for____________ months when the balance of the Note will be due and payable.

❑ (3) Interest only in monthly installments for the first ___________ month(s) and thereafter in installments of $________________ ❑ including interest ❑ plus interest (check one box only) beginning ___________________ after the date of the Note and continuing monthly thereafter for____________ months when the balance of the Note will be due and payable.

D. **DEED OF TRUST.** The deed of trust securing the Note will provide for the following:

(1) PROPERTY TRANSFERS: (check one box only)

❑ (a) Consent Not Required: The Property may be sold, conveyed or leased without the consent of Seller, provided any subsequent buyer assumes the Note.

❑ (b) Consent Required: If all or any part of the Property is sold, conveyed, leased for a period longer than 3 years, leased with an option to purchase, or otherwise sold (including any contract for deed), without Seller's prior written consent, which consent may be withheld in Seller's sole discretion, Seller may declare the balance of the Note

Initialed for identification by Buyer_____________ and Seller__________ TREC NO. 26-7

FIGURE 8-3 Seller Financing Addendum
Source: Reprinted with permission of Texas Real Estate Commission

Seller Financing Addendum Concerning Page 2 of 2 11-2-2015

____

(Address of Property)

to be immediately due and payable. The creation of a subordinate lien, any conveyance under threat or order of condemnation, any deed solely between buyers, or the passage of title by reason of the death of a buyer or by operation of law will not entitle Seller to exercise the remedies provided in this paragraph.

NOTE: *Under (a) or (b), Buyer's liability to pay the Note will continue unless Buyer obtains a release of liability from Seller.*

(2) TAX AND INSURANCE ESCROW: (check one box only)

❑ (a) Escrow Not Required: Buyer shall furnish Seller, before each year's ad valorem taxes become delinquent, evidence that all ad valorem taxes on the Property have been paid. Buyer shall annually furnish Seller evidence of paid-up casualty insurance naming Seller as a mortgagee loss payee.

❑ (b) Escrow Required: With each installment Buyer shall deposit in escrow with Seller a pro rata part of the estimated annual ad valorem taxes and casualty insurance premiums for the Property. Buyer shall pay any deficiency within 30 days after notice from Seller. Buyer's failure to pay the deficiency will be a default under the deed of trust. Buyer is not required to deposit any escrow payments for taxes and insurance that are deposited with a superior lienholder. The casualty insurance must name Seller as a mortgagee loss payee.

(3) PRIOR LIENS: Any default under any lien superior to the lien securing the Note will be a default under the deed of trust securing the Note.

____________________ ____________________

Buyer Seller

____________________ ____________________

Buyer Seller

The form of this contract has been approved by the Texas Real Estate Commission for use with similarly approved or promulgated contract forms. TREC forms are intended for use only by trained real estate license holders. No representation is made as to the legal validity or adequacy of any provision in any specific transactions. It is not intended for complex transactions. Texas Real Estate Commission, P.O. Box 12188, Austin, TX 78711-2188, 512-936-3000 (http://www.trec.texas.gov) TREC No. 26-7. This form replaces TREC No. 26-6.

TREC NO. 26-7

FIGURE 8-3 (Continued)

Paragraph D(2) discusses the method by which taxes and insurance payments will be made. Most sellers will typically prefer Paragraph D(2)(b) "escrow required" so they do not have to worry about these payments being made.

FORECLOSURES AND SHORT SALES

Foreclosure

Once the financing takes place and the lender perfects its lien on the property, there may come a time when the purchaser can no longer make payments on the loan. At this point, the property owner should attempt a payment plan with the lender. If this is not possible, the property owner might attempt a short sale or a deed in lieu of foreclosure, which will be discussed later in this chapter. The last possibility when the property owner cannot pay his or her mortgage is a foreclosure.

The typical deed of trust provides a power of sale clause, which authorizes the trustee to sell the property at public auction in case the debtor defaults on payment of the loan. However, there are additional requirements that must be met by the trustee in order to proceed with this non-judicial foreclosure. A sale of real property under a power of sale clause of a deed of trust must be a public sale at auction held between 10 a.m. and 4 p.m. of the first Tuesday of a month. The sale must take place at the county courthouse in the county where the land is located or other county designated location.[1] If the property is the debtor's residence, the lender must serve the debtor with written notice by certified mail stating that the debtor is in default under the deed of trust and give the debtor at least 20 days to cure the default before notice of sale can be given.[2] Notice of the foreclosure sale must be given to the debtor. This notice of sale, which must include a statement of the earliest time at which the sale will begin, must be given at least 21 days before the date of the sale by: (1) posting at the appropriate county courthouse door a written notice designating the county where the property will be sold; (2) filing in the appropriate county clerk's office a copy of the notice posted; and (3) serving written notice of the sale by certified mail on each debtor who is obligated to pay the debt.[3] Notice served on the debtor must state the name and address of the sender of the notice and contain, in addition to any other statements required under this section, a statement that is conspicuous, printed in boldface or underlined type, and substantially similar to the following: "Assert and protect your rights as a member of the armed forces of the United States. If you are or your spouse is serving on active military duty, including active military duty as a member of the Texas National Guard or the National Guard of another state or as a member of a reserve component of the armed forces of the United States, please

[1] Tex. Prop. Code § 51.002(a).
[2] Tex. Prop. Code § 51.002(d).
[3] Tex. Prop. Code § 51.002(b).

send written notice of the active duty military service to the sender of this notice immediately."[4]

If the price for which real property is sold at a foreclosure sale is less than the unpaid balance of the indebtedness secured by the real property, the lender can pursue the debtor for any deficiency. An action by the lender for deficiency against the debtor must be brought within two years of the foreclosure sale.[5] In a deficiency action, the debtor has the right to present evidence to the judge or jury as fact finder contesting the fair market value of the property as of the date of the foreclosure sale.[6] If the court determines that the fair market value of the property was greater than the sales price at the foreclosure sale, then the debtor will be entitled to an offset against the deficiency for the difference.[7] For instance, if the debtor owed $100,000 on the property, but the property was sold for only $75,000 at the foreclosure sale, then the debtor would have a $25,000 deficiency. However, if the debtor is able to prove that the fair market value of the property was in fact $100,000, then the debtor would be permitted to offset the entire deficiency. If the debtor does not contest the fair market value, then the sale price at foreclosure will be used to determine the deficiency.[8] Any amounts received from the lender for private mortgage insurance (PMI) must be credited to any deficiency prior to the lender bringing a deficiency action.[9]

Short Sales

A seller on the brink of foreclosure may try to sell the home rather than face foreclosure. However, trying to obtain a high enough sales price to satisfy the loan in a sluggish market can be difficult. In these circumstances the seller might attempt a short sale. A **short sale** is used when the seller must sell the property for less than the total debt remaining on the loan. See figure 8-4. During negotiations, the seller should inform the buyer that a short sale is intended.

For a short sale to take place, the lender must agree to accept the proceeds of any sale even though they will not satisfy the entire debt. The lender is merely agreeing to the sale and may or may not excuse the difference that the seller still owes. However, there is no guarantee that the lender will approve the short sale. From a tactical perspective, the seller should contact the lender before trying a short sale to find out under what terms, particularly sales price, the lender will accept the short sale. For a buyer considering a short sale, this is an important question to ask as a preapproved short sale with known terms generally reduces the overall negotiation time.

---

[4] Tex. Prop. Code § 51.002(i).
[5] Tex. Prop. Code § 51.003(a).
[6] Tex. Prop. Code § 51.003(b).
[7] Tex. Prop. Code § 51.003(c).
[8] Tex. Prop. Code § 51.003(c).
[9] Tex. Prop. Code § 51.003(d).

PROMULGATED BY THE TEXAS REAL ESTATE COMMISSION (TREC) 12-05-11

SHORT SALE ADDENDUM

ADDENDUM TO CONTRACT CONCERNING THE PROPERTY AT

____
(Street Address and City)

A. This contract involves a "short sale" of the Property. As used in this Addendum, "short sale" means that:

(1) Seller's net proceeds at closing will be insufficient to pay the balance of Seller's mortgage loan; and

(2) Seller requires:
(a) the consent of the lienholder to sell the Property pursuant to this contract; and
(b) the lienholder's agreement to:
(i) accept Seller's net proceeds in full satisfaction of Seller's liability under the mortgage loan; and
(ii) provide Seller an executed release of lien against the Property in a recordable format.

B. As used in this Addendum, "Seller's net proceeds" means the Sales Price less Seller's Expenses under Paragraph 12 of the contract and Seller's obligation to pay any brokerage fees.

C. The contract to which this Addendum is attached is binding upon execution by the parties and the earnest money and the Option Fee must be paid as provided in the contract. The contract is contingent on the satisfaction of Seller's requirements under Paragraph A(2) of this Addendum (Lienholder's Consent and Agreement). Seller shall apply promptly for and make every reasonable effort to obtain Lienholder's Consent and Agreement, and shall furnish all information and documents required by the lienholder. Except as provided by this Addendum, neither party is required to perform under the contract while it is contingent upon obtaining Lienholder's Consent and Agreement.

D. If Seller does not notify Buyer that Seller has obtained Lienholder's Consent and Agreement on or before ______________________________, this contract terminates and the earnest money will be refunded to Buyer. Seller must notify Buyer immediately if Lienholder's Consent and Agreement is obtained. For purposes of performance, the effective date of the contract changes to the date Seller provides Buyer notice of the Lienholder's Consent and Agreement (Amended Effective Date).

E. This contract will terminate and the earnest money will be refunded to Buyer if the Lienholder refuses or withdraws its Consent and Agreement prior to closing and funding. Seller shall promptly notify Buyer of any lienholder's refusal to provide or withdrawal of a Lienholder's Consent and Agreement.

F. If Buyer has the unrestricted right to terminate this contract, the time for giving notice of termination begins on the effective date of the contract, continues after the Amended Effective Date and ends upon the expiration of Buyer's unrestricted right to terminate the contract under Paragraph 23.

G. For the purposes of this Addendum, time is of the essence. Strict compliance with the times for performance stated in this Addendum is required.

H. Seller authorizes any lienholder to furnish to Buyer or Buyer's representatives information relating to the status of the request for a Lienholder's Consent and Agreement.

I. If there is more than one lienholder or loan secured by the Property, this Addendum applies to each lienholder.

______________________	______________________
Buyer	Seller
______________________	______________________
Buyer	Seller

The form of this addendum has been approved by the Texas Real Estate Commission for use only with similarly approved or promulgated forms of contracts. Such approval relates to this contract form only. TREC forms are intended for use only by trained real estate licensees. No representation is made as to the legal validity or adequacy of any provision in any specific transactions. It is not intended for complex transactions. Texas Real Estate Commission, P.O. Box 12188, Austin, TX 78711-2188, (512) 936-3000 (http://www.trec.texas.gov) TREC No. 45-1. This form replaces TREC No. 45-0.

TREC NO. 45-1

FIGURE 8-4 Short Sale Addendum
Source: Reprinted with permission of Texas Real Estate Commission

Lenders take into consideration several factors to determine whether to accept a short sale. A significant factor is whether the property's market value is less than the remaining debt. If the property is worth more than the debt, then there is no incentive for the lender to accept a short sale when a foreclosure sale would likely net a higher price. Other factors lenders often consider take into account problems that cannot otherwise be solved by a payment arrangement or loan refinance. These factors include the extent of default on the debt, significant hardships faced by the seller that would prevent repayment, such as loss of job, and lack of additional assets that could be used to pay the loan.

In addition, many lenders prefer that the buyer accept the property "as is" to alleviate the need for extra funds to be used for repairs. Therefore, the buyer should take repairs into consideration when making an offer. Furthermore, during any short sale transaction, the lender, rather than the seller, makes the decisions. Therefore, reaching a final agreement for the sale can take longer. In addition, the lender's participation during the entire transaction can potentially extend the time it takes to close on the deal.

The short sale is often confused with a deed in lieu of foreclosure. A **deed in lieu of foreclosure** is a deed that is used for the seller to convey title of the property to the lender, rather than a third party, in exchange for a release from the mortgage. Most lenders prefer that the seller attempt the short sale process first before proceeding with a deed in lieu of foreclosure. If the lender is unable to obtain the full mortgage debt amount at sale after receiving the deed in lieu of foreclosure, the seller may still be responsible for any deficiency. The lender may be able to void a deed in lieu of foreclosure within four years after the deed is executed and foreclosed under the original deed of trust if: (1) the debtor fails to disclose to the lender a lien or other encumbrance on the property before executing the deed in lieu of foreclosure; and (2) the lender has no personal knowledge of the undisclosed lien or encumbrance on the property.[10]

LIENS

There are several additional types of liens that can attach to real estate other than mortgages. This section will address some of the liens that can attach to real estate and are exempt under the homestead laws thereby permitting the property to be sold to satisfy the underlying debt. Property (ad valorem) tax liens, materialman's liens, and liens for preexisting indebtedness will be discussed.

Property (Ad Valorem) Tax Liens

One power the government has over real property is the power of taxation, which can be enforced through a lien. A property (ad valorem) tax lien is a lien on real

---

[10] Tex. Prop. Code § 51.006(b).

property to secure payment of property taxes. On January 1 of each year, a tax lien attaches to real property to secure the payment of all taxes, penalties, and interest ultimately imposed for the year on the property, whether or not the taxes are imposed in the year the lien attaches.[11] Property tax bills are considered delinquent if not paid by February 1 of the following year.[12] At any time after the property tax becomes delinquent, the taxing authority may file suit to foreclose the lien securing payment of the tax, to enforce personal liability for the tax, or both.[13]

In a real estate transaction, the seller must be prepared to show that there are no delinquent taxes at closing. This information can be obtained by the title company acting as escrow agent for the transaction. The county taxing authority is not required to file a property tax lien in the county deed records so delinquent tax information must be obtained directly from the tax office.[14] Since taxes cover the entire year, the taxes will be prorated through the closing date. If the taxes are not paid at or prior to closing, the buyer will have to pay all taxes for the current year as new owner of the property.

Mechanic's, Contractor's, or Materialman's Liens

A materialman's lien is a lien that can be attached to real property to secure payment for a house, building, or other improvements to the property. To fix a lien on a homestead, the contractor and the owner must execute a written contract setting forth the terms of the agreement.[15] In addition, before a residential construction contract is signed by the owner, the contractor must deliver to the owner a disclosure statement informing him or her about materialman's liens in Texas.[16]

If the property owner fails to pay for the project, the contractor will take steps to enforce his or her lien. The contractor claiming the lien as a result of a residential construction project must file an affidavit with the county clerk not later than the 15th day of the third calendar month after the day on which the indebtedness accrues and provide the property owner with notice.[17] For a residential construction project, the contractor must bring suit to foreclose the lien within one year after the last day for filing the affidavit or within one year after completion, termination, or abandonment of the work under the original contract, whichever is later.[18] A materialman's lien can be foreclosed only through a judicial foreclosure and the property subject to the lien will be ordered sold.[19]

---

[11] Tex. Tax Code § 32.01(a).
[12] Tex. Tax Code § 31.02.
[13] Tex. Tax Code § 33.41(a).
[14] Tex. Prop. Code § 51.008.
[15] Tex. Prop. Code § 53.254(a).
[16] Tex. Prop. Code § 53.255(a).
[17] Tex. Prop. Code § 53.052(b).
[18] Tex. Prop. Code § 53.158(b).
[19] Tex. Prop. Code § 53.154.

Preexisting Indebtedness

A lien for preexisting indebtedness attaches to real property for non-payment of a debt that arose prior to the acquisition of the homestead. The most common type of preexisting indebtedness is homeowners association dues. Homeowners association assessments are considered a preexisting indebtedness because they become an obligation of the property at the time the subdivision plat is created. The purchaser then buys the property subject to the assessments.

The owner of real property located in a subdivision with a mandatory homeowners association will be required to pay certain fees and assessments to the homeowners association. If the owner fails to pay assessments or other charges as required, a lien can be filed in the county deed records.[20] This is why it is crucial that the buyer seek information from the seller regarding the presence of mandatory membership in a homeowners association, as well as the association's fees and assessments.

THE REAL ESTATE FINANCING MARKET, TECHNIQUES, AND LOAN PROGRAMS

The Real Estate Financing Market

As discussed in an earlier chapter, there are several traditional financing methods that a buyer can use to purchase real estate. These include assumption, seller financing, third party conventional, VA, and FHA financing. But there are various loan programs as well as creative financing techniques that can be used as well. Unfortunately, the financing options nowadays are not as flexible as they once were. The Great Recession of 2008, instigated by the fallout of the housing market, led to a decrease in the loan options available. Current loans can be of two types—conforming and nonconforming. A **conforming loan** is a loan that conforms to Fannie Mae (FNMA) and Freddie Mac (FHLMC) guidelines. Fannie Mae and Freddie Mac purchase the majority of mortgage loans creating a secondary real estate market. This secondary market frees up funds for lenders to make additional loans. If lenders wish to take advantage of this market, the loan must conform to the requisite guidelines. These entities were taken over by the Federal Housing Finance Agency (FHFA) after the recession.

A non-conforming loan is a loan that does not conform to the Fannie Mae and Freddie Mac guidelines. The most common type of non-conforming loan is a jumbo loan. A jumbo loan is a loan for an amount that exceeds the Fannie Mae and Freddie Mac guidelines. Terms on a jumbo loan are typically stricter than traditional conforming loans.

[20] Tex. Prop. Code § 209.0094.

Financing Techniques

Assumptions

There are not only special loan programs available in Texas, but there are also different financing techniques. For example, an **assumption** transaction is the purchase of real property subject to a mortgage whereby the purchaser accepts liability under an existing note, and the seller remains liable to the lender. This is true unless the lender executes a release of liability. An assumption may arise between a lender, a seller, and a buyer. In an assumption situation, a note exists between the lender and the seller. The buyer assumes the note. The seller has delegated the duty to pay to the buyer. If the buyer fails to pay, the lender is still entitled to collect payment from the seller, in the absence of a release of liability of the seller. The buyer in this case is said to be primarily liable, and the seller is secondarily liable. Thus, if the buyer fails to pay, the seller will be responsible for making the payment or risk foreclosure and a poor credit rating. Since the seller does still have some liability under the note, most sellers will have the buyer execute a **deed of trust to secure assumption**. When this document is properly executed and recorded in the county deed records, it allows the seller to foreclose on the property if the seller has to make a delinquent payment to the lender on behalf of the buyer.

The Loan Assumption Addendum (TREC 41-2) is used any time the property is obtained through an assumption. See figure 8-5. Paragraph A provides for credit documentation to be delivered by the buyer to the seller. Paragraph B provides for credit approval. If the buyer's information is not delivered on time, the seller has the right to terminate the contract. If the documentation is delivered on time, the seller can terminate the contract if the seller deems the buyer's credit is unacceptable. If the seller does not terminate, the seller is deemed to have accepted the buyer's credit. Therefore, if the seller sends a termination via fax, a return receipt should be obtained. Paragraph C provides for assumption of a first or second lien note by the buyer. Space is provided for the inclusion of the name of the lienholder, the unpaid balance at closing, and the current monthly payment. The buyer's first payment will be the first payment due after closing. In addition, under the assumption the buyer assumes all obligations under the note.

When dealing with an assumption transaction, it is important to estimate the unpaid balance at closing as accurately as possible, because the contract provides that if the total unpaid balance of all loans varies by greater than $500 at closing, either party may terminate the contract unless the other party agrees to cover the difference in the variance at closing. To ensure accuracy, it is wise to check all figures with the mortgage company before proceeding.

In addition, space is provided for insertion of the maximum assumption or transfer fee. If the amount required by the lender exceeds this amount and the seller elects not to pay the difference, the buyer may terminate the contract and have the earnest money refunded. Furthermore, if the interest rate exceeds the

PROMULGATED BY THE TEXAS REAL ESTATE COMMISSION (TREC) 12-05-11

LOAN ASSUMPTION ADDENDUM
TO CONTRACT CONCERNING THE PROPERTY AT

____
(Address of Property)

A. CREDIT DOCUMENTATION. To establish Buyer's creditworthiness, Buyer shall deliver to Seller within_________days after the effective date of this contract ❑ credit report ❑ verification of employment, including salary ❑ verification of funds on deposit in financial institutions ❑ current financial statement and ❑____
____.
Buyer hereby authorizes any credit reporting agency to furnish copies of Buyer's credit reports to Seller at Buyer's sole expense.

B. CREDIT APPROVAL. If the credit documentation described in Paragraph A is not delivered within the specified time, Seller may terminate this contract by notice to Buyer within 7 days after expiration of the time for delivery, and the earnest money will be paid to Seller. If the credit documentation is timely delivered, and Seller determines in Seller's sole discretion that Buyer's credit is unacceptable, Seller may terminate this contract by notice to Buyer within 7 days after expiration of the time for delivery and the earnest money will be refunded to Buyer. If Seller does not terminate this contract within the time specified, Seller will be deemed to have approved Buyer's creditworthiness.

C. ASSUMPTION. Buyer's assumption of an existing note includes all obligations imposed by the deed of trust securing the note.

❑ (1) The unpaid principal balance of a first lien promissory note payable to______________ ____________________________which unpaid balance at closing will be $ ______________. The total current monthly payment including principal, interest and any reserve deposits is $ ______________. Buyer's initial payment will be the first payment due after closing.

❑ (2) The unpaid principal balance of a second lien promissory note payable to ____________ ____________________________which unpaid balance at closing will be $ ______________. The total current monthly payment including principal, interest and any reserve deposits is $ ______________. Buyer's initial payment will be the first payment due after closing.

If the unpaid principal balance of any assumed loan as of the Closing Date varies from the loan balance stated above, the ❑ cash payable at closing ❑ Sales Price will be adjusted by the amount of any variance. If the total principal balance of all assumed loans varies in an amount greater than $500 at closing, either party may terminate this contract and the earnest money will be refunded to Buyer unless the other party elects to pay the excess of the variance.

D. LOAN ASSUMPTION TERMS. Buyer may terminate this contract and the earnest money will be refunded to Buyer if the noteholder requires:
(1) payment of an assumption fee in excess of $ _________in C(1) or $ ____________in C(2) and Seller declines to pay such excess, or
(2) an increase in the interest rate to more than ______% in C(1) or______% in C(2), or
(3) any other modification of the loan documents.

E. CONSENT BY NOTEHOLDER. If the noteholder fails to consent to the assumption of the loan, either Seller or Buyer may terminate this contract by notice to the other party and the earnest money will be refunded to the Buyer.

F. SELLER'S LIENS. Unless Seller is released from liability on any assumed note, a vendor's lien and deed of trust to secure assumption will be required. The vendor's lien will automatically be released on delivery of an executed release by noteholder.

Initialed for identification by Buyer ___ and Seller__________ TREC NO. 41-2

FIGURE 8-5 Loan Assumption Addendum
Source: Reprinted with permission of Texas Real Estate Commission

Loan Assumption Addendum Concerning Page 2 of 2 12-05-11

____
(Address of Property)

G. TAX AND INSURANCE ESCROW. If noteholder maintains an escrow account for ad valorem taxes, casualty insurance premiums or mortgage insurance premiums, Seller shall transfer the escrow account to Buyer without any deficiency. Buyer shall reimburse Seller for the amount in the transferred accounts.

NOTICE TO BUYER: If you are concerned about the possibility of future adjustments, monthly payments, interest rates or other terms, do not sign the contract without examining the notes and deeds of trust.

NOTICE TO SELLER: Your liability to pay the notes assumed by Buyer will continue unless you obtain a release of liability from the noteholders. If you are concerned about future liability, you should use the TREC Release of Liability Addendum.

______________________ Buyer	______________________ Seller
______________________ Buyer	______________________ Seller

TREC TEXAS REAL ESTATE COMMISSION

This form has been approved by the Texas Real Estate Commission for use with similarly approved or promulgated contract forms. Such approval relates to this form only. TREC forms are intended for use only by trained real estate licensees. No representation is made as to the legal validity or adequacy of any provision in any specific transactions. It is not suitable for complex transactions. Texas Real Estate Commission, P.O. Box 12188, Austin, TX 78711-2188, 512-936-3000 (http://www.trec.texas.gov) TREC No. 41-2. This form replaces TREC No. 41-1.

FIGURE 8-5 (Continued)

predetermined amount or there is any modification to the loan documents, the buyer may terminate the contract and have the earnest money refunded.

In assumption transactions, the seller will seek a release from the underlying loan by using the Addendum for Release of Liability on Assumed Loan and/or Restoration of Seller's VA Entitlement (TREC 12-3). See figure 8-6. When this form is used, it gives the seller the right to seek a release of liability from the lender within a designated number of days from the effective date of the contract. Three to five days is usually sufficient time to apply. If the release is not obtained, it gives the seller the right to terminate the contract or continue with the deal. It is rare that lenders will release the seller. When a release is not obtained, a vendor's lien and deed of trust to secure assumption are utilized to protect the seller in case the buyer fails to make payments. As mentioned earlier, the buyer has the primary responsibility to pay, but if he or she does not, then the seller will be responsible for the payment. If the seller does ultimately make a payment, the vendor's lien and deed of trust to secure assumption will allow the seller to regain title if the seller chooses. Obviously, if the seller is released from liability, there is no need for the vendor's lien and deed of trust to secure assumption.

The last paragraph deals with notice to the buyer and seller. The Notice to Buyer provides that the note may be adjusted at closing or thereafter. If the buyer is concerned about future adjustments, he or she should not sign the contract without reviewing the necessary documents. The buyer may wish to see an attorney at this point. The Notice to Seller advises the seller that he or she will remain liable under the note unless a release of liability is obtained from the lender. If the seller is concerned about future liability, a promulgated Release of Liability Addendum should be used. For practical purposes, sellers do not typically want to be responsible for someone else's debt, so the Addendum for Release of Liability on Assumed Loan and/or Restoration of Seller's VA Entitlement should be included with all assumption transactions.

It is helpful to know that assumption transactions are rare nowadays. A couple of decades ago lenders got wise to assumption techniques and devised what are called due on sale clauses. A **due on sale clause** basically states that when a sale takes place, the seller must pay the amount due on the note to the bank. If the note is paid off, there would be no note for a prospective buyer to assume. Hence, no assumption transaction would ensue.

Third Party Financing

The most common type of financing is third party lender financing. A third party lender can refer to a "lending institution, including a bank, trust company, banking association, savings and loan association, mortgage company, investment bank, credit union, life insurance company, and governmental agency, that customarily provides financing or an affiliate of a lending institution."[21] For third

[21] Tex. Prop. Code § 5.201(2).

PROMULGATED BY THE TEXAS REAL ESTATE COMMISSION (TREC) 12-05-11

ADDENDUM FOR RELEASE OF LIABILITY ON ASSUMED LOAN AND/OR RESTORATION OF SELLER'S VA ENTITLEMENT

TO CONTRACT CONCERNING THE PROPERTY AT

____

(Address of Property)

❑ **A. RELEASE OF SELLER'S LIABILITY ON LOAN TO BE ASSUMED:**

Within ____________ days after the effective date of this contract Seller and Buyer shall apply for release of Seller's liability from (a) any conventional lender, (b) VA and any lender whose loan has been guaranteed by VA, or (c) FHA and any lender whose loan has been insured by FHA. Seller and Buyer shall furnish all required information and documents. If any release of liability has not been approved by the Closing Date: (check one box only)

❑ (1) This contract will terminate and the earnest money will be refunded to Buyer.

❑ (2) Failure to obtain release approval will not delay closing.

❑ **B. RESTORATION OF SELLER'S ENTITLEMENT FOR VA LOAN:**

Within ___________ days after the effective date of this contract Seller and Buyer shall apply for restoration of Seller's VA entitlement and shall furnish all information and documents required by VA. If restoration has not been approved by the Closing Date: (check one box only)

❑ (1) This contract will terminate and the earnest money will be refunded to Buyer.

❑ (2) Failure to obtain restoration approval will not delay closing.

NOTICE: VA will not restore Seller's VA entitlement unless Buyer: (a) is a veteran, (b) has sufficient unused VA entitlement and (c) is otherwise qualified. If Seller desires restoration of VA entitlement, paragraphs A and B should be used.

Seller shall pay the cost of securing the release and restoration.

Seller's deed will contain any loan assumption clause required by FHA, VA or any lender.

Buyer	Seller
Buyer	Seller

TREC TEXAS REAL ESTATE COMMISSION

This form has been approved by the Texas Real Estate Commission for use with similarly approved or promulgated contract forms. Such approval relates to this form only. TREC forms are intended for use only by trained real estate licensees. No representation is made as to the legal validity or adequacy of any provision in any specific transactions. It is not suitable for complex transactions. Texas Real Estate Commission, P.O. Box 12188, Austin, TX 78711-2188, 512-936-3000 (http://www.trec.texas.gov) TREC No. 12-3. This form replaces TREC No. 12-2.

TREC No. 12-3

FIGURE 8-6 Release of Liability on Assumed Loan and/or Restoration of Seller's VA Entitlement
Source: Reprinted with permission of Texas Real Estate Commission

party lender financing, the real estate professional must use the promulgated Third Party Financing Addendum (TREC 40-7). See figure 8-7. The Third Party Financing Addendum provides a checklist of the various types of financing typically available in a residential real estate transaction. This addendum is not used where the transaction is in all cash.

Paragraph A addresses the various types of financing for which the form can be used, which will be detailed in the remaining paragraphs. Paragraph B of the Third Party Financing Addendum concerns approval of financing. Under this paragraph there is both buyer approval and property approval. Buyer approval, addressed in paragraph B1, concerns those things related to the buyer that impact approval, such as income, assets, or credit history. Paragraph B2, addressing property approval, concerns those things related to the property that impact approval, such as repairs, title insurance issues, or insufficient appraisal. Time is of the essence applies when terminating under paragraph B. The Addendum Concerning Right to Terminate Due to Lender's Appraisal (TREC 49-0) would be used when terminating under paragraph B2. See figure 8-8. Paragraph C clarifies that financing for the purchase will be secured by a lien. And paragraph E addresses the authorization to release information to necessary parties.

Conventional Financing

Paragraph A1 provides for conventional financing. In most cases, the third party financing the transaction will be a lender such as a bank or mortgage company, but in some instances, the third party may be a party outside the transaction who is lending money for the purchase. This does not include FHA-insured or VA-guaranteed financing sources. The blanks provide information on the principal amount of the loan, the length of the loan term, interest rate, and term of the interest rate. Paragraph A1(a) is checked if there is going to be a first mortgage loan and both paragraphs A1(a) and A1(b) are checked if there will be a first and second mortgage. For a fixed-rate note, the term of the interest rate will be the term of the note. For a variable-rate note, the term of the rate will be for one year.

The PMI premium referenced in this paragraph refers to private mortgage insurance. **Private mortgage insurance** is insurance that covers the bank when more than 80% is loaned for the purchase of real estate. Therefore, if the purchaser puts 20% or more down, the loan will be issued without PMI. If the purchaser puts less than 20% down, the loan will be issued with PMI. To avoid having to pay the PMI, it is possible for the purchaser to obtain two loans, one for 80% and the other for 20%, so that PMI need not be financed. The purchaser can consult a financial advisor to determine if this would be beneficial. Third party conventional financing can also be used with an assumption, a Texas Veterans Housing Assistance Program Loan, or a seller financing transaction. Terms for a Texas veterans loan are provided in paragraph A2.

11-15-18

TREC
TEXAS REAL ESTATE COMMISSION

PROMULGATED BY THE TEXAS REAL ESTATE COMMISSION (TREC)

THIRD PARTY FINANCING ADDENDUM

TO CONTRACT CONCERNING THE PROPERTY AT

____

(Street Address and City)

1. **TYPE OF FINANCING AND DUTY TO APPLY AND OBTAIN APPROVAL:** Buyer shall apply promptly for all financing described below and make every reasonable effort to obtain approval for the financing, including but not limited to furnishing all information and documents required by Buyer's lender. (Check applicable boxes):

❑ A. CONVENTIONAL FINANCING:

❑ (1) A first mortgage loan in the principal amount of $______________ (excluding any financed PMI premium), due in full in ______ year(s), with interest not to exceed _____% per annum for the first _______ year(s) of the loan with Origination Charges as shown on Buyer's Loan Estimate for the loan not to exceed _______% of the loan.

❑ (2) A second mortgage loan in the principal amount of $_____________ (excluding any financed PMI premium), due in full in __________ year(s), with interest not to exceed _____% per annum for the first ________ year(s) of the loan with Origination Charges as shown on Buyer's Loan Estimate for the loan not to exceed ________% of the loan.

❑ B. TEXAS VETERANS LOAN: A loan(s) from the Texas Veterans Land Board of $_______________ for a period in the total amount of _______ years at the interest rate established by the Texas Veterans Land Board.

❑ C. FHA INSURED FINANCING: A Section ________________ FHA insured loan of not less than $_________________(excluding any financed MIP), amortizable monthly for not less than ________ years, with interest not to exceed _______% per annum for the first _______ year(s) of the loan with Origination Charges as shown on Buyer's Loan Estimate for the loan not to exceed ______ % of the loan.

❑ D. VA GUARANTEED FINANCING: A VA guaranteed loan of not less than $________________ (excluding any financed Funding Fee), amortizable monthly for not less than ______ years, with interest not to exceed ______% per annum for the first _____ year(s) of the loan with Origination Charges as shown on Buyer's Loan Estimate for the loan not to exceed _______% of the loan.

❑ E. USDA GUARANTEED FINANCING: A USDA-guaranteed loan of not less than $____________ (excluding any financed Funding Fee), amortizable monthly for not less than _______ years, with interest not to exceed _____% per annum for the first _______ year(s) of the loan with Origination Charges as shown on Buyer's Loan Estimate for the loan not to exceed _____% of the loan.

❑ F. REVERSE MORTGAGE FINANCING: A reverse mortgage loan (also known as a Home Equity Conversion Mortgage loan) in the original principal amount of $ _____________ (excluding any financed PMI premium or other costs), with interest not to exceed _____% per annum for the first _______ year(s) of the loan with Origination Charges as shown on Buyer's Loan Estimate for the loan not to exceed ____% of the loan. The reverse mortgage loan ❑will ❑ will not be an FHA insured loan.

2. **APPROVAL OF FINANCING**: Approval for the financing described above will be deemed to have been obtained when Buyer Approval and Property Approval are obtained.

A. BUYER APPROVAL *(Check one box only)*:

❑ This contract is subject to Buyer obtaining Buyer Approval. If Buyer cannot obtain Buyer Approval, Buyer may give written notice to Seller within ______ days after the effective date of this contract and this contract will terminate and the earnest money will be refunded to Buyer. If Buyer does not terminate the contract under this provision, the contract shall no longer be subject to the Buyer obtaining Buyer Approval. Buyer Approval will be deemed to have been obtained when (i) the terms of the loan(s)

Initialed for identification by Buyer____ _____ and Seller_____ _____ TREC NO. 40-8

FIGURE 8-7 Third Party Financing Addendum
Source: Reprinted with permission of Texas Real Estate Commission

Third Party Financing Addendum Concerning

11-15-18
Page 2 of 2

____
(Address of Property)

described above are available and (ii) lender determines that Buyer has satisfied all of lender's requirements related to Buyer's assets, income and credit history.

☐ This contract is not subject to Buyer obtaining Buyer Approval.

B. PROPERTY APPROVAL: If Buyer's lender determines that the Property does not satisfy lender's underwriting requirements for the loan (including but not limited to appraisal, insurability, and lender required repairs) Buyer, not later than 3 days before the Closing Date, may terminate this contract by giving Seller: (i) notice of termination; and (ii) a copy of a written statement from the lender setting forth the reason(s) for lender's determination. If Buyer terminates under this paragraph, the earnest money will be refunded to Buyer. If Buyer does not terminate under this paragraph, Property Approval is deemed to have been obtained.

C. **Time is of the essence for this paragraph and strict compliance with the time for performance is required.**

3. SECURITY: Each note for the financing described above must be secured by vendor's and deed of trust liens.

4. FHA/VA REQUIRED PROVISION: If the financing described above involves FHA insured or VA financing, it is expressly agreed that, notwithstanding any other provision of this contract, the purchaser (Buyer) shall not be obligated to complete the purchase of the Property described herein or to incur any penalty by forfeiture of earnest money deposits or otherwise: (i) unless the Buyer has been given in accordance with HUD/FHA or VA requirements a written statement issued by the Federal Housing Commissioner, Department of Veterans Affairs, or a Direct Endorsement Lender setting forth the appraised value of the Property of not less than $____________________; or (ii) if the contract purchase price or cost exceeds the reasonable value of the Property established by the Department of Veterans Affairs.

A. The Buyer shall have the privilege and option of proceeding with consummation of the contract without regard to the amount of the appraised valuation or the reasonable value established by the Department of Veterans Affairs.

B. If FHA financing is involved, the appraised valuation is arrived at to determine the maximum mortgage the Department of Housing and Urban Development will insure. HUD does not warrant the value or the condition of the Property. The Buyer should satisfy himself/herself that the price and the condition of the Property are acceptable.

C. If VA financing is involved and if Buyer elects to complete the purchase at an amount in excess of the reasonable value established by the VA, Buyer shall pay such excess amount in cash from a source which Buyer agrees to disclose to the VA and which Buyer represents will not be from borrowed funds except as approved by VA. If VA reasonable value of the Property is less than the Sales Prices, Seller may reduce the Sales Price to an amount equal to the VA reasonable value and the sale will be closed at the lower Sales Price with proportionate adjustments to the down payment and the loan amount.

5. AUTHORIZATION TO RELEASE INFORMATION:

A. Buyer authorizes Buyer's lender to furnish to Seller or Buyer or their representatives information relating to the status of the approval for the financing.

B. Seller and Buyer authorize Buyer's lender, title company, and escrow agent to disclose and furnish a copy of the closing disclosures and settlement statements provided in relation to the closing of this sale to the parties' respective brokers and sales agents provided under Broker Information.

______________________________	______________________________
Buyer	Seller
______________________________	______________________________
Buyer	Seller

TREC
TEXAS REAL ESTATE COMMISSION

This form has been approved by the Texas Real Estate Commission for use with similarly approved or promulgated contract forms. Such approval relates to this form only. TREC forms are intended for use only by trained real estate license holders. No representation is made as to the legal validity or adequacy of any provision in any specific transactions. It is not intended for complex transactions. Texas Real Estate Commission, P.O. Box 12188, Austin, TX 78711-2188, (512) 936-3000 (http://www.trec.texas.gov) TREC No. 40-8. This form replaces TREC No. 40-7.

TREC NO. 40-8

FIGURE 8-7 (Continued)

PROMULGATED BY THE TEXAS REAL ESTATE COMMISSION (TREC) 11-15-18

TREC
TEXAS REAL ESTATE COMMISSION

ADDENDUM CONCERNING RIGHT TO TERMINATE DUE TO LENDER'S APPRAISAL

Use only if the Third Party Financing Addendum is attached to the contract and the transaction does not involve FHA insured or VA guaranteed financing

CONCERNING THE PROPERTY AT:______________________________________
(Street Address and City)

The financing described in the Third Party Financing Addendum attached to the contract for the sale of the above-referenced Property does not involve FHA or VA financing. *(Check one box only)*

❑ (1) **WAIVER.** Buyer waives Buyer's right to terminate the contract under Paragraph 2B of the Third Party Financing Addendum if Property Approval is not obtained because the opinion of value in the appraisal does not satisfy lender's underwriting requirements.

If the lender reduces the amount of the loan due to the opinion of value, the cash portion of Sales Price is increased by the amount the loan is reduced due to the appraisal.

❑ (2) **PARTIAL WAIVER.** Buyer waives Buyer's right to terminate the contract under Paragraph 2B of the Third Party Financing Addendum if:

(i) Property Approval is not obtained because the opinion of value in the appraisal does not satisfy lender's underwriting requirements; and

(ii) the opinion of value is $________________ or more.

If the lender reduces the amount of the loan due to the opinion of value, the cash portion of Sales Price is increased by the amount the loan is reduced due to the appraisal.

❑ (3) **ADDITIONAL RIGHT TO TERMINATE.** In addition to Buyer's right to terminate under Paragraph 2B of the Third Party Financing Addendum, Buyer may terminate the contract within _______ days after the Effective Date if:

(i) the appraised value, according to the appraisal obtained by Buyer's lender, is less than $________________; and

(ii) Buyer delivers a copy of the appraisal to the Seller.

If Buyer terminates under this paragraph, the earnest money will be refunded to Buyer.

____________________ ____________________
Buyer Seller

____________________ ____________________
Buyer Seller

TREC
TEXAS REAL ESTATE COMMISSION

The form of this addendum has been approved by the Texas Real Estate Commission for use only with similarly approved or promulgated forms of contracts. Such approval relates to this contract form only. TREC forms are intended for use only by trained real estate license holders. No representation is made as to the legal validity or adequacy of any provision in any specific transactions. It is not intended for complex transactions. Texas Real Estate Commission, P.O. Box 12188, Austin, TX 78711-2188, (512) 936-3000 (www.trec.texas.gov) TREC No. 49-1.

TREC NO. 49-1

FIGURE 8-8 Addendum Concerning Right to Terminate Due to Lender's Appraisal
Source: Reprinted with permission of Texas Real Estate Commission

FHA Financing

For FHA-insured financing, paragraph A3 would be used. The Federal Housing Administration is an agency within the Department of Housing and Urban Development responsible for insuring large real estate loans. Under a FHA-insured loan, the Federal Housing Administration insures the lender whenever more than 80% is loaned on the purchase of real estate. The determination of the down payment and amount financed can be obtained from an FHA loan chart available through most mortgage companies. The provisions for the FHA financing are similar to the provisions for conventional financing. Paragraph D of the Third Party Financing Addendum also applies to FHA financing.

VA Financing

VA-guaranteed financing is also very similar to third party conventional financing and is contained in paragraph A4. The Veterans Administration is an agency of the United States government that is responsible for providing benefits to veterans. A VA guaranteed loan is a loan that is guaranteed by the Veterans Administration. This loan provides the lender with a guarantee that if the purchaser defaults, the lender will be compensated up to a designated amount. The VA process is tied to entitlements however. Therefore, a veteran will often have to sell his or her home and recoup VA entitlements before a new loan can be obtained. The Addendum for Release of Liability on Assumed Loan and/or Restoration of Seller's VA Entitlement (TREC 12-3) can be used to give the seller the right to seek restoration of his or her VA entitlements within a designated number of days from the effective date of the contract. Three to five days is usually sufficient time to apply. If the restoration is not obtained, it gives the seller the right to terminate the contract or continue with the deal. Paragraph D of the Third Party Financing Addendum also applies to VA financing.

USDA-Guaranteed Financing

USDA-guaranteed financing in paragraph A5 refers to direct single-family housing loan programs operated by the Rural Housing Service (RHS) of the U.S. Department of Agriculture (USDA). The Rural Housing Service guarantees the loan in case the borrower defaults. A section 502 loan allows persons who do not currently own adequate housing, and who cannot obtain other credit, the opportunity to acquire and build dwellings in rural areas.[22] It provides a means for low- and very low-income people to obtain decent and safe housing in rural areas.[23] A rural area is defined for purposes of this loan program as "(1) open country which is not part of or associated with an urban area or (2) any town, village, city, or place, including the immediate adjacent densely settled area, which is not part

---

[22] 7 C.F.R. § 3550.51-3550.100.

[23] 7 C.F.R. § 3550.2.

of or associated with an urban area and which (i) has a population not in excess of 10,000 if it is rural in character; or (ii) has a population in excess of 10,000 but not in excess of 20,000, is not contained within a Metropolitan Statistical Area, and has a serious lack of mortgage credit for low- and moderate-income households as determined by the Secretary of Agriculture and the Secretary of HUD."[24] The borrower's debt ratios and the maximum income limits for the county will determine the amount of loan for which the borrower can qualify.[25] Currently these are fixed-rate loans for no more than 33 years or 30 years for manufactured homes.[26] There is 100% financing available with no down payment.[27] However, there is a guarantee fee associated with this loan as well as an annual fee.

Home Equity Conversion Mortgage (HECM) for Purchase (Reverse Mortgage for Purchase)

Paragraph A6 of the Third Party Financing Addendum addresses reverse mortgage financing. A traditional reverse mortgage, or home equity conversion mortgage (HECM), is a loan secured by a homeowner's equity in his or her home similar to a home equity loan. Both options are used to increase the homeowner's cash flow. However, the key difference between a reverse mortgage and a home equity loan is that with a reverse mortgage the homeowner does not need to pay back the loan as long as he or she continues to live on the property. A reverse mortgage is only available to individuals 62 years of age or older.[28] The homeowner maintains title to the property during the term of the loan.[29] A single family home or condominium will qualify.[30] Because the reverse mortgage process is so complex, the borrower is required to participate in a HECM counseling session.[31]

A reverse mortgage (HECM) for purchase is similar to the traditional reverse mortgage because it permits the homeowner to access equity in his or her home; however, the homeowner is creating the equity up front in a new home from which the reverse mortgage can be given. The Texas Constitution permits reverse mortgages for the purchase of homestead property that the borrower will occupy as a principal residence.[32] The reverse mortgage for purchase can only be used if the borrower has sufficient funds to pay the difference between the sales price including closing costs and the loan proceeds that would be received from the reverse mortgage. If the borrower had significant equity in his or her previous home, then this requirement is likely satisfied. As with the traditional reverse mortgage the homeowner does not need to pay back the loan as long as

[24] 7 C.F.R. § 3550.10.
[25] 7 C.F.R. § 3550.63.
[26] 7 C.F.R. § 3550.67.
[27] 7 C.F.R. § 3550.63.
[28] 12 U.S.C. § 1715v(a)(2).
[29] 24 C.F.R. § 206.35.
[30] 24 C.F.R. § 206.45(b).
[31] 24 C.F.R. § 206.41.
[32] Tex. Const. Art. 16, § 50.

he or she continues to live on the property. Without pursuing this option, the only other way the borrower would have to avoid mortgage payments would be to purchase the new home outright, which may not leave the borrower with many liquid assets for emergencies. The TREC Third Party Financing Addendum can be attached to the promulgated sales contract if the purchaser is considering a reverse mortgage for purchase.

Loan Programs

Not all mortgages are created equal. There are several types of loan programs and techniques that can be used. For instance, The Texas Veterans' Land Board administers two loan programs in Texas. These are the Veterans' Land Loan Program and the Veterans' Housing Assistance Program. The Veterans' Land Loan Program provides loans to veterans for the purchase of land. A veteran is defined as a person who:

> (A)(i) served not less than 90 days, unless sooner discharged by reason of a service-connected disability, on active duty in the Army, Navy, Air Force, Coast Guard, United States Public Health Service or Marine Corps of the United States after September 16, 1940, and who on the date of filing an application has not been dishonorably discharged from the branch of the service in which the person served; (ii) has at least 20 years of active or reserve military service as computed when determining the person's eligibility to receive retired pay under applicable federal law; (iii) has enlisted or received an appointment in the Texas National Guard, who has completed all initial active duty training required as a condition of the enlistment or appointment, and who on the date of filing the person's application has not been dishonorably discharged from the Texas National Guard; or (iv) served in the armed forces of the Republic of Vietnam between February 28, 1961, and May 7, 1975, if the board adopts a rule regarding these veterans under subsection (b);
>
> (B) at the time of the person's enlistment, induction, commissioning, appointment, or drafting was a bona fide resident of this state or has resided in this state at least one year immediately before the date of filing an application; and
>
> (C) at the time of the person's application is a bona fide resident of this state. The term includes the unmarried surviving spouse of a veteran who died or who is identified as missing in action if the deceased or missing veteran meets the requirements of this section, with the exception that the deceased or missing veteran need not have served 90 days under paragraph (A)(i) of this subdivision, and if the deceased or missing veteran was a bona fide resident of this state at the time of enlistment, induction, commissioning, appointment, or drafting.[33]

[33] Tex. Nat. Res. Code § 161.001(7).

To qualify for the loan, the land must be situated entirely in Texas, contain at least one acre, and have insurable title. If more than one tract of land is selected the tracts must be contiguous, or, if not contiguous, then one tract must meet the minimum acreage requirement, and the use, location, and value of the tracts would permit the board, in its sole discretion, to consider the combination of the tracts as one tract. Last, the land must have direct access to a public road or, in the alternative, a perpetual access easement with specific requirements set by the board must be conveyed.[34] The Veterans' Land Board originates all land loans under this program, rather than a third party lender. Additional information can be found at their website, http://www.glo.texas.gov/vlb/.

The Veterans' Housing Assistance Program provides home mortgage loans to veterans for housing within Texas. The term "veteran" has the same meaning as indicated above. The home acquired through the loan program does not have to be new construction. But it must be on a permanent foundation. Mobile homes are not eligible for financing through this program. In addition, the home must be occupied by the veteran within 60 days of closing and must be maintained as the veteran's principal residence for three consecutive years from the date of purchase.[35] Origination through this program is with a lender.

FINANCING LEGISLATION

There are several laws that are implicated in the financing process. Federal financing legislation is found in section I of the Federal Consumer Credit Protection Act, the Truth in Lending Act. The purpose of the Federal Truth in Lending Act is to provide a "meaningful disclosure of credit terms so that the consumer will be able to compare more readily the various credit terms available to him and avoid the uninformed use of credit."[36] Rulemaking authority for implementation of this statute was originally governed by the Federal Reserve Board, but was recently given to the Bureau of Consumer Financial Protection as a result of the Dodd-Frank Wall Street Reform and Consumer Protection Act. Regulation Z was drafted to implement the statute.[37]

Regulation Z provides, in part, that consumers have the right to cancel certain credit transactions that involve a lien on their principal dwelling. In addition, the regulation provides a means for fair and timely resolution of credit billing disputes. Regulation Z requires a maximum interest rate to be stated in variable-rate contracts secured by the consumer's dwelling. Furthermore, it imposes limitations on home-equity plans and mortgages. And it also prohibits certain acts or practices in connection with credit secured by a consumer's principal dwelling.[38]

[34] 40 T.A.C. § 175.3(a).
[35] 40 T.A.C. § 177.8.
[36] 15 U.S.C. § 1601.
[37] 12 C.F.R. Part 1026.
[38] 12 C.F.R. § 1026.1(b).

Regulation Z applies to each individual or business that offers or extends credit when four conditions are met: (i) the credit is offered or extended to consumers; (ii) the offering or extension of credit is done regularly; (iii) the credit is subject to a finance charge or is payable by a written agreement in more than four installments; and (iv) the credit is primarily for personal, family, or household purposes.[39]

Two important disclosures that must be made to consumers are the finance charge and annual percentage rate (APR). The term "**finance charge**" is defined as "the sum of all charges, payable directly or indirectly by the person to whom the credit is extended, and imposed directly or indirectly by the creditor as an incident to the extension of credit."[40] "**Annual percentage rate**," on the other hand, is defined as "that nominal annual percentage rate which will yield a sum equal to the amount of the finance charge when it is applied to the unpaid balances of the amount financed, calculated according to the actuarial method of allocating payments made on a debt between the amount financed and the amount of the finance charge, pursuant to which a payment is applied first to the accumulated finance charge and the balance is applied to the unpaid amount financed."[41] A sample disclosure form is contained in figure 8-9, which shows both of these amounts conspicuously in bold typeface.[42]

Through the Dodd-Frank Wall Street Reform and Consumer Protection Act, Congress also ordered the creation of two important disclosures that lenders need to make to consumers. These two disclosures, the Loan Estimate and Closing Disclosure, are classified under the general category of Truth in Lending Act/RESPA Integrated Disclosures (TRID). The Loan Estimate is intended to provide a good faith cost estimate to a prospective purchaser after the loan application is submitted.[43] A sample form is contained in figure 8-10.[44] The Closing Disclosure will be provided to the consumer within three business days of closing and is intended to give the consumer time to compare the costs disclosed with those in the loan estimate.[45] This form will be discussed in more detail in a later chapter.

COMPUTERIZED LOAN ORIGINATION (CLO)

Prequalification for a loan is often sought by prospective purchasers interested in purchasing real estate. The process of prequalification involves determining how much the prospective purchaser may be able to borrow, but it does not involve a formal loan application process nor the collection of resources typically obtained during the loan application process. Unfortunately, merely prequalifying for a

---

[39] 12 C.F.R. § 1026.1(c)(1).
[40] 15 U.S.C. § 1605(a).
[41] 15 U.S.C. § 1606(a)(1)(A).
[42] 12 C.F.R. Part 1026, App. H, Form H-2.
[43] 12 C.F.R. § 1026.37.
[44] 12 C.F.R. Part 1026, App. H, Form H-24A.
[45] 12 C.F.R. § 1026.38.

H-2—Loan Model Form

ANNUAL PERCENTAGE RATE The cost of your credit as a yearly rate.	FINANCE CHARGE The dollar amount the credit will cost you.	Amount Financed The amount of credit provided to you or on your behalf.	Total of Payments The amount you will have paid after you have made all payments as scheduled.
%	$	$	$

You have the right to receive at this time an itemization of the Amount Financed.
☐ I want an itemization. ☐ I do not want an itemization.

Your payment schedule will be:

Number of Payments	Amount of Payments	When Payments Are Due

Insurance
Credit life insurance and credit disability insurance are not required to obtain credit, and will not be provided unless you sign and agree to pay the additional cost.

Type	Premium	Signature
Credit Life		I want credit life insurance. __________ Signature
Credit Disability		I want credit disability insurance. __________ Signature
Credit Life and Disability		I want credit life and disability insurance. __________ Signature

You may obtain property insurance from anyone you want that is acceptable to (creditor). If you get the insurance from (creditor), you will pay $_______________

Security: You are giving a security interest in:
☐ the goods or property being purchased.
☐ (brief description of other property).

Filing fees $ ____________ **Non-filing insurance $** ____________

Late Charge: If a payment is late, you will be charged $ ____________ /__________ % of the payment.

Prepayment: If you pay off early, you
☐ may ☐ will not have to pay a penalty.
☐ may ☐ will not be entitled to a refund of part of the finance charge.

See your contract documents for any additional information about nonpayment, default, any required repayment in full before the scheduled date, and prepayment refunds and penalties.

____
e means an estimate

FIGURE 8-9 Loan Model Form

Save this Loan Estimate to compare with your Closing Disclosure.

Loan Estimate

DATE ISSUED
APPLICANTS

PROPERTY
SALE PRICE

LOAN TERM
PURPOSE
PRODUCT
LOAN TYPE ☐ Conventional ☐ FHA ☐ VA ☐ ____________
LOAN ID #
RATE LOCK ☐ NO ☐ YES, until
Before closing, your interest rate, points, and lender credits can change unless you lock the interest rate. All other estimated closing costs expire on

Loan Terms	**Can this amount increase after closing?**
Loan Amount	
Interest Rate	
Monthly Principal & Interest *See Projected Payments below for your Estimated Total Monthly Payment*	
	Does the loan have these features?
Prepayment Penalty	
Balloon Payment	

Projected Payments	
Payment Calculation	
Principal & Interest Mortgage Insurance Estimated Escrow *Amount can increase over time*	
Estimated Total Monthly Payment	
Estimated Taxes, Insurance & Assessments *Amount can increase over time*	**This estimate includes** **In escrow?** ☐ Property Taxes ☐ Homeowner's Insurance ☐ Other: *See Section G on page 2 for escrowed property costs. You must pay for other property costs separately.*

Costs at Closing	
Estimated Closing Costs	Includes in Loan Costs + in Other Costs – in Lender Credits. *See page 2 for details.*
Estimated Cash to Close	Includes Closing Costs. *See Calculating Cash to Close on page 2 for details.*

Visit **www.consumerfinance.gov/mortgage-estimate** for general information and tools.

LOAN ESTIMATE PAGE 1 OF 3 • LOAN ID #

FIGURE 8-10 Loan Estimate
Source: files.consumerfinance.gov

Closing Cost Details

Loan Costs

A. Origination Charges

% of Loan Amount (Points)

B. Services You Cannot Shop For

C. Services You Can Shop For

D. TOTAL LOAN COSTS (A + B + C)

Other Costs

E. Taxes and Other Government Fees

Recording Fees and Other Taxes
Transfer Taxes

F. Prepaids

Homeowner's Insurance Premium (months)
Mortgage Insurance Premium (months)
Prepaid Interest (per day for days @)
Property Taxes (months)

G. Initial Escrow Payment at Closing

Homeowner's Insurance per month for mo.
Mortgage Insurance per month for mo.
Property Taxes per month for mo.

H. Other

I. TOTAL OTHER COSTS (E + F + G + H)

J. TOTAL CLOSING COSTS

D + I
Lender Credits

Calculating Cash to Close

Total Closing Costs (J)
Closing Costs Financed (Paid from your Loan Amount)
Down Payment/Funds from Borrower
Deposit
Funds for Borrower
Seller Credits
Adjustments and Other Credits
Estimated Cash to Close

LOAN ESTIMATE PAGE 2 OF 3 • LOAN ID #

FIGURE 8-10 (Continued)

Additional Information About This Loan

LENDER
NMLS/___ LICENSE ID
LOAN OFFICER
NMLS/___ LICENSE ID
EMAIL
PHONE

MORTGAGE BROKER
NMLS/___ LICENSE ID
LOAN OFFICER
NMLS/___ LICENSE ID
EMAIL
PHONE

Comparisons	Use these measures to compare this loan with other loans.
In 5 Years	Total you will have paid in principal, interest, mortgage insurance, and loan costs. Principal you will have paid off.
Annual Percentage Rate (APR)	Your costs over the loan term expressed as a rate. This is not your interest rate.
Total Interest Percentage (TIP)	The total amount of interest that you will pay over the loan term as a percentage of your loan amount.

Other Considerations

Appraisal	We may order an appraisal to determine the property's value and charge you for this appraisal. We will promptly give you a copy of any appraisal, even if your loan does not close. You can pay for an additional appraisal for your own use at your own cost.
Assumption	If you sell or transfer this property to another person, we ☐ will allow, under certain conditions, this person to assume this loan on the original terms. ☐ will not allow assumption of this loan on the original terms.
Homeowner's Insurance	This loan requires homeowner's insurance on the property, which you may obtain from a company of your choice that we find acceptable.
Late Payment	If your payment is more than ___ days late, we will charge a late fee of ______________
Refinance	Refinancing this loan will depend on your future financial situation, the property value, and market conditions. You may not be able to refinance this loan.
Servicing	We intend ☐ to service your loan. If so, you will make your payments to us. ☐ to transfer servicing of your loan.

Confirm Receipt

By signing, you are only confirming that you have received this form. You do not have to accept this loan because you have signed or received this form.

Applicant Signature Date Co-Applicant Signature Date

LOAN ESTIMATE PAGE 3 OF 3 • LOAN ID #

FIGURE 8-10 (Continued)

loan does not guarantee approval in the future. And because prequalification does not involve a credit decision, federal credit disclosures are not required.

In contrast to prequalification is preapproval for a loan. With preapproval, the prospective purchaser has not yet selected a property to purchase, but initiates the formal loan application process. **Loan origination** is the process by which a prospective purchaser initiates a new loan application with a lender. The most commonly used loan application is the Uniform Residential Loan Application available through Fannie Mae. Once the prospective purchaser completes the application, the lender is required to provide the borrower with the required federal credit disclosures since preapproval is a credit decision. Next, the lender will gather additional information to support the application. This additional information can include the borrower's W-2 forms or past tax returns, copies of bank statements, verification of employment, and a credit report. Once granted, preapprovals are conditioned on the purchaser's circumstances remaining unchanged on the closing date.

Loan origination can also take place when a sales contract is in place on a particular piece of property. After the application is completed and the requisite disclosures are given to the borrower, the lender will gather additional information to support the application. In addition, a preliminary title report and appraisal will be ordered for the prospective collateral property.

Unfortunately, traditional loan origination involves prospective purchasers meeting directly with lenders for loans. This makes the process of applying for a loan tedious for buyers. However, real estate sales offices nowadays can provide computerized loan origination (CLO) to permit a one-stop loan shopping experience for real estate purchasers. Specifically, **computerized loan origination** is a computerized network of lenders that real estate brokers can use to allow the purchaser to comparison shop for a mortgage loan. The buyer's loan application information is input electronically to determine the buyer's eligibility for a loan and, if applicable, the types of loans available and the terms of those loans. In addition, the required federal credit disclosures are displayed immediately with CLO for each loan being considered rather than received days after submitting a traditional application to a lender. Since everything is provided up front to the prospective borrower, the prospective borrower has the opportunity to assess numerous variables associated with several loans in a short period of time. Most importantly, preliminary loan approval can be immediately obtained. Furthermore, the application can continue to be monitored for a firm denial or acceptance within a few days.

Discussion Questions

SIMPLE QUALIFYING ASSUMPTION TRANSACTION

You are a broker for Brown and Son Brokerage located at 777 Polter, Dallas, Texas 74748, working for Cynthia Martin. Ms. Martin asks you to find a house for her near the hospital. She would prefer an assumption. You locate a home for $80,000 that will allow a qualifying assumption. The property is located at 1222 Ivory Surf Road, Dallas, Texas 74747, also known as Lot 13, Block 43, NCB 1343, Ivory Bluff Subdivision in Dallas County. The property is currently owned by Jeff Carton and the property is not subject to mandatory membership in a homeowners association. The house was constructed in 1953, but was recently remodeled. Ms. Martin would like the washer and dryer to stay. She is also willing to put exact cash down in the amount of $10,000 and assume the loan balance of $65,000 at a current rate of 10% payable to Francisco Mortgage. The seller requests that the buyer apply for lienholder approval within three days; if approval is not obtained, the contract will terminate. The assumption transfer fee is $150. The seller also requests verification of the buyer's employment and a credit report.

The buyer writes an earnest money check for $2,000 payable to Apricot Hill Title located at 511 Pecan Avenue, Dallas, Texas 74749. The buyer requests a policy of title insurance and a survey to be performed at the seller's expense. In addition, the buyer requests an appraisal to be paid for by the buyer, which is to be reimbursed by the seller at closing. The buyer has received the seller's disclosure notice and the buyer accepts the property as it is, but requests the seller to complete repairs on the sidewalk in the backyard. The buyer wants to take possession in the next six weeks, but the seller wants to stay in the house for the next eight weeks, if possible. Sammy Fisk is the listing agent for Hyposink Inc. located at 111 Soleburg, Dallas, Texas 74749, license number 1414141. The listing broker agrees to pay any cooperating broker a commission of 2.5% of the total sales price.

1. Which residential sales contract would you use?
2. Using the information provided, complete the residential sales contract.
3. Which other promulgated forms might you include with the residential sales contract?

SIMPLE NON-QUALIFYING ASSUMPTION TRANSACTION

You are a broker with Champion Brokerage located at 1515 North Hampton, Suburbia, Texas 74112, license number 4444444 working for Jenny Rodriguez. Ms. Rodriguez asks you to look for a non-qualifying assumption somewhere near the interstate for no more than $120,000. You locate a property at 14530 West Hickoc Lane, Suburbia, Texas 74111, also known as Lot 11, Block 34, NCB

1134 and situated in Lone Star subdivision in Peacock County. This property was owned by Leslie Tomkins, who is deceased. The property is, however, being sold by the executor, Tammy Wallas, to her estate. The property was only recently constructed and is subject to mandatory membership in the homeowners association. The listing price is $111,000 and the loan amount is $85,500 at an interest rate of 11.5% with Hipot Mortgage Company. The transfer fee is $175. Ms. Rodriguez wants to make an exact cash down offer of $15,000. She writes a check in the amount of $1,500 for earnest money payable to Shark Title, Inc. located at 13000 West Pedro, Ste. 1100, Suburbia, Texas 74112.

The seller wants verification of employment. The buyer requests a policy of title insurance and a survey, but the buyer will cover the expense. The buyer wants to take possession in two weeks. The seller will provide a home warranty for one year not to exceed $400. The buyer is not requesting an appraisal, but has offered an option fee of $200 to the seller to keep the option to terminate open for 10 days. The listing and selling associate is Mike Peteres of Xero Brokerage Company located at 14111 South Preston, Ste. 100, Suburbia, Texas 74111, license number 6666666. The listing broker agrees to pay any cooperating broker a commission of 3.5% of the total sales price. The seller is requesting a release from liability under the assumption.

1. Which residential sales contract would you use?
2. Using the information provided, complete the residential sales contract.
3. Which other promulgated forms might you include with the residential sales contract?

SELLER-FINANCED TRANSACTION

You are a sales agent for Happiness Realty Company located at 444 Terrimont, Plymouth, Texas 71111, license number 8888888 working with Robert Prescott and his wife, Sheila Prescott. The Prescotts ask you to prepare an offer of $20,000 cash down on a property located at 1710 South Eastland, Plymouth, Texas 71111, also known as Lot 10, Block 10, NCB 1010, Separation Point subdivision, Plymouth County, Texas. This property is currently owned by Ruth Adams and her sister, Jessica Adams-Richland, and is not subject to mandatory membership in a homeowners association. The house was built in 1980. The Prescotts are requesting seller financing on the remainder of the $84,000 sales price. The sellers agree for financing at 9%.

The sellers request that the buyers make 120 payments of $763 beginning 15 days after the note and continuing monthly for 10 years. Sellers prohibit future assumptions. Taxes and insurance payments shall not be paid into escrow, but the sellers reserve the right to verify that all taxes and insurance has been paid.

The buyers present a cashier's check for $3,000 as earnest money payable to Selling Title Company located at 1500 South Mississippi Avenue, Plymouth, Texas

71111. The buyers are requesting title insurance and an appraisal to be paid for by the seller, but the buyers will reimburse the seller for the appraisal at closing. The buyers also request a survey to determine whether they can enclose and add on approximately 200 square feet to the garage. A seller's disclosure notice has already been given to the buyers and the buyers accept the property in its present condition except the buyers want the seller to fix the wall in the living room where the water damage occurred. The buyers want to be in the house within the next 30 days. The seller will provide a home warranty for one year not to exceed $400. Hampton Parks is the listing agent working with ABC Realty at 17155 South 12th Street, Ste. 111, Plymouth, Texas 71111, license number 71664218. The listing broker agrees to pay any cooperating broker a commission of 4.0% of the total sales price.

1. Which residential sales contract would you use?
2. Using the information provided, complete the residential sales contract.
3. Which other forms are required to be included with the contract in a seller-financed transaction?
4. Which other promulgated forms might you include with the residential sales contract?

THIRD PARTY CONVENTIONAL TRANSACTION

You are a sales agent for Harper Realty, Inc. working with Robert Sonyan. Mr. Sonyan asks you to prepare an offer of $72,000 on the property located at 7654 Hickory Barge, Depot, Texas 72222, also known as Lot 23, Block 22, NCB 2322 in Gutman County. This property is currently owned by Gutman County and was constructed within the last year. The property is not subject to mandatory membership in a homeowners association. The property is listed for $75,000. Mr. Sonyan wants to present his offer with 10% down and finance the remainder. The seller requests that he seek approval for the loan within five days due. If the buyer fails to obtain a loan within 30 days, the contract will terminate. The loan will be due in full in 30 years, with interest at a fixed rate not to exceed 10%.

The buyer writes a check for $2,000 as earnest money payable to Chesapeake Title located at 2008 Hamer Avenue, Depot, Texas 72223. The buyer requests a policy of title insurance, a survey, and an appraisal to be furnished at the seller's expense. The buyer has not received a seller's disclosure statement, but accepts the property in its present condition except for any lender-required repairs. The buyer wants to take possession in about six weeks and at that time the seller will transfer the property by special warranty deed. The total discount points offered are two, with the seller to pay half. The contract is also subject to the buyer being able to sell his other property located at 7777 Carnation Road, Depot, Texas 72222. Sally Forth is the listing agent for Peper Pep Realty located at 811 North Elm, Ste. 111, Depot, Texas 72222, license number 8181811. The listing broker agrees to pay any cooperating broker a commission of 3.0% of the total sales price.

1. Which residential sales contract would you use?
2. Using the information provided, complete the residential sales contract.
3. Which other promulgated forms might you include with the residential sales contract?

VA TRANSACTION

May South and her husband, Virgil, enter the office of Compath Realty. They look at some in-house listings and they decide to make an offer on a home listed by John Jackson. The property is located at 150 Cheviar Blvd, Hoover, Texas 74111 at Lot 18, Block 14, ncb 181, Forth Right Subdivision, Fedly County, Texas. The property is subject to mandatory membership in a homeowners association. The Souths want to offer a sales price of $100,000 with zero down with a VA-guaranteed loan. They write a check of $1,000 payable to Farm Title, Inc. at 255 Blossom Avenue, Ste 444, Hoover, Texas 74111. The buyers have received the Seller's Disclosure Notice and find that the home was built in 1977. The buyers want to take possession in 45 days and they would like the seller to pay for all fees. In addition, the buyers offer an option fee of $100 to keep the option to terminate open for seven days. Neither party has an attorney. Compath Realty is representing both the buyers and the seller in an intermediary relationship.

1. Which residential sales contract would you use?
2. Using the information provided, complete the residential sales contract.
3. Which other promulgated forms might you include with the residential sales contract?

FHA TRANSACTION

Philip Lepon enters Store Realty to find a home. Associate Edith Chism takes down some preliminary information and pulls several possible properties off of the MLS. Mr. Lepon subsequently view the home of Neal and Pat Samuels and wants to make an offer. The property is located at 4811 Air Mountain Lane, Cart, Texas 76666 at Lot 48, Block 11, NCB 4811, Tire Path Subdivision, Mathis County, Texas. The property is not subject to mandatory membership in a homeowners association. In addition, Mr. Lepon would like the sofa to be included in the sale. The listed price is $72,000 but Mr. Lepon wants to offer $65,000. He writes a check for $1,500 payable to Paper Title at 186 West Commercial, Cart, Texas 76663. Mr. Lepon has received the Seller's Disclosure Notice and finds out that the property was constructed in 1982. He is willing to accept the property as is except for lender-required repairs. The buyer wants to close in 60 days. The buyer wants the seller to pay for the title insurance and the buyer agrees to pay for the survey and will reimburse for appraisal fees at closing. Neither party has an attorney. The listing broker is Cart Realty at 53 Rathborne St., Cart, Texas

76664. The listing associate is Tim Philips. The cooperating broker is Store Realty at 154 South Texas Street, Cart, Texas 76666. The cooperating associate is Jeanette Matthews.

1. Which residential sales contract would you use?
2. Using the information provided, complete the residential sales contract.
3. Which other forms are required to be included with an FHA residential sales contract?
4. Which other promulgated forms might you include with the residential sales contract?
5. What document would be required to transfer the sofa in the sale?

CHAPTER

9

CONVEYANCE OF TITLE

KEY TERMS

actual notice
administratrix
administrator
adverse possession
bargain and sale deed
codicil
deed
execution
executor
executrix
general warranty deed
grantee
grantor
grantor-grantee index
habendum clause
inquiry notice
Letters of Administration
Letters Testamentary
premise
probate proceeding
quitclaim deed
record notice
special warranty deed
testator
testatrix
title
tract index
warranty clause
will

TITLE

Title to property refers to proof of ownership of property. This chapter will focus on title conveyances. There are two types of title conveyances that can be made. The first is a voluntary conveyance, also referred to as a voluntary alienation. A voluntary conveyance is a conveyance made intentionally by the property owner. The two types of voluntary conveyances that will be discussed include conveyances by deed and by will. The second type of title conveyance is the involuntary conveyance, also referred to as involuntary alienation. Involuntary conveyances are conveyances that occur unintentionally through no choice of the property owner. The involuntary conveyances that will be discussed in this chapter include conveyances by intestacy and adverse possession. However, other types of involuntary conveyances discussed throughout the book include foreclosure, escheat, and eminent domain.

VOLUNTARY ALIENATION

Deeds

At the closing of the real estate sales transaction, the seller will convey title to the real estate to the purchaser. The conveyance of title is in the form of a **deed**. And a certified copy of this deed obtained from the county deed records represents the purchaser's proof of ownership for the property. Conveying property by deed is a form of voluntary alienation or conveyance. In the standard deed, the seller is referred to as the **grantor** while the purchaser of the property is referred to as the **grantee**. There are various forms of title ownership as well as different types of deeds used in Texas, and each category is equally important.

When a deed is created, there are several parts typically included. The first is the premise. The **premise** is the portion of a deed that describes the subject property. This description may be a metes and bounds description or a recorded lot and block description. The premise describes the parties to the conveyance. The parties must be described with as much specificity as possible. Care should be taken to avoid nicknames and abbreviations. The premise also recites the consideration taken. In Texas, deeds typically only recite nominal consideration of 10 and no/100 dollars. The last portion of the premise is the granting clause. The granting clause is merely a clause that contains standard conveyancing language, such as "grant, sell, and convey."

The second common portion of a deed is the habendum clause. This clause typically begins with the phrase "To have and to hold." The **habendum clause** describes the estate transferred to the grantee by the grantor. Freehold estates, discussed in an earlier chapter, are usually encountered in the habendum clause of a deed. The third clause, characteristic of warranty deeds, is the warranty clause and serves to distinction the various types of deeds in Texas. This clause typically includes the term "warrant." The **warranty clause** is a clause that states the warranties contained under the deed. Another part that is common to a deed in Texas is the execution. The **execution** refers to the signature of the grantor. It is possible to have an informal deed, but the document cannot be recorded without an acknowledgment by a notary public or an attestation by credible witnesses. In Texas, the deed is not effective to put third parties on notice of the interest in the property unless it is recorded.

Wills

Knowledge of the laws of wills and descent and distribution is useful for real estate professionals because title to real estate may be passed by a person at his or her death. The primary means by which a person transfers property at death is by a will. A **will** is a legal document that allows a person to voluntarily distribute his or her assets upon death. The person who creates a will is called a **testator**, if male, and a **testatrix**, if female. The will has no effect until the testator or testatrix dies. A testator or testatrix may revoke or change the will at any time before he or she dies. An amendment to a will is referred to as a **codicil**.

In addition, the document is not enforceable until it is validated by the court. The means by which a will is validated in Texas is by way of a **probate proceeding**. In Texas, it is very important that the real estate of a deceased individual go through a probate proceeding to clear title to the property. If too much time passes and an attempt is made to sell the property, there may be a problem. When a person dies, an application for probate along with the will is filed at the court and set for hearing. At the initial hearing, the court will validate the will and appoint the executor or executrix. The **executor** is a man who is chosen by the testator or testatrix to effect the directions in the will and to dispose of property according to the will provisions. The **executrix** is a female executor. This person will be responsible for paying the debts of the estate, which might include selling estate property, and distributing any remaining property to the beneficiaries. Title to the property will be conveyed to the beneficiaries by deed.

In the real estate profession, one must be careful when listing and selling property of a deceased individual. The most important point to remember is that the property cannot be listed with the authority of anyone other than the title holder. A will designating the person as the beneficiary of the real estate is not sufficient authority. The probate court will have to validate the will and appoint an executor or executrix. The executor or executrix is the only person who has the authority to list and sell the real estate. Proof of this executor's or executrix's authority is in the form of **Letters Testamentary**. An original certified copy of the Letters Testamentary must be obtained before listing the property and kept in the transaction file. A photocopy will not suffice. Furthermore, when conveyancing the deceased owner's real estate, the sales contract, rather than listing the deceased owner as seller, will typically include language showing that the action was taken by the executor. Therefore, in the parties' description under the contract, the seller might be indicated as "______________________ (executor's name), executor of the estate of ______________________________ (deceased owner's name), deceased."

INVOLUNTARY ALIENATION

Intestacy Law

There are also a number of ways that property may be involuntarily conveyed in Texas. The first way in which property may be conveyed involuntarily arises when a person dies without a will. When a person dies without a will, he or she is referred to as intestate. When a property owner dies intestate, Texas statutory intestacy law dictates the distribution of his or her property. See figure 9-1. This is a form of involuntary alienation or conveyance because the property owner has not indicated how his or her property is to be distributed. The procedure for distribution of the decedent's assets under Texas law is very similar to the situation involving a will. However, where no will is involved, the male person chosen by the court to effectuate the terms of the statute and to dispose of the property is referred to as an **administrator**. An **administratrix** is a female administrator. This person will be responsible for paying the debts of the estate, which might include selling estate property, and distributing any remaining property to the heirs designated in the intestacy statute. Title to the property will be conveyed to the heirs by deed.

When an administrator or administratrix attempts to list the real estate, he or she must show adequate authority to do so. The authority is in the form of Letters of Administration. An original certified copy of the **Letters of Administration** must be obtained before listing the property and kept in the transaction file. As was the case for the Letters Testamentary, a photocopy will not suffice. Furthermore, when conveyancing the deceased owner's real estate, the sales contract, rather than listing the deceased as the seller in the transaction, will typically include language showing that the action was taken by an administrator. Therefore, in the parties description of the contract, the seller might be indicated as "______________________ (administrator's name), administrator of the estate of ______________________ (deceased owner's name), deceased." If there are no heirs to receive the property through the intestacy law, then title to the property will vest to the state of Texas through an escheat proceeding.[1]

Adverse Possession

Another form of involuntary conveyance involves adverse possession. **Adverse possession** is defined as "an actual and visible appropriation of real property, commenced and continued under a claim of right that is inconsistent with and is hostile to the claim of another person."[2] Misplaced fence lines do not generally involve issues of adverse possession, but are generally treated as encroachments.

Under the adverse possession laws, the property owner must bring an action to remove the adverse possessor within a requisite time period, depending on the type of possession involved, or the possessor may be able to acquire title. There are five limitations periods that apply to adverse possession cases in Texas. These are the 3-, 5-, 10-, 15-, and 25-year limitations periods. If the possessor has satisfied the requisite statutory requirements, then he or she can file a trespass to try title action to establish title to the property.

The three-year statute requires that the property owner bring suit against a possessor in "peaceable and adverse possession under title or color of title not later than three years after the day the cause of action accrues."[3] "Peaceable possession" is defined as "possession of real property that is continuous and is not

[1] Tex. Prop. Code § 71.001.

[2] Tex. Civ. Prac. & Rem. Code § 16.021.

[3] Tex. Civ. Prac. & Rem. Code § 16.024.

The Texas Intestacy Statute
(Texas Estates Code Chapter 201)

--Deceased was married at the time of death--

Community Property

No Children or Descendants

All community property of the deceased spouse passes to the survivor.

Children or Descendants

If all of the deceased's children are children of both the deceased spouse and the surviving spouse, then all community property of the deceased spouse passes to the survivor.

If any of the deceased's children are not children of the surviving spouse, then all community property of the deceased passes to the deceased's children.

Separate Property

No Children or Descendants

Personal Property:

All separate property passes to the surviving spouse.

Real Property:

Half goes to the spouse; half is distributed as if it were individual property.

Children or Descendants

Personal Property:

One-third goes to the spouse; two-thirds go to the children.

Real Property:

Life estate in one-third to spouse; indefeasibly vested remainder in one-third to the children; two-thirds fee simple absolute to the children.

---Deceased was not married at the time of death---

Individual Property

No Children or Descendants

Then to father and mother in equal proportions; if only one is alive, then pass the portion on to the siblings and their descendants. If both father and mother are dead, then it all goes to siblings and their descendants. If there are none, then the inheritance shall be divided into moieties one of which will go to the maternal kindred and the other will go to the paternal kindred. If none surviving then goes down to collaterals.

Children or Descendants

All goes to the children.

FIGURE 9-1 Texas Intestacy Distribution
Source: © 2021 Mbition LLC

interrupted by an adverse suit to recover the property." A claim under this statute might be brought if a possessor attempted to acquire title to the property legitimately, but possibly didn't record his or her deed.

The five-year statute requires that the property owner bring suit not later than five years after the day the cause of action accrues to recover real property held in peaceable and adverse possession by another who (1) cultivates, uses, or enjoys the property; (2) pays applicable taxes on the property; and (3) claims the property under a duly registered deed.[4]

The most common adverse possession statute; however, is the 10-year statute. The 10-year statute requires the property owner to "bring suit not later than 10 years after the day the cause of action accrues to recover real property held in peaceable and adverse possession by another who cultivates, uses, or enjoys the property." If the possessor does not have a title instrument, then the number of acres that can be acquired through adverse possession cannot exceed 160 acres. However, if the acreage is enclosed and the acreage enclosed is larger than 160 acres, then the possessor can acquire rights to the entire tract enclosed.[5]

A 15-year combined limitations statute concerns adverse possession by a co-tenant heir.[6] Co-tenant heirs are created as a result of intestacy laws whereby multiple heirs acquire a shared ownership interest in property. Some of the heirs may be interested in owning more than they received, while others may not care what they own. As a result, the interested heirs may attempt to adversely possess those portions of the property owned by the disinterested heirs. The initial period of adverse possession is 10 years; however, the possessor must then file an affidavit putting any other heirs on notice of the claim. The possessor must then wait five years before filing suit.

The last two statutes are 25-year statutes. The first statute requires that the property owner "bring suit not later than 25 years after the day the cause of action accrues to recover real property held in peaceable and adverse possession by another who cultivates, uses, or enjoys the property."[7] The second statute does not require that the person cultivate, use or enjoy the property, but merely requires that the person brings his or her claim in good faith and under a deed or other instrument purporting to convey the property that is recorded in the county deed records.[8]

The key difference between these 25-year statutes and the others is that this statute of limitations applies regardless of whether the property owner is or has been under a legal disability. A person is under a legal disability "if the person is: (1) younger than 18 years of age, regardless of whether the person is married; (2) of unsound mind; or (3) serving in the United States Armed Forces during

[4] Tex. Civ. Prac. & Rem. Code § 16.025.
[5] Tex. Civ. Prac. & Rem. Code § 16.026.
[6] Tex. Civ. Prac. & Rem. Code § 16.0265.
[7] Tex. Civ. Prac. & Rem. Code § 16.027.
[8] Tex. Civ. Prac. & Rem. Code § 16.028.

time of war."[9] For the 3-, 5-, and 10-year statutes, the limitations period is tolled during the property owner's period of disability.

CONVEYANCE OF ESTATES

Since freehold estates are ownership interests in the property, they are the only types of estates that can be conveyed. Since there are multiple types of freehold estates that can be conveyed in Texas, the language used for each conveyance will vary. The typical way that a grant of a fee simple absolute, the largest freehold estate, is made is by using any words that show an intent to convey full property rights. For example, "To Have and To Hold unto said Grantee and its successors and assigns, forever." Conveyance of defeasible fee interests varies based on the type. Special language such as "while" or "so long as" is commonly used to create the fee simple determinable interest. For example, "To Have and To Hold unto said Grantee and its successors and assigns *so long as* the premises are used as a farm." Special language such as "if," "but if," or "on condition that" is used to create the fee simple subject to a condition subsequent. For example, "To Have and To Hold unto said Grantee and its successors and assigns *on the condition that* no alcohol is sold on the premises." Language typically used to create a fee simple determinable or a fee simple subject to a condition subsequent is sufficient to create the fee simple subject to an executory interest in a third party. For example, "To Have and To Hold unto said Grantee and its successors and assigns *so long as* the premises are used as a farm, if not then to Beth."

The conveyance can also involve a life estate with some future freehold interest. A regular life estate is a life estate measured by the life of the grantee. For example, Mike conveys "To Have and To Hold unto said Grantee for life." The two primary types of future freehold estates are the reversion and the remainder. A reversion refers to a future estate that returns to the original grantor after the termination of the present freehold estate. By conveying "To Have and To Hold unto said Grantee for life," without additional instructions, the estate will revert back to the original grantor when the grantee dies. A remainder is a future estate that transfers to a third party, not the original grantor, after the termination of the present estate. A remainder may be either vested (complete) or contingent (conditional) depending on the type of conveyance made to the third party. Vested remainders are established without satisfying any conditions and can be (1) indefeasibly vested, (2) vested subject to total divestment, or (3) vested subject to open. Indefeasibly vested remainders simply terminate in a third party. For example, "To Have and To Hold unto said Grantee for life, then to Bob." Vested remainders subject to total divestment are remainders that terminate in a third party, but which can be divested. For example, "To Have and To Hold unto said Grantee for life, then to Dawn if Dawn survives Grantee." Vested remainders

[9] Tex. Civ. Prac. & Rem. Code § 16.022.

subject to open terminate in an open class of individuals. For example, "To Have and To Hold unto said Grantee for life, then to Grantee's heirs." The contingent remainder, in contrast to the vested remainders, requires some condition precedent be satisfied before the interest will pass. For example, "To Have and To Hold unto said Grantee for life, then to Ben if Ben survives Grantee, otherwise to Chris."

PUBLIC RECORDS

In Texas, a deed is valid even if it is not recorded; however, the deed will not operate to put third parties on notice of the purchaser's interest until the deed is recorded. Recording is the process of filing a document in the county deed records for the county in which the property is located. This record puts third-party creditors on notice of the grantee's new property interest by making property ownership information public. In addition, the recording process itself protects the ultimate grantee from fraud by preventing a prior grantor from hiding any interest in the property. The ultimate goal of recording is to make the title stable.

What Can Be Recorded

Certain documents can be recorded in Texas. The deed, evidencing the conveyance of title to land, is one document that can be recorded. Also, a deed of trust, evidencing a lender's security interest in the real estate can be recorded. Often, an option on the purchase of real estate, particularly commercial real estate, will be recorded. In addition, an installment land contract will be recorded to protect the buyer from the seller selling to another during the executory period.

Recording Indices

When an item is recorded in the deed records, it exists as a volume and page number. If a third party is interested in the information contained in the records, he or she must search by way of an index system. In Texas there are two primary types of recording indices available. The first is the **grantor-grantee index**. This index lists the documents according to their grantors and grantees. If a title search is conducted using this method, the examiner will work backwards in the title from grantee to grantor to make sure the chain of title is unbroken.

The second type of recording index available in Texas is the **tract index**. Rather than listing the documents by their respective grantors and grantees, the tract index lists the document by the property description. The big advantage of this method over the grantor-grantee index is that a title examiner can find stray conveyances that would not be traceable through the grantor-grantee index.

Recording Acts

Before there were statutes available that dictated rules for recording, case law determined the rules. Under these prestatutory laws, the first person to take the deed had title. The basic premise behind this law was that once the grantor conveyed his or her interest in the real estate to the grantee, there was no longer anything left to give. Because of the harsh results of this law, most of the states enacted some type of recording statute. In the United States, there are currently three types of statutes recognized. These are the race statute, the race-notice statute, and the notice statute. Texas adopted the notice statute.[10]

Under the notice statute, the grantee must be a bona fide purchaser without notice of a prior claim. In order to be a bona fide purchaser, the grantee must pay some type of value for the premises. Value in this instance must bear some relation to the fair market value of the property. In addition, this bona fide purchaser must be without notice of a prior claim.

In determining whether a person qualifies as a bona fide purchaser, there are three types of notice recognized in Texas. First, there is **actual notice**. Actual notice is expressly given notice. This may be expressed verbally or in writing. For instance, someone tells the purchaser that there is an outstanding claim to the property. The second type of notice is **record notice**. Record notice can be obtained by looking in the county deed records. For instance, by looking in the deed records, the purchaser finds that there is a tax lien on the property. The last type of notice found in Texas is inquiry notice. **Inquiry notice** applies when a person finds something unusual that prompts further inquiry. For example, the prospective purchaser goes to a listed property to look around and there is someone living on the property, and the prospective purchaser has been told that the seller is living in Colorado. A reasonable person would inquire as to the true circumstances.

Requirements for Recording

In Texas, six requirements must be satisfied before a document may be filed in the deed records. The document must:

a. be in the English language;
b. contain the mailing address of each grantee;
c. be signed by the grantor;
d. contain the signature of the grantor;
e. be acknowledged by a notary or attested to by at least two credible witnesses; and
f. be accompanied by a filing fee.

---

[10] Tex. Prop. Code § 13.001.

PROOF OF OWNERSHIP

Regardless of whether title has been conveyed voluntarily or involuntarily, proof of ownership will be in the form of a deed. There are, however, several types of deeds recognized in Texas. These include the general warranty deed, special warranty deed, bargain and sale deed, and quitclaim deed.

General Warranty Deed

A **general warranty deed** is a deed that conveys title to the property and warrants title to the property against all defects in title that arose both before and after the grantor took title to the property. In real estate transactions in Texas, the general warranty deed is the most common type of deed used to convey real estate and is the default deed specified in the TREC 20-14 form. If any other deed is to be used in the real estate transaction, it should be specified in paragraph 11 of the promulgated residential sales contract. A sample general warranty deed is shown in figure 9-2. The key distinction in this deed from the remaining types of deeds is the warranty clause. Note that the grantor agrees to "warrant and forever defend all and singular the said premises. . . against every person whomsoever lawfully claiming or to claim the same, or any part thereof."

The State of Texas,
County of ______________

GENERAL WARRANTY DEED

Know all men by these presents, That I, ________________, (Grantor) of the __________ (give name of city, town, or county), in the state aforesaid, for and in consideration of ___________ dollars, to me in hand paid by ______________, have granted, sold, and conveyed, and by these presents do grant, sell, and convey unto the said ____________, (Grantee) of the ______________ (give name of city, town, or county), in the state of _____________, all that certain _____________ (describe) the premises).

To have and to hold the above described premises, together with all and singular the rights and appurtenances thereto in any wise belonging, unto the said ___________, (Grantee) his heirs or assigns forever.

And I do hereby bind myself, my heirs, executors, and administrators to warrant and forever defend all and singular the said premises unto the said ____________, his heirs, and assigns, against every person whomsoever, lawfully claiming or to claim the same, or any part thereof.

Witness my hand, this ____________ day of _______________, A.D. ________.

Signed and delivered in the presence of ________________________________

FIGURE 9-2 General Warranty Deed
Source: © 2021 Mbition LLC

Special Warranty Deed

A **special warranty deed** conveys title to the property, but warrants only against the grantor's own acts and not the acts of others. For example, the grantor agrees to "warrant and forever defend all and singular the said premises . . . against every person whomsoever lawfully claiming or claim the same, or any part thereof, by, through, or under Grantor, but not otherwise." This type of deed is more commonly used in conveyances by governmental entities.

Bargain and Sale Deed

A **bargain and sale deed** conveys title to the property, but it does not contain any warranties. The bargain and sale deed will not contain the last paragraph seen in the General Warranty Deed in figure 9-2, but may often contain a sentence that states, "This conveyance is made without warranty, express or implied." This type of deed is commonly used by fiduciaries to transfer property, for instance, out of a trust or will. It is also commonly used to transfer property pursuant to a divorce settlement.

Quitclaim Deed

A **quitclaim deed** transfers whatever interest the grantor has in the property. No warranties of any kind are made similar to the bargain and sale deed. However, the conveyancing language is different in a quitclaim deed. Instead of the "grant, sell, and convey" language seen with the other three deeds, the quitclaim deed specifies that the grantor "quitclaims" the property. In Texas, quitclaim deeds are typically used when correction to the deeds is necessary.

Discussion Questions

1. What types of deeds are generally available for use in a real estate transfer?
2. Explain what happens to a married person's separate real property if he or she dies intestate either with or without children.
3. Explain what happens to a married person's community property if he or she dies intestate either with or without children in common with the surviving spouse.
4. Identify the type of recording statute used in Texas and explain what is necessary to establish priority of title if there is a conflict.
5. What types of clauses are typically found in a general warranty deed and how do these clauses differ in the other types of deeds?

6. If an executor or administrator needs to sell real estate to satisfy the debts of the estate, what type of authority must each representative show the license holder before the license holder may list the property?
7. What are the various types of interests that can pass in a deed under the habendum clause and how are the different contract forms implicated in each situation?

CHAPTER

10

TRANSACTION PROCESS AND CLOSING

KEY TERMS

closing
Closing Disclosure
covenant against encumbrances
covenant of further assurances
covenant of general warranty
covenant of quiet enjoyment
covenant of seisin
covenant of the right to convey

TRANSACTION PROCESS

After the real estate sales contract is signed by both parties, there is quite a lot of work to get done before closing can take place. If the buyer has elected a termination option, the buyer must pay an option fee, the receipt of which will be acknowledged by the seller or the seller's broker on the promulgated contract form. The executed contract and the earnest money must be taken to the title company and the title company will acknowledge receipt of both on the promulgated contract form. What takes place afterwards varies based on what was requested in the contract. However, in a typical real estate transaction that involves financing this can include financing approval, title searches, surveys, appraisals, inspections, and environmental assessments.

SAMPLE CHECKLIST

The following checklist can be used as a guide to make sure each component of the transaction process is completed after the title company acknowledges receipt of the executed contract and earnest money.

- Buyer should apply for loan approval immediately, if applicable. The deadline for the buyer to terminate the contract without penalty if approval cannot be obtained is set forth in the Third Party Financing Addendum.

- Seller should give an existing survey to the title company and buyer (by the deadline included in the contract, which is typically within the first 5–7 days) along with the T-47 Residential Real Property Affidavit. See figure 10-1. In the alternative, a new survey should be sought immediately by the party designated in the contract and by the deadline indicated.
- Buyer should order a home inspection immediately, particularly if the termination option has been selected. The deadline for the buyer to terminate the contract without penalty is set forth in the termination option paragraph of the promulgated sales contract. Enough time should be allocated between the inspection and this termination date to give the buyer sufficient time to negotiate with the seller to make certain repairs.
- Buyer should seek an environmental assessment of the property immediately, if applicable. The deadline for the buyer to terminate the contract without penalty if an adverse report is obtained is specified in the Environmental Assessment, Threatened or Endangered Species, and Wetlands Addendum.
- Any property appraisal (mandatory if a lender is involved) should take place after the termination option deadline.
- Within 20 days the buyer should receive the title commitment for review.
- Buyer should contact an insurance company for a homeowner's insurance policy, at least 2–3 weeks before closing.
- Before closing, buyer should do a final walk-through.
- Before closing, both buyer and seller should receive statements concerning their settlement costs so each knows how much money to bring to the closing table.

LOAN APPROVAL

For loans involving a third-party lender, the prospective purchaser must go through the loan approval process. This begins with a loan application. Additional documentation then may be requested by the lender. This documentation may include a credit report, employment verification, bank fund verification, and any other necessary documentation. Once all of the information has been obtained, the loan officer will review all available loan programs to provide the prospective purchaser with the best available rates and terms. A loan package will then be compiled and presented to the underwriter for approval.

There are two aspects to loan approval that must be considered. The first aspect that must be considered is buyer approval. Buyer approval is considered to have been obtained when the terms of the loan(s) are available and the lender determines that the buyer has satisfied all of the lender's requirements related to the buyer's assets, income, and credit history. If the buyer cannot obtain buyer approval, then the buyer may give written notice to the seller and the contract

T-47 RESIDENTIAL REAL PROPERTY AFFIDAVIT
(MAY BE MODIFIED AS APPROPRIATE FOR COMMERCIAL TRANSACTIONS)

Date:______________________________ GF No.______________________________
Name of Affiant(s):____
Address of Affiant:____
Description of Property:____
County______________________________, Texas

"Title Company" as used herein is the Title Insurance Company whose policy of title insurance is issued in reliance upon the statements contained herein.

Before me, the undersigned notary for the State of ______________, personally appeared Affiant(s) who after by me being sworn, stated:

1. We are the owners of the Property. (Or state other basis for knowledge by Affiant(s) of the Property, such as lease, management, neighbor, etc. For example, "Affiant is the manager of the Property for the record title owners.")

2. We are familiar with the property and the improvements located on the Property.

3. We are closing a transaction requiring title insurance and the proposed insured owner or lender has requested area and boundary coverage in the title insurance policy(ies) to be issued in this transaction. We understand that the Title Company may make exceptions to the coverage of the title insurance as Title Company may deem appropriate. We understand that the owner of the property, if the current transaction is a sale, may request a similar amendment to the area and boundary coverage in the Owner's Policy of Title Insurance upon payment of the promulgated premium.

4. To the best of our actual knowledge and belief, since ____________________________ there have been no:

   a. construction projects such as new structures, additional buildings, rooms, garages, swimming pools or other permanent improvements or fixtures;

   b. changes in the location of boundary fences or boundary walls;

   c. construction projects on immediately adjoining property(ies) which encroach on the Property;

   d. conveyances, replattings, easement grants and/or easement dedications (such as a utility line) by any party affecting the Property.

   EXCEPT for the following (If None, Insert "None" Below:)

5. We understand that Title Company is relying on the truthfulness of the statements made in this affidavit to provide the area and boundary coverage and upon the evidence of the existing real property survey of the Property. This Affidavit is not made for the benefit of any other parties and this Affidavit does not constitute a warranty or guarantee of the location of improvements.

6. We understand that we have no liability to Title Company that will issue the policy(ies) should the information in this Affidavit be incorrect other than information that we personally know to be incorrect and which we do not disclose to the Title Company.

____

____

SWORN AND SUBSCRIBED this ______ day of ________________, 20______.

____
Notary Public

FIGURE 10-1 T-47 Residential Real Property Affidavit

will terminate and the earnest money will be refunded to the buyer. If the buyer fails to give the requisite notice, then the contingency is removed and the parties move forward with the contract. The second aspect that must be considered is property approval. Property approval is deemed to have been obtained when the property has satisfied the lender's underwriting requirements for the loan, including but not limited to appraisal, insurability, and lender-required repairs. If property approval is not obtained, then the buyer may terminate the contract by giving notice to the seller before closing and the earnest money will be refunded to the buyer.

Once approved, the prospective purchaser will be notified of the approval and any requirements that must be satisfied before the loan will close. Loan approval is an important first step in the closing process. The lender will draft the promissory note and deed of trust documents and send them to the title company for signature at closing. Once the prospective purchaser signs the loan documents at closing, the lender will fund the loan.

REAL ESTATE SETTLEMENT PROCEDURES ACT (RESPA)

The procedure for the settlement of most transactions is governed by the Real Estate Settlement Procedures Act (RESPA).[1] RESPA was enacted in 1974 to ensure "(1) more effective advance disclosure to home buyers and sellers of settlement costs; (2) the elimination of kickbacks or referral fees that tend to increase unnecessarily the costs of certain settlement services; (3) a reduction in the amounts home buyers are required to place in escrow accounts established to insure the payment of real estate taxes and insurance; and (4) significant reform and modernization of local recordkeeping of land title information." Enforcement of RESPA is governed by Regulation X found in the Code of Federal Regulations.

Among its other guidelines, RESPA requires that a standard closing statement be issued. This form must clearly itemize all charges imposed upon both the borrower and the seller in connection with the settlement of the real estate transaction and must indicate whether any title insurance premium included in the charges covers or insures the lender's interest in the property, the borrower's interest, or both.[2] This closing statement is referred to as a **Closing Disclosure.**[3] A sample form is contained in figure 10-2.[4] This document must be used in all closing transactions involving a federally related mortgage loan in which there is a borrower and a seller.

A "federally related mortgage loan" is a loan (other than temporary financing such as a construction loan) that is secured by a first or subordinate lien on residential real property (including individual units of condominiums

[1] 12 U.S.C. § 2601.
[2] 12 U.S.C. § 2603; 12 C.F.R. § 1024.8.
[3] 12 C.F.R. § 1026.38.
[4] 12 C.F.R. Part 1026, App. H. Form H-25A.

Closing Disclosure

This form is a statement of final loan terms and closing costs. Compare this document with your Loan Estimate.

Closing Information	Transaction Information	Loan Information
Date Issued	**Borrower**	**Loan Term**
Closing Date		**Purpose**
Disbursement Date		**Product**
Settlement Agent	**Seller**	
File #		**Loan Type** ☐Conventional ☐FHA ☐VA ☐ ______
Property	**Lender**	**Loan ID #**
Sale Price		**MIC #**

Loan Terms		Can this amount increase after closing?
Loan Amount		
Interest Rate		
Monthly Principal & Interest *See Projected Payments below for your Estimated Total Monthly Payment*		
		Does the loan have these features?
Prepayment Penalty		
Balloon Payment		

Projected Payments	
Payment Calculation	
Principal & Interest	
Mortgage Insurance	
Estimated Escrow *Amount can increase over time*	
Estimated Total Monthly Payment	
Estimated Taxes, Insurance & Assessments *Amount can increase over time* *See page 4 for details*	**This estimate includes** **In escrow?** ☐ Property Taxes ☐ Homeowner's Insurance ☐ Other: *See Escrow Account on page 4 for details. You must pay for other property costs separately.*

Costs at Closing	
Closing Costs	Includes in Loan Costs + in Other Costs – in Lender Credits. *See page 2 for details.*
Cash to Close	Includes Closing Costs. *See Calculating Cash to Close on page 3 for details.*

CLOSING DISCLOSURE PAGE 1 OF 5 • LOAN ID #

FIGURE 10-2 Closing Disclosure
Source: files.consumerfinance.gov

Closing Cost Details

Loan Costs	Borrower-Paid At Closing	Borrower-Paid Before Closing	Seller-Paid At Closing	Seller-Paid Before Closing	Paid by Others
A. Origination Charges					
01 % of Loan Amount (Points)					
02					
03					
04					
05					
06					
07					
08					
B. Services Borrower Did Not Shop For					
01					
02					
03					
04					
05					
06					
07					
08					
09					
10					
C. Services Borrower Did Shop For					
01					
02					
03					
04					
05					
06					
07					
08					
D. TOTAL LOAN COSTS (Borrower-Paid)					
Loan Costs Subtotals (A + B + C)					

Other Costs	Borrower-Paid At Closing	Borrower-Paid Before Closing	Seller-Paid At Closing	Seller-Paid Before Closing	Paid by Others
E. Taxes and Other Government Fees					
01 Recording Fees Deed: Mortgage:					
02					
F. Prepaids					
01 Homeowner's Insurance Premium (mo.)					
02 Mortgage Insurance Premium (mo.)					
03 Prepaid Interest (per day from to)					
04 Property Taxes (mo.)					
05					
G. Initial Escrow Payment at Closing					
01 Homeowner's Insurance per month for mo.					
02 Mortgage Insurance per month for mo.					
03 Property Taxes per month for mo.					
04					
05					
06					
07					
08 Aggregate Adjustment					
H. Other					
01					
02					
03					
04					
05					
06					
07					
08					
I. TOTAL OTHER COSTS (Borrower-Paid)					
Other Costs Subtotals (E + F + G + H)					
J. TOTAL CLOSING COSTS (Borrower-Paid)					
Closing Costs Subtotals (D + I)					
Lender Credits					

CLOSING DISCLOSURE PAGE 2 OF 5 • LOAN ID #

FIGURE 10-2 (Continued)

Calculating Cash to Close

Use this table to see what has changed from your Loan Estimate.

	Loan Estimate	Final	Did this change?
Total Closing Costs (J)			
Closing Costs Paid Before Closing			
Closing Costs Financed (Paid from your Loan Amount)			
Down Payment/Funds from Borrower			
Deposit			
Funds for Borrower			
Seller Credits			
Adjustments and Other Credits			
Cash to Close			

Summaries of Transactions

Use this table to see a summary of your transaction.

BORROWER'S TRANSACTION

K. Due from Borrower at Closing	
01 Sale Price of Property	
02 Sale Price of Any Personal Property Included in Sale	
03 Closing Costs Paid at Closing (J)	
04	
Adjustments	
05	
06	
07	
Adjustments for Items Paid by Seller in Advance	
08 City/Town Taxes to	
09 County Taxes to	
10 Assessments to	
11	
12	
13	
14	
15	
L. Paid Already by or on Behalf of Borrower at Closing	
01 Deposit	
02 Loan Amount	
03 Existing Loan(s) Assumed or Taken Subject to	
04	
05 Seller Credit	
Other Credits	
06	
07	
Adjustments	
08	
09	
10	
11	
Adjustments for Items Unpaid by Seller	
12 City/Town Taxes to	
13 County Taxes to	
14 Assessments to	
15	
16	
17	
CALCULATION	
Total Due from Borrower at Closing (K)	
Total Paid Already by or on Behalf of Borrower at Closing (L)	
Cash to Close ☐ From ☐ To Borrower	

SELLER'S TRANSACTION

M. Due to Seller at Closing	
01 Sale Price of Property	
02 Sale Price of Any Personal Property Included in Sale	
03	
04	
05	
06	
07	
08	
Adjustments for Items Paid by Seller in Advance	
09 City/Town Taxes to	
10 County Taxes to	
11 Assessments to	
12	
13	
14	
15	
16	
N. Due from Seller at Closing	
01 Excess Deposit	
02 Closing Costs Paid at Closing (J)	
03 Existing Loan(s) Assumed or Taken Subject to	
04 Payoff of First Mortgage Loan	
05 Payoff of Second Mortgage Loan	
06	
07	
08 Seller Credit	
09	
10	
11	
12	
13	
Adjustments for Items Unpaid by Seller	
14 City/Town Taxes to	
15 County Taxes to	
16 Assessments to	
17	
18	
19	
CALCULATION	
Total Due to Seller at Closing (M)	
Total Due from Seller at Closing (N)	
Cash ☐ From ☐ To Seller	

CLOSING DISCLOSURE PAGE 3 OF 5 • LOAN ID #

FIGURE 10-2 (Continued)

Additional Information About This Loan

Loan Disclosures

Assumption
If you sell or transfer this property to another person, your lender
☐ will allow, under certain conditions, this person to assume this loan on the original terms.
☐ will not allow assumption of this loan on the original terms.

Demand Feature
Your loan
☐ has a demand feature, which permits your lender to require early repayment of the loan. You should review your note for details.
☐ does not have a demand feature.

Late Payment
If your payment is more than ___ days late, your lender will charge a late fee of ________________

Negative Amortization (Increase in Loan Amount)
Under your loan terms, you
☐ are scheduled to make monthly payments that do not pay all of the interest due that month. As a result, your loan amount will increase (negatively amortize), and your loan amount will likely become larger than your original loan amount. Increases in your loan amount lower the equity you have in this property.
☐ may have monthly payments that do not pay all of the interest due that month. If you do, your loan amount will increase (negatively amortize), and, as a result, your loan amount may become larger than your original loan amount. Increases in your loan amount lower the equity you have in this property.
☐ do not have a negative amortization feature.

Partial Payments
Your lender
☐ may accept payments that are less than the full amount due (partial payments) and apply them to your loan.
☐ may hold them in a separate account until you pay the rest of the payment, and then apply the full payment to your loan.
☐ does not accept any partial payments.
If this loan is sold, your new lender may have a different policy.

Security Interest
You are granting a security interest in ________________

____

____

You may lose this property if you do not make your payments or satisfy other obligations for this loan.

Escrow Account
For now, your loan
☐ will have an escrow account (also called an "impound" or "trust" account) to pay the property costs listed below. Without an escrow account, you would pay them directly, possibly in one or two large payments a year. Your lender may be liable for penalties and interest for failing to make a payment.

Escrow		
Escrowed Property Costs over Year 1		Estimated total amount over year 1 for your escrowed property costs:
Non-Escrowed Property Costs over Year 1		Estimated total amount over year 1 for your non-escrowed property costs: You may have other property costs.
Initial Escrow Payment		A cushion for the escrow account you pay at closing. See Section G on page 2.
Monthly Escrow Payment		The amount included in your total monthly payment.

☐ will not have an escrow account because ☐ you declined it ☐ your lender does not offer one. You must directly pay your property costs, such as taxes and homeowner's insurance. Contact your lender to ask if your loan can have an escrow account.

No Escrow		
Estimated Property Costs over Year 1		Estimated total amount over year 1. You must pay these costs directly, possibly in one or two large payments a year.
Escrow Waiver Fee		

In the future,
Your property costs may change and, as a result, your escrow payment may change. You may be able to cancel your escrow account, but if you do, you must pay your property costs directly. If you fail to pay your property taxes, your state or local government may (1) impose fines and penalties or (2) place a tax lien on this property. If you fail to pay any of your property costs, your lender may (1) add the amounts to your loan balance, (2) add an escrow account to your loan, or (3) require you to pay for property insurance that the lender buys on your behalf, which likely would cost more and provide fewer benefits than what you could buy on your own.

CLOSING DISCLOSURE PAGE 4 OF 5 • LOAN ID #

FIGURE 10-2 (Continued)

Loan Calculations

Total of Payments. Total you will have paid after you make all payments of principal, interest, mortgage insurance, and loan costs, as scheduled.	
Finance Charge. The dollar amount the loan will cost you.	
Amount Financed. The loan amount available after paying your upfront finance charge.	
Annual Percentage Rate (APR). Your costs over the loan term expressed as a rate. This is not your interest rate.	
Total Interest Percentage (TIP). The total amount of interest that you will pay over the loan term as a percentage of your loan amount.	

Questions? If you have questions about the loan terms or costs on this form, use the contact information below. To get more information or make a complaint, contact the Consumer Financial Protection Bureau at **www.consumerfinance.gov/mortgage-closing**

Other Disclosures

Appraisal
If the property was appraised for your loan, your lender is required to give you a copy at no additional cost at least 3 days before closing. If you have not yet received it, please contact your lender at the information listed below.

Contract Details
See your note and security instrument for information about
- what happens if you fail to make your payments,
- what is a default on the loan,
- situations in which your lender can require early repayment of the loan, and
- the rules for making payments before they are due.

Liability after Foreclosure
If your lender forecloses on this property and the foreclosure does not cover the amount of unpaid balance on this loan,

☐ state law may protect you from liability for the unpaid balance. If you refinance or take on any additional debt on this property, you may lose this protection and have to pay any debt remaining even after foreclosure. You may want to consult a lawyer for more information.

☐ state law does not protect you from liability for the unpaid balance.

Refinance
Refinancing this loan will depend on your future financial situation, the property value, and market conditions. You may not be able to refinance this loan.

Tax Deductions
If you borrow more than this property is worth, the interest on the loan amount above this property's fair market value is not deductible from your federal income taxes. You should consult a tax advisor for more information.

Contact Information

	Lender	Mortgage Broker	Real Estate Broker (B)	Real Estate Broker (S)	Settlement Agent
Name					
Address					
NMLS ID					
__ License ID					
Contact					
Contact NMLS ID					
Contact __ License ID					
Email					
Phone					

Confirm Receipt

By signing, you are only confirming that you have received this form. You do not have to accept this loan because you have signed or received this form.

Applicant Signature Date Co-Applicant Signature Date

CLOSING DISCLOSURE PAGE 5 OF 5 • LOAN ID #

FIGURE 10-2 (Continued)

and cooperatives) designed principally for the occupancy of from one to four families, including any such secured loan, the proceeds of which are used to prepay or pay off an existing loan secured by the same property; and

- is made in whole or in part by any lender the deposits or accounts of which are insured by any agency of the federal government, or is made in whole or in part by any lender that is regulated by any agency of the federal government, or
- is made in whole or in part, or insured, guaranteed, supplemented, or assisted in any way, by the secretary or any other officer or agency of the federal government or under or in connection with a housing or urban development program administered by the secretary or a housing or related program administered by any other such officer or agency; or
- is intended to be sold by the originating lender to the Federal National Mortgage Association, the Government National Mortgage Association, the Federal Home Loan Mortgage Corporation, or a financial institution from which it is to be purchased by the Federal Home Loan Mortgage Corporation; or
- is made in whole or in part by any "creditor," as defined in 15 U.S.C. § 1602(f)(1), who makes or invests in residential real estate loans aggregating more than $1,000,000 per year, except that for the purpose of this chapter, the term "creditor" does not include any agency or instrumentality of any state."[5]

There are however a number of exemptions to the use of the form. These exemptions apply to business purpose loans, temporary financing, loans on vacant land, assumptions without lender approval, loan conversions, and secondary market transactions.[6]

INSPECTIONS

Inspections are another necessary step to the transaction process. The prospective buyer will have some idea of issues associated with the property by viewing the Seller's Disclosure Notice. The Seller's Disclosure Notice should be provided to the buyer before the buyer makes an offer on the property. Obviously, if there are problems, the prospective buyer can take this into account when proposing the offer. The preferred time when the prospective buyer should get this document is before he or she goes out to see the property. The prospective buyer shouldn't waste his or her time if certain problems would preclude making an offer.

If the parties contract for the property before the buyer receives the Seller's Disclosure Notice, the buyer can still walk away from the deal if the seller is not otherwise exempt from providing the notice. If the buyer does not receive the

[5] 12 U.S.C. § 2602(1).

[6] 12 C.F.R. § 1024.5.

notice by the time indicated in the real estate sales contract, he or she can terminate at any time and for any reason and receive his or her earnest money back. Even if the notice is delivered by the time indicated, the buyer can still terminate for any reason within seven days after the buyer's receipt of the notice or before closing, whichever occurs first and receive his or her earnest money back.

Once the contract is signed, the prospective purchaser may have the property inspected by a licensed inspector of his or her choice and a report prepared. See figure 10-3. The inspection is typically paid for by the buyer since the buyer is choosing the inspector. In order to conduct the inspection, the seller must permit access to the property at reasonable times. The parties can define what constitutes "reasonable times" in paragraph 11 of the promulgated residential sales contract. In addition, the seller must also make sure the utilities are kept on during the term of the contract so any necessary inspections can be made. Any hydrostatic testing, however, must be separately authorized in writing by the seller. See figure 10-4.

The buyer may accept the property as it is or "as is" with specified repairs to be performed for the buyer at the seller's expense. Accepting the property "as is" does not preclude the buyer from inspecting the property, negotiating repairs, or terminating the contract during the option period. Depending on the extent of repairs requested, it may be wise for the seller to counteroffer with a cap to the seller's expense for the repairs under the contract.

Neither party is obligated to pay for lender-required repairs, which include treatments for wood-destroying insects, unless otherwise agreed in writing. These repairs are negotiable. If the buyer agrees to pay for the repairs and/or treatments, then this should be provided in paragraph 11. If the seller agrees to pay for the repairs and/or treatments, then this should be provided in paragraph 7D. A monetary cap might be included to limit the parties' liability. When setting the cap, care should be taken in setting the cap below 5% of the sales price. If the cost of lender-required repairs exceeds 5% of the sales price, then the buyer may terminate the contract and have his or her earnest money refunded. If the parties cannot agree as to who pays for lender-required repairs, the contract terminates and the earnest money is refunded to the buyer.

The promulgated residential sales contract sets out a time schedule for the completion of indicated repairs by the seller. By default, the repairs must be completed by the seller before the closing date, but the parties may make a different agreement. Repairs and treatments must be performed by persons who regularly provide these repairs and the necessary permits are required. This can become quite expensive after the contract is created. Many brokers will recommend to their sellers that certain obvious repairs be done before the house is listed and a contract is signed. This is so the repairs do not have to be performed by persons who regularly provide the repairs. If the buyer wishes, he or she can seek any transferable warranties received by the seller on the repairs. If the seller fails to

TREC
TEXAS REAL ESTATE COMMISSION

PROPERTY INSPECTION REPORT

Prepared For: ______________________________
(Name of Client)

Concerning: ______________________________
(Address or Other Identification of Inspected Property)

By: ______________________________ ______________
(Name and License Number of Inspector) (Date)

____
(Name, License Number of Sponsoring Inspector)

PURPOSE, LIMITATIONS AND INSPECTOR / CLIENT RESPONSIBILITIES

This property inspection report may include an inspection agreement (contract), addenda, and other information related to property conditions. If any item or comment is unclear, you should ask the inspector to clarify the findings. It is important that you carefully read ALL of this information.

This inspection is subject to the rules ("Rules") of the Texas Real Estate Commission ("TREC"), which can be found at www.trec.texas.gov.

The TREC Standards of Practice (Sections 535.227-535.233 of the Rules) are the minimum standards for inspections by TREC-licensed inspectors. An inspection addresses only those components and conditions that are present, visible, and accessible at the time of the inspection. While there may be other parts, components or systems present, only those items specifically noted as being inspected were inspected. The inspector is NOT required to turn on decommissioned equipment, systems, utility services or apply an open flame or light a pilot to operate any appliance. The inspector is NOT required to climb over obstacles, move furnishings or stored items. The inspection report may address issues that are code-based or may refer to a particular code; however, this is NOT a code compliance inspection and does NOT verify compliance with manufacturer's installation instructions. The inspection does NOT imply insurability or warrantability of the structure or its components. Although some safety issues may be addressed in this report, this inspection is NOT a safety/code inspection, and the inspector is NOT required to identify all potential hazards.

In this report, the inspector shall indicate, by checking the appropriate boxes on the form, whether each item was inspected, not inspected, not present or deficient and explain the findings in the corresponding section in the body of the report form. The inspector must check the Deficient (D) box if a condition exists that adversely and materially affects the performance of a system or component or constitutes a hazard to life, limb or property as specified by the TREC Standards of Practice. General deficiencies include inoperability, material distress, water penetration, damage, deterioration, missing components, and unsuitable installation. Comments may be provided by the inspector whether or not an item is deemed deficient. The inspector is not required to prioritize or emphasize the importance of one deficiency over another.

Some items reported may be considered life-safety upgrades to the property. For more information, refer to Texas Real Estate Consumer Notice Concerning Recognized Hazards or Deficiencies below.

THIS PROPERTY INSPECTION IS NOT A TECHNICALLY EXHAUSTIVE INSPECTION OF THE STRUCTURE, SYSTEMS OR COMPONENTS. This inspection may not reveal all deficiencies. A real estate inspection helps to reduce some of the risk involved in purchasing a home, but it cannot eliminate these risks, nor can the inspection anticipate future events or changes in performance due to changes in use or occupancy. If is recommended that you obtain as much information as is available about this property, including seller's disclosures, previous inspection reports, engineering reports, building/remodeling permits, and reports performed for and by relocation companies, municipal inspection departments, lenders, insurers, and appraisers. You should also attempt to determine whether repairs, renovation, remodeling, additions, or other such activities have taken place at this property. It is not the inspector's responsibility to confirm that information obtained from these sources is complete or accurate or that this inspection is consistent with the opinions expressed in previous or future reports.

ITEMS IDENTIFIED IN THE REPORT DO NOT OBLIGATE ANY PARTY TO MAKE REPAIRS OR TAKE OTHER ACTIONS, NOR IS THE PURCHASER REQUIRED TO REQUEST THAT THE SELLER TAKE ANY ACTION. When a deficiency is reported, it is the client's responsibility to obtain further evaluations and/or cost estimates from qualified service professionals. Any such follow-up should take place prior to the expiration of any time limitations such as option periods.

Promulgated by the Texas Real Estate Commission (TREC) P.O. Box 12188, Austin, TX 78711-2188 (512) 936-3000 (http://www.trec.texas.gov).

Page 1 of

FIGURE 10-3 REI 7-5 Property Inspection Report

Report Identification: ______________________________

Evaluations by qualified tradesmen may lead to the discovery of additional deficiencies which may involve additional repair costs. Failure to address deficiencies or comments noted in this report may lead to further damage of the structure or systems and add to the original repair costs. The inspector is not required to provide follow-up services to verify that proper repairs have been made.

Property conditions change with time and use. For example, mechanical devices can fail at any time, plumbing gaskets and seals may crack if the appliance or plumbing fixture is not used often, roof leaks can occur at any time regardless of the apparent condition of the roof, and the performance of the structure and the systems may change due to changes in use or occupancy, effects of weather, etc. These changes or repairs made to the structure after the inspection may render information contained herein obsolete or invalid. This report is provided for the specific benefit of the client named above and is based on observations at the time of the inspection. If you did not hire the inspector yourself, reliance on this report may provide incomplete or outdated information. Repairs, professional opinions or additional inspection reports may affect the meaning of the information in this report. It is recommended that you hire a licensed inspector to perform an inspection to meet your specific needs and to provide you with current information concerning this property.

TEXAS REAL ESTATE CONSUMER NOTICE CONCERNING HAZARDS OR DEFICIENCIES

Each year, Texans sustain property damage and are injured by accidents in the home. While some accidents may not be avoidable, many other accidents, injuries, and deaths may be avoided through the identification and repair of certain hazardous conditions. Examples of such hazards include:

- malfunctioning, improperly installed, or missing ground fault circuit protection (GFCI) devices for electrical receptacles in garages, bathrooms, kitchens, and exterior areas;
- malfunctioning arc fault protection (AFCI) devices;
- ordinary glass in locations where modern construction techniques call for safety glass;
- malfunctioning or lack of fire safety features such as smoke alarms, fire-rated doors in certain locations, and functional emergency escape and rescue openings in bedrooms;
- malfunctioning carbon monoxide alarms;
- excessive spacing between balusters on stairways and porches;
- improperly installed appliances;
- improperly installed or defective safety devices;
- lack of electrical bonding and grounding; and
- lack of bonding on gas piping, including corrugated stainless steel tubing (CSST).

To ensure that consumers are informed of hazards such as these, the Texas Real Estate Commission (TREC) has adopted Standards of Practice requiring licensed inspectors to report these conditions as "Deficient" when performing an inspection for a buyer or seller, if they can be reasonably determined.

These conditions may not have violated building codes or common practices at the time of the construction of the home, or they may have been "grandfathered" because they were present prior to the adoption of codes prohibiting such conditions. While the TREC Standards of Practice do not require inspectors to perform a code compliance inspection, TREC considers the potential for injury or property loss from the hazards addressed in the Standards of Practice to be significant enough to warrant this notice.

Contract forms developed by TREC for use by its real estate license holders also inform the buyer of the right to have the home inspected and can provide an option clause permitting the buyer to terminate the contract within a specified time. Neither the Standards of Practice nor the TREC contract forms require a seller to remedy conditions revealed by an inspection. The decision to correct a hazard or any deficiency identified in an inspection report is left to the parties to the contract for the sale or purchase of the home.

INFORMATION INCLUDED UNDER "ADDITIONAL INFORMATION PROVIDED BY INSPECTOR", OR PROVIDED AS AN ATTACHMENT WITH THE STANDARD FORM, IS NOT REQUIRED BY THE COMMISSION AND MAY CONTAIN CONTRACTUAL TERMS BETWEEN THE INSPECTOR AND YOU, AS THE CLIENT. THE COMMISSION DOES NOT REGULATE CONTRACTUAL TERMS BETWEEN PARTIES. IF YOU DO NOT UNDERSTAND THE EFFECT OF ANY CONTRACTUAL TERM CONTAINED IN THIS SECTION OR ANY ATTACHMENTS, CONSULT AN ATTORNEY.

ADDITIONAL INFORMATION PROVIDED BY INSPECTOR

Page 2 of ___

REI 7-5 (5/4/2015)

FIGURE 10-3 (Continued)

Report Identification: ______________________________

I=Inspected **NI=Not Inspected** **NP=Not Present** **D=Deficient**

I NI NP D

I. STRUCTURAL SYSTEMS

☐ ☐ ☐ ☐ **A. Foundations**
Type of Foundation(s):
Comments:

☐ ☐ ☐ ☐ **B. Grading and Drainage**
Comments:

☐ ☐ ☐ ☐ **C. Roof Covering Materials**
Types of Roof Covering:
Viewed From:
Comments:

☐ ☐ ☐ ☐ **D. Roof Structures and Attics**
Viewed From:
Approximate Average Depth of Insulation:
Comments:

☐ ☐ ☐ ☐ **E. Walls (Interior and Exterior)**
Comments:

☐ ☐ ☐ ☐ **F. Ceilings and Floors**
Comments:

☐ ☐ ☐ ☐ **G. Doors (Interior and Exterior)**
Comments:

☐ ☐ ☐ ☐ **H. Windows**
Comments:

☐ ☐ ☐ ☐ **I. Stairways (Interior and Exterior)**
Comments:

☐ ☐ ☐ ☐ **J. Fireplaces and Chimneys**
Comments:

☐ ☐ ☐ ☐ **K. Porches, Balconies, Decks, and Carports**
Comments:

☐ ☐ ☐ ☐ **L. Other**
Comments:

Page 3 of ___

REI 7-5 (5/4/2015)

FIGURE 10-3 (Continued)

Report Identification: ____________________

I=Inspected **NI=Not Inspected** **NP=Not Present** **D=Deficient**

I NI NP D

II. ELECTRICAL SYSTEMS

☐ ☐ ☐ ☐ **A. Service Entrance and Panels**
Comments:

☐ ☐ ☐ ☐ **B. Branch Circuits, Connected Devices, and Fixtures**
Type of Wiring:
Comments:

III. HEATING, VENTILATION AND AIR CONDITIONING SYSTEMS

☐ ☐ ☐ ☐ **A. Heating Equipment**
Type of Systems:
Energy Sources:
Comments:

☐ ☐ ☐ ☐ **B. Cooling Equipment**
Type of Systems:
Comments:

☐ ☐ ☐ ☐ **C. Duct Systems, Chases, and Vents**
Comments:

IV. PLUMBING SYSTEMS

☐ ☐ ☐ ☐ **A. Plumbing Supply, Distribution Systems and Fixtures**
Location of water meter:
Location of main water supply valve:
Static water pressure reading:
Comments:

☐ ☐ ☐ ☐ **B. Drains, Wastes, and Vents**
Comments:

☐ ☐ ☐ ☐ **C. Water Heating Equipment**
Energy Sources:
Capacity:
Comments:

☐ ☐ ☐ ☐ **D. Hydro-Massage Therapy Equipment**
Comments:

☐ ☐ ☐ ☐ **E. Other**
Comments:

Page 4 of ___

REI 7-5 (5/4/2015)

FIGURE 10-3 (Continued)

Report Identification: ______________________________

I=Inspected **NI=Not Inspected** **NP=Not Present** **D=Deficient**

I NI NP D

V. APPLIANCES

☐ ☐ ☐ ☐ **A. Dishwashers**
Comments:

☐ ☐ ☐ ☐ **B. Food Waste Disposers**
Comments:

☐ ☐ ☐ ☐ **C. Range Hood and Exhaust Systems**
Comments:

☐ ☐ ☐ ☐ **D. Ranges, Cooktops, and Ovens**
Comments:

☐ ☐ ☐ ☐ **E. Microwave Ovens**
Comments:

☐ ☐ ☐ ☐ **F. Mechanical Exhaust Vents and Bathroom Heaters**
Comments:

☐ ☐ ☐ ☐ **G. Garage Door Operators**
Comments:

☐ ☐ ☐ ☐ **H. Dryer Exhaust Systems**
Comments:

☐ ☐ ☐ ☐ **I. Other**
Comments:

VI. OPTIONAL SYSTEMS

☐ ☐ ☐ ☐ **A. Landscape Irrigation (Sprinkler) Systems**
Comments:

☐ ☐ ☐ ☐ **B. Swimming Pools, Spas, Hot Tubs, and Equipment**
Type of Construction:
Comments:

☐ ☐ ☐ ☐ **C. Outbuildings**
Comments:

Page 5 of ___

REI 7-5 (5/4/2015)

FIGURE 10-3 (Continued)

Report Identification: ______________________________

I=Inspected **NI=Not Inspected** **NP=Not Present** **D=Deficient**

I	NI	NP	D	
☐	☐	☐	☐	**D. Private Water Wells** (A coliform analysis is recommended.) *Type of Pump:* *Type of Storage Equipment:* *Comments:*
☐	☐	☐	☐	**E. Private Sewage Disposal (Septic) Systems** *Type of System:* *Location of Drain Field:* *Comments:*
☐	☐	☐	☐	**F. Other** *Comments:*

Page 6 of ___

REI 7-5 (5/4/2015)

FIGURE 10-3 (Continued)

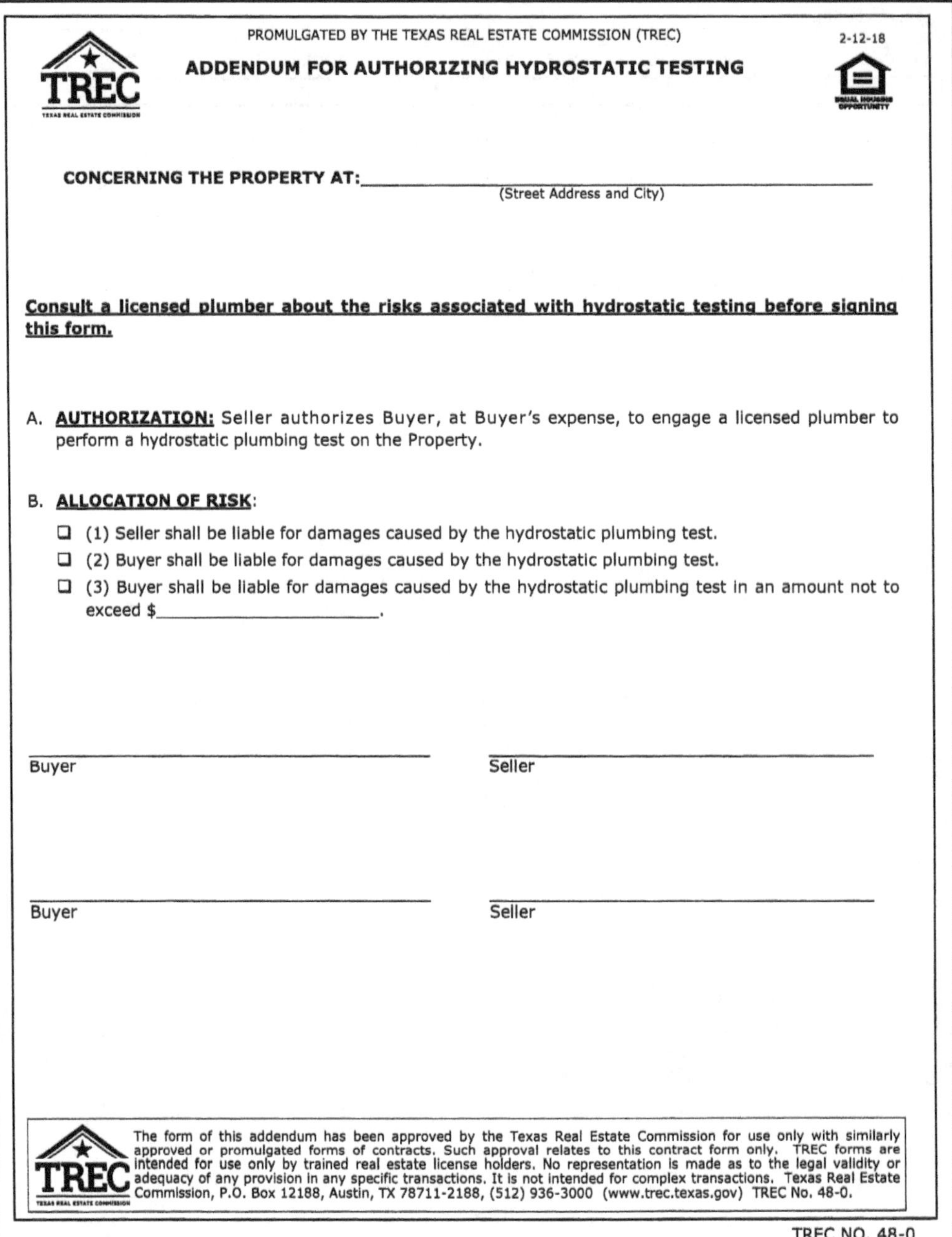

PROMULGATED BY THE TEXAS REAL ESTATE COMMISSION (TREC) 2-12-18

TREC
TEXAS REAL ESTATE COMMISSION

ADDENDUM FOR AUTHORIZING HYDROSTATIC TESTING

EQUAL HOUSING OPPORTUNITY

CONCERNING THE PROPERTY AT:____
(Street Address and City)

Consult a licensed plumber about the risks associated with hydrostatic testing before signing this form.

A. **AUTHORIZATION:** Seller authorizes Buyer, at Buyer's expense, to engage a licensed plumber to perform a hydrostatic plumbing test on the Property.

B. **ALLOCATION OF RISK:**

- ☐ (1) Seller shall be liable for damages caused by the hydrostatic plumbing test.
- ☐ (2) Buyer shall be liable for damages caused by the hydrostatic plumbing test.
- ☐ (3) Buyer shall be liable for damages caused by the hydrostatic plumbing test in an amount not to exceed $____________________.

____________________ ____________________
Buyer Seller

____________________ ____________________
Buyer Seller

TREC
TEXAS REAL ESTATE COMMISSION

The form of this addendum has been approved by the Texas Real Estate Commission for use only with similarly approved or promulgated forms of contracts. Such approval relates to this contract form only. TREC forms are intended for use only by trained real estate license holders. No representation is made as to the legal validity or adequacy of any provision in any specific transactions. It is not intended for complex transactions. Texas Real Estate Commission, P.O. Box 12188, Austin, TX 78711-2188, (512) 936-3000 (www.trec.texas.gov) TREC No. 48-0.

TREC NO. 48-0

FIGURE 10-4 Addendum for Authorizing Hydrostatic Testing
Source: Reprinted with permission of Texas Real Estate Commission

complete the repairs by the closing date, the buyer can seek default remedies or extend the closing date to allow the seller to finish the repairs.

The buyer may purchase a residential service contract to be reimbursed by the seller at closing. A space is provided in the sales contract to limit the cost of the residential service contract. The Disclosure of Relationship with Residential Service Company form (TREC RSC-2) can be used to disclose any relationship the broker may have with a residential service company.

TITLE WORK

A buyer of real estate in Texas must realize that title is never perfect. All one can hope for in Texas is marketable title. Therefore, purchasers in Texas want some assurance that the title is marketable. If it isn't marketable, then it is important to be aware of the remedies. This is where title work is helpful.

Deed warranties

There are three methods of title assurance that may be available to the buyer in a real estate transaction. These are (1) deed warranties, (2) title insurance, and (3) lawyer's title opinion. The first is the deed warranties. If a grantor conveys title to real estate by either a general or special warranty deed, then he or she is providing specific warranties to the grantee. A portion of these warranties apply to the present transfer, and the remainder of the warranties apply in the future. These warranties are respectively referred to as present warranties and future warranties. See figure 10-5.

Present Warranties

Present warranties have specific characteristics. First, a present warranty may only be breached when the deed is delivered. If no breach has occurred by that point, then the only applicable warranties are future warranties. In addition, the statute of limitations on a breach of a present warranty begins to run from the time of delivery. Third, the present warranty does not run with the land. That is, the present warranty as between the grantor and the grantee does not attach to the property and pass from owner to owner.

There are actually three types of present warranties that exist in a warranty deed. The first is the covenant of seisin. The **covenant of seisin** states that the grantor of the property warrants that he or she owns the property that he or she purports to convey. The second type of present warranty is the **covenant of the right to convey**. Under the covenant of the right to convey, the grantor warrants that he or she has the right to convey the property. In other words, the grantor

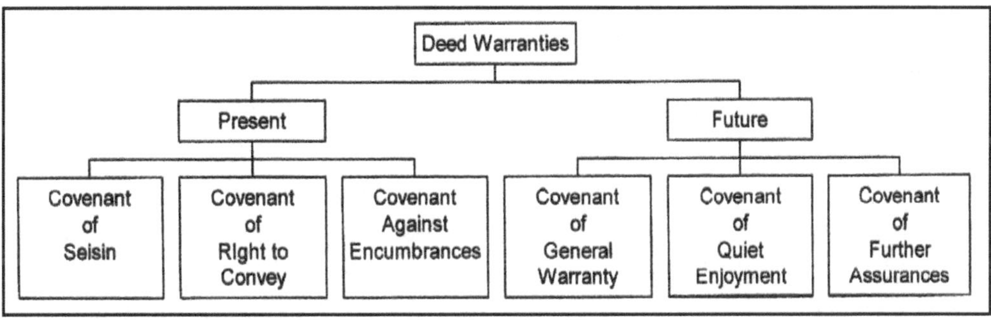

FIGURE 10-5 Deed Warranties
Source: © 2021 Mbition LLC

is warranting that he or she has the authority to convey the property. The third type of present warranty is the **covenant against encumbrances.** In this covenant, the grantor warrants that there are no encumbrances on the property. Certain encumbrances might include liens, easements, covenants, and possibly oil, gas, and mineral interests.

Future Warranties

In addition to the present warranties, a warranty deed contains future warranties. Because the future warranties relate to a different time frame, there are specific characteristics that apply to future warranties. First, the future warranty is not breached until a grantee is evicted from the real estate itself or is somehow damaged by an outstanding claim. Second, the statute of limitations on a future warranty does not begin to run until the grantee has been evicted from the premises or the damage occurs. Last, the future warranty does run with the land for subsequent transfers.

There are three types of future warranties recognized under the warranty deed. The first type of warranty is the **covenant of general warranty** in which the grantor warrants that he or she will defend the property against any lawful claims and compensate the grantee for any loss that he or she suffers by the assertion of superior title by a third party. The second future warranty is the **covenant of quiet enjoyment** in which the grantor warrants that the grantee will not be disturbed in his or her possession and enjoyment of the property by the assertion of superior title by a third party. This warranty is typically considered interchangeable with the covenant of general warranty. The third future warranty in the warranty deed is the **covenant of further assurances** in which the grantor promises that he or she will execute any other documents required to perfect the title that has been conveyed to the grantee.

Recourse for a Buyer

If any of these deed warranties is breached, the recourse of the buyer depends on the type of warranty deed that was used in the real estate transaction. Since general warranty deeds warrant title to the property against all defects in title that arose both before and after the grantor took title to the property, the buyer can sue the grantor even for title defects that arose during ownership by previous owners. It would be up to the grantor therefore to pursue any prior owner if the grantor purchased the property with a warranty deed. By contrast, if the buyer purchased the property with a special warranty deed, the buyer would only be able to sue the grantor for title defects that arose during the grantor's ownership and not for those defects that arose from prior owners.

Unfortunately, while the buyer may have the right to sue in these instances and be able to obtain a judgment because of the title defects, the reality is that the buyer may not be able to collect any money on the judgment. The reason for this is because the judgment is considered a general debt and therefore cannot be collected out of the grantor's exempt homestead property. Since most individuals do not own more than the homestead exemptions, the buyer may end up with a judgment and no ability to collect. This is why title insurance, or alternatively lawyer title opinions, are so useful: they give the buyer the ability to collect if there is a problem.

Title Insurance

Title insurance is the most common method of title assurance in Texas and is typically obtained for property located in a subdivision. Title insurance is insurance against loss or damage resulting from title defects. Title insurance has one advantage over warranties contained in warranty deeds in that the company issuing the policy of title insurance, the title company, agrees to defend at its expense all litigation against the insured based upon the defect covered under the policy. If however the defect is not covered by the policy, the buyer may still be able to sue the grantor for the defect if a warranty deed was used.

The policy of title insurance is an insurance policy that protects the insured owner, in an owner policy, and lender, in a mortgagee policy, if any, from loss due to defects in the title. The policy does not pass from owner to owner. Title insurance, however, only covers matters of record. Title insurance is required with third-party financing situations, such as third party conventional, VA, and FHA financing, so that the lender's investment is protected against loss caused by some title defect. Unfortunately, it is not required in all cash, seller financing, and assumption transactions; however, it is highly recommended given the issues associated with seeking recovery for title defects on the deed warranties alone. In these situations a prospective purchaser may choose not to get a title policy. Alternatively, the party may request only a title search on the premises. A request for a title search only can be included in paragraph 11; however, a title search alone is insufficient to protect against defects in the title. A license holder should make it clear that the buyer should obtain a lawyer's title opinion or obtain a policy of title insurance. If a policy of title insurance is requested, then the seller typically pays for the issuance of the policy, but as with all provisions under the promulgated residential sales contract, the determination of who ultimately pays for the policy can be negotiated between the parties.

The standard title insurance will be subject to specific exclusions indicated by the title company as well as a list of standard exceptions listed in paragraph 6A. It is important to note that Texas also recognizes a concept called express insurance. This express insurance may allow the party to insure around some of the standard exceptions. The purchaser can consult a title company for additional information on express insurance and whether it might benefit him or her.

Paragraph 6B of the promulgated residential sales contract deals with deadlines for the title commitment. When the title company receives the contract it will first conduct a title search of the property to confirm ownership and find any liens on the property. Paragraph 6B provides that a title commitment must be delivered to the buyer within 20 days after the title company gets the contract. The title commitment is used to inform the prospective purchaser about the title to the property. If it's not delivered by that time, the time for delivery is automatically extended up to 15 days or 3 days before closing, whichever is earlier. But if due to factors beyond the seller's control the documents cannot be delivered, then the buyer can terminate the contract and request his or her earnest money back. If the transaction proceeds to closing, the title company will issue a title insurance policy for the property.

Lawyer's Title Opinion

An alternative to a title insurance policy is a lawyer's title opinion. The lawyer's title opinion is sought for much larger tracts of land and may be specifically requested by any lender involved. A lawyer's title opinion has an advantage over warranties contained in warranty deeds in that the lawyer who issues the opinion may be sued for malpractice if the buyer discovers any title defects. Due to the cost associated with the opinion, the buyer pays the lawyer directly.

If the lawyer's title opinion is necessary, then it is mandatory in third-party conventional transactions, VA transactions, and FHA transactions. In all-cash transactions, seller financing transactions, and assumption transactions, the lawyer's title opinion would be discretionary.

PREPARATION FOR CLOSING

If the parties to the contract are successful, the real estate transaction will close. But as the time for closing approaches, there are certain preparations that should be made for the closing. First, the prospective purchaser should inspect the loan documents the day before closing to ensure there are no changes since the preliminary documents only list estimates. Second, the prospective purchaser needs to purchase homeowner's insurance, which will take effect on the day of closing. Third, the prospective purchaser with his or her agent must plan and con duct the final walk-through inspection. At this time the prospective purchaser can confirm that the seller has moved out, all necessary repairs have been completed, and all personal property to be conveyed has been left. Third, any issues that came about as a result of the walk-through inspection should be resolved. Fourth, the prospective purchaser should make sure that he or she has received a commitment of title insurance to make sure there are no issues that need to be resolved before closing. Last, the prospective purchaser should contact the respective utility companies to ensure that utility service is transferred when the prospective purchaser takes possession. These steps will help ensure a smooth transition at closing.

PRORATIONS

At closing, taxes, interest, maintenance fees, assessments, dues, and rents will be prorated through the closing date. Note that if the taxes are not paid at or prior to closing, the buyer will have to pay all taxes for the current year as new owner of the property. Sample calculations for proration of taxes and insurance are included in figures 10-6 and 10-7.

CLOSING AND FUNDING

Closing of the deal is simply the final settlement of the transaction and the date for closing is specified in the promulgated real estate sales contract. The closing date will vary depending on the type of financing involved. Where no lender is involved, the transaction can be between one and three weeks. If a lender is involved, such as in third-party conventional, FHA, or VA financing, the transaction can take anywhere between one and two months. This can vary if the buyer is prequalified for a loan. Note that if either party fails to close on the date indicated without a valid legal excuse, the non-defaulting party may exercise his or her breach of contract remedies.

At closing, the seller must be prepared to show that there are no delinquent taxes, and the seller must furnish a general warranty deed conveying good and indefeasible title. If any other deed is to be used to transfer title to the property, then that fact must be indicated in paragraph 11 of the promulgated residential sales contract and the buyer should be given the ability to seek legal counsel if he

Proration of Taxes

The closing of the real estate sale occurs on June 22. Taxes for the current year are $840 and have not been paid. The seller will owe the following amount for taxes to the buyer on the day of closing.

Proration through last full month

($840 + 12 months in a year) × 5 months = $350

Proration through the closing date

($840 + 360 days in a statutory year) × 22 days = $51.33

Addition to find the total proration of taxes owed by the seller

$350 + $51.33 = $401.33

FIGURE 10-6 Proration of Taxes
Source: © 2021 Mbition LLC

Proration of Insurance

The closing of the real estate sale occurs on February 14. Insurance for the year of $1200 has already been paid by the seller at the beginning of the year. The buyer must pay the seller for the unused portion at closing.

<u>Portion used in January</u>

($1200 + 12 months in a year) × 1 month = $100

<u>Portion used through closing</u>

($1200 + 360 days in a statutory year) × 14 days = $46.67

<u>Total portion used by seller is</u>

$100 + $46.67 = <u>$146.67</u>

<u>Total amount buyer must pay seller for unused portion is</u>

$1200 − $146.67 = <u>$1053.33</u>

FIGURE 10-7 Proration of Insurance
Source: © 2021 Mbition LLC

or she desires. In addition, the seller must provide a copy of any existing residential lease to the buyer.

This process is conducted by the escrow officer. At closing, the seller will transfer the title to the real estate, usually in the form of a general warranty deed, and the buyer will transfer the proceeds. The parties do not generally close at the same time. The seller typically goes first because he or she is signing over the title, but if the transaction is for all cash the buyer may go first just to make sure the money for the deal is obtained. Real estate licenses and/or attorneys who helped the parties to the transaction may also be present at the closing with their respective clients.

In most cases possession by the buyer will take place upon "closing and funding" of the loan. This concept is important because there may be instances where closing and funding do not occur on the same day. For instance, if closing takes place on a Friday, most lenders will not fund the loan until Monday, unless a release of funds is obtained. There may also be instances where a purchaser actually prequalified for a loan, but the buyer created more debt between the time the contract was signed and the time for closing, which prevented the loan from funding. This may occur in instances where the new buyer goes shopping for all new furniture and appliances before the transaction is closed and reaches the limit on his or her credit cards.

If the buyer is to take possession of the premises before closing, then a promulgated Buyer's Temporary Residential Lease should be used. If the seller is to remain in the premises beyond the closing date, then a promulgated Seller's Temporary Residential Lease should be used. If no form is used, then a tenancy at sufferance relationship will arise, in which case the terms of the tenancy will be established after a dispute arises between the parties. It is important that the license holder inform the parties involved, particularly the property owner, to make sure they have adequate homeowner's insurance coverage on the premises. Most insurance companies require that the policies be amended to reflect the tenancy situation.

The documents required from the parties during the closing will also vary depending on the type of transaction involved. However, a typical closing checklist is provided below:

SELLER

- deed for signature
- Closing Disclosure
- money for any amounts due

BUYER

- owner's policy of title insurance
- promissory note (if financing is involved)
- deed of trust (if financing is involved)
- Closing Disclosure
- money for any amounts due
- disclosures required by law
- transferable warranties, if applicable

The list of expense items owed at closing is detailed in the sales contract. Paragraph 12A contains a detailed list of closing expenses that is self-explanatory and provides for a VA loan funding fee, private mortgage insurance, or FHA mortgage insurance premium, which the lender can require. A termination provision is contained in paragraph 12B that allows a party to the contract to terminate the contract if any expense exceeds an amount indicated in the contract, unless the other party agrees to pay the excess. This is the primary reason it is important to include some type of cap on the expense amounts designated in the contract.

After the closing procedure, certain documents must be recorded. The closer will present the deed for recording. Some title companies may send an extra copy of the deed to be stamped with the volume and page number and returned to the buyer for his or her records. Otherwise, the buyer can order a certified copy of the deed at a later date. In addition, the old lender will record a release of the seller's previous lien, although it will not generally send a copy of the release to the seller. The seller should follow up with the lender to confirm that a release was filed and obtain a copy for his or her records. Furthermore, the buyer's lender will record the new mortgage instrument, the deed of trust. Once recorded, the buyer should obtain a copy for his or her records. Once all of these documents have been filed in the county deed records, the title company will issue the new owner and mortgagee policy, if any.

Discussion Questions

1. What issues are implicated during the closing process?
2. What are the types of title assurance available in Texas? What are the advantages and disadvantages of each?

APPENDIX
COMMON CONTRACT EXAMPLES AND MISTAKES

This appendix facilitates discussion of common contract mistakes by providing contract examples and common areas of concern associated with those contract examples.

I. CONTRACT EXAMPLES

1. All Cash Transaction 1

You are a salesperson for Sawyer Realty, Inc. working with Eric and Tammy Williams. The Williams ask you to prepare an all-cash offer of $60,000 on the property located at 111 East Oak Lane, Orange, Texas 72143, also known as Lot 18, Block 45, NCB 1220, Fountain Creek Subdivision in Bloom County. This property is currently owned by Richard and Maria Guzman and was constructed in 1976. The property is subject to mandatory membership in the homeowners association. Mrs. Williams wants the 25-cubic-foot refrigerator and the 20-cubic-foot freezer included in the sale. Mr. Guzman does not want the satellite dish included in the transaction. The buyers would like a one-year home warranty paid for by the seller.

The buyers write a check for $2,500 as earnest money to "Lucky Lake Title, Inc." located at 1508 West 7th Street, Orange, Texas 72143. In addition, the buyers include another check for $500 as an option fee. The buyers are not concerned with a policy of title insurance; however, they do want a survey. In addition, the sale is subject to the buyers being able to install a 30-foot-by-30-foot swimming pool in the backyard. Seller will provide a home warranty. Buyers are not requesting an appraisal. Richard Guzman is the listing agent working for Acme Brokerage, Inc. located at 101 South 10th Street, Orange, Texas 72143, license number 804918. The listing broker agrees to pay any cooperating broker a commission of 2.5% of the total sales price. The buyers would like to close in two weeks. Using the appropriate residential sales contract, complete an offer from the buyer to the seller. See figure App-1 for a sample offer.

PROMULGATED BY THE TEXAS REAL ESTATE COMMISSION (TREC) 2-12-18

ONE TO FOUR FAMILY RESIDENTIAL CONTRACT (RESALE)

NOTICE: Not For Use For Condominium Transactions

1. PARTIES: The parties to this contract are Richard Guzman and wife Maria Guzman (Seller) and Eric Williams and wife, Tammy Williams (Buyer). Seller agrees to sell and convey to Buyer and Buyer agrees to buy from Seller the Property defined below.

2. PROPERTY: The land, improvements and accessories are collectively referred to as the "Property".

A. LAND: Lot 18 Block 45, NCB 1220, Fountain Creek Subdivision Addition, City of Orange, County of Bloom, Texas, known as 111 East Oak Lane 72143 (address/zip code), or as described on attached exhibit.

B. IMPROVEMENTS: The house, garage and all other fixtures and improvements attached to the above-described real property, including without limitation, the following **permanently installed and built-in items,** if any: all equipment and appliances, valances, screens, shutters, awnings, wall-to-wall carpeting, mirrors, ceiling fans, attic fans, mail boxes, television antennas, mounts and brackets for televisions and speakers, heating and air-conditioning units, security and fire detection equipment, wiring, plumbing and lighting fixtures, chandeliers, water softener system, kitchen equipment, garage door openers, cleaning equipment, shrubbery, landscaping, outdoor cooking equipment, and all other property owned by Seller and attached to the above described real property.

C. ACCESSORIES: The following described related accessories, if any: window air conditioning units, stove, fireplace screens, curtains and rods, blinds, window shades, draperies and rods, door keys, mailbox keys, above ground pool, swimming pool equipment and maintenance accessories, artificial fireplace logs, and controls for: (i) garage doors, (ii) entry gates, and (iii) other improvements and accessories.

D. EXCLUSIONS: The following improvements and accessories will be retained by Seller and must be removed prior to delivery of possession: satellite dish system and equipment.

E. RESERVATIONS: Any reservation for oil, gas, or other minerals, water, timber, or other interests is made in accordance with an attached addendum.

3. SALES PRICE:

A. Cash portion of Sales Price payable by Buyer at closing .... $ 60,000.00

B. Sum of all financing described in the attached: ❑ Third Party Financing Addendum, ❑ Loan Assumption Addendum, ❑ Seller Financing Addendum .... $ ------0------

C. Sales Price (Sum of A and B).. $ 60,000.00

4. LICENSE HOLDER DISCLOSURE: Texas law requires a real estate license holder who is a party to a transaction or acting on behalf of a spouse, parent, child, business entity in which the license holder owns more than 10%, or a trust for which the license holder acts as a trustee or of which the license holder or the license holder's spouse, parent or child is a beneficiary, to notify the other party in writing before entering into a contract of sale. Disclose if applicable: Richard Guzman is a real estate license holder acting on his own behalf.

5. EARNEST MONEY: Within 3 days after the Effective Date, Buyer must deliver $ 2,500.00 as earnest money to Lucky Lake Title, Inc., as escrow agent, at 1508 West 7th Street (address). Buyer shall deliver additional earnest money of $ N/A to escrow agent within N/A days after the Effective Date of this contract. If Buyer fails to deliver the earnest money within the time required, Seller may terminate this contract or exercise Seller's remedies under Paragraph 15, or both, by providing notice to Buyer before Buyer delivers the earnest money. If the last day to deliver the earnest money falls on a Saturday, Sunday, or legal holiday, the time to deliver the earnest money is extended until the end of the next day that is not a Saturday, Sunday, or legal holiday. **Time is of the essence for this paragraph.**

N/A **6. TITLE POLICY AND SURVEY:**

A. TITLE POLICY: Seller shall furnish to Buyer at ❑ Seller's ❑ Buyer's expense an owner policy of title insurance (Title Policy) issued by ______________ (Title Company) in the amount of the Sales Price, dated at or after closing, insuring Buyer against loss under the provisions of the Title Policy, subject to the promulgated exclusions (including existing building and zoning ordinances) and the following exceptions:

(1) Restrictive covenants common to the platted subdivision in which the Property is located.

(2) The standard printed exception for standby fees, taxes and assessments.

Initialed for identification by Buyer______ ______ and Seller ______ ______ TREC NO. 20-14

FIGURE APP-1 Sample Offer

Source: Reprinted with permission of Texas Real Estate Commission

(3) Liens created as part of the financing described in Paragraph 3.
(4) Utility easements created by the dedication deed or plat of the subdivision in which the Property is located.
(5) Reservations or exceptions otherwise permitted by this contract or as may be approved by Buyer in writing.
(6) The standard printed exception as to marital rights.
(7) The standard printed exception as to waters, tidelands, beaches, streams, and related matters.
(8) The standard printed exception as to discrepancies, conflicts, shortages in area or boundary lines, encroachments or protrusions, or overlapping improvements:
❑(i) will not be amended or deleted from the title policy; or
❑(ii) will be amended to read, "shortages in area" at the expense of ❑Buyer ❑Seller.
(9) The exception or exclusion regarding minerals approved by the Texas Department of Insurance.

B. COMMITMENT: Within 20 days after the Title Company receives a copy of this contract, Seller shall furnish to Buyer a commitment for title insurance (Commitment) and, at Buyer's expense, legible copies of restrictive covenants and documents evidencing exceptions in the Commitment (Exception Documents) other than the standard printed exceptions. Seller authorizes the Title Company to deliver the Commitment and Exception Documents to Buyer at Buyer's address shown in Paragraph 21. If the Commitment and Exception Documents are not delivered to Buyer within the specified time, the time for delivery will be automatically extended up to 15 days or 3 days before the Closing Date, whichever is earlier. If the Commitment and Exception Documents are not delivered within the time required, Buyer may terminate this contract and the earnest money will be refunded to Buyer.

C. SURVEY: The survey must be made by a registered professional land surveyor acceptable to the Title Company and Buyer's lender(s). (Check one box only)

❑(1) Within _______ days after the Effective Date of this contract, Seller shall furnish to Buyer and Title Company Seller's existing survey of the Property and a Residential Real Property Affidavit promulgated by the Texas Department of Insurance (T-47 Affidavit). **If Seller fails to furnish the existing survey or affidavit within the time prescribed, Buyer shall obtain a new survey at Seller's expense no later than 3 days prior to Closing Date.** If the existing survey or affidavit is not acceptable to Title Company or Buyer's lender(s), Buyer shall obtain a new survey at ❑Seller's ❑Buyer's expense no later than 3 days prior to Closing Date.

☑(2) Within 10 days after the Effective Date of this contract, Buyer shall obtain a new survey at Buyer's expense. Buyer is deemed to receive the survey on the date of actual receipt or the date specified in this paragraph, whichever is earlier.

❑(3) Within _______ days after the Effective Date of this contract, Seller, at Seller's expense shall furnish a new survey to Buyer.

D. OBJECTIONS: Buyer may object in writing to defects, exceptions, or encumbrances to title: disclosed on the survey other than items 6A(1) through (7) above; disclosed in the Commitment other than items 6A(1) through (9) above; or which prohibit the following use or activity: 30 foot x 30 foot swimming pool.
Buyer must object the earlier of (i) the Closing Date or (ii) 5 days after Buyer receives the Commitment, Exception Documents, and the survey. Buyer's failure to object within the time allowed will constitute a waiver of Buyer's right to object; except that the requirements in Schedule C of the Commitment are not waived by Buyer. Provided Seller is not obligated to incur any expense, Seller shall cure any timely objections of Buyer or any third party lender within 15 days after Seller receives the objections (Cure Period) and the Closing Date will be extended as necessary. If objections are not cured within the Cure Period, Buyer may, by delivering notice to Seller within 5 days after the end of the Cure Period: (i) terminate this contract and the earnest money will be refunded to Buyer; or (ii) waive the objections. If Buyer does not terminate within the time required, Buyer shall be deemed to have waived the objections. If the Commitment or Survey is revised or any new Exception Document(s) is delivered, Buyer may object to any new matter revealed in the revised Commitment or Survey or new Exception Document(s) within the same time stated in this paragraph to make objections beginning when the revised Commitment, Survey, or Exception Document(s) is delivered to Buyer.

E. TITLE NOTICES:
(1) ABSTRACT OR TITLE POLICY: Broker advises Buyer to have an abstract of title covering the Property examined by an attorney of Buyer's selection, or Buyer should be furnished with or obtain a Title Policy. If a Title Policy is furnished, the Commitment should be promptly reviewed by an attorney of Buyer's choice due to the time limitations on Buyer's right to object.
(2) MEMBERSHIP IN PROPERTY OWNERS ASSOCIATION(S): The Property ☑is ❑is not

FIGURE APP-1 (Continued)

subject to mandatory membership in a property owners association(s). If the Property is subject to mandatory membership in a property owners association(s), Seller notifies Buyer under §5.012, Texas Property Code, that, as a purchaser of property in the residential community identified in Paragraph 2A in which the Property is located, you are obligated to be a member of the property owners association(s). Restrictive covenants governing the use and occupancy of the Property and all dedicatory instruments governing the establishment, maintenance, or operation of this residential community have been or will be recorded in the Real Property Records of the county in which the Property is located. Copies of the restrictive covenants and dedicatory instruments may be obtained from the county clerk. **You are obligated to pay assessments to the property owners association(s). The amount of the assessments is subject to change. Your failure to pay the assessments could result in enforcement of the association's lien on and the foreclosure of the Property.**

Section 207.003, Property Code, entitles an owner to receive copies of any document that governs the establishment, maintenance, or operation of a subdivision, including, but not limited to, restrictions, bylaws, rules and regulations, and a resale certificate from a property owners' association. A resale certificate contains information including, but not limited to, statements specifying the amount and frequency of regular assessments and the style and cause number of lawsuits to which the property owners' association is a party, other than lawsuits relating to unpaid ad valorem taxes of an individual member of the association. These documents must be made available to you by the property owners' association or the association's agent on your request.

If Buyer is concerned about these matters, the TREC promulgated Addendum for Property Subject to Mandatory Membership in a Property Owners Association(s) should be used.

(3) STATUTORY TAX DISTRICTS: If the Property is situated in a utility or other statutorily created district providing water, sewer, drainage, or flood control facilities and services, Chapter 49, Texas Water Code, requires Seller to deliver and Buyer to sign the statutory notice relating to the tax rate, bonded indebtedness, or standby fee of the district prior to final execution of this contract.

(4) TIDE WATERS: If the Property abuts the tidally influenced waters of the state, §33.135, Texas Natural Resources Code, requires a notice regarding coastal area property to be included in the contract. An addendum containing the notice promulgated by TREC or required by the parties must be used.

(5) ANNEXATION: If the Property is located outside the limits of a municipality, Seller notifies Buyer under §5.011, Texas Property Code, that the Property may now or later be included in the extraterritorial jurisdiction of a municipality and may now or later be subject to annexation by the municipality. Each municipality maintains a map that depicts its boundaries and extraterritorial jurisdiction. To determine if the Property is located within a municipality's extraterritorial jurisdiction or is likely to be located within a municipality's extraterritorial jurisdiction, contact all municipalities located in the general proximity of the Property for further information.

(6) PROPERTY LOCATED IN A CERTIFICATED SERVICE AREA OF A UTILITY SERVICE PROVIDER: Notice required by §13.257, Water Code: The real property, described in Paragraph 2, that you are about to purchase may be located in a certificated water or sewer service area, which is authorized by law to provide water or sewer service to the properties in the certificated area. If your property is located in a certificated area there may be special costs or charges that you will be required to pay before you can receive water or sewer service. There may be a period required to construct lines or other facilities necessary to provide water or sewer service to your property. You are advised to determine if the property is in a certificated area and contact the utility service provider to determine the cost that you will be required to pay and the period, if any, that is required to provide water or sewer service to your property. The undersigned Buyer hereby acknowledges receipt of the foregoing notice at or before the execution of a binding contract for the purchase of the real property described in Paragraph 2 or at closing of purchase of the real property.

(7) PUBLIC IMPROVEMENT DISTRICTS: If the Property is in a public improvement district, §5.014, Property Code, requires Seller to notify Buyer as follows: As a purchaser of this parcel of real property you are obligated to pay an assessment to a municipality or county for an improvement project undertaken by a public improvement district under Chapter 372, Local Government Code. The assessment may be due annually or in periodic installments. More information concerning the amount of the assessment and the due dates of that assessment may be obtained from the municipality or county levying the assessment. The amount of the assessments is subject to change. Your failure to pay the assessments could result in a lien on and the foreclosure of your property.

(8) TRANSFER FEES: If the Property is subject to a private transfer fee obligation, §5.205, Property Code, requires Seller to notify Buyer as follows: The private transfer fee

FIGURE APP-1 (Continued)

Contract Concerning 111 East Oak Lane 72143 (Address of Property) Page 4 of 10 2-12-18

obligation may be governed by Chapter 5, Subchapter G of the Texas Property Code.

(9) PROPANE GAS SYSTEM SERVICE AREA: If the Property is located in a propane gas system service area owned by a distribution system retailer, Seller must give Buyer written notice as required by §141.010, Texas Utilities Code. An addendum containing the notice approved by TREC or required by the parties should be used.

(10) NOTICE OF WATER LEVEL FLUCTUATIONS: If the Property adjoins an impoundment of water, including a reservoir or lake, constructed and maintained under Chapter 11, Water Code, that has a storage capacity of at least 5,000 acre-feet at the impoundment's normal operating level, Seller hereby notifies Buyer: "The water level of the impoundment of water adjoining the Property fluctuates for various reasons, including as a result of: (1) an entity lawfully exercising its right to use the water stored in the impoundment; or (2) drought or flood conditions."

7. PROPERTY CONDITION:

A. ACCESS, INSPECTIONS AND UTILITIES: Seller shall permit Buyer and Buyer's agents access to the Property at reasonable times. Buyer may have the Property inspected by inspectors selected by Buyer and licensed by TREC or otherwise permitted by law to make inspections. Any hydrostatic testing must be separately authorized by Seller in writing. Seller at Seller's expense shall immediately cause existing utilities to be turned on and shall keep the utilities on during the time this contract is in effect.

B. SELLER'S DISCLOSURE NOTICE PURSUANT TO §5.008, TEXAS PROPERTY CODE (Notice): (Check one box only)

☑ (1) Buyer has received the Notice.

☐ (2) Buyer has not received the Notice. Within _______ days after the Effective Date of this contract, Seller shall deliver the Notice to Buyer. If Buyer does not receive the Notice, Buyer may terminate this contract at any time prior to the closing and the earnest money will be refunded to Buyer. If Seller delivers the Notice, Buyer may terminate this contract for any reason within 7 days after Buyer receives the Notice or prior to the closing, whichever first occurs, and the earnest money will be refunded to Buyer.

☐ (3)The Seller is not required to furnish the notice under the Texas Property Code.

C. SELLER'S DISCLOSURE OF LEAD-BASED PAINT AND LEAD-BASED PAINT HAZARDS is required by Federal law for a residential dwelling constructed prior to 1978.

D. ACCEPTANCE OF PROPERTY CONDITION: "As Is" means the present condition of the Property with any and all defects and without warranty except for the warranties of title and the warranties in this contract. Buyer's agreement to accept the Property As Is under Paragraph 7D(1) or (2) does not preclude Buyer from inspecting the Property under Paragraph 7A, from negotiating repairs or treatments in a subsequent amendment, or from terminating this contract during the Option Period, if any.

(Check one box only)

☑ (1) Buyer accepts the Property As Is.

☐ (2) Buyer accepts the Property As Is provided Seller, at Seller's expense, shall complete the following specific repairs and treatments: ____
____.

(Do not insert general phrases, such as "subject to inspections" that do not identify specific repairs and treatments.)

E. LENDER REQUIRED REPAIRS AND TREATMENTS: Unless otherwise agreed in writing, neither party is obligated to pay for lender required repairs, which includes treatment for wood destroying insects. If the parties do not agree to pay for the lender required repairs or treatments, this contract will terminate and the earnest money will be refunded to Buyer. If the cost of lender required repairs and treatments exceeds 5% of the Sales Price, Buyer may terminate this contract and the earnest money will be refunded to Buyer.

F. COMPLETION OF REPAIRS AND TREATMENTS: Unless otherwise agreed in writing: (i) Seller shall complete all agreed repairs and treatments prior to the Closing Date; and (ii) all required permits must be obtained, and repairs and treatments must be performed by persons who are licensed to provide such repairs or treatments or, if no license is required by law, are commercially engaged in the trade of providing such repairs or treatments. At Buyer's election, any transferable warranties received by Seller with respect to the repairs and treatments will be transferred to Buyer at Buyer's expense. If Seller fails to complete any agreed repairs and treatments prior to the Closing Date, Buyer may exercise remedies under Paragraph 15 or extend the Closing Date up to 5 days if necessary for Seller to complete the repairs and treatments.

G. ENVIRONMENTAL MATTERS: Buyer is advised that the presence of wetlands, toxic substances, including asbestos and wastes or other environmental hazards, or the presence of a threatened or endangered species or its habitat may affect Buyer's intended use of the Property. If Buyer is concerned about these matters, an addendum promulgated by TREC or required by the parties should be used.

Initialed for identification by Buyer______ ______ and Seller _______ ______ TREC NO. 20-14

FIGURE APP-1 (Continued)

Contract Concerning 111 East Oak Lane 72143 (Address of Property) Page 5 of 10 2-12-18

H. RESIDENTIAL SERVICE CONTRACTS: Buyer may purchase a residential service contract from a residential service company licensed by TREC. If Buyer purchases a residential service contract, Seller shall reimburse Buyer at closing for the cost of the residential service contract in an amount not exceeding $ 400.00. Buyer should review any residential service contract for the scope of coverage, exclusions and limitations. **The purchase of a residential service contract is optional. Similar coverage may be purchased from various companies authorized to do business in Texas.**

8. BROKERS' FEES: All obligations of the parties for payment of brokers' fees are contained in separate written agreements.

9. CLOSING:

A. The closing of the sale will be on or before [date in two weeks], 20_____, or within 7 days after objections made under Paragraph 6D have been cured or waived, whichever date is later (Closing Date). If either party fails to close the sale by the Closing Date, the non-defaulting party may exercise the remedies contained in Paragraph 15.

B. At closing:

(1) Seller shall execute and deliver a general warranty deed conveying title to the Property to Buyer and showing no additional exceptions to those permitted in Paragraph 6 and furnish tax statements or certificates showing no delinquent taxes on the Property.

(2) Buyer shall pay the Sales Price in good funds acceptable to the escrow agent.

(3) Seller and Buyer shall execute and deliver any notices, statements, certificates, affidavits, releases, loan documents and other documents reasonably required for the closing of the sale and the issuance of the Title Policy.

(4) There will be no liens, assessments, or security interests against the Property which will not be satisfied out of the sales proceeds unless securing the payment of any loans assumed by Buyer and assumed loans will not be in default.

(5)If the Property is subject to a residential lease, Seller shall transfer security deposits (as defined under §92.102, Property Code), if any, to Buyer. In such an event, Buyer shall deliver to the tenant a signed statement acknowledging that the Buyer has acquired the Property and is responsible for the return of the security deposit, and specifying the exact dollar amount of the security deposit.

10. POSSESSION:

A. Buyer's Possession: Seller shall deliver to Buyer possession of the Property in its present or required condition, ordinary wear and tear excepted: ☑upon closing and funding ☐according to a temporary residential lease form promulgated by TREC or other written lease required by the parties. Any possession by Buyer prior to closing or by Seller after closing which is not authorized by a written lease will establish a tenancy at sufferance relationship between the parties. **Consult your insurance agent prior to change of ownership and possession because insurance coverage may be limited or terminated. The absence of a written lease or appropriate insurance coverage may expose the parties to economic loss.**

B. Leases:

(1)After the Effective Date, Seller may not execute any lease (including but not limited to mineral leases) or convey any interest in the Property without Buyer's written consent.

(2) If the Property is subject to any lease to which Seller is a party, Seller shall deliver to Buyer copies of the lease(s) and any move-in condition form signed by the tenant within 7 days after the Effective Date of the contract.

11. SPECIAL PROVISIONS: (Insert only factual statements and business details applicable to the sale. TREC rules prohibit license holders from adding factual statements or business details for which a contract addendum, lease or other form has been promulgated by TREC for mandatory use.)

12. SETTLEMENT AND OTHER EXPENSES:

A. The following expenses must be paid at or prior to closing:

(1) Expenses payable by Seller (Seller's Expenses):

(a) Releases of existing liens, including prepayment penalties and recording fees; release of Seller's loan liability; tax statements or certificates; preparation of deed; one-half of escrow fee; and other expenses payable by Seller under this contract.

(b) Seller shall also pay an amount not to exceed $ N/A to be applied in the following order: Buyer's Expenses which Buyer is prohibited from paying by FHA, VA, Texas Veterans Land Board or other governmental loan programs, and then to other Buyer's Expenses as allowed by the lender.

Initialed for identification by Buyer______ ______ and Seller ______ ______ TREC NO. 20-14

FIGURE APP-1 (Continued)

(2) Expenses payable by Buyer (Buyer's Expenses): Appraisal fees; loan application fees; origination charges; credit reports; preparation of loan documents; interest on the notes from date of disbursement to one month prior to dates of first monthly payments; recording fees; copies of easements and restrictions; loan title policy with endorsements required by lender; loan-related inspection fees; photos; amortization schedules; one-half of escrow fee; all prepaid items, including required premiums for flood and hazard insurance, reserve deposits for insurance, ad valorem taxes and special governmental assessments; final compliance inspection; courier fee; repair inspection; underwriting fee; wire transfer fee; expenses incident to any loan; Private Mortgage Insurance Premium (PMI), VA Loan Funding Fee, or FHA Mortgage Insurance Premium (MIP) as required by the lender; and other expenses payable by Buyer under this contract.

B. If any expense exceeds an amount expressly stated in this contract for such expense to be paid by a party, that party may terminate this contract unless the other party agrees to pay such excess. Buyer may not pay charges and fees expressly prohibited by FHA, VA, Texas Veterans Land Board or other governmental loan program regulations.

13. PRORATIONS: Taxes for the current year, interest, maintenance fees, assessments, dues and rents will be prorated through the Closing Date. The tax proration may be calculated taking into consideration any change in exemptions that will affect the current year's taxes. If taxes for the current year vary from the amount prorated at closing, the parties shall adjust the prorations when tax statements for the current year are available. If taxes are not paid at or prior to closing, Buyer shall pay taxes for the current year.

14. CASUALTY LOSS: If any part of the Property is damaged or destroyed by fire or other casualty after the Effective Date of this contract, Seller shall restore the Property to its previous condition as soon as reasonably possible, but in any event by the Closing Date. If Seller fails to do so due to factors beyond Seller's control, Buyer may (a) terminate this contract and the earnest money will be refunded to Buyer (b) extend the time for performance up to 15 days and the Closing Date will be extended as necessary or (c) accept the Property in its damaged condition with an assignment of insurance proceeds, if permitted by Seller's insurance carrier, and receive credit from Seller at closing in the amount of the deductible under the insurance policy. Seller's obligations under this paragraph are independent of any other obligations of Seller under this contract.

15. DEFAULT: If Buyer fails to comply with this contract, Buyer will be in default, and Seller may (a) enforce specific performance, seek such other relief as may be provided by law, or both, or (b) terminate this contract and receive the earnest money as liquidated damages, thereby releasing both parties from this contract. If Seller fails to comply with this contract, Seller will be in default and Buyer may (a) enforce specific performance, seek such other relief as may be provided by law, or both, or (b) terminate this contract and receive the earnest money, thereby releasing both parties from this contract.

16. MEDIATION: It is the policy of the State of Texas to encourage resolution of disputes through alternative dispute resolution procedures such as mediation. Any dispute between Seller and Buyer related to this contract which is not resolved through informal discussion will be submitted to a mutually acceptable mediation service or provider. The parties to the mediation shall bear the mediation costs equally. This paragraph does not preclude a party from seeking equitable relief from a court of competent jurisdiction.

17. ATTORNEY'S FEES: A Buyer, Seller, Listing Broker, Other Broker, or escrow agent who prevails in any legal proceeding related to this contract is entitled to recover reasonable attorney's fees and all costs of such proceeding.

18. ESCROW:

A. ESCROW: The escrow agent is not (i) a party to this contract and does not have liability for the performance or nonperformance of any party to this contract, (ii) liable for interest on the earnest money and (iii) liable for the loss of any earnest money caused by the failure of any financial institution in which the earnest money has been deposited unless the financial institution is acting as escrow agent.

B. EXPENSES: At closing, the earnest money must be applied first to any cash down payment, then to Buyer's Expenses and any excess refunded to Buyer. If no closing occurs, escrow agent may: (i) require a written release of liability of the escrow agent from all parties, (ii) require payment of unpaid expenses incurred on behalf of a party, and (iii) only deduct from the earnest money the amount of unpaid expenses incurred on behalf of the party receiving the earnest money.

C. DEMAND: Upon termination of this contract, either party or the escrow agent may send a release of earnest money to each party and the parties shall execute counterparts of the release and deliver same to the escrow agent. If either party fails to execute the release, either party may make a written demand to the escrow agent for the earnest money. If only one party makes written demand for the earnest money, escrow agent shall promptly

FIGURE APP-1 (Continued)

Contract Concerning 111 East Oak Lane 72143 (Address of Property) Page 7 of 10 2-12-18

provide a copy of the demand to the other party. If escrow agent does not receive written objection to the demand from the other party within 15 days, escrow agent may disburse the earnest money to the party making demand reduced by the amount of unpaid expenses incurred on behalf of the party receiving the earnest money and escrow agent may pay the same to the creditors. If escrow agent complies with the provisions of this paragraph, each party hereby releases escrow agent from all adverse claims related to the disbursal of the earnest money.

D. DAMAGES: Any party who wrongfully fails or refuses to sign a release acceptable to the escrow agent within 7 days of receipt of the request will be liable to the other party for (i) damages; (ii) the earnest money; (iii) reasonable attorney's fees; and (iv) all costs of suit.

E. NOTICES: Escrow agent's notices will be effective when sent in compliance with Paragraph 21. Notice of objection to the demand will be deemed effective upon receipt by escrow agent.

19. **REPRESENTATIONS:** All covenants, representations and warranties in this contract survive closing. If any representation of Seller in this contract is untrue on the Closing Date, Seller will be in default. Unless expressly prohibited by written agreement, Seller may continue to show the Property and receive, negotiate and accept back up offers.

20. **FEDERAL TAX REQUIREMENTS:** If Seller is a "foreign person," as defined by Internal Revenue Code and its regulations, or if Seller fails to deliver an affidavit or a certificate of non-foreign status to Buyer that Seller is not a "foreign person," then Buyer shall withhold from the sales proceeds an amount sufficient to comply with applicable tax law and deliver the same to the Internal Revenue Service together with appropriate tax forms. Internal Revenue Service regulations require filing written reports if currency in excess of specified amounts is received in the transaction.

21. **NOTICES:** All notices from one party to the other must be in writing and are effective when mailed to, hand-delivered at, or transmitted by fax or electronic transmission as follows:

To Buyer at:		**To Seller at:**	101 South 10th Street
			Orange, Texas 72143
Phone:	( )	Phone:	( )
Fax:	( )	Fax:	( )
E-mail:		E-mail:	

22. **AGREEMENT OF PARTIES:** This contract contains the entire agreement of the parties and cannot be changed except by their written agreement. Addenda which are a part of this contract are (Check all applicable boxes):

- ☐ Third Party Financing Addendum
- ☐ Seller Financing Addendum
- ☑ Addendum for Property Subject to Mandatory Membership in a Property Owners Association
- ☐ Buyer's Temporary Residential Lease
- ☐ Loan Assumption Addendum
- ☐ Addendum for Sale of Other Property by Buyer
- ☐ Addendum for Reservation of Oil, Gas and Other Minerals
- ☐ Addendum for "Back-Up" Contract
- ☐ Addendum for Coastal Area Property
- ☐ Addendum for Authorizing Hydrostatic Testing
- ☐ Addendum Concerning Right to Terminate Due to Lender's Appraisal
- ☐ Environmental Assessment, Threatened or Endangered Species and Wetlands Addendum
- ☐ Seller's Temporary Residential Lease
- ☐ Short Sale Addendum
- ☐ Addendum for Property Located Seaward of the Gulf Intracoastal Waterway
- ☑ Addendum for Seller's Disclosure of Information on Lead-based Paint and Lead-based Paint Hazards as Required by Federal Law
- ☐ Addendum for Property in a Propane Gas System Service Area
- ☑ Other (list): Nonrealty Items Addendum

Initialed for identification by Buyer_____ _____ and Seller _____ _____ TREC NO. 20-14

FIGURE APP-1 (Continued)

Contract Concerning 111 East Oak Lane 72143 (Address of Property) Page 8 of 10 2-12-18

23. TERMINATION OPTION: For nominal consideration, the receipt of which is hereby acknowledged by Seller, and Buyer's agreement to pay Seller $ 500.00 (Option Fee) within 3 days after the Effective Date of this contract, Seller grants Buyer the unrestricted right to terminate this contract by giving notice of termination to Seller within 7 days after the Effective Date of this contract (Option Period). Notices under this paragraph must be given by 5:00 p.m. (local time where the Property is located) by the date specified. If no dollar amount is stated as the Option Fee or if Buyer fails to pay the Option Fee to Seller within the time prescribed, this paragraph will not be a part of this contract and Buyer shall not have the unrestricted right to terminate this contract. If Buyer gives notice of termination within the time prescribed, the Option Fee will not be refunded; however, any earnest money will be refunded to Buyer. The Option Fee ☑will ☐will not be credited to the Sales Price at closing. **Time is of the essence for this paragraph and strict compliance with the time for performance is required.**

24. CONSULT AN ATTORNEY BEFORE SIGNING: TREC rules prohibit real estate license holders from giving legal advice. READ THIS CONTRACT CAREFULLY.

Buyer's Attorney is:	Attorney not selected	Seller's Attorney is:	
Phone:	( )	Phone:	( )
Fax:	( )	Fax:	( )
E-mail:		E-mail:	

EXECUTED the ____ day of ____________________, 20____ (Effective Date).
(BROKER: FILL IN THE DATE OF FINAL ACCEPTANCE.)

Buyer ______________ Seller ______________

Buyer ______________ Seller ______________

TREC

TEXAS REAL ESTATE COMMISSION

The form of this contract has been approved by the Texas Real Estate Commission. TREC forms are intended for use only by trained real estate license holders. No representation is made as to the legal validity or adequacy of any provision in any specific transactions. It is not intended for complex transactions. Texas Real Estate Commission, P.O. Box 12188, Austin, TX 78711-2188, (512) 936-3000 (http://www.trec.texas.gov) TREC NO. 20-14. This form replaces TREC NO. 20-13.

TREC NO. 20-14

FIGURE APP-1 (Continued)

BROKER INFORMATION
(Print name(s) only. Do not sign)

Sawyers Realty, Inc. 123456	Acme Brokerage 804918
Other Broker Firm License No.	Listing Broker Firm License No.
represents ☐ Buyer only as Buyer's agent ☑ Seller as Listing Broker's subagent	represents ☐ Seller and Buyer as an intermediary ☑ Seller only as Seller's agent
Student Salesperson	Richard Guzman
Associate's Name License No.	Listing Associate's Name License No.
Associate's Email Address Phone	Listing Associate's Email Address Phone
	Barnaby Boss
Licensed Supervisor of Associate License No.	Licensed Supervisor of Listing Associate License No.
	101 South 10th Street,
Other Broker's Address Phone	Listing Broker's Office Address Phone
	Orange TX 72143
City State Zip	City State Zip
	Selling Associate's Name License No.
	Selling Associate's Email Address Phone
	Licensed Supervisor of Selling Associate License No.
	Selling Associate's Office Address
	City State Zip

Listing Broker has agreed to pay Other Broker 2.5% of the total sales price when the Listing Broker's fee is received. Escrow agent is authorized and directed to pay Other Broker from Listing Broker's fee at closing.

TREC NO. 20-14

FIGURE APP-1 (Continued)

Contract Concerning 111 East Oak Lane 72143 (Address of Property) Page 10 of 10 2-12-18

OPTION FEE RECEIPT

Receipt of $______________ (Option Fee) in the form of ____________________ is acknowledged.

Seller or Listing Broker | Date

EARNEST MONEY RECEIPT

Receipt of $______________ Earnest Money in the form of ____________________ is acknowledged.

Escrow Agent | Received by | Email Address | Date/Time

Address | Phone

City | State | Zip | Fax

CONTRACT RECEIPT

Receipt of the Contract is acknowledged.

Escrow Agent | Received by | Email Address | Date

Address | Phone

City | State | Zip | Fax

ADDITIONAL EARNEST MONEY RECEIPT

Receipt of $______________ additional Earnest Money in the form of ____________________ is acknowledged.

Escrow Agent | Received by | Email Address | Date/Time

Address | Phone

City | State | Zip | Fax

TREC NO. 20-14

FIGURE APP-1 (Continued)

2. All Cash Transaction 2

Below is a general fact scenario explaining the offer proposed by the prospective buyer, a counteroffer by the seller, and the final acceptance of the buyer. Using the appropriate residential sales contract, indicate the terms of the offer, counteroffer, and acceptance. Also denote any assumptions you make based on what is commonly done in the marketplace. See figure App-2 for a sample completed contract form.

Michael Worton enters the office of Dysnee Realty, located at 444 Salesman Avenue, San Antonio, Texas, 78200, License No. 000001, for some help in locating a house to purchase. The associate available at the time is Daf E. Duk. Mr. Duk gives Mr. Worton an agency disclosure notice, which Mr. Worton proudly signs. After discussing the firm's practices regarding agency relationships, Mr. Worton decides to hire the brokerage company as his exclusive representative for which he will pay a 2.5% commission. Excited that Mr. Worton has cash to burn, Mr. Duk begins a search of a home that meets Mr. Worton's specifications. After looking through the MLS, Mr. Duk locates three properties that match Mr. Worton's specifications. After doing an initial walk-through on the three houses, Mr. Worton decides to make an offer on the house located at 111 West Fifth Street in San Antonio, Texas 78200 (Lot 11, Block 11, ncb 111, Eleven Subdivision). The sellers are Billy and Sue Martin. They are a married couple; however, the home is Billy Martin's separate property even though his wife currently lives in the home as her primary residence. The home is listed through Fred F. Stone located at 1212 Broker Avenue, San Antonio, Texas 78200, License 000000. The listing associate is Barn E. Ruble. The listing agent is only willing to pay a cooperating seller's broker 3% and a cooperating buyer's broker 2% of the sales price.

Mr. Worton notices in the MLS that the seller is not including the drapes and the satellite dish in the sale. The seller has however offered to include the refrigerator in the sale with a full price offer. The refrigerator is a GE Profile Stainless with bottom freezer, Model No. PD522SFSBLSS and Serial No. FLO50458. Mr. Worton would be interested in the refrigerator. The MLS also indicates that the home is not located within a homeowners association.

The home is listed at $60,000.00; however, since the seller's disclosure notice revealed that the home had previous termite damage, Mr. Worton does not want to offer so high a price. Mr. Worton offers $55,000 as a sales price that he will pay with cash. He is willing to put $200 earnest money down and he executes a check payable to Acme Title Co. located at 117 West Pecan Avenue. Mr. Worton does not request a title policy, survey, or appraisal. He does however want the one-year home warranty not to exceed $355 that the sellers indicated in the MLS.

The property was constructed in 1976; however, the buyer accepts the property in its present condition except that he would like the seller to have the roof replaced. The buyer wants to close in the next three weeks because his apartment lease will be up by that time.

Mr. Duk faxes the offer over to Mr. Stone for review by the sellers. A sales contract had just one hour previously been entered into between the sellers and Mr. Baker, another prospective buyer. Mr. Duk gets approval from Mr. Worton to submit the offer as a backup offer. The offer is faxed to Mr. Stone for the sellers' review.

The sellers propose a counteroffer indicating a preferred closing date of two months. Since the sellers have a great deal of equity in the house, they ask for the full listing price of $60,000. The seller also puts a cap on the roof repair not to exceed $1,500.

The counteroffer is proposed back to Mr. Duk for review by Mr. Worton. Mr. Worton accepts all of the changes on February 22 at 2:00 p.m. The contract is sent to the title company that same day and received by Ginger Jones.

PROMULGATED BY THE TEXAS REAL ESTATE COMMISSION (TREC) 2-12-18

TREC
TEXAS REAL ESTATE COMMISSION

ONE TO FOUR FAMILY RESIDENTIAL CONTRACT (RESALE)

NOTICE: Not For Use For Condominium Transactions

1. PARTIES: The parties to this contract are Billy Martin and wife, Sue Martin (Seller) and Michael Worton, a single person (Buyer). Seller agrees to sell and convey to Buyer and Buyer agrees to buy from Seller the Property defined below.

2. PROPERTY: The land, improvements and accessories are collectively referred to as the "Property".

A. LAND: Lot 11 Block 11, NCB 111, Eleven Subdivision Addition, City of San Antonio, County of Bexar, Texas, known as 111 West Fifth Street 78200 (address/zip code), or as described on attached exhibit.

B. IMPROVEMENTS: The house, garage and all other fixtures and improvements attached to the above-described real property, including without limitation, the following **permanently installed and built-in items,** if any: all equipment and appliances, valances, screens, shutters, awnings, wall-to-wall carpeting, mirrors, ceiling fans, attic fans, mail boxes, television antennas, mounts and brackets for televisions and speakers, heating and air-conditioning units, security and fire detection equipment, wiring, plumbing and lighting fixtures, chandeliers, water softener system, kitchen equipment, garage door openers, cleaning equipment, shrubbery, landscaping, outdoor cooking equipment, and all other property owned by Seller and attached to the above described real property.

C. ACCESSORIES: The following described related accessories, if any: window air conditioning units, stove, fireplace screens, curtains and rods, blinds, window shades, draperies and rods, door keys, mailbox keys, above ground pool, swimming pool equipment and maintenance accessories, artificial fireplace logs, and controls for: (i) garage doors, (ii) entry gates, and (iii) other improvements and accessories.

D. EXCLUSIONS: The following improvements and accessories will be retained by Seller and must be removed prior to delivery of possession: draperies and rods, satellite dish system and equipment, controls for satellite dish.

E. RESERVATIONS: Any reservation for oil, gas, or other minerals, water, timber, or other interests is made in accordance with an attached addendum.

3. SALES PRICE:

A. Cash portion of Sales Price payable by Buyer at closing .... $ ~~55,000.00~~ 60,000.00 BM SM 11A 2/22/YR MW 2p 2/22/YR

B. Sum of all financing described in the attached: ☐ Third Party Financing Addendum, ☐ Loan Assumption Addendum, ☐ Seller Financing Addendum .... $ ---0---

C. Sales Price (Sum of A and B)... $ ~~55,000.00~~ 60,000.00 BM SM 11AM 2/22/YR MW 2pm 2/22/YR

4. LICENSE HOLDER DISCLOSURE: Texas law requires a real estate license holder who is a party to a transaction or acting on behalf of a spouse, parent, child, business entity in which the license holder owns more than 10%, or a trust for which the license holder acts as a trustee or of which the license holder or the license holder's spouse, parent or child is a beneficiary, to notify the other party in writing before entering into a contract of sale. Disclose if applicable: N/A

5. EARNEST MONEY: Within 3 days after the Effective Date, Buyer must deliver $ 200.00 as earnest money to Acme Title Co., as escrow agent, at 117 West Pecan Avenue 78200 (address). Buyer shall deliver additional earnest money of $ N/A to escrow agent within N/A days after the Effective Date of this contract. If Buyer fails to deliver the earnest money within the time required, Seller may terminate this contract or exercise Seller's remedies under Paragraph 15, or both, by providing notice to Buyer before Buyer delivers the earnest money. If the last day to deliver the earnest money falls on a Saturday, Sunday, or legal holiday, the time to deliver the earnest money is extended until the end of the next day that is not a Saturday, Sunday, or legal holiday. **Time is of the essence for this paragraph.**

N/A **6. TITLE POLICY AND SURVEY:**

A. TITLE POLICY: Seller shall furnish to Buyer at ☐ Seller's ☐ Buyer's expense an owner policy of title insurance (Title Policy) issued by ______ (Title Company) in the amount of the Sales Price, dated at or after closing, insuring Buyer against loss under the provisions of the Title Policy, subject to the promulgated exclusions (including existing building and zoning ordinances) and the following exceptions:

(1) Restrictive covenants common to the platted subdivision in which the Property is located.

(2) The standard printed exception for standby fees, taxes and assessments.

Initialed for identification by Buyer MW ______ and Seller BM SM TREC NO. 20-14

FIGURE APP-2 Sample Completed Contract

Contract Concerning 111 West Fifth Street 78200 (Address of Property) Page 2 of 10 2-12-18

(3) Liens created as part of the financing described in Paragraph 3.
(4) Utility easements created by the dedication deed or plat of the subdivision in which the Property is located.
(5) Reservations or exceptions otherwise permitted by this contract or as may be approved by Buyer in writing.
(6) The standard printed exception as to marital rights.
(7) The standard printed exception as to waters, tidelands, beaches, streams, and related matters.
(8) The standard printed exception as to discrepancies, conflicts, shortages in area or boundary lines, encroachments or protrusions, or overlapping improvements:
❑(i) will not be amended or deleted from the title policy; or
❑(ii) will be amended to read, "shortages in area" at the expense of ❑Buyer ❑Seller.
(9) The exception or exclusion regarding minerals approved by the Texas Department of Insurance.

B. COMMITMENT: Within 20 days after the Title Company receives a copy of this contract, Seller shall furnish to Buyer a commitment for title insurance (Commitment) and, at Buyer's expense, legible copies of restrictive covenants and documents evidencing exceptions in the Commitment (Exception Documents) other than the standard printed exceptions. Seller authorizes the Title Company to deliver the Commitment and Exception Documents to Buyer at Buyer's address shown in Paragraph 21. If the Commitment and Exception Documents are not delivered to Buyer within the specified time, the time for delivery will be automatically extended up to 15 days or 3 days before the Closing Date, whichever is earlier. If the Commitment and Exception Documents are not delivered within the time required, Buyer may terminate this contract and the earnest money will be refunded to Buyer.

N/A C. SURVEY: The survey must be made by a registered professional land surveyor acceptable to the Title Company and Buyer's lender(s). (Check one box only)

❑(1) Within _______ days after the Effective Date of this contract, Seller shall furnish to Buyer and Title Company Seller's existing survey of the Property and a Residential Real Property Affidavit promulgated by the Texas Department of Insurance (T-47 Affidavit). **If Seller fails to furnish the existing survey or affidavit within the time prescribed, Buyer shall obtain a new survey at Seller's expense no later than 3 days prior to Closing Date.** If the existing survey or affidavit is not acceptable to Title Company or Buyer's lender(s), Buyer shall obtain a new survey at ❑Seller's ❑Buyer's expense no later than 3 days prior to Closing Date.

❑(2) Within _______ days after the Effective Date of this contract, Buyer shall obtain a new survey at Buyer's expense. Buyer is deemed to receive the survey on the date of actual receipt or the date specified in this paragraph, whichever is earlier.

❑(3) Within _______ days after the Effective Date of this contract, Seller, at Seller's expense shall furnish a new survey to Buyer.

D. OBJECTIONS: Buyer may object in writing to defects, exceptions, or encumbrances to title: disclosed on the survey other than items 6A(1) through (7) above; disclosed in the Commitment other than items 6A(1) through (9) above; or which prohibit the following use or activity: N/A.

Buyer must object the earlier of (i) the Closing Date or (ii) 5 days after Buyer receives the Commitment, Exception Documents, and the survey. Buyer's failure to object within the time allowed will constitute a waiver of Buyer's right to object; except that the requirements in Schedule C of the Commitment are not waived by Buyer. Provided Seller is not obligated to incur any expense, Seller shall cure any timely objections of Buyer or any third party lender within 15 days after Seller receives the objections (Cure Period) and the Closing Date will be extended as necessary. If objections are not cured within the Cure Period, Buyer may, by delivering notice to Seller within 5 days after the end of the Cure Period: (i) terminate this contract and the earnest money will be refunded to Buyer; or (ii) waive the objections. If Buyer does not terminate within the time required, Buyer shall be deemed to have waived the objections. If the Commitment or Survey is revised or any new Exception Document(s) is delivered, Buyer may object to any new matter revealed in the revised Commitment or Survey or new Exception Document(s) within the same time stated in this paragraph to make objections beginning when the revised Commitment, Survey, or Exception Document(s) is delivered to Buyer.

E. TITLE NOTICES:
(1) ABSTRACT OR TITLE POLICY: Broker advises Buyer to have an abstract of title covering the Property examined by an attorney of Buyer's selection, or Buyer should be furnished with or obtain a Title Policy. If a Title Policy is furnished, the Commitment should be promptly reviewed by an attorney of Buyer's choice due to the time limitations on Buyer's right to object.
(2) MEMBERSHIP IN PROPERTY OWNERS ASSOCIATION(S): The Property ❑is ☑is not

Initialed for identification by Buyer MW ______ and Seller BM SM TREC NO. 20-14

FIGURE APP-2 (Continued)

subject to mandatory membership in a property owners association(s). If the Property is subject to mandatory membership in a property owners association(s), Seller notifies Buyer under §5.012, Texas Property Code, that, as a purchaser of property in the residential community identified in Paragraph 2A in which the Property is located, you are obligated to be a member of the property owners association(s). Restrictive covenants governing the use and occupancy of the Property and all dedicatory instruments governing the establishment, maintenance, or operation of this residential community have been or will be recorded in the Real Property Records of the county in which the Property is located. Copies of the restrictive covenants and dedicatory instruments may be obtained from the county clerk. **You are obligated to pay assessments to the property owners association(s). The amount of the assessments is subject to change. Your failure to pay the assessments could result in enforcement of the association's lien on and the foreclosure of the Property.**

Section 207.003, Property Code, entitles an owner to receive copies of any document that governs the establishment, maintenance, or operation of a subdivision, including, but not limited to, restrictions, bylaws, rules and regulations, and a resale certificate from a property owners' association. A resale certificate contains information including, but not limited to, statements specifying the amount and frequency of regular assessments and the style and cause number of lawsuits to which the property owners' association is a party, other than lawsuits relating to unpaid ad valorem taxes of an individual member of the association. These documents must be made available to you by the property owners' association or the association's agent on your request.

If Buyer is concerned about these matters, the TREC promulgated Addendum for Property Subject to Mandatory Membership in a Property Owners Association(s) should be used.

(3) STATUTORY TAX DISTRICTS: If the Property is situated in a utility or other statutorily created district providing water, sewer, drainage, or flood control facilities and services, Chapter 49, Texas Water Code, requires Seller to deliver and Buyer to sign the statutory notice relating to the tax rate, bonded indebtedness, or standby fee of the district prior to final execution of this contract.

(4) TIDE WATERS: If the Property abuts the tidally influenced waters of the state, §33.135, Texas Natural Resources Code, requires a notice regarding coastal area property to be included in the contract. An addendum containing the notice promulgated by TREC or required by the parties must be used.

(5) ANNEXATION: If the Property is located outside the limits of a municipality, Seller notifies Buyer under §5.011, Texas Property Code, that the Property may now or later be included in the extraterritorial jurisdiction of a municipality and may now or later be subject to annexation by the municipality. Each municipality maintains a map that depicts its boundaries and extraterritorial jurisdiction. To determine if the Property is located within a municipality's extraterritorial jurisdiction or is likely to be located within a municipality's extraterritorial jurisdiction, contact all municipalities located in the general proximity of the Property for further information.

(6) PROPERTY LOCATED IN A CERTIFICATED SERVICE AREA OF A UTILITY SERVICE PROVIDER: Notice required by §13.257, Water Code: The real property, described in Paragraph 2, that you are about to purchase may be located in a certificated water or sewer service area, which is authorized by law to provide water or sewer service to the properties in the certificated area. If your property is located in a certificated area there may be special costs or charges that you will be required to pay before you can receive water or sewer service. There may be a period required to construct lines or other facilities necessary to provide water or sewer service to your property. You are advised to determine if the property is in a certificated area and contact the utility service provider to determine the cost that you will be required to pay and the period, if any, that is required to provide water or sewer service to your property. The undersigned Buyer hereby acknowledges receipt of the foregoing notice at or before the execution of a binding contract for the purchase of the real property described in Paragraph 2 or at closing of purchase of the real property.

(7) PUBLIC IMPROVEMENT DISTRICTS: If the Property is in a public improvement district, §5.014, Property Code, requires Seller to notify Buyer as follows: As a purchaser of this parcel of real property you are obligated to pay an assessment to a municipality or county for an improvement project undertaken by a public improvement district under Chapter 372, Local Government Code. The assessment may be due annually or in periodic installments. More information concerning the amount of the assessment and the due dates of that assessment may be obtained from the municipality or county levying the assessment. The amount of the assessments is subject to change. Your failure to pay the assessments could result in a lien on and the foreclosure of your property.

(8) TRANSFER FEES: If the Property is subject to a private transfer fee obligation, §5.205, Property Code, requires Seller to notify Buyer as follows: The private transfer fee

FIGURE APP-2 (Continued)

Contract Concerning 111 West Fifth Street 78200 (Address of Property) Page 4 of 10 2-12-18

obligation may be governed by Chapter 5, Subchapter G of the Texas Property Code.

(9) PROPANE GAS SYSTEM SERVICE AREA: If the Property is located in a propane gas system service area owned by a distribution system retailer, Seller must give Buyer written notice as required by §141.010, Texas Utilities Code. An addendum containing the notice approved by TREC or required by the parties should be used.

(10) NOTICE OF WATER LEVEL FLUCTUATIONS: If the Property adjoins an impoundment of water, including a reservoir or lake, constructed and maintained under Chapter 11, Water Code, that has a storage capacity of at least 5,000 acre-feet at the impoundment's normal operating level, Seller hereby notifies Buyer: "The water level of the impoundment of water adjoining the Property fluctuates for various reasons, including as a result of: (1) an entity lawfully exercising its right to use the water stored in the impoundment; or (2) drought or flood conditions."

7. PROPERTY CONDITION:

A. ACCESS, INSPECTIONS AND UTILITIES: Seller shall permit Buyer and Buyer's agents access to the Property at reasonable times. Buyer may have the Property inspected by inspectors selected by Buyer and licensed by TREC or otherwise permitted by law to make inspections. Any hydrostatic testing must be separately authorized by Seller in writing. Seller at Seller's expense shall immediately cause existing utilities to be turned on and shall keep the utilities on during the time this contract is in effect.

B. SELLER'S DISCLOSURE NOTICE PURSUANT TO §5.008, TEXAS PROPERTY CODE (Notice): (Check one box only)

☑ (1) Buyer has received the Notice.

☐ (2) Buyer has not received the Notice. Within ______ days after the Effective Date of this contract, Seller shall deliver the Notice to Buyer. If Buyer does not receive the Notice, Buyer may terminate this contract at any time prior to the closing and the earnest money will be refunded to Buyer. If Seller delivers the Notice, Buyer may terminate this contract for any reason within 7 days after Buyer receives the Notice or prior to the closing, whichever first occurs, and the earnest money will be refunded to Buyer.

☐ (3) The Seller is not required to furnish the notice under the Texas Property Code.

C. SELLER'S DISCLOSURE OF LEAD-BASED PAINT AND LEAD-BASED PAINT HAZARDS is required by Federal law for a residential dwelling constructed prior to 1978.

D. ACCEPTANCE OF PROPERTY CONDITION: "As Is" means the present condition of the Property with any and all defects and without warranty except for the warranties of title and the warranties in this contract. Buyer's agreement to accept the Property As Is under Paragraph 7D(1) or (2) does not preclude Buyer from inspecting the Property under Paragraph 7A, from negotiating repairs or treatments in a subsequent amendment, or from terminating this contract during the Option Period, if any.

(Check one box only)

☐ (1) Buyer accepts the Property As Is.

☑ (2) Buyer accepts the Property As Is provided Seller, at Seller's expense, shall complete the following specific repairs and treatments: replacement of the roof not to exceed $1500 BM SM MW 2/22/18 MW 2/22/18

(Do not insert general phrases, such as "subject to inspections" that do not identify specific repairs and treatments.)

E. LENDER REQUIRED REPAIRS AND TREATMENTS: Unless otherwise agreed in writing, neither party is obligated to pay for lender required repairs, which includes treatment for wood destroying insects. If the parties do not agree to pay for the lender required repairs or treatments, this contract will terminate and the earnest money will be refunded to Buyer. If the cost of lender required repairs and treatments exceeds 5% of the Sales Price, Buyer may terminate this contract and the earnest money will be refunded to Buyer.

F. COMPLETION OF REPAIRS AND TREATMENTS: Unless otherwise agreed in writing: (i) Seller shall complete all agreed repairs and treatments prior to the Closing Date; and (ii) all required permits must be obtained, and repairs and treatments must be performed by persons who are licensed to provide such repairs or treatments or, if no license is required by law, are commercially engaged in the trade of providing such repairs or treatments. At Buyer's election, any transferable warranties received by Seller with respect to the repairs and treatments will be transferred to Buyer at Buyer's expense. If Seller fails to complete any agreed repairs and treatments prior to the Closing Date, Buyer may exercise remedies under Paragraph 15 or extend the Closing Date up to 5 days if necessary for Seller to complete the repairs and treatments.

G. ENVIRONMENTAL MATTERS: Buyer is advised that the presence of wetlands, toxic substances, including asbestos and wastes or other environmental hazards, or the presence of a threatened or endangered species or its habitat may affect Buyer's intended use of the Property. If Buyer is concerned about these matters, an addendum promulgated by TREC or required by the parties should be used.

Initialed for identification by Buyer MW ______ and Seller BM SM TREC NO. 20-14

FIGURE APP-2 (Continued)

H. RESIDENTIAL SERVICE CONTRACTS: Buyer may purchase a residential service contract from a residential service company licensed by TREC. If Buyer purchases a residential service contract, Seller shall reimburse Buyer at closing for the cost of the residential service contract in an amount not exceeding $ 355.00. Buyer should review any residential service contract for the scope of coverage, exclusions and limitations. **The purchase of a residential service contract is optional. Similar coverage may be purchased from various companies authorized to do business in Texas.**

8. BROKERS' FEES: All obligations of the parties for payment of brokers' fees are contained in separate written agreements.

9. CLOSING:

A. The closing of the sale will be on or before ~~[date in three weeks]~~ [date in two months] BM 11am SM 2/22/yr MW 3pm 2/22/yr, 20____, or within 7 days after objections made under Paragraph 6D have been cured or waived, whichever date is later (Closing Date). If either party fails to close the sale by the Closing Date, the non-defaulting party may exercise the remedies contained in Paragraph 15.

B. At closing:

(1) Seller shall execute and deliver a general warranty deed conveying title to the Property to Buyer and showing no additional exceptions to those permitted in Paragraph 6 and furnish tax statements or certificates showing no delinquent taxes on the Property.

(2) Buyer shall pay the Sales Price in good funds acceptable to the escrow agent.

(3) Seller and Buyer shall execute and deliver any notices, statements, certificates, affidavits, releases, loan documents and other documents reasonably required for the closing of the sale and the issuance of the Title Policy.

(4) There will be no liens, assessments, or security interests against the Property which will not be satisfied out of the sales proceeds unless securing the payment of any loans assumed by Buyer and assumed loans will not be in default.

(5) If the Property is subject to a residential lease, Seller shall transfer security deposits (as defined under §92.102, Property Code), if any, to Buyer. In such an event, Buyer shall deliver to the tenant a signed statement acknowledging that the Buyer has acquired the Property and is responsible for the return of the security deposit, and specifying the exact dollar amount of the security deposit.

10. POSSESSION:

A. Buyer's Possession: Seller shall deliver to Buyer possession of the Property in its present or required condition, ordinary wear and tear excepted: ☑ upon closing and funding ☐ according to a temporary residential lease form promulgated by TREC or other written lease required by the parties. Any possession by Buyer prior to closing or by Seller after closing which is not authorized by a written lease will establish a tenancy at sufferance relationship between the parties. **Consult your insurance agent prior to change of ownership and possession because insurance coverage may be limited or terminated. The absence of a written lease or appropriate insurance coverage may expose the parties to economic loss.**

B. Leases:

(1) After the Effective Date, Seller may not execute any lease (including but not limited to mineral leases) or convey any interest in the Property without Buyer's written consent.

(2) If the Property is subject to any lease to which Seller is a party, Seller shall deliver to Buyer copies of the lease(s) and any move-in condition form signed by the tenant within 7 days after the Effective Date of the contract.

11. SPECIAL PROVISIONS: (Insert only factual statements and business details applicable to the sale. TREC rules prohibit license holders from adding factual statements or business details for which a contract addendum, lease or other form has been promulgated by TREC for mandatory use.)

N/A

12. SETTLEMENT AND OTHER EXPENSES:

A. The following expenses must be paid at or prior to closing:

(1) Expenses payable by Seller (Seller's Expenses):

(a) Releases of existing liens, including prepayment penalties and recording fees; release of Seller's loan liability; tax statements or certificates; preparation of deed; one-half of escrow fee; and other expenses payable by Seller under this contract.

(b) Seller shall also pay an amount not to exceed $ N/A to be applied in the following order: Buyer's Expenses which Buyer is prohibited from paying by FHA, VA, Texas Veterans Land Board or other governmental loan programs, and then to other Buyer's Expenses as allowed by the lender.

FIGURE APP-2 (Continued)

Contract Concerning 111 West Fifth Street 78200 (Address of Property) Page 6 of 10 2-12-18

(2) Expenses payable by Buyer (Buyer's Expenses): Appraisal fees; loan application fees; origination charges; credit reports; preparation of loan documents; interest on the notes from date of disbursement to one month prior to dates of first monthly payments; recording fees; copies of easements and restrictions; loan title policy with endorsements required by lender; loan-related inspection fees; photos; amortization schedules; one-half of escrow fee; all prepaid items, including required premiums for flood and hazard insurance, reserve deposits for insurance, ad valorem taxes and special governmental assessments; final compliance inspection; courier fee; repair inspection; underwriting fee; wire transfer fee; expenses incident to any loan; Private Mortgage Insurance Premium (PMI), VA Loan Funding Fee, or FHA Mortgage Insurance Premium (MIP) as required by the lender; and other expenses payable by Buyer under this contract.

B. If any expense exceeds an amount expressly stated in this contract for such expense to be paid by a party, that party may terminate this contract unless the other party agrees to pay such excess. Buyer may not pay charges and fees expressly prohibited by FHA, VA, Texas Veterans Land Board or other governmental loan program regulations.

13. PRORATIONS: Taxes for the current year, interest, maintenance fees, assessments, dues and rents will be prorated through the Closing Date. The tax proration may be calculated taking into consideration any change in exemptions that will affect the current year's taxes. If taxes for the current year vary from the amount prorated at closing, the parties shall adjust the prorations when tax statements for the current year are available. If taxes are not paid at or prior to closing, Buyer shall pay taxes for the current year.

14. CASUALTY LOSS: If any part of the Property is damaged or destroyed by fire or other casualty after the Effective Date of this contract, Seller shall restore the Property to its previous condition as soon as reasonably possible, but in any event by the Closing Date. If Seller fails to do so due to factors beyond Seller's control, Buyer may (a) terminate this contract and the earnest money will be refunded to Buyer (b) extend the time for performance up to 15 days and the Closing Date will be extended as necessary or (c) accept the Property in its damaged condition with an assignment of insurance proceeds, if permitted by Seller's insurance carrier, and receive credit from Seller at closing in the amount of the deductible under the insurance policy. Seller's obligations under this paragraph are independent of any other obligations of Seller under this contract.

15. DEFAULT: If Buyer fails to comply with this contract, Buyer will be in default, and Seller may (a) enforce specific performance, seek such other relief as may be provided by law, or both, or (b) terminate this contract and receive the earnest money as liquidated damages, thereby releasing both parties from this contract. If Seller fails to comply with this contract, Seller will be in default and Buyer may (a) enforce specific performance, seek such other relief as may be provided by law, or both, or (b) terminate this contract and receive the earnest money, thereby releasing both parties from this contract.

16. MEDIATION: It is the policy of the State of Texas to encourage resolution of disputes through alternative dispute resolution procedures such as mediation. Any dispute between Seller and Buyer related to this contract which is not resolved through informal discussion will be submitted to a mutually acceptable mediation service or provider. The parties to the mediation shall bear the mediation costs equally. This paragraph does not preclude a party from seeking equitable relief from a court of competent jurisdiction.

17. ATTORNEY'S FEES: A Buyer, Seller, Listing Broker, Other Broker, or escrow agent who prevails in any legal proceeding related to this contract is entitled to recover reasonable attorney's fees and all costs of such proceeding.

18. ESCROW:

A. ESCROW: The escrow agent is not (i) a party to this contract and does not have liability for the performance or nonperformance of any party to this contract, (ii) liable for interest on the earnest money and (iii) liable for the loss of any earnest money caused by the failure of any financial institution in which the earnest money has been deposited unless the financial institution is acting as escrow agent.

B. EXPENSES: At closing, the earnest money must be applied first to any cash down payment, then to Buyer's Expenses and any excess refunded to Buyer. If no closing occurs, escrow agent may: (i) require a written release of liability of the escrow agent from all parties, (ii) require payment of unpaid expenses incurred on behalf of a party, and (iii) only deduct from the earnest money the amount of unpaid expenses incurred on behalf of the party receiving the earnest money.

C. DEMAND: Upon termination of this contract, either party or the escrow agent may send a release of earnest money to each party and the parties shall execute counterparts of the release and deliver same to the escrow agent. If either party fails to execute the release, either party may make a written demand to the escrow agent for the earnest money. If only one party makes written demand for the earnest money, escrow agent shall promptly

Initialed for identification by Buyer MW _____ and Seller BM SM TREC NO. 20-14

FIGURE APP-2 (Continued)

provide a copy of the demand to the other party. If escrow agent does not receive written objection to the demand from the other party within 15 days, escrow agent may disburse the earnest money to the party making demand reduced by the amount of unpaid expenses incurred on behalf of the party receiving the earnest money and escrow agent may pay the same to the creditors. If escrow agent complies with the provisions of this paragraph, each party hereby releases escrow agent from all adverse claims related to the disbursal of the earnest money.

D. DAMAGES: Any party who wrongfully fails or refuses to sign a release acceptable to the escrow agent within 7 days of receipt of the request will be liable to the other party for (i) damages; (ii) the earnest money; (iii) reasonable attorney's fees; and (iv) all costs of suit.

E. NOTICES: Escrow agent's notices will be effective when sent in compliance with Paragraph 21. Notice of objection to the demand will be deemed effective upon receipt by escrow agent.

19. **REPRESENTATIONS:** All covenants, representations and warranties in this contract survive closing. If any representation of Seller in this contract is untrue on the Closing Date, Seller will be in default. Unless expressly prohibited by written agreement, Seller may continue to show the Property and receive, negotiate and accept back up offers.

20. **FEDERAL TAX REQUIREMENTS:** If Seller is a "foreign person," as defined by Internal Revenue Code and its regulations, or if Seller fails to deliver an affidavit or a certificate of non-foreign status to Buyer that Seller is not a "foreign person," then Buyer shall withhold from the sales proceeds an amount sufficient to comply with applicable tax law and deliver the same to the Internal Revenue Service together with appropriate tax forms. Internal Revenue Service regulations require filing written reports if currency in excess of specified amounts is received in the transaction.

21. **NOTICES:** All notices from one party to the other must be in writing and are effective when mailed to, hand-delivered at, or transmitted by fax or electronic transmission as follows:

To Buyer at:	**To Seller at:**
Michael Worton c/o Daf E. Duk	Billy and Sue Martin c/o Bar E. Ruble
444 Salesman Ave., San Antonio, TX 78200	1212 Broker Avenue, San Antonio, TX 78200
Phone: ( )	Phone: ( )
Fax: ( )	Fax: ( )
E-mail:	E-mail:

22. **AGREEMENT OF PARTIES:** This contract contains the entire agreement of the parties and cannot be changed except by their written agreement. Addenda which are a part of this contract are (Check all applicable boxes):

- ☐ Third Party Financing Addendum
- ☐ Seller Financing Addendum
- ☐ Addendum for Property Subject to Mandatory Membership in a Property Owners Association
- ☐ Buyer's Temporary Residential Lease
- ☐ Loan Assumption Addendum
- ☐ Addendum for Sale of Other Property by Buyer
- ☐ Addendum for Reservation of Oil, Gas and Other Minerals
- ☑ Addendum for "Back-Up" Contract
- ☐ Addendum for Coastal Area Property
- ☐ Addendum for Authorizing Hydrostatic Testing
- ☐ Addendum Concerning Right to Terminate Due to Lender's Appraisal
- ☐ Environmental Assessment, Threatened or Endangered Species and Wetlands Addendum
- ☐ Seller's Temporary Residential Lease
- ☐ Short Sale Addendum
- ☐ Addendum for Property Located Seaward of the Gulf Intracoastal Waterway
- ☑ Addendum for Seller's Disclosure of Information on Lead-based Paint and Lead-based Paint Hazards as Required by Federal Law
- ☐ Addendum for Property in a Propane Gas System Service Area
- ☑ Other (list): Nonrealty Items Addendum

FIGURE APP-2 (Continued)

Contract Concerning 111 West Fifth Street 78200 (Address of Property) Page 8 of 10 2-12-18

23. TERMINATION OPTION: For nominal consideration, the receipt of which is hereby acknowledged by Seller, and Buyer's agreement to pay Seller $ N/A (Option Fee) within 3 days after the Effective Date of this contract, Seller grants Buyer the unrestricted right to terminate this contract by giving notice of termination to Seller within N/A days after the Effective Date of this contract (Option Period). Notices under this paragraph must be given by 5:00 p.m. (local time where the Property is located) by the date specified. If no dollar amount is stated as the Option Fee or if Buyer fails to pay the Option Fee to Seller within the time prescribed, this paragraph will not be a part of this contract and Buyer shall not have the unrestricted right to terminate this contract. If Buyer gives notice of termination within the time prescribed, the Option Fee will not be refunded; however, any earnest money will be refunded to Buyer. The Option Fee ☐will ☐will not be credited to the Sales Price at closing. **Time is of the essence for this paragraph and strict compliance with the time for performance is required.**

24. CONSULT AN ATTORNEY BEFORE SIGNING: TREC rules prohibit real estate license holders from giving legal advice. READ THIS CONTRACT CAREFULLY.

Buyer's Attorney is: ____________	Seller's Attorney is: ____________
____________	____________
Phone: ( )	Phone: ( )
Fax: ( )	Fax: ( )
E-mail:	E-mail:

EXECUTED the ____ day of ____________, 20____ (Effective Date).
(BROKER: FILL IN THE DATE OF FINAL ACCEPTANCE.)

Buyer	Seller
Buyer	Seller

TREC — TEXAS REAL ESTATE COMMISSION

The form of this contract has been approved by the Texas Real Estate Commission. TREC forms are intended for use only by trained real estate license holders. No representation is made as to the legal validity or adequacy of any provision in any specific transactions. It is not intended for complex transactions. Texas Real Estate Commission, P.O. Box 12188, Austin, TX 78711-2188, (512) 936-3000 (http://www.trec.texas.gov) TREC NO. 20-14. This form replaces TREC NO. 20-13.

TREC NO. 20-14

FIGURE APP-2 (Continued)

Contract Concerning 111 West Fifth Street 78200 (Address of Property) Page 9 of 10 2-12-18

BROKER INFORMATION
(Print name(s) only. Do not sign)

Dysnee Realty — Other Broker Firm; License No.: 00001	Fred F. Stone — Listing Broker Firm; License No.: 000000
represents ☑ Buyer only as Buyer's agent ☐ Seller as Listing Broker's subagent	represents ☐ Seller and Buyer as an intermediary ☑ Seller only as Seller's agent
Daf E. Duk — Associate's Name; License No.	Barn E. Ruble — Listing Associate's Name; License No.
Associate's Email Address; Phone	Listing Associate's Email Address; Phone
Licensed Supervisor of Associate; License No.	Fred F. Stone — Licensed Supervisor of Listing Associate; License No.
444 Salesman Ave. — Other Broker's Address; Phone	1212 Broker Avenue — Listing Broker's Office Address; Phone
San Antonio (City), TX (State), 78200 (Zip)	San Antonio (City), TX (State), 78200 (Zip)
	Selling Associate's Name; License No.
	Selling Associate's Email Address; Phone
	Licensed Supervisor of Selling Associate; License No.
	Selling Associate's Office Address
	City; State; Zip

Listing Broker has agreed to pay Other Broker 2% of the total sales price when the Listing Broker's fee is received. Escrow agent is authorized and directed to pay Other Broker from Listing Broker's fee at closing.

TREC NO. 20-14

FIGURE APP-2 (Continued)

Contract Concerning 111 West Fifth Street 78200 (Address of Property) Page 10 of 10 2-12-18

OPTION FEE RECEIPT

Receipt of $__________ (Option Fee) in the form of __________ is acknowledged.

Seller or Listing Broker | Date

EARNEST MONEY RECEIPT

Receipt of $ 200.00 Earnest Money in the form of check is acknowledged.

Escrow Agent	Received by	Email Address	Date/Time
Acme Title Co.	Ginger Jones		

Address			Phone
117 West Pecan Avenue			

City	State	Zip	Fax
San Antonio	TX	78200	

CONTRACT RECEIPT

Receipt of the Contract is acknowledged.

Escrow Agent	Received by	Email Address	Date
Acme Title Co.	Ginger Jones		

Address			Phone
117 West Pecan Avenue			

City	State	Zip	Fax
San Antonio	TX	78200	

ADDITIONAL EARNEST MONEY RECEIPT

Receipt of $__________ additional Earnest Money in the form of __________ is acknowledged.

Escrow Agent | Received by | Email Address | Date/Time

Address | Phone

City | State | Zip | Fax

TREC NO. 20-14

FIGURE APP-2 (Continued)

II. COMMON AREAS OF CONCERN

1. All Cash Transaction 1

Relationship of the buyers and sellers

According to the example, "You are working with Eric and Tammy Williams. … This property is currently owned by Richard and Maria Guzman." The assumption from the scenario is that both the buyers and the sellers are married couples. However, the parties could be friends or siblings. This will need to be clarified up front. For married parties, issues of common law marriage, community property, and survivorship should be considered. For co-owners, survivorship issues also should be considered since Texas is a tenancy in common state. See generally Chapter 2.

Agency status of representative working with the buyers

The example provides, "You are working with Eric and Tammy Williams." The use of the word "with" is intended to reflect a seller subagent representation whereas the use of the word "for" would denote buyer representative status. For a discussion of agency relationships and contracts used for those relationships, see generally Chapter 5.

Age of the house

According to the scenario, "This property was constructed in 1976." The construction date automatically implicates the use of a Lead Based Paint Addendum. However, environmental hazards such as mold and asbestos should also be considered given the age of the house. See generally Chapter 7 for discussion of these addenda.

Homeowner's association

The example provides, "The property is subject to mandatory membership in the homeowner's association." Mandatory membership in an association automatically implicates the use of the Addendum for Property Subject to Mandatory Membership in a Property Owners Association to allow the buyer to gather information about the association and the membership fees. For a discussion of this addendum in detail, see generally Chapter 7.

Non-realty items

According to the example, "Mrs. Williams wants the 25 cubic foot refrigerator and the 20 cubic foot freezer included in the sale." This implicates the use of a Non-Realty Items Addendum. The make, model, and serial number for the items should be obtained for accurate identification on the form to ensure what is contracted for remains the same at closing. For additional discussion of personal property and the Non-Realty Items Addendum, see generally Chapter 2.

Option fee

According to the contract example, "the buyers include another check for $500 as an Option Fee." The inclusion of an option fee implicates a preliminary inspection after which time the buyers may exercise their right to get out of the contract or seek a contract amendment. For further discussion about the use of the option, see generally Chapter 5.

Title insurance, survey, and appraisal

The contract scenario provides, "The buyers are not concerned with a policy of title insurance; however, they do want a survey." In addition, the scenario provides "Buyers are not requesting an appraisal." For an all cash transaction, the title insurance, survey and appraisal are all discretionary. However, due to concerns about the risks associated with obtaining unmarketable title, the sales contract provides, "Broker advises Buyer to have an abstract of title covering the Property examined by an attorney of Buyer's selection, or Buyer should be furnished with or obtain a Title Policy." An in house brokerage form additionally may be used to obtain the buyer's signature when the buyer elects to waive the title policy. For further discussion of marketable title and title insurance, see generally Chapter 10.

Swimming pool

According to the contract example, "In addition, the sale is subject to the buyers being able to install a 30 ft. by 30 ft. swimming pool in the backyard." The buyers have requested a survey, which will provide some information about installation and will give them grounds to object if the installation is not possible. In addition, since the property is located in a mandatory homeowner's association, then there may be an Architectural Review Committee that should be consulted as well. Objections to the survey are addressed in Paragraph 6 of the sales contract.

Seller is a real estate professional

The scenario provides, "Richard Guzman is the listing agent working for Acme Brokerage, Inc." Since the seller is also a real estate professional, then notice must be provided in Paragraph 4 of the sales contract. For additional discussion of this notice, see generally Chapter 1.

Closing date

According to the scenario, "The buyers would like to close in two weeks." A typical all cash transaction can close in a short timeframe as long as there are no additional third parties involved. However, in this example, the buyers have included an option fee, which implicates an inspection. Furthermore, a survey has been requested. Therefore, the closing date may need to be set later. For a sample checklist associated with a real estate closing, see generally Chapter 10.

2. All Cash Transaction 2

Agency disclosure

The contract example provides, "Michael Worton enters the office of Dysnee Realty, located at 444 Salesman Avenue, San Antonio, Texas, 78200, License No. 000001, for some help in locating a house to purchase. The associate available at the time is Daf E. Duk. Mr. Duk gives Mr. Worton an agency disclosure notice which Mr. Worton proudly signs." This implicates the use of the agency disclosure form, the Information about Brokerage Services. This form is required to be furnished, in most cases, before the first substantive communication. For further discussion of the use of the Information about Brokerage Services, see generally Chapter 5.

Homestead

According to the contract scenario, "The sellers are Billy and Sue Martin. They are a married couple however the home is Billy Martin's separate property even though his wife currently lives in the home as her primary residence." This implicates the issue of homestead. Even though the property is Mr. Martin's separate property, the fact that his wife currently lives on the property renders the property homestead. Therefore, her signature is required to sell the property. For further discussion of community and separate property, see generally Chapter 2. For further discussion of homestead property, see generally Chapter 4.

Buyer's broker commission

The contract example provides, "After discussing the firm's practices regarding agency relationships, Mr. Worton decides to hire the brokerage company as his exclusive representative for which he will pay a 2.5% commission. ... The listing agent is only willing to pay a cooperating seller's broker 3% and a cooperating buyer's broker 2% of the sales price." This implicates the creation of a buyer representation agreement. The assumption with many buyers who hire representatives is that the seller will cover the buyer's commission expense; however, that is not always the case. Although, the buyer's representative can recover 2% from the seller's representative in this example, an additional 0.5% will be the buyer's responsibility. For further discussion of buyer agency, see generally Chapter 5.

Fixtures

The contract scenario provides, "Mr. Worton notices in the MLS that the seller is not including the drapes ... in the sale." Since the draperies are automatically included in the sale per the sales contract, they must be specifically excluded from the sale. For further discussion of fixtures, see generally Chapter 2.

Non-realty items and negotiation

According to the example, "The seller has however offered to include the refrigerator in the sale with a full price offer. The refrigerator is a GE Profile Stainless with bottom freezer; Model No. PD522SFSBLSS and Serial No. FLO50458. ... Mr. Worton would be interested in the refrigerator." This implicates two issues. First, the refrigerator is a non-realty item, which implicates the use of a Non-Realty Items Addendum. The make, model, and serial number for the items are available so they can be accurately identified on the form. For additional discussion of personal property and the Non-Realty Items Addendum, see generally Chapter 2. Second, the seller indicated that the personal property would only be available with a full price offer. Mr. Worton did not offer full price initially, but can still request the personal property, although the request may be rejected. For further discussion of outright rejections and counteroffers, see generally Chapter 6.

Deed restrictions

According to the scenario, "The MLS also indicates that the home is not located within a homeowner's association." The lack of a homeowner's association does not necessarily mean that there are no restrictions on the use of the property. For example, there may be restrictions in the deed that limit use. For further discussion of deed restrictions, see generally Chapter 4.

Earnest money

The contract example provides, "He is willing to put $200.00 earnest money down and he executes a check payable to Acme Title Co. located at 117 West Pecan Avenue." Although earnest money is not required for a real estate transaction, it does show the buyer's good faith toward the transaction. The question here is whether $200 constitutes sufficient good faith. For further discussion of earnest money, see generally Chapter 6.

Title policy, survey, and appraisal

According to the contract example, "Mr. Worton does not request a title policy, survey or appraisal." For an all cash transaction, the title insurance, survey and appraisal are all discretionary. However, due to concerns about the risks associated with obtaining unmarketable title, the sales contract provides, "Broker advises Buyer to have an abstract of title covering the Property examined by an attorney of Buyer's selection, or Buyer should be furnished with or obtain a Title Policy." An in house brokerage form additionally may be used to obtain the buyer's signature when the buyer elects to waive the title policy. For further discussion of marketable title and title insurance, see generally Chapter 10.

Age of the house

According to the contract scenario, "The property was constructed in 1976." The construction date automatically implicates the use of a Lead Based Paint Addendum. However, environmental hazards such as mold and asbestos should also be considered given the age of the house. See generally Chapter 7 for discussion of these addenda.

Limited repairs

The example provides, "The buyer accepts the property in its present condition except that he would like the seller to have the roof replaced." The buyer's representative should have the buyer exercise caution with an "as is" offer in light of the age of the house, discussed above. The contract further provides, "The seller also puts a cap on the roof repair not to exceed $1,500.00." The cap allows the seller to budget for the repair, but the buyer's representative must be able to determine whether the cap is sufficient to complete the repair. Further information concerning repairs is available in paragraph 7 of the sales contract.

Closing date

According to the contract scenario, "The buyer wants to close in the next three weeks because his apartment lease will be up by that time. … The sellers propose a counteroffer indicating a preferred closing date of two months." A typical all cash transaction can close in a short timeframe as long as there are no additional third parties involved. Here, the buyer has not requested much so the three weeks could work; however, the sellers have requested considerably more time before closing. If the sellers cannot agree to the earlier closing date, a Buyer's Temporary Residential Lease may be implicated to allow the buyer to move in early when the lease is up. For a sample checklist associated with a real estate closing, see generally Chapter 10. For further discussion of temporary leases, see generally Chapter 5.

Backup contract

The example provides, "A sales contract had just one hour previously been entered into between the sellers and Mr. Baker, another prospective buyer. Mr. Duk gets approval from Mr. Worton to submit the offer as a backup offer." This implicates use of the Addendum for "Back-Up" Contract form. If the seller accepts, then this form would create a second contract contingent on the termination of the first contract. For further information about multiple offers and backup contracts, see generally Chapter 6.

GLOSSARY

A

acceptance an action taken by the offeree upon receipt of the offer which manifests his or her agreement to the terms of the offer by the means indicated in the offer.

accord an executory agreement to accept performance in future satisfaction of a contractual duty.

actual notice notice that has been expressly given. This may be expressed orally or in writing.

Addendum for Backup Contract states that the backup contract does not take effect until the termination of the pending residential sales contract.

additional consideration consideration combined with the promise or performance of a preexisting legal duty that creates a valid enforceable agreement.

administrator where no will is involved, the male person chosen by the court to effectuate the terms of the statute and to dispose of the property.

administratrix where no will is involved, the female person chosen by the court to effectuate the terms of the statute and to dispose of the property.

adverse possession an actual and visible appropriation of real property, commenced and continued under a claim of right that is inconsistent with and is hostile to the claim of another person.

amendment modification.

Amendment to Contract TREC 39-3 form used for amendment of a contract.

anticipatory repudiation (also called anticipatory breach) a breach of contract that occurs before the time for performance is due under the contract in which (1) the renunciation is made before the time for performance is due, (2) the defaulting party makes the renunciation with positive and unconditional words or actions, and (3) the words must be unequivocal, that is, understood.

annual percentage rate that nominal annual percentage rate which will yield a sum equal to the amount of the finance charge when it is applied to the unpaid balances of the amount financed, calculated according to the actuarial method of allocating payments made on a debt between the amount financed and the amount of the finance charge, pursuant to which a payment is applied first to the accumulated finance charge and the balance is applied to the unpaid amount financed.

assignee the party who receives the rights under the contract.

assignment a transfer of all intangible rights to do or not do something under a contract.

assignor a party who transfers rights under a contract.

assumption the purchase of real property -subject to a mortgage whereby the purchaser accepts liability under an existing note and the seller remains liable to the lender unless the lender executes a release of liability. An assumption may arise between a lender, as obligee, a seller, as delegating party, and a buyer, as delegate.

B

backup offer a second offer presented during the pendency of a contract.

bargain and sale deed a deed that conveys title to the property but does not contain any warranties. This type of deed is commonly used by fiduciaries to transfer property, for instance, out of a trust or will.

benefit of the bargain damages the difference between the benefit received and the benefit promised to the nondefaulting party under the contract.

bilateral contract a contract whereby one party to the contract makes a promise in exchange for a promise by the second contracting party. This is the most common type of contract.

bill of sale a written instrument that may be used by the parties to a real estate contract to transfer title of personal property from the seller to the purchaser.

breach of contract occurs any time a party to the contract fails to perform without a legal excuse.

Broker-Lawyer Committee committee created, in part, to draft and revise contract forms and addenda capable of uniform use by real estate license holders.

buyer agency is created in employment -agreements between brokers and purchasers. The agreements are called buyer representation agreements.

buyer representation agreement creates an agency relationship between the real estate broker and the buyer in a real estate sales transaction.

Buyer's Temporary Residential Lease form used when a buyer is to take possession of the premises before closing.

C

client a person or entity who has contracted with the real estate licensee for professional services and advice.

closing the final settlement transaction consisting of the transfer of the title to the real estate by the seller, usually in the form of a general -warranty deed, and the transfer of the proceeds by the buyer.

Closing Disclosure document intended to give the consumer time to compare the costs disclosed with those in the loan estimate.

codicil an amendment to a will.

common law fraud fraud that arises under case decisions.

common law marriage a legal marriage in which a person claiming to be a spouse can show three elements: an oral or written agreement, (2) cohabitation with the other spouse, and (3) the couple represented themselves as a married couple.

communication a direct or indirect act of transmitting information.

community property property owned in -common between spouses each having a one-half undivided interest in the property by virtue of their marital status.

computerized loan origination a computerized network of lenders that real estate brokers can use to allow the purchaser to comparison shop for a mortgage loan.

condition precedent a condition that must occur before a party to a contract is obligated to perform under the contract.

condition subsequent a condition that exists after the parties enter into a contract that will -terminate one of the parties' obligation to perform under the contract.

condominium ownership ownership of the unit plus an undivided ownership in the land underneath and an undivided ownership interest in the common elements on the premises, such as stairways and sidewalks.

conforming loan a loan that conforms to Fannie Mae (FNMA) and Freddie Mac (FHLMC) guidelines.

consideration the inducement to a contract, often referred to as a bargained-for exchange between the parties to an agreement. Promises that are the result of a bargained-for exchange are enforceable and each party must experience both a benefit and a detriment.

constitutional county court this court has a jurisdictional amount of between $200.01 and $5,000 and overlaps the jurisdiction of the justice court. It also has subject matter jurisdiction to issue writs necessary to enforce its jurisdiction and limited probate jurisdiction where there is no other court exercising probate authority.

contract a promise or a set of promises for the breach of which the law gives a remedy, or the performance of which the law in some way recognizes as a duty.

contract clause the part of the United States Constitution that provides that no state shall pass a law that impairs the obligation under a contract.

contract for deed a creative financing technique usually seen with people who cannot obtain traditional financing, for instance, because of a bad debt, no down payment, or they won't qualify for a loan.

contribution the right of a defendant to recover proportional shares of a judgment from others whose negligence contributed to the injury of the consumer.

cooperative involves ownership of the unit and the common areas, but the ownership is held by a corporation.

co-ownership ownership of real or personal property by two or more persons.

counteroffer a proposal, made by the offeree, that relates to the same matter as the original offer, but proposes a substitute for portions of the original proposal. Where a counteroffer is made, the original offer is rejected and a new offer is put up for negotiation by the offeree.

county court at law this court has a jurisdictional amount of between $200.01 and $100,000.00. It also has subject matter jurisdiction in probate proceedings where there is no statutory probate court. In counties where the population exceeds two million the county court at law has jurisdiction over suits to the title of real or personal property.

covenant against encumbrances the grantor warrants that there are no encumbrances on the property. Certain encumbrances might include liens, easements, covenants, and possibly oil, gas and mineral interests.

covenant of further assurances the grantor promises that he or she will execute any other documents required to perfect the title that has been conveyed to the grantee.

covenant of general warranty the grantor warrants that he or she will defend the property against any lawful claims and compensate the grantee for any loss that he or she suffers by the assertion of superior title by a third party.

covenant of quiet enjoyment the grantor warrants that the grantee will not be disturbed in his or her possession and enjoyment of the property by the assertion of superior title by a third party. This warranty is typically considered interchangeable with the covenant of general warranty.

covenant of seisin the grantor of the property warrants that he or she owns the property that he or she purports to convey.

covenant of the right to convey the grantor warrants that he or she has the right to convey the property. In other words, the grantor is warranting that he or she has the authority to convey the property.

customer a person who is working with a real estate licensee to the extent necessary to complete the transaction, but he or she has not specifically contracted with the licensee for professional services or advice.

D

damages pecuniary compensation that can be recovered in a court of law by a person who has suffered a loss as a result of a breach of contract.

death or insanity physical or mental condition of the offeror that terminates an offer.

debt a specified sum of money the buyer is obligated to pay to the lender as well the lender's right to receive and enforce the payment.

Deceptive Trade Practices Consumer Protection Act (DTPA) law enacted to protect consumers against false, misleading, and deceptive business practices; unconscionable actions; and breaches of warranty and to provide efficient and economical procedures to secure such protection.

Declaration of Informal Marriage affidavit establishing proof of marital status.

deed the conveyance of title.

deed in lieu of foreclosure a deed that is used for the seller to convey title of the property to the lender, rather than a third party, in exchange for a release from the mortgage.

deed of trust the security interest in Texas.

deed of trust to secure assumption recorded in the county deed records this document allows the seller to foreclose on the property if the seller has to make a delinquent payment to the lender on behalf of the buyer.

defeasible fee a fee simple absolute that can be defeated by the happening of some event.

delegate the party to whom the duty or obligation is delegated.

delegating party the party making the delegation.

delegation the transfer of certain duties or obligations under a contract.

destruction of the subject matter the partial or complete loss of the property indicated in the offer due to some Act of God or a governmental taking causing the termination of an offer before it is accepted.

direct communication a communication made directly to the intended party.

direct revocation the more common type of revocation that involves a statement made by the offeror or the offeror's -representative to the offeree or the offeree's represen tative indicating the desire to withdraw the offer.

discharge is the termination of an obligation under a contract.

district court this highest trial court has a jurisdictional amount in excess of $500 and has subject matter jurisdiction over suits (1) for enforcement of a lien on land, (2) on behalf of the State for escheat, (3) for divorce, (4) for eminent domain, (5) for recovery of land (trespass to try title), and (6) for trial of the right to property valued at $500 or more and levied on under a writ of execution, sequestration, or attachment.

diversity of citizenship jurisdiction the suit must involve citizens from different states, and there must be an amount in controversy in excess of $75,000.

due on sale clause clause that states that when a sale takes place, the seller must pay the amount due on the note to the bank.

durable power of attorney authority that -continues while the principal is alive and even if the principal becomes incompetent.

E

easement appurtenant an easement designed to benefit another tract of land, rather than an individual.

easement in gross a personal easement that attaches to the individual grantee rather than to a tract of land.

eminent domain the power of the government to take private property for public use for just compensation.

encumbrance an interest in property that diminishes its value, but does not prohibit the owner from disposing of the property.

escheat occurs when there are no heirs to receive property upon the death of the property owner, such as can occur when a person dies without a will, or intestate, in Texas so the property passes to the State.

estate an interest that one or more persons hold in land.

exclusive agency listing a listing where the -broker is entitled to a commission only if he or she sells the property during the listing period. The owner does not owe a commission if he or she sells the property during that same time. This type of agency is more advantageous to the seller than to the broker. The broker is still entitled to exclusivity; however, if the broker fails to find a buyer and the seller does find a buyer, the broker does not get paid.

exclusive right to sell listing gives the broker the authority to sell the property, but entitles the broker to a commission regardless of whether the broker or the property owner sells the property during the term of the listing. This is the most common type of listing used in Texas in residential sales. The exclusivity of the relationship means that the seller cannot go to another broker during the listing period.

executed contract a contract which has been completely performed by the parties that takes effect immediately or a contract which conveys an immediate right.

execution the signature of the grantor.

executor a male person who is chosen by the testator or testatrix to effectuate the directions in the will and to dispose of property according to the will provisions.

executory contract a contract that has not been fully completed.

executory period the time when closing takes place.

executrix is a female person who is -chosen by the testator or testatrix to effectuate the directions in the will and to dispose of property according to the will provisions.

express contract a contract created by a verbal or written expression of the parties.

expression of intent a statement made by a person in which the person seeks to accomplish a specific goal.

F

family homestead is created by a family, that is, (1) two or more persons must (2) live together, (3) with some moral or legal obligation, and (4) there must be some dependence on the head of the family for support.

federal question jurisdiction some federal law must have an implication in the case.

fee simple absolute the largest estate that may be conveyed. This estate is considered the default estate in Texas. When a conveyance of this estate is made, the grantor effectively grants 100% of the surface, subsurface, and air rights to the grantee. The typical way that a grant of a fee simple absolute is made is by using any words that show an intent to convey full property rights.

fee simple subject to a condition subsequent an estate that will terminate upon the happening of some event. This estate is very similar to the fee simple determinable; however, the future estate held by the grantor is a right of entry. In addition, if the event does occur, the estate does not automatically terminate, the grantor merely has the right to reenter the premises to claim possession. Where the interest is reclaimed, the original grantor again takes a fee simple absolute to the property. Special language such as "if," "but if," or "on condition that" is typically used to create the fee simple subject to a condition subsequent.

fee simple subject to an executory interest an estate that will terminate upon the happening of some event; however, the future estate is held by a third party rather than the original grantor. This future interest in the third party is referred to as an executory interest. If the event occurs and the fee terminates, it will automatically terminate in this designated third party thereby creating a fee simple in the third party. Language typically used to create a fee simple determinable or a fee simple subject to a condition subsequent is sufficient to create this estate.

finance charge the sum of all charges, payable directly or indirectly by the person to whom the credit is extended, and imposed directly or indirectly by the creditor as an incident to the extension of credit.

fixity the permanence of the property as an investment.

fixtures items attached to the land.

freehold estate ownership rights of indefinite duration that can be conveyed voluntarily by deed or by will.

frustration of purpose nothing has happened to impede performance, but the purpose has been frustrated in some way by the happening of an event. To establish frustration of the purpose under the contract (1) there must have been a supervening act, (2) this act must have been unforeseeable at the time the contract was entered into, (3) the purpose or object of the contract was known and recognized by both parties at the time they entered into the contract, and (4) the supervening act totally destroys the purpose of the contract.

Full Faith and Credit clause states that contracts and other legal documents executed in one state are valid in all other states.

future freehold estate a freehold estate that has a future right of possession. The two primary types of future freehold estates are the reversion and the remainder.

G

general agency an agency whereby the agent is given authorization to conduct several transactions. Because of the nature of this type of agency, the principal is responsible for all acts of the agent performed within the scope of the agency.

general breach of contract arises where a party to the contract fails to perform on the date and time indicated for performance.

general partnership a business arrangement that involves two or more persons.

general power of attorney gives the attorney in fact full power to handle a principal's assets.

general warranty deed a deed that conveys title to the property and warrants title to the property against all defects in title that arose both before and after the grantor took title to the property. In real estate transactions in Texas, the general warranty deed is the most common type of deed used to convey real estate.

good faith an honest intention to -contract and the absence of the intent to defraud.

grantee the purchaser of the property.

grantor the seller of the property.

grantor–grantee index lists the documents according to their grantors and grantees.

gratuitous consideration where either party to the transaction intends to make a gift there is typically no detriment that is induced and therefore there is no consideration; thus, a promise to make a gift, in itself, is insufficient to create a valid contract.

gross lease lease for a flat sum of rent

ground lease lease for a flat sum of rent, but the rent is paid to the landlord for vacant land

guardianship a legal arrangement whereby one person, the guardian, is given the legal right and duty to care for another, the ward, and the ward's property.

H

habendum clause describes the estate transferred to the grantee by the grantor.

I

illegality that which is contrary to the principles of law, morals, or public policy.

Immobile the inability to be moved from place to place.

implied contract a contract that is not created by any expression of the parties, but is inferred from the circumstances of the transaction.

impossibility of performance one party's duty to perform under the contract is discharged when, without any fault of that party, it becomes impossible to perform.

imputed communication often referred to as imputed notice, a concept whereby communication to an agent is considered communication to his or her principal.

inception of title doctrine property is considered either separate or community at the beginning of title. If in the first moment a legal right is acquired in property and the person is single, then the property is separate property. If he or she is married at that time, then the property is community property.

indemnity a right whereby one party agrees to indemnify, or restore, another upon the occurrence of some anticipated loss.

independent contractor typical business arrangement between real estate salespersons and their sponsoring brokers in Texas. Where there is no control by the employer, the employee functions as an independent contractor and is responsible for his or her own actions, expenses, fees, and other miscellaneous business overhead. The parties can contract either verbally or in writing.

Indestructibility inability to be destroyed.

indirect communication a communication made indirectly to the intended party by way of a third party or third-party device.

indirect revocation a revocation whereby the offeror says or does something that indicates a desire to withdraw the offer and which is known by the offeree.

Information About Brokerage Services an agency disclosure form that complies with the Texas Real Estate License Act.

inquiry a question proposed concerning a piece of property with the intent that an answer be forthcoming but does not constitute an offer.

inquiry notice notice used when a person finds something unusual which prompts them to inquire further.

Interest a right in property.

interpleader a proceeding to determine the rights of disputing parties to property held by a neutral third party. The money is put in the court's custody. The parties can then fight in court for custody of the monies. Since the neutral third party has no interest in the property itself, there may be liability for distributing the property to one party over the other without the consent of both parties.

intoxicated individual a person who is under the influence of an intoxicant. The intoxicant can consist of alcohol, illicit drugs, prescription medication, or over-the-counter medication.

invitation to offer invites parties to make offers on a particular piece of property.

J

joint tenancy a type of co-ownership not recognized in Texas, this relationship was recognized at common law and created under the four unities: time, title, interest, and possession.

justice court this court has a jurisdictional amount of between $.01 and $5,000; however, it has exclusive jurisdiction over those cases from $.01 to $200. In addition to an exclusive jurisdictional amount, the justice court has exclusive subject matter jurisdiction over eviction proceedings.

L

Land ground, soil, or earth.

lapse of time a way an offer can be terminated when a specified time stated in the offer has elapsed.

Lead-Based Paint Disclosure Addendum approved by TREC provides a brief warning statement in the first paragraph. This is followed by the seller's disclosure of the presence of lead hazards as well as records and reports available to the seller. Keep in mind if an earlier prospective purchaser had an inspection done, and lead was found, the seller must disclose that information to any subsequent prospective purchasers.

lease written or oral agreement between a landlord and tenant that establishes or modifies the terms, conditions, rules, or other provisions regarding the use and occupancy of a dwelling

lease purchase agreement landlord gives the tenant the right, up front, to purchase the property at a later date with specific terms

Letters of Administration proof of adequate authority of an administrator or administratrix to list the real estate.

Letters of Guardianship certified papers issued when a guardianship is created.

letters of intent used by parties to negotiations to express their intent with regard to matters involved in the transaction. These letters do not constitute offers.

Letters Testamentary the proof necessary before a realtor can list or sell a property from an executor or executrix.

lien theory a bank with a mortgage on property merely holds a lien on the property during the term of the debt while the purchaser holds legal title to the property.

life estate an estate measured by a life or lives in being.

life estate pur autre vie a life estate measured by the life of another.

limited partnership a business association that involves two or more persons; however, the partners involved can have a different role as either general partners or limited partners.

liquidated damages the sum that a party to a contract agrees to pay if he or she breaches the contract and is used to predict damages if a contract is breached.

lis pendens a notice of pending suit. The general purpose of a lis pendens is to put third parties on notice of the facts and issues involved in the lawsuit.

listing agreement the written agency relationship between a seller and broker.

loan origination the process by which a prospective purchaser initiates a new loan application with a lender.

M

Mediation Addendum form attached when the parties to a residential real estate transaction wish their future disputes to be handled by some type of mediation.

mental capacity the ability of a person to understand the nature and effect of the acts in which he or she is engaged and the business that he or she is transacting.

mentally infirm individual is a person of weak mental health.

merger the termination of one contract by its inclusion into another.

minors individuals (1) who are under the age of eighteen, (2) who have never been married, and (3) who have not had their disability of minority removed by a court order.

misrepresentation an untrue statement of material fact.

mitigation of damages the principle that an injured party cannot recover damages that could reasonably have been avoided.

modification the amendment of a contract. When the original contract is modified by agreement of the parties, the terms of the original contract are discharged.

multiple listing service a system available, usually through a local board of realtors, that disseminates a broker's information on listed properties to other member brokers and through which participants offer cooperation on transactions as well as specific compensation.

multiple offers a situation where the seller receives several offers simultaneously concerning a parcel of real estate.

mutual assent agreement of the parties in the form of the offer and acceptance.

mutual rescission a mutual agreement to cancel a contract.

N

necessaries board, lodging, wearing apparel, medicine, medical attendance, and education.

net lease requires the tenant to pay not only rent, but also the expenses of the property

net listing a listing in which the broker's commission is any amount above the agreed on sales price.

net proceeds are the amount of proceeds left after closing expenses and indebtedness have been paid.

nominal consideration consideration that bears no relation to the real value of the contract.

non-freehold estate an estate of fixed duration.

Non-realty Items addenda used as attachments to the residential sales contract that allows the transfer of the personal property to occur almost simultaneously with the transfer of the real property in the same transaction.

novation substitutes a new party for an original party to the contract, and completely releases the original party to the contract from all liability under that -contract.

O

obligee the party to whom a duty is owed.

obligor the party who is obligated to perform under the contract.

offer a proposal to act or perform communicated by one party to another with the intent that the proposal be accepted to form a contract.

offeree the person to whom an offer is communicated.

offeror the person proposing the offer.

open listing a listing where the seller can go to several different brokers to list the property, and the first broker that sells it gets the commission.

option contract in the context of a residential real estate transaction, an agreement between the buyer and seller in which the seller accepts a certain option fee from the buyer. In exchange, the buyer will be allowed to terminate the sales contract for any reason by the end of the preestablished option period.

P

parol evidence rule states that terms set forth in a writing intended by the parties to be a final expression of their agreement may not be contradicted or modified by evidence of a prior agreement or a contemporaneous oral agreement.

part performance doctrine exception to the writing requirement of the Statute of Frauds that allows for the enforcement of an oral agreement. To enforce the oral agreement, the purchaser must show that (1) there was an oral agreement, (2) partial consideration was paid, (3) the purchaser took possession of the property, and (4) the purchaser made permanent and valuable improvements to the property.

partially integrated a contract not considered to be the exclusive contract of the parties.

partnership an association of two or more persons to carry on a business for profit.

past consideration an act completed before the contract is created and that cannot create a valid contract.

pecuniary consideration (money) consideration that can be used to form a valid contract.

percentage lease lease for a small base rent with an additional rent payment based on a percentage of gross profits on the premises

personal property consists of movable property.

personal services contracts where the contract is personal to the party performing the service. Death or incapacity of a party to the contract may operate to discharge that party in the absence of a contrary contractual provision.

physical exchange consideration in the form of property given in exchange for property sufficient to establish a valid contract.

plat a map of an area of land that incorporates the rural metes and bounds description of the entire property, but is subdivided as necessary for the subdivision project.

police power the power of the government to make laws that control land use for the health, safety, and welfare of the people.

possibility of reverter the future estate of the fee simple determinable estate.

power of attorney a written instrument whereby one person, the principal, appoints another, the attorney in fact, as his or her agent and gives the agent authority to perform certain acts on behalf of the principal.

power of sale clause clause that gives the trustee authority to sell the property at public auction (nonjudicial foreclosure) if the debtor defaults.

precontractual liability liability that arises due to failed negotiations between the parties before a contract is formed.

preexisting legal duty a duty a party is already obligated to perform.

premise the portion of a deed that describes the sub ject property and the parties to the conveyance. The description of the subject property may be a metes and bounds description or possibly a recorded lot and block description.

present freehold estates estates that have a present right of possession.

private mortgage insurance insurance that covers the bank when more than 80% is loaned for the purchase of real estate.

probate proceeding the means by which a will is validated in Texas to clear title to the property.

promissory estoppel the enforcement of an agreement without consideration when there has been a promise made calculated to induce reliance and actual reliance on the promise by the injured party has caused some injustice as a result of the agreement not being enforced.

promissory note is a written promise by the maker to pay a specified sum at a specified time to a person named in the agreement, the payee. This document is a -contract between the lender and the borrower. Since this document is merely a contract, it is not typically recorded.

promulgated forms capable of uniform use by real estate licensees. These forms for the most part are mandatory.

Q

quitclaim deed a deed that transfers what-ever interest the grantor has in the property. No warranties of any kind are made. In Texas, quitclaim deeds are typically limited in use to instances involving corrections to deeds.

R

ratification the confirmation of a previous contract.

real estate land and anything permanently affixed to the land, such as buildings, fences, and those things attached to the buildings, such as light fixtures, plumbing and heating fixtures, or other such items which would be personal property (movable property) if not attached.

real estate lien note in real estate sales transactions, the promissory note.

real property consists of the land and everything attached to the land.

record notice notice which can be obtained by looking in the county deed records.

recording the process of filing a document in the county deed records for the county in which the property is located, putting third party creditors on notice of the grantee's new property interest by making property ownership information public and making the title stable. The recording process also protects the ultimate grantee from fraud by preventing a prior grantor from hiding any interest in the property.

reformation an equitable remedy used by the parties to correct a written contract to accurately reflect the terms of the intended agreement when the contract does not embody the intended terms.

rejection refers to the express refusal, either written or verbal, by the offeree to accept the terms of the offer.

Release of Earnest Money form this form dictates that the parties are released of all liability under the contract and indicates who is to receive the earnest money upon termination of the contract.

remainder a future estate that transfers to a third party, not the original grantor, after the termination of the present estate. A remainder may be either vested (complete) or contingent (conditional) depending on the type of conveyance made to the third party.

rescission cancellation of the contract.

restitution an equitable remedy under which an injured party is restored to his or her original position before the injury occurred and placed in the position that he or she would have been in had the breach not occurred. Also, the reasonable value of the performance the nondefaulting party to a contract can recover for the value of services he or she gave to the nondefaulting party irrespective of whether the nondefaulting party would have lost money on the contract and would have been unable to recover in a suit on the contract.

reversion a future estate that returns to the original grantor after the termination of the present freehold estate.

revocation the direct or indirect act of withdrawing the offer by the offeror.

right of entry the future estate of the fee simple subject to a condition subsequent estate.

right of first refusal gives the tenant the right to make the first offer to purchase the property

rural use homestead cannot be situated in a built up, urbanized area and is limited to 200 acres, which may be noncontiguous.

S

satisfaction the time when the accord is fully performed.

scarcity relates to the supply and demand for a property.

security a resource to be used in case the buyer fails in the principal obligation.

security interest a form of interest in property which provides that the property may be sold if the purchaser defaults on his or her obligation. The security interest in Texas is referred to as a deed of trust.

seller agency employment contracts between brokers and sellers. The contracts involved are called listing agreements.

seller financing a transaction in which the seller, rather than a lending institution, finances the transaction.

Seller's Disclosure Notice form where the seller indicates everything he or she knows about the property and represents that the document was completed to the best of his or her knowledge.

Seller's Temporary Residential Lease form used if the seller is to remain in the property after closing.

separate property property owned during marriage by a spouse in his or her own name or right. Separate property, in Texas, includes (1) all property owned before marriage; (2) property gained through gift, devise, or descent; (3) personal injury recoveries except for lost wages; and (4) property made separate by agreement.

short sale used when the seller must sell the property for less than the total debt remaining on the loan.

single adult homestead created by a single adult, that is, a party who is at least 18 years of age, or a person with the disability of minority removed by a court and who is not married or the constituent of a family.

situs people's preference for property in a particular location.

sole proprietorship business ownership by one individual.

special agency an agency relationship between the parties established by a contract. The agreement establishes the licensee as the agent and the client, either the seller or the buyer, as the principal. The agent is given authorization for only limited situations; therefore, the principal is not responsible for the acts of the agent.

special power of attorney gives the -attorney in fact limited power to handle a principal's assets. This is typically done in a list form.

special warranty deed a deed that conveys title to the property and warrants only against the grantor's own acts and not the acts of others. This type of deed is more commonly used in conveyances by governmental entities.

specific performance a remedy that requires exact performance by the defaulting party under the contract.

sponsoring broker the broker that the new salesperson works with once he or she passes the exam and becomes licensed. The real estate salesperson in Texas cannot practice his or her trade, nor accept a fee, without a sponsoring broker.

Statute of Frauds based on an old English statute passed in 1677, requires certain contracts to be in writing and signed by the party to be charged or by his or her authorized agent. This statute provides that contracts for the sale of goods priced at $500 or more, contracts for the sale of land, contracts that cannot be performed within a year, and contracts for surety ship all must be in writing to be enforceable in a court of law.

substantial performance the doctrine that recognizes that performance under a contract that deviates slightly from the terms of the contract will be considered complete performance under the contract less the damages that result from deviation from the contract. Substantial performance limits the damages awarded where the defaulting party has substantially performed under the contract and damages are measured according to the loss in value rather than the cost to complete the project. This doctrine is limited to those instances where (1) the cost to complete the construction is grossly disproportionate to the loss in value, and (2) the defaulting party acted in good faith.

substitution changes one party for another under the contract, but the party who is substituted is still liable under the contract.

surface water water of the ordinary flow, underflow, and tides of every flowing river, natural stream, and lake, and of every bay or arm of the Gulf of Mexico, and the storm water, floodwater, and rainwater of every river, natural stream, canyon, ravine, depression, and watershed in the state.

survey the process by which real estate is measured to determine boundaries in addition to total size.

T

tenancy at sufferance created when a tenant remains in possession of the premises after termination of the lease

tenancy at will tenancy for an indefinite and uncertain length of time and might be tied to a specific event

tenancy for years tenancy with a fixed duration

tenancy from period to period tenancy without a fixed duration. Tenancy rolls over from some specific period to the next

tenancy in common the type of co-ownership recognized in Texas where the tenant in common holds an undivided interest in the property, and there is no automatic right of survivorship between the tenants.

Termination of Listing Agreement a form commonly used by the parties to terminate the listing agreement by mutual agreement.

testator the male person who creates a will.

testatrix the female person who creates a will.

Texas Constitution sets forth the primary law of the state and the organization and regulation of the state government.

Texas Real Estate Commission (TREC) consists of nine members appointed for six-year terms by the governor with the advice and consent of the Texas senate and responsible for the administration of the Texas Real Estate License Act. Six of these members are required to have operated as real estate brokers for at least five years preceding their appointments. The remaining three members must be representatives of the general public who are not real estate licensees.

Texas Real Estate License Act governs the real estate profession. The administration of the Texas Real

Estate License Act was vested in the Texas Real Estate Commission.

time is of the essence provision a provision requiring that all times indicated under a contract be interpreted exactly; more common in commercial real estate transactions.

title proof of ownership of property.

title theory a bank with a mortgage on the property holds title to the property until the underlying debt on the real estate is paid.

totally integrated a contract considered to be the complete agreement of the parties.

tract index lists the document by the property description.

trust clause clause that specifies that the conveyance under the deed of trust is made in trust to secure payment of the underlying debt in the promissory note.

U

unenforceable contract a contract which for some reason cannot be enforced. A valid contract may be incapable of enforcement where the four-year statute of limitations has lapsed.

Uniform Vendor and Purchaser Risk Act this law states that the risk of the loss is on the seller *unless* the buyer is in possession.

unilateral contract a contract in which only one person has made a promise, more familiar in reward situations.

uniqueness a characteristic of real property.

United States Constitution sets forth the fundamental law of the United States and the principles relating to the organization and regulation of the federal government.

urban use use of the property located in an urban area. To constitute an urban use, a person may use the property for a residential purpose.

V

valid contract is a contract which has all of the essential elements of a contract and is enforceable in a court of law. A valid contract may also be unenforceable.

valuable consideration consideration that bears a substantial relation to the real value of the contract and is sufficient to create a valid contract.

void contract a contract that does not exist under the law, that is, the contract has failed to include all of the essential elements necessary to the creation of a valid contract. This type of contract is unenforceable.

voidable contract a valid contract which may be legally avoided at the option of one of the parties.

W

warranty clause states the warranties contained under the deed. Another part that is common to a deed in Texas is the execution.

Wetlands those areas that are inundated or saturated by surface or ground water at a frequency and duration sufficient to support, and that under normal circumstances do support, a prevalence of vegetation typically adapted for life in saturated soil conditions. Wetlands generally include swamps, marshes, bogs and similar areas.

will a legal document that disposes of a person's assets upon his or her death.

INDEX

D

E

F

G

M

Q

R

U